Got God?

A 365 Day Devotional for Regular People

Julie Taylor, RN

Got God?

A 365 Day Devotional for Regular People

©2022 Julie Taylor, RN

print ISBN: 978-1-66787-166-0
ebook ISBN: 978-1-66787-167-7

INTRODUCTION

Faith isn't a magic wand, it's a journey in change of spirit. Just because we *believe* in God, doesn't mean we're actually *following* Him. Clarify, strengthen, and renew your invisible, yet dynamic, relationship with God within the journey of this devotional. Whether you've been reading prayer books for years, and are looking for an in-depth, thought-provoking daily read to get your spirit on track, or just dipping your toe into the deeper waters of faith, contained in the pages of this book lies a closer relationship with your Heavenly Father.

Plagued by mistakes that we repeat over and over, pain and suffering in our lives we don't understand, and prayers that never seem to be answered leave many of us frustrated, confused and disillusioned with God. It's in understanding our relationship with God that allows us to draw closer to Him. God's love and mercy is for **everyone**, no matter what we've done, or think we've done. Shine, because Christ died for you, and dies a little each day without you nearer. Allow peace to envelop your heart as you devote this time to the Lord. Pray on, brothers and sisters.

```
Pray for it, or repent because of it, but seek God through the life of Jesus.
-J.J. Taylor, RN
```

EXPLAINING WHAT'S WHAT

Matthew 13:15, ERV

15 "Yes, the minds of these people are now closed. They have ears, but they don't listen. They have eyes, but they refuse to see. If their minds were not closed, they might see with their eyes; they might hear with their ears; they might understand with their minds. Then they might turn back to me and be healed."

Matthew-book of Matthew

13:15- CHAPTER # 13, VERSE # 15

ESV-Version of the bible used for reference, Easy To Read Version

Verse: "Yes, the minds of these people are now closed. They have ears, but they don't listen. They have eyes, but they refuse to see. If their minds were not closed, they might see with their eyes; they might hear with their ears; they might understand with their minds. Then they might turn back to me and be healed."

Old Testament Order:

Genesis

Exodus

Leviticus

Numbers

Deuteronomy

Joshua

Judges

Ruth

1 Samuel

2 Samuel

1 Kings

2 Kings

1 Chronicles

2 Chronicles

Ezra

Nehemiah

Job

Psalms

Proverbs

Ecclesiastes

Song of Solomon

Isaiah

Jeremiah

Lamentations

Ezekiel

Daniel

Hosea

Joel

Amos

Obadiah

Jonah

Micah

Micah

Nahum

Zephaniah

Haggai

Zechariah

Malachi

New Testament Order

Matthew

Mark

Luke

John

Acts

Romans

1 Corinthians

2 Corinthians

Galatians

Ephesians

Philippians

Colossians

1 Thessalonians

2 Thessalonians

1 Timothy

2 Timothy

Titus

Philemon

Hebrews

James

1 Peter

2 Peter

1 John

2 John

3 John

Jude

Revelation

Bible Versions Used:

21st Century KJV (KJ21)

American Standard Version (ASV)

BRG Bible (BRG)

CSB (CSB)

Common English Bible (CEB)

Complete Jewish Bible (CJB)

Contemporary English Version (CEV)

Disciples' Literal New Testament (DLNT)

Douay-Rheims 1899 American Edition (DRA)

Easy-to-Read Version (ERV)

English Standard Version (ESV)

1599 Geneva Bible (GNV)

GOD'S WORD Translation (GW)

Good News Translation (GNT)

International Children's Bible (ICB)

International Standard Version (ISV)

King James Version (KJV)

New American Standard Bible (NASB)

New Catholic Bible (NCB)

New English Translation (NET)

New International Version (NIV)

New King James Version (NKJV)

New Life Version (NLV)

New Living Translation (NLT)

Free Online Bible Resources:

biblegateway.com

biblestudytools.com

biblehub.com

bible.com

Matthew 13:15

ESV

"Yes, the minds of these people are now closed.

They have ears, but they don't listen.

They have eyes, but they refuse to see.

If their minds were not closed,

they might see with their eyes;

they might hear with their ears;

they might understand with their minds.

Then they might turn back to me and be healed."

January 1
Resolute in Jesus

Deuteronomy 13:4, ESV

4 You shall walk after the Lord your God and **fear him** and **keep His commandments** and **obey His voice**, and you shall serve him and hold fast to him.

1 Samuel 12:24, ESV

24 Only fear the Lord and **serve him faithfully with all your heart**. For consider what great things he has done for you.

It's a New Year, so let's be honest, most of us probably spend more time on our cell phones than we do praying to Jesus. Many people profess to believe in Jesus Christ, but don't really pray or go to church. Our belief, even our *love* for our Savior doesn't mean we're truly giving our relationship with Him our first priority in our lives (Matthew 22:36-37). A relationship requires equal communication and commitment, and the amount of encounters with another reflects their priority in our lives. Jesus has proved His commitment through His resurrection on the cross, and communicates to us through prayer, the bible, and the Holy Spirit. Just believing is great, but only just the start of something larger. We can show we love and serve Christ through our prayers, our actions, our behaviors and words, as they reflect what is in our hearts. God calls on us to be committed to Him, but are we, really? In this New Year, be *resolute* in your relationship with Jesus Christ through the Holy Spirit.

Resolution, our *dedication*, should be to Christ Jesus, and not only our hearts by loving Him, but in our actions by serving Him. We do this by communicating with Him through prayer, devotion to Him by our service, and giving him our burdens and thoughts. When we do these things, we are allowing the Holy Spirit to guide our lives (Proverbs 3:5-6). So, no matter where we find ourselves this day in our relationship with Christ, we can all be *resolute* to praying a little more, sharing a little more, listening a little more, and obeying a little more. Spending a few more minutes to ourselves without distraction is important to reacquaint ourselves with our Lord and Savior, and in those quiet thoughts the Holy Spirit can be heard (Matthew 6:6). Turning off all external distractions, we should incur to be still, and give ourselves a couple of minutes peace of mind at the beginning and end of the day. We should all ask ourselves, have I shared all I could with Jesus today?

1 Corinthians 15:56-58, GW/ERV

56 Sin gives death its sting, and God's standards give sin its power. 57 Thank God that he gives us the victory through our Lord Jesus Christ. 58 Therefore, my beloved brothers, be **steadfast**, immovable, always abounding in the work of the Lord, knowing that in the Lord your labor is not in vain.

January 2
Faith

Philippians 4:13, ESV

13 I can do all things through him who strengthens me.

Hebrews 11:6, ESV

6 And without faith it is impossible to please him, for whoever would draw near to God must believe that he exists and that he rewards those who seek him.

Many of us would have to admit saying, "Just leave it to me, I'll do it," at least once in our lives. We are often more comfortable with our own efforts, even our own half-hearted efforts, than we are with someone else's. Our social norms have placed a great deal of emphasis on being self-sufficient, independent, capable, and that seeking help for anything is typically a sign of weakness. It is by our faith that we can get through trying or tempting moments in our lives with grace and discipline, certainly not by anything we could do ourselves. It is in the discipline of our faith, or trust in God, that gives us the power to manage any solution with God's grace (Ephesians 3:20). The discipline of our faith tells us to forgive people who cross us, and to offer forgiveness to our enemies. The discipline of our faith tells us not to brag or be arrogant, but to know that all of us are a work in progress under the guidance of the Lord. Our faith assures us that God will never abandon us, and that we are forgiven our sins when we repent to Him with humility.

Faith is trust, trust takes time to build, and many people have difficulty placing full trust in others. Humans are sinful, prone to wickedness, and carry the potential to disappoint where God is always the same (Hebrews 13:8). Humans change their minds and let one another down, God's love is steadfast and permanent. God loved His human creation so much, He sent a piece of Himself down in the form of a man, Jesus, to die for our sins (John 3:16). Loving and generous, God proves His love for us each day, allowing us another opportunity to repent and grow in Him. God's power waits for us in the form of the Holy Spirit, which dwells inside of us (1 Corinthians 3:16). Listening to that 'voice' in our heads trying to steer us toward more wholesome choices, less sinful desires, and kinder words for our brothers and sisters is the Holy Spirit at work within us. When we're patient with ourselves, and when we pray through our difficulties, we're accessing God's power within us. When we do this knowing we'll receive God's mercy and grace, we're leaning on our faith. Trust on, and be patient, AMEN.

Hebrews 11:1, ESV

1 Now faith is the assurance of things hoped for, the conviction of things not seen.

Romans 10:17, ESV

17 So faith comes from hearing, and hearing through the word of Christ.

January 3
Why Do We Need Jesus?

Genesis 6:12, KJ21

12 And God looked upon the earth, and behold, it was corrupt; for all flesh had corrupted His way upon the earth.

Matthew 28:18, ESV

18 And Jesus came and said to them, "All authority in heaven and on earth has been given to me."

Ask yourself, do you think everyone who commits a moral sin should be punished? Most people would agree, that yes, people who commit moral sins should be punished. Now ask yourself, have I ever committed a sin? If you answered no, you might need to rethink your answer. According to the bible, God see's us all the same, as a sinful race. For those who have answered correctly, this is precisely why we need Jesus. If it weren't for Jesus, our sin brings our souls to a spiritual death, but we have an opportunity at *everlasting* spiritual life through Him (Romans 6:23). Although our society creates and enforces our worldly laws, our Lord in Heaven rules over our souls, and the judgement we will receive at the end of our lives.

God sent Jesus to die for our sins, the only perfectly sin-less man who ever walked the Earth. Jesus was the perfect, and ultimate sacrifice, dying for the sins of all who believe in Him. Our sinful world crucified Him on the cross, and He died, was buried, and on the third day resurrected (John 11:25). Upon His resurrection Jesus bestowed upon us the gift of the Holy spirit, that whoever *follows* Him will have the Holy spirits assistance and guidance until Jesus comes for us at the end of our lives. When Adam took the bite of the forbidden fruit, he poisoned *all mankind* as we are **all** descendants from Adam, to be slaves of our sin (Romans 5:12). Just as one man condemned all mankind, another man saved it. Without this belief in Jesus, along with the conviction to be righteous by His example, everlasting life cannot bless your soul, and in this way God's love is conditional. The Good News is, it's never too late to repent our sinful old ways, and ask Jesus to guide our lives.

Hebrews 9:13-14, NLT

13 Under the old system, the blood of goats and bulls and the ashes of a heifer could cleanse people's bodies from ceremonial impurity. 14 Just think how much more the blood of Christ will purify our consciences from sins so that we can worship the living God. For by the power of the eternal Spirit, Christ offered himself to God as a perfect sacrifice for our sins.

Romans 5:18, ESV

18 Therefore, as one trespass led to condemnation for all men, so one act of righteousness leads to justification and life for all men.

January 4
Understanding the Holy Spirit

John 14:26, CEV

26 Jesus said, "The Holy Spirit will come and help you, because God will send the Spirit to take my place. The Spirit will teach you everything and will remind you of what I said while I was with you."

Acts 2:38, ESV

38 And Peter said to them, "Repent and be baptized every one of you in the name of Jesus Christ for the forgiveness of your sins, and you will receive the gift of the Holy Spirit.

If someone asked us what the Holy Spirit was, how would we answer them? God is the Almighty, all-knowing, all-powerful creator of the universe. Jesus Christ, the son of God, was sent to teach us how to live as God's children, and died so that our souls could live forever in heaven. The Holy Spirit is a little more enigmatic. God is spirit, born from Jesus' love and sacrifice through His resurrection, the Holy Spirit is something that dwells inside of us and is with us always (Ezekiel 36:27). An invisible force binding us to Jesus, when we profess our belief in Him and repent our sins we are blessed with the Holy Spirit. We utilize the Holy Spirit each time we pray, and this is how we communicate to Jesus (Romans 8:26). Most of us lead lives that are too busy and hectic to provide an environment conducive to hearing the Holy Spirit. We need to be calm, quiet, and at peace to hear the Holy Spirit. Through our lives busy with work, kids, deadlines, and family obligations, we need to remember to take quiet, personal time to nurture our connection through the Holy Spirit as we strengthen our relationship in Jesus Christ. It's in these quiet moments we can hear the Holy Spirit, 'whispering' to our subconscious, influencing our thoughts, feelings and attitudes (John 14:15-17).

We can only hear the Holy Spirit when we aren't too busy to hear Him, and are calm and open-minded. We need to be at peace to hear the Holy Spirit. Our emotions can give us insight to what's in our hearts, but can cloud righteous judgment. When we devote our time and energy to utilizing the Holy Spirit inside of each of us, we're given the tools we need to understand how to stay in God's good graces, and are given the knowledge that we need to lead us to the peace, goodness and fulfilment that we seek (Galatians 5:22-23). That may sound a lot more daunting than it really is. God isn't going to give any of us anything we cannot handle (1 Corinthians 10:13), and we need to be able to trust God on that. Serving God means we pray daily and follow the Holy Spirit inside of us as we yield to God's path for us. How about you, how strong is *your* relationship with the Holy Spirit dwelling inside of you?

Isaiah 11:2, ESV

2 And the Spirit of the Lord shall rest upon him, the Spirit of wisdom and understanding, the Spirit of counsel and might, the Spirit of knowledge and the fear of the Lord.

January 5
Praying

Proverbs 15:8, ERV

8 The Lord hates the offerings of the wicked, but he is happy to hear the prayers of those who live right.

1 Thessalonians 5:17, ESV

17 pray without ceasing.

Matthew 6:7-8, ERV

7 "And when you pray, don't be like the people who don't know God. They say the same things again and again. They think that if they say it enough, their god will hear them. 8 Don't be like them. Your Father knows what you need before you ask him."

Prayer is a Christ follower's secret weapon. We can derive strength, advice, comfort, hope, forgiveness and love through prayer. Some people are afraid to pray, thinking they may sound silly or inarticulate. Other people aren't sure if they're allowed to pray directly to Jesus, even though He instructed us on this personally (John 14:6). Since all humans are fallible except Jesus, why would we want to pray to anyone else? In the bible, Jesus describes how to pray, endorsing this activity plainly. God knows our steps before we do, and knows our heart, but like any loving parent wants us to seek Him. Praying is our conduit for righteousness through Christ Jesus, it's how we repent, it's how we fill ourselves up with the goodness of Christ in the way of strength, hope, patience, and grace. As a matter of fact, what kind of person wants to keep someone else from connecting with Jesus? No one with Holy intentions.

The bible is full of references to prayer and how important it is. In the passage below, Jesus teaches the 'Lord's prayer,' encouraging prayer to His disciples. Knowing no human would ever be righteous enough for everlasting life in God's Holy presence, Jesus was sent to show us what God wants from our lives, what He seeks from our attitudes, hearts, spirits, and souls. If we are to follow Jesus and not other humans, we must seek Him routinely. God knows our hearts, and if we are sincere in our prayers, or if we're holding things back. We must also pursue kinder, purer hearts through prayer in order to change what truly motivates them. Jesus not only advocated for daily prayer, He even teaches us all how to do it properly. As followers of the one true Christ, we shouldn't let anyone tell us anything different, or lead us astray from Christ's own words.

Matthew 6:9-13, ERV

9 Jesus said, "So this is how you should pray: 'Our Father in heaven, we pray that your name will always be kept holy. 10 We pray that your kingdom will come— that what you want will be done here on earth, the same as in heaven. 11 Give us the food we need for today. 12 Forgive our sins, just as we have forgiven those who did wrong to us. 13 Don't let us be tempted, but save us from the Evil One.'"

January 6
Our Covenant

Our covenant with God (Exodus 34:10) holds the information we need to follow Him, and remain Holy. In the passage below, God gives Moses the ten commandments, and warns that 'anyone who sins against God becomes His enemy that He will punish.' Yikes. God created us, created the Universe that surrounds us, and we aren't supposed to understand it all in minutia (Ecclesiastes 3:11). We are limited in our knowledge of the Heavens and the spiritual Universe, that is why we are measured by the depth of our faith and service to our devotion. Jesus explained to His disciples the significance of two commandments, and how the entire structure of God's directives rests upon them. This is significant because it means that God's commandments might have originated out of God's 'chosen' Israel, but **all people are invited to seek God** in repentance, and to adhere to those commandments in their own life-no matter the century we're living in (Isaiah 40:8, 1 Peter 1:25). God doesn't expire.

If we aren't totally devoted to God, He knows. Don't be afraid to ask God tough questions in prayer, seeking a deeper knowledge in our creator breeds understanding and love. We need to understand the covenant in order to obey it as God commands. Since we are all God's creation, we are brothers and sisters under one Father God (Genesis 9:18-19). Submitting ourselves, in humility, to a superior entity might be difficult for the proud or the conceited. Remember that God is in control of our souls, but the Devil is in control of the world we live in (1 John 5:19). Our covenant with God is something the Devil wishes to destroy, and our eternal salvation with it. Read up on the covenant, then think about how they affect your daily life, are you *as* faithful as you *could* be?

> Exodus 20:3-8, 12-17, ESV
>
> 3 "You shall have no other gods before me. 4 You shall not make for yourself a carved image, or any likeness of anything that is in heaven above, or that is in the earth beneath, or that is in the water under the earth. 5 You shall not bow down to them or serve them, for I the Lord your God am a jealous God, People who sin against me become my enemies, and I will punish them. And I will punish their children, their grandchildren, and even their great- grandchildren, 6 but showing steadfast love to thousands of those who love me and keep my commandments. 7 You shall not take the name of the Lord your God in vain, for the Lord will not hold him guiltless who takes His name in vain. 8 Remember the Sabbath day, to keep it holy. 12 Honor your father and your mother, that your days may be long in the land that the Lord your God is giving you. 13 You shall not murder. 14 You shall not commit adultery. 15 You shall not steal. 16 You shall not bear false witness against your neighbor. 17 You shall not covet your neighbor's house; you shall not covet your neighbor's wife, or His male servant, or His female servant, or His ox, or His donkey, or anything that is your neighbor's."

January 7
The Bible

Matthew 4:4, ESV

4 But he answered, "It is written, "'Man shall not live by bread alone, but by every word that comes from the mouth of God.'"

2 Timothy 3:16, ESV

16 All Scripture is breathed out by God and profitable for teaching, for reproof, for correction, and for training in righteousness.

As Christ-followers we must understand and respect the significance of the bible. A book of mystery, the bible was written by different people, and in a time and day that seems light-years away from our current worlds. A collection of scriptures that not only defines how we are to live our lives, the bible also highlights the life and death of Jesus Christ, and God's love for us through His relationship with the nation of Israel. The bible also describes God's love for us through Jesus, and ultimately describes the creation and intention of the Holy Spirit. Comprising the word of our Almighty God, the bible contains God's laws and commandments, and examples of the spiritual code He intended for us to live by. Sometimes the bible can be hard to understand, but it's meant to be a guide in our journey to become more like Christ.

Over and over again, the bible talks about living righteously (Ezekiel 18:5-9). Lying, cheating, swearing, stealing, greed, vanity, and frivolous sexual activity are all described in the bible as sins we need to cleanse ourselves of, and things to avoid. But the bible doesn't stop there, we are also told to be patient, graceful, forgiving, loving and strong to ourselves and others as Jesus was. We are told to pray, and ask for forgiveness, and then actually *want* to be better people who are really making an effort in their lives to be. We may not understand everything in the bible, but if we're able to derive meaning from the lessons the bible is teaching us, then we're on the right track. Keep reading, keep praying, keep seeking improvement in the right places. Maybe we should nickname the bible, 'the righteousness handbook?'

1 Corinthians 2:12, ESV

12 Now we have received not the spirit of the world, but the Spirit who is from God, that we might understand the things freely given us by God.

Hebrews 4:12, ESV

12 For the word of God is living and active, sharper than any two-edged sword, piercing to the division of soul and of spirit, of joints and of marrow, and discerning the thoughts and intentions of the heart.

January 8
Righteousness 101

Colossians 3:5-10, ESV/ERV

5 Put to death therefore what is earthly in you: fornication, uncleanness, inordinate affection, evil concupiscence, and covetousness, which is idolatry. 6 God will show His anger against those who don't obey him, because they do these evil things. 7 In these you too once walked, when you were living in them. 8 But now you must put them all away: anger, wrath, malice, slander, and obscene talk from your mouth. 8 But now put these things out of your life: anger, losing your temper, doing or saying things to hurt others, and saying shameful things. 9 Don't lie to each other. You have taken off those old clothes—the person you once were and the bad things you did then. 10 Now you are wearing a new life, a life that is new every day. You are growing in your understanding of the one who made you. You are becoming more and more like him.

In this passage we can get a good example of how to live in Jesus' righteousness. Our words, behaviors and attitudes reflect who we are, what we think, and what's truly in our hearts. We must pray for purer hearts, and the desire to help our fellow man, if we don't come by those feelings naturally. As Christ-followers, we serve as *Christ* served through good works, but what does that mean? Helping one another, building each other up, acts of service to the poor, needy and underserved is what Christ meant by good works. Many people are usually focused on themselves, not given to *wanting* to go out of their way for another. Just because we are naturally greedy and selfish doesn't mean we *can't* change, with God anything is possible (Matthew 19:26). When we pledge to be more righteous we are taking on additional struggle, the pressure to avoid temptation instead of submitting to it. Many people attempt a more righteous lifestyle and become frustrated, and eventually walk away from their faith not wanting to avoid temptations. Other people are under false beliefs, and practice their religion separate from their personal lives thinking that what they do doesn't really matter in the grand scheme of things. Other people talk about their religion to anyone who'll listen, but don't change their attitude or behavior. What's in our hearts directs our actions, behaviors, words and attitudes, praying regularly for a more righteous heart is wise and prudent Holy maintenance. We cannot hide what's truly in our hearts from God, and His love through Jesus is the only way to a more virtuous heart (John 14:6). We must be patient with ourselves, and allow ourselves to learn from our sins instead of using them as building blocks that imprison our souls.

Micah 6:8, CEB

8 He has told you, human one, what is good and what the Lord requires from you: to do justice, embrace faithful love, and walk humbly with your God.

January 9
Importance of Repentance

2 Corinthians 7:10, ERV

10 The kind of sorrow God wants makes people decide to change their lives. This leads them to salvation, and we cannot be sorry for that. But the kind of sorrow the world has will bring death.

Acts 3:19, ERV

19 So you must change your hearts and lives. Come back to God, and he will forgive your sins.

Perhaps we've caught ourself passing judgement, or coveting what someone else has, or partaking in crude humor, after all, we are natural born sinners. Once we've learned what we've done wrong, we can apologize to Christ in prayer for those specific things. If we never know what we've done wrong, we cannot hand it over and rid ourselves of it, but are doomed to repeat the mistake. Here we can become discouraged if we are unable to see our mistakes for any reason; maybe we are too focused on one issue when it's another the Lord wants us to work on, or maybe we have trouble admitting or focusing on anything that reminds us of our imperfections. Forgiveness is when we're remorseful for our sins, and repentance is the effort we put into not committing that sin again. This is important because if we're not repentant, we can't be washed of our sins, and we'll end up in hell for our wickedness. Hell isn't a pleasant thought (Matthew 13:50).

Life isn't a competition to see who can become the best follower of Christ, really. It's about our individual walk with Christ, our devotion to faith and service through him, to live as righteous a life as we can by following His example. The bible urges us not to compare ourselves, not to pass judgement, and lift one another up. That doesn't sound much like a competition. We must look *inward* at *ourselves* to see what is motivating our behavior, and this leads us closer to understanding our mistakes. Seeking forgiveness for our sins through prayers to Jesus, we begin the journey to repentance. Repentance leads us to change our hearts and minds, focusing on the righteous thoughts and behaviors of Christ's example.

Ezekiel 18:32, GW

32 "I don't want anyone to die," declares the Almighty Lord. "Change the way you think and act!"

2 Peter 3:9, ISV

9 The Lord is not slow about His promise, as some people understand slowness, but is being patient with you. He does not want anyone to perish, but everyone to find room for repentance.

January 10
Mistakes

John 3:20-21, ERV

20 Everyone who does evil hates the light. They will not come to the light, because the light will show all the bad things they have done. 21 But anyone who follows the true way comes to the light. Then the light will show that whatever they have done was done through God.

Mistakes, we all make them, and we all react to them differently. Some of us don't like admitting that we make them on a regular basis, some of us use them against ourselves, and others ignore them all together, hoping they'll magically disappear. Some followers of Christ think that simply accepting Jesus into their hearts makes them invulnerable to committing any *more* sins. Mistakes humble us, and remind us just how much we need Jesus to *make* us holy. When we place our pride in our own accomplishments, we are being vain, and our focus is wrongly placed. When we chastise ourselves for not being perfect we are assuming judgment, taking away final judgement which rightfully belongs to God, our focus is wrongly placed. If we ignore our mistakes we are destined to repeat them, never progressing in our faith, our spiritual growth, or our intellectual capacity. In the bible, even Christ's disciples admit to sinning and making mistakes (James 3:2, Psalm 19:12, 1 John 2:1), highlighting the need for the sovereign Messiah we have in Christ Jesus. The point is, we should never be *comfortable* or *tolerant* of our wrongs, all are sins bad (James 2:10, Proverbs 28:13-14).

Not everyone may like hearing this, but God wants us to not only achieve humility, but maintain it as a resting place for our souls (Isaiah 66:2). We all fall short in the eyes of God, we may do it differently, but all humans sin. We are meant to know and understand that God is the superior being in our world, and not highlighting our weaknesses out of cruelty, but to offer guidance and sanctuary for our souls. God is purifying those who will let him (Jeremiah 9:7). When we can stop looking inward, stop focusing on ourselves, and begin looking toward *Jesus* as our example, He will show us what we need to focus on. In trusting Jesus to guide us, we are taking the first steps toward a more humble, righteous spirit. When we walk in this light, learning from our mistakes with humility, we learn and grow stronger from them. This isn't because of how awesome we are as humans, but because of God's generosity, grace and love for us (1 Corinthians 1:30).

Proverbs 24:16, ERV

16 Good people might fall again and again, but they always get up. It is the wicked who are defeated by their troubles.

January 11
Humility

Luke 18:9-14, ESV

9 There were some people who thought they were very good and looked down on everyone else. Jesus used this story to teach them: 10 "Two men went up into the temple to pray, one a Pharisee and the other a tax collector. 11 The Pharisee, standing by himself, prayed thus: 'God, I thank you that I am not like other men, extortioners, unjust, adulterers, or even like this tax collector. 12 I fast twice a week; I give tithes of all that I get.' 13 But the tax collector, standing far off, would not even lift up His eyes to heaven, but beat His breast, saying, 'God, be merciful to me, a sinner!' 14 I tell you, this man went down to His house justified, rather than the other. For everyone who exalts himself will be humbled, but the one who humbles himself will be exalted."

Some people may think of humiliation or shame when they think of the word, 'humility.' This is not what Jesus meant by humility sought in righteousness through Him. The bible teaches that arrogance, pride in oneself, pride in one's knowledge all stem from conceit, and seeing oneself as better than others. In loving and understanding God, we also understand that no one is created to be better than anyone else (except Jesus). Everything good within us comes from the direct results of our own quests for righteousness, which is from the Lord (Deuteronomy 10:14, James 1:17). This is why we read prayers of thanksgiving, prayers of rejoicing, and celebrations for the Lord over and over in the bible, because of His divine mercy. When we humble ourselves to the knowledge that we cannot achieve righteousness without Jesus, we become grateful for His special gift in the way He desires. If you had died for someone you would also be justified in wanting them to love you and be eternally grateful!

It can be easy for some people to argue that being proud of oneself is a positive quality, and only builds healthy confidence and self-esteem. Ask yourself, what are you proud of? Is it the accomplishments we've achieved through worldly things, or is it through a deeper spiritual faith and good works according to Christ Jesus? When we exalt ourselves, we put ourselves before Christ. Our self-esteem should be built on the fact that whatever we need, our God will provide, we merely need to seek it, and not from anything we ourselves will ever accomplish (Ephesians 2:5-10). This doesn't mean that we're completely inept beings, just that we are all smaller pieces of a much bigger, more powerful, spiritual Heavenly Kingdom, and shouldn't presume to be more than we are, or were designed to be.

James 4:10, ESV

10 Humble yourselves before the Lord, and he will exalt you.

January 12
God and Humanity: a Love Story

Genesis 6:11-12, ESV

11 Now the earth was corrupt in God's sight, and the earth was filled with violence. 12 And God saw the earth, and behold, it was corrupt, for all flesh had corrupted their way on the earth.

Genesis 6:7, ESV

7 So the Lord said, "I will blot out man whom I have created from the face of the land, man and animals and creeping things and birds of the heavens, for I am sorry that I have made them."

Genesis 8:21-22, ESV

21 And when the Lord smelled the pleasing aroma, the Lord said in His heart, "I will never again curse the ground because of man, for the intention of man's heart is evil from His youth. Neither will I ever again strike down every living creature as I have done. 22 While the earth remains, seedtime and harvest, cold and heat, summer and winter, day and night, shall not cease."

Every good love story seems to follow a similar storyline: hero meets heroine and love blooms, but then something goes wrong that threatens their love and there is a struggle to regain their one true happiness. God's love for an evil, corrupt humanity is the original love story. Through Passover, and other similar type events in History, God has given humanity a way back to His salvation. God came down to Earth personally, in the form of Jesus Christ, and died for the humanity he created that had corrupted themselves, saving our souls from eternal death and damnation. This is the ultimate form of love (John 15:13).

Love is wonderful in all its forms, but it takes work. Effort is required to maintain the Holy, righteous lifestyle Christ-followers are called to, as well as pious devotion to God and our Savior, Jesus. Just how invested we become in our relationship with God is totally up to us, but He's made it clear where *He* stands. He wants us all to come back to Him, be devoted to Him, repent, and we'll be forgiven and welcomed back into His kingdom (2 Chronicles 7:14). It's up to us how this love story ends, will we return to God, repent, and assure Him of our faith wholeheartedly? Or will we turn our backs on Him, and continue to live our own, sinful lives making our own choices, continuing to pursue our worldly pleasures instead of righteousness despite Him?

1 John 4:9, ESV

9 In this the love of God was made manifest among us, that God sent His only Son into the world, so that we might live through him.

January 13
Why Does God Allow Suffering?

1 Peter 2:19-21, ICB

19 A person might have to suffer even when he has done nothing wrong. But if he thinks of God and bears the pain, this pleases God. 20 If you are punished for doing wrong, there is no reason to praise you for bearing punishment. But if you suffer for doing good, and you are patient, then that pleases God. 21 That is what you were called to do. Christ suffered for you. He gave you an example to follow. So you should do as he did.

We all suffer from time to time, and tend to view suffering as unfair, unjust and undeserved when we experience it. Why do we think we are exempt from suffering? Why do we think we are an accurate judge of what's fair or just? Where was it promised that life would be full of pleasant experiences, triumphs and uninterrupted gratification? We are arrogant to assume any of these, in any respect. Humans slip into patterns of arrogant thinking all too easily. Our lives are designed and run by God, whether we want to admit it or not, and He's got a plan we are intended to follow (Psalm 33:11). Anytime we stray from that path, God is going to try and get us back on what He considers is the right track for us (Proverbs 3:12). It is important to remember, here, that we always have a choice.

We learn and grow stronger from the trials in our lives, perhaps we're meant to learn something about *our* wrongdoings in our suffering. Still maybe, we could be serving as an example for *another's* lesson in *their own* wrongdoings, but all is done for the purpose of personal and spiritual growth. We can let the suffering in our lives make us bitter, or we can examine it, learn from it and let it make us better, stronger people. We can do this much faster, more efficiently, and certainly more accurate when we tap into Jesus' power through the Holy Spirit. So calm down, take a deep breath and relax. Pray to Jesus about your suffering, and ask for comfort and direction, that's all we have to do to get through it (1 Peter 5:6-7). If we chose to deny this, we don't grow stronger from our suffering, just more bitter and unfulfilled. The lessons we allow the Holy Spirit to teach us, through our suffering grows into wisdom that leads to salvation through Christ Jesus. Our Savior is the only guarantee in life.

2 Timothy 3:12-15, ICB

12 Everyone who wants to live the way God wants, in Christ Jesus, will be persecuted. 13 People who are evil and cheat other people will go from bad to worse. They will fool others, but they will also be fooling themselves. 14 But you should continue following the teachings that you learned. You know that these teachings are true. And you know you can trust those who taught you. 15 You have known the Holy Scriptures since you were a child. The Scriptures are able to make you wise. And that wisdom leads to salvation through faith in Christ Jesus.

January 14
Ask and You Shall Receive

James 1:5, ESV

5 If any of you lacks wisdom, let him ask God, who gives generously to all without reproach, and it will be given him. 6 But let him ask in faith, with no doubting, for the one who doubts is like a wave of the sea that is driven and tossed by the wind.

What if we don't know what we need when we're praying? We would all like a little more money to pay our bills, or more time in a day to get things done, or maybe one more conversation with someone dear to us who's past. In God, we learn that all things are possible. Serving an all-powerful, all-knowing, yet invisible God is as difficult as it sounds. Only the bible offers clear instruction on God's will for our lives, and its contents are complicated and confusing to many of us. In reading the word of God we will learn God's laws and commandments, the propensity of humans to sin, of God's eternal love for us, what love really looks like, and how Jesus saved us all just to name a few! People who aren't reading the bible for themselves either aren't interested in what God has to say, or place their faith in others' interpretation of the bible. God isn't a mere moral guide for us to take advantage of when *we* think we need him. God is king of all creation, designed us to need Him, and only God can show us our true potential (2 Peter 1:5-12).

Sometimes it takes a great deal of soul searching to reveal what our hearts are in need of deep down, and our growing relationship with God can illuminate this in a way we never could on our own. Maybe we'll find we need advice, direction, renewed hope, a deeper faith, or a clearer sense of purpose, that seems to be trapped under years of neglected emotions and daily tasks thought to be more important. If we find ourselves unsure, we pray for direction, reassurance and a deeper faith, and God is faithful to hear us (John 14:14). If we need clarity, we ask for it, and if we need patience we must ask for that too. We know when we're praying that God knows our hearts and hears our cries. We understand that God works through the Holy Spirit inside of us to guide our lives. Through this journey in finding a clearer, deeper connection with God, we learn hidden truths our hearts have suppressed. It's in this knowing that we find comfort and understanding, and we find hope which renews our faith, and ultimately, this guides our paths. God works through us in mysterious and enigmatic ways which we will never fully understand (Isaiah 55:8-9), but our faith reassures us that He will sustain us when we ask for it. So, the answer to the above question is, it doesn't matter, just pray. If we don't know what we need, then we pray for direction until we do. If we have direction but face obstacles, then we pray to learn a way around those obstacles. Either way, we must trust that the Lord will provide the guidance we seek.

Matthew 7:7-8, ESV

7 "Ask, and it will be given to you; seek, and you will find; knock, and it will be opened to you. 8 For everyone who asks receives, and the one who seeks finds, and to the one who knocks it will be opened."

January 15
Prayer Is Important

Philippians 4:6, ESV

6 do not be anxious about anything, but in everything by prayer and supplication with thanksgiving let your requests be made known to God.

Matthew 6:5-6, ESV

5 "And when you pray, you must not be like the hypocrites. For they love to stand and pray in the synagogues and at the street corners, that they may be seen by others. Truly, I say to you, they have received their reward. 6 But when you pray, go into your room and shut the door and pray to your Father who is in secret. And your Father who sees in secret will reward you."

If God already knows what we're thinking, and what we're going to do before we do it, why must we always be in prayer with Him? Prayer is the tool we use to communicate with God. To love and serve God is to share our concerns, anxieties, and upcoming decisions with Him in order to allow Him a closer presence in our lives. As humans we sin daily, and need to offer ourselves to God daily in prayer for the forgiveness of those sins. All relationships are a two-way effort, so we must do our parts. How many times did you pray yesterday, and did you share anything with God or just complain and make requests? Our gift from God is to be heard, loved, forgiven and understood, but we spend far less time than we should in prayer. We must commit to spending a little more time with our heavenly Father in prayers of thanks, and prayers of sharing.

As sinners we need close spiritual guidance, but we are usually so busy in our daily lives that we don't spend the time we should in devotion to God. Think about the moments you could have been more patient, a little more compassionate, understanding or generous and use those moments as a blueprint for self-change. We shouldn't be muttering to God under our breath while we clean up in the kitchen, or while we're putting our laundry away, or while we're working on our budgets. Rather, in a quiet place with the door closed to outside interruption spend a few private moments devoting ourselves to God in prayer. The 'Lord's prayer' is always a good place to begin (Matthew 6:7-14). Practice speaking with God, not just about your transgressions and wrongs, but also your concerns, your needs and desires, and the people or things in your life you are grateful for. And, do this in a peaceful environment, where your focus is only on God. More than just building trust in our faith, we are *loving* our Heavenly Father back when we share our hearts with Him. Take a moment to think about the things that take up the most space in your daily thoughts, and share them with God in prayer today.

Jeremiah 29:12, ESV

12 "Then you will call upon me and come and pray to me, and I will hear you."

January 16
Frustration!

Psalm 34:18, ERV

18 The Lord is close to those who have suffered disappointment. He saves those who are discouraged.

James 1:20, ERV

20 Anger does not help you live the way God wants.

Sometimes we need a little more patience and grace to get through our day in order to *not* behave or react foolishly to our daily frustrations, moments of anger, and disappointments. Other times still, this can be an understatement. Our expectations can leave us bitterly disappointed when things don't turn out the way we want them, or need them to. We can all get angry at traffic when driving, get frustrated standing in a long line, or disappointed in our families or communities, and we can let those irritations really gnaw at us. Usually, before we've properly delt with *one* negative challenge we're focused on another, and, before you know it, the whole day has soured our attitudes. We don't always think of prayer as a remedy, but that's exactly what it's for. It can be difficult to stop and pray when we're angry, irritated, frustrated or disappointed, but that's just what God wants us to do (Philippians 4:6).

God wants us to know that Jesus bears our burdens if we'd just let Him. God is ready to provide solutions for our lives, but we must ask for His help. We must stop what we're doing, tune everything else out, and focus on Jesus for a couple of minutes. When we 'vent' our frustrations, we really should be praying those feelings away to Jesus in prayer, not to any friend, family member or colleague who will listen. Our Sovereign Lord can't work His miracles in us if we don't give more than a few seconds of our attention daily, and can even be considered turning away from God (Jeremiah 7:24). We can't take our jobs, family, money, awards, or friends to heaven when we're called (1 Timothy 6:7), so why should they get more of our hearts than Christ Jesus? Pray; Upload all anxious thoughts and worries, all fears and concerns, all anger and contempt, all disappointment and heartbreak, to Jesus in a prayer. Salvation.

Proverbs 15:18, ESV

18 A hot-tempered man stirs up strife, but he who is slow to anger quiets contention.

Isaiah 41:10, ESV

10 "fear not, for I am with you; be not dismayed, for I am your God; I will strengthen you, I will help you, I will uphold you with my righteous right hand."

January 17
Pride vs. Humility

Proverbs 11:2, ESV

2 When pride comes, then comes disgrace, but with the humble is wisdom.

Accomplishments and awards often reflect many hours of hard work, and perhaps, a little talent. Physical abilities or weight loss, knowledge, possessions, and wealth are also achievements that come after much effort has been invested into a set goal. We can all think of many things in our lives we could say we're 'proud' of, but what does that pride say about us? The health, or success of our family, giving up bad habits, and even rehabilitating our attitudes all seem like triumphs worthy of a little pride. Pride and humility are opposite words, and both describe character. When we are proud we are more *than a little* satisfied with our own achievements, acquisitions, and accomplishments. If we are humble, we have a much more modest opinion of our importance. Many of us would consider this to be a no-brainer, and so, what? In the bible, repeatedly, humility is praised over pride (James 4:6). In fact, God doesn't like proud people, He thinks they have such a high opinion of themselves that they don't think they need Him (Psalm 10:3-4). God humbles the proud, and we see evidence of this in many of the stories of kings being rebuked for their arrogance (Daniel 4:28-37).

If we think we've accomplished all that we're so very proud of all on our own, this is our first mistake. When we give ourselves credit for what God has provided, enlightened us to, or blessed us with, we're ignoring His grace, generosity, love, and very presence in our lives. Likewise, when we judge our own lives, or the lives of those around us, demanding justice or fair treatment from the Lord we are, again, displaying arrogance. God decides what each person's life will contain, both good and bad (Isaiah 45:7), it's only our refusal to accept this that causes us trouble. We can only be humble when we realize that **God** is in control of our lives, quite divinely, and the only thing we can truly control is how we respond to that. Acceptance, repentance, and gratitude should replace our indignance, stubbornness, and arrogance. If we look around us all we see are sinners (Romans 3:23), not one of us is better than another in the eyes of God, no matter what our society tells us. Our world, our society, our government, even our churches and schools are run by sinners; both good and bad. The bible explains that all humans sin, and will continue to sin, (Genesis 6:5). This is our handicap in the quest to show God how devoted we can be to Him, and His covenant with humanity (Hebrews 9:15). Instead of feeling proud, honored, delighted, or satisfied, we should simply, and humbly, be thankful to God for all we have. Praise God for His patience, love, and grace for all who seek Him, AMEN!

Proverbs 15:33, ICB

33 The fear of the Lord is instruction in wisdom. If you want to be honored, you must not be proud.

January 18
For Some, Seeing Is Believing

John 20:24-28, ESV

24 Now Thomas, one of the twelve, called the Twin, was not with them when Jesus came. 25 So the other disciples told him, "We have seen the Lord." But he said to them, "Unless I see in His hands the mark of the nails, and place my finger into the mark of the nails, and place my hand into His side, I will never believe." 26 Eight days later, His disciples were inside again, and Thomas was with them. Although the doors were locked, Jesus came and stood among them and said, "Peace be with you." 27 Then he said to Thomas, "Put your finger here, and see my hands; and put out your hand, and place it in my side. Do not disbelieve, but believe." 28 Thomas answered him, "My Lord and my God!"

We can't see a Wi-Fi signal, but we can tell when we don't have one. We cannot see electricity, but we know that it exists because it provides power to communities worldwide. We don't see the wind blow, but we know it exists because we can *feel it*. God is *spirit*, and many people misunderstand or simply don't believe in Him. We all have different levels of belief, but the struggle to understand, and get closer to an invisible, mysterious God has baffled humans since the beginning of time. Humans had been so focused on themselves and their environment for so long, that even Jesus had trouble explaining who He was, not to mention the complexities of a spiritual kingdom of Heaven (Matthew 16:13-17)(John 3:11-12).

Although some people will admit to believing in the human spirit, or the depth of human emotions, they continue to disbelieve, or place their full trust in a God they cannot see. When people don't see God in their lives they aren't looking with the right eyes. If God were visible to us today, there wouldn't be any reason to *prove our devotion* to Him. To know God is to understand Him, so open a bible, get to know Him better! People have difficulty accepting things they don't understand, and some are too proud to admit they don't understand God. We must be humble, penitent, and thankful instead of bittersweet, disappointed, impatient, or demanding to success-fully communicate with our Lord. Many people might still be struggling because they refuse to accept that they are a divine creation of the Almighty God, and created in His image. May the light of the Lord illuminate the mind of our brothers and sisters in darkness. Praise be to God, Amen.

1 John 4:2-3, ESV

2 By this you know the Spirit of God: every spirit that confesses that Jesus Christ has come in the flesh is from God, 3 and every spirit that does not confess Jesus is not from God. This is the spirit of the antichrist, which you heard was coming and now is in the world already.

January 19
Money

1 Timothy 6:10, ERV/GW

10 Certainly, the love of money is the root of all kinds of evil. Some people who have set their hearts on getting rich have wandered away from the faith and have caused themselves a lot of grief.

Ecclesiastes 5: 10, GNT/ESV

10 If you love money, you will never be satisfied; if you long to be rich, you will never get all you want. It is useless ; this also is vanity.

Money, we need it to secure a domicile for our families, to provide food, clothing and transportation to and from our place of employment. Money provides the means of acquiring things *necessary* to our survival, but it also provides us with an opportunity to acquire things that are unnecessary, as well as unwholesome. Also, the more wealth you acquire, the more you desire. Money can be a double-edged sword, and tricks us into succumbing to worldly desires to acquire more of what we *don't* need. We tell ourselves, "We're building a *nest egg* for the family," or, "I've worked hard, I *deserve* to play hard," thinking we won't let money consume our souls (Mark 8:36). Before long, we are greedy, selfish, money-grubbing misers looking with suspicion and contempt at our brothers and sisters in Christ. We can easily forget that we have to work hard, and suffer tribulations in life, *because* of *the depravity of man* that started in the book of Genesis (Genesis 3:10-19). We mustn't lose our focus, or the knowledge that we need God, and in our lives we honor Him by emulating the life of Christ as best we can.

As Christ's followers, we must be mindful that the pursuit of greater financial security is the root of evil motivations, greed, pride, and vanity. Money is only significant to the extent we have what we need to survive, shelter, food, clothing, transportation to and from work. The bible teaches that good, righteous Christ-followers should be donating something to those less fortunate, whether it's food, clothing, or monetary donations to the needy (Deuteronomy 15:11, Matthew 25:34-46). If we are lucky enough to experience wealth, as followers of Christ, the bible encourages us to be philanthropic to the poor, less fortunate, and in need. Donate to a local church or community center, or to a food bank, but remember that humility and love for our fellow neighbor should be our motivation.

Matthew 16:26-27, BRG Bible

26 For what is a man profited, if he shall gain the whole world, and lose His own soul? or what shall a man give in exchange for His soul? 27 For the Son of man shall come in the glory of His Father with His angels; and then he shall reward every man according to His works.

Acts 20:35, ERV

35 Jesus said, "I always showed you that you should work just as I did and help people who are weak. I taught you to remember the words of the Lord Jesus: 'You will have a greater blessing when you give than when you receive.'"

January 20
Patience

Romans 12:12, ESV

12 Rejoice in hope, be patient in tribulation, be constant in prayer.

Romans 15:5, GNT

5 All patience and encouragement come from God. And I pray that will allow you to live in harmony with each other by following the example of Christ Jesus.

Waiting in line, not getting the result we were expecting, being let down by a friend, a quick temper looking for an outlet are all ways our patience can be tested. As humans, we all have our breaking point that tests our perseverance and faith. Expectations are difficult to avoid, and humans are just as good at disappointing as they are at setting themselves up for disappointment. When we've lost our patience, we become angry, flustered, and our attitudes are tested. Some of us yell and lose our tempers, honking our horn and asking to speak to the manager when our patience is tested. Faithful Christ-followers pray. When we need something we don't have, we pray. When we have unwanted emotions or stress that we don't need, we pray. It's only when we're exhibiting patience that we'll begin to see our circumstances in a clearer light. When we're in a patient state of mind we are able to see and accept God's will, and not rebuke against it. After all, God's will is firm like a brick wall, so fighting it will just be more painful than just accepting the lesson for what it's intended to be.

When we lose our patience we shouldn't panic, we should pray. (Proverbs 14:29) Praying helps us to regain the balance lost from our tumultuous emotions, and puts our anxieties at the feet of Christ where they belong. When we focus on our own, human solutions, to our problems, revenge, or the support of other humans we only invite more inadequacies to the suffering. God may not answer our prayer in the time-line we desire, and the response may not be the gold-star solution we had imagined it should be. Faith is patience and trust, especially through trying times. And we can have patience in our faith because we know that God will never forsake us, and we know that God's love for us is eternal (Jeremiah 31:3). Impatience, anger, and frustration all narrow our perspectives, removing the clear thinking required to see the solution before us. Praying allows the Lord to guide our steps, and places the power and grace to change our circumstances at the feet of the Lord, where it belongs. We will always be subject to the whim of our changing emotions, but patience in the Lord through prayer is our secret weapon.

Isaiah 30:18, GW

18 The Lord is waiting to be kind to you. He rises to have compassion on you. The Lord is a God of justice. Blessed are all those who wait for him.

January 21
Why We Suffer

Isaiah 45:7, GNV

7 "I form the light, and create darkness: I make peace, and create evil: I the Lord do all these things."

Isaiah 48:10, ERV

10 "Look, I will make you pure, but not in the way you make silver pure. I will make you pure by giving you troubles."

Romans 8: 17, ERV

17 If we are God's children, we will get the blessings God has for His people. He will give us all that he has given Christ. But we must suffer like Christ suffered. Then we will be able to share His glory.

Life hurts. Our hearts break sometimes, our hope is crushed by others, and we are all made to suffer loss. We suffer because Christ suffered. If we want to end our life's journey in heaven, never to suffer again, we must endure as Christ endured. We will all endure suffering of different sorts in our lives, there are no exceptions. The real question is, *when* you suffer, whom are you turning to? Jesus wants us to turn to him, and show him patience in our faith while waiting for him to take the suffering from us. When we suffer calamity after calamity it can be easy to lose our patience, our focus, and even our faith. We can become angry, bitter, and resentful at the trials God throws at us, but all are designed to bring us back to God (Zechariah 13:9).

Jesus is ready to forgive our lack of faith, we must only repent. Nothing is impossible through Christ (Philippians 4:13). Suffering is a test of faith, and a lesson. We can only grow stronger from these tests of our faith, and by relying on prayer through the Holy Spirit. In learning to pray for what we need, learning to *fully* give up our burdens to the Lord, we strengthen our faith. When we endure tribulations and seek guidance and comfort in the Lord, we please him. In this attitude of patience and faith, we are calm enough to see things through the Holy Spirits eyes. This is when changes and solutions are presented to us. All good things come to those who not only wait, but seek the Lord through the waiting. This is how we endure.

James 1:12, ESV

12 Blessed is the man who remains steadfast under trial, for when he has stood the test he will receive the crown of life, which God has promised to those who love him.

January 22
Be Humbled

Matthew 23:12, GW

12 Whoever honors himself will be humbled, and whoever humbles himself will be honored.

James 4:10, ERV

10 Be humble before the Lord, and he will make you great.

It's normal to be proud of academic achievements, philanthropic work, or a large, well-earned paycheck. But what is the reason for the goals we set? If we are seeking success, fame, recognition, respect of our peers, or the admiration of others we are choosing in vain. Don't do good work just to outdo another or look favorably in someone's eyes, doing the right thing for the wrong reason is still wrong (Galatians 6:7-9). We should strive to accomplish things in our life because it feels good to be a person who pleases the Lord, to help others, and do the right thing. It's not enough to just *do* good things for others, but the reason *why* we do these things is even more important that the act itself. True greatness isn't measured in the amount of awards one can acquire, the amount of friends one can accumulate, or the amount of academic accolades one can be awarded. All we have, all we are, all we can become is due to the grace and will of the Lord (Jeremiah 17:10). Therefore, since we're all sinners, we're only arrogant and proud out of natural wickedness. We must work harder at being better people for Christ.

True greatness is measured by the life of our Lord Jesus Christ, and the example He set, not how our world views greatness. Our perspective must change to match that of Jesus' before we can truly change, but we need to get over our egos before we approach the Lord. Our desire to impress should only extend to the *Lord*, no one else's opinion really matters. We often lose sight of that as we are surrounded by other humans, some of whom will never stop the foolish race to be better than another. Once we can view greatness from the *Lord's* perspective, we will know what behaviors are truly congruent with greatness, we'll want to seek them. Humility means we don't see ourselves any better, or worse, than all the other sinners walking around in human bodies (Philippians 2:3-4). The motives for our behavior must be authentic, we must truly *want* the Lord to view us more favorably. Ask yourself if the Lord saw your behavior today, would *He* be proud?

Ephesians 4:2, ERV

2 Always be humble and gentle. Be patient and accept each other with love.

Isaiah 13:11, GW

11 "I will punish the world for its evil and the wicked for their wrongdoing. I will put an end to arrogant people and humble the pride of tyrants."

January 23
Unconditional Love?

Matthew 12:31-32, ERV

31 "So I tell you, people can be forgiven for every sinful thing they do and for every bad thing they say against God. But anyone who speaks against the Holy Spirit will not be forgiven. 32 You can even speak against the Son of Man and be forgiven. But anyone who speaks against the Holy Spirit **will never be forgiven** — not now or in the future."

God's love for us is so deep that he sent His only son to die a horrible death on the cross in order to cleanse our sinful spirits, therefore giving us eternal life. But is this love *unconditional*? Many people believe in God, but do not knowingly follow His commandments, or repent for their sins. In order to get in God's good graces and secure our spot in heaven's everlasting rapture, we must *believe* in the almighty God, Jesus Christ, and Christ's crucifixion for our sins (John 3:16). We must also keep the Lords commandments, seek regular forgiveness for our sins, and believe in and respect the Holy Spirit, or risk not being forgiven (Luke 3:8, Matthew 6:15, 7:2). Yikes! God has repeatedly explained this in the bible, and pleads with us over and over to accept these facts into our hearts, and accept His omnipresent love and forgiveness. We should *want* to love and serve our creator, our Lord and savior.

Loving God in the way He's asked us to (John 14:15) may be difficult for us at times, but the reward is spiritual salvation and eternal life in Heaven with our Lord, what a wonderful gift! Accepting Jesus into our hearts means accepting, and undertaking, the lifelong quest for righteousness we all must undertake to become the holy versions of ourselves God asks for (1 Peter 1:16). We must remember that *all* love is conditional, and, as such should be treasured, respected and mutually reciprocal. This ensures our fear in God, all actions come with consequences. Authentic love should be respected, appreciated and equally shared between all parties. Eternal life, and love, for our spirits free from pain, suffering and mourning is worth loving and serving a generous and easily loveable God.

Romans 8:38-39, ERV

38-39 Yes, I am sure that nothing can separate us from God's love — not death, life, angels, or ruling spirits. I am sure that nothing now, nothing in the future, no powers, nothing above us or nothing below us — nothing in the whole created world — will ever be able to separate us from the love God has shown us in Christ Jesus our Lord.

January 24
Prone to Sin

Genesis 6:5, ESV

5 Then the Lord saw that the wickedness of man was great on the earth, and that every intent of the thoughts of His heart was only evil **continually**.

Romans 3:10-11, ESV

10 as it is written: "None is righteous, no, not one; 11 no one understands; **no one seeks for God**."

Many of us read these scriptures and think to ourselves, "How did sin sneak into my life when I'm just trying to survive one day to the next with a moderate amount of comfort?" When we decide to go after what we want instead of being grateful for what we've been given, we're turning to sin. Sin is in the world all around us, and allowing ourselves to become contaminated or tainted by that sin is a real danger. Pride and arrogance, lies, adultery committed against one another, or against God's rules, sexual immorality, violence, vengeance, greed and lust are all common sins clearly described in the bible. What's more, all of us have committed one or more of these sins in our lifetimes, and we are all called to repent. God is faithful to cleanse us of our iniquities (1 John 1:9), if we would just humble ourselves before Him. When we humble ourselves before Jesus we admit that we've sinned, and vow not to commit that sin again.

Can any of us really say we'll never lie, or have a moment of pride, or become tempted by an indulgence that is wrong again? Humans are clearly flawed, and we clearly need the Sovereign power of the Almighty God to guide and correct us when we stray. Some unfortunate people think that life is an opportunity to acquire, satisfy temptations and urges, and gain as much knowledge, wealth, possessions or status as they can. Perhaps people think they don't need God, that all they have is because of their own will and determination. God created all things (John 1:3), God will have the final word and judgement over us all (Ecclesiastes 12:14), and God is the source of all good and bad in our lives (Isaiah 45:7), to deny this is either ignorance, or lack of faith. Humans are prone to sin, and must fight off temptations while adhering to God's commandments, which is no easy feat. The more we continue to turn to sinful behaviors and choices, focused on things the world thinks are important, the farther we stray from God's grace and protection. Whether we want to admit it, or we're still in an arrogant denial, God is in control of our lives, and the only real choice we each have is how faithful are we going to be to Him.

Psalm 36:1-3, ERV

1 Deep in the hearts of the wicked a voice tells them to do wrong. They have no respect for God. 2 They lie to themselves. They don't see their own faults, so they are not sorry for what they do. 3 Their words are wicked lies. They have stopped doing anything wise or good.

January 25
God's Plan

Romans 11:28-31, ICB

28 The Jews refuse to accept the Good News, so they are God's enemies. This has happened to help you non-Jews. But the Jews are still God's chosen people, and God loves them very much. He loves them because of the promises he made to their ancestors. 29 God never changes His mind about the people he calls and the things he gives them. 30 At one time you refused to obey God. But now you have received mercy, because those people refused to obey. 31 And now the Jews refuse to obey, because God showed mercy to you. But this happened so that they also can receive mercy from God.

God's plan from the beginning was to include **all** of humanity that prove faithful to Him to be joined with Him in His everlasting kingdom, and He wants pure hearts. The bible beautifully narrates the relationship between our Heavenly Father and the humanity He created that is prone to sinning against Him. Over and over, humans would stray from God and His laws, committing sins and partaking in wickedness, then come back to God apologetic and repent (Hosea 6:1, Lamentations 3:40 Jeremiah 3:22). This cycle repeats itself to the present day, and all of humanity is entrenched in sin against the one, Almighty God. Being holy, as God expects, is difficult for a sinful humanity, and that is the whole point. Who will prove to love God enough to work hard at being worthy, and considered righteous, in the eyes of God? Here's a secret; being holy is something that is only possible with God's help (Matthew 19:26). We are *meant* to need God, to turn to Him for all our needs, and follow His direction in our daily lives. We must do all of the work He directs us to, and we must remain humble when He corrects our mistakes. Prayer, humility, repentance, and purity of heart are the ways to secure God's approval, and we can obtain this because of the grace given to us by Jesus (Titus 3:3-7). When Jesus died for all of humanities sins, we all became eligible for eternal life through Him, we need only to believe. Following Jesus was God's way of sending us an example to live by, and to die by. Jesus died for us, so we're expected to die following Him, this is the only way to Heaven. Not just believing, but actually living our lives the way God demands, the way Jesus led by example, is what it means to be holy in the eyes of God. We are all like the people of Israel as told in the bible, sinful and, hopefully, seeking the one and true God. The bottom line is that no one is exempt from God's laws, His teachings, His discipline or His expectations. All humanity belongs to God, so His master plan includes **all** of humanity.

Luke 24:46-48, NIV

46 He told them, "This is what is written: The Messiah will suffer and rise from the dead on the third day, 47 and repentance for the forgiveness of sins will be preached in his name to all nations, beginning at Jerusalem. 48 You are witnesses of these things."

January 26
Get Better by God

Psalm 19:12, GW

12 Who can notice every mistake? Forgive my hidden faults.

Romans 6:1-2, ERV

1 So do you think we should continue sinning so that God will give us more and more grace? 2 Of course not! Our old sinful life ended. It's dead. So how can we continue living in sin?

God knows we sin. He knows we're going to sin tomorrow. We need to remember that the goal is a slow and steady progression to a more Christ-like and holy life. Consider swearing less if you're a person prone to that, as a step toward a more righteous lifestyle. Maybe smile at a stranger once in a while, show a little more love toward your fellow man. When co-workers or colleagues huddle up and begin gossiping, we walk away for the moment instead of partaking in the judgement of others. Perhaps instead of watching the downfall of humanity through shows about conquest and competition, or eavesdropping on other people's calumny on social media, maybe read a chapter of the bible in a quiet corner. It's hard to admit that we have flaws that need correcting, but then again, we were all made imperfect in the eyes of God. We cannot all rest in the consolation that we are *all* imperfect, but we *can* all be improved through following Christ Jesus. We all share Jesus' gift equally, and with equal opportunity, as there is always enough of His love for everyone.

If you're going to make changes to your life for the better, make sure you're doing it for the right reason, and following the direction of the Holy Spirit. Don't put on false platitudes with God, He'll see right through it (Proverbs 15:3), and we can't progress if we're lying to ourselves (1 John 1:8). Our wholesome self-improvement shouldn't just last for a day, or a week, these are *life* and lifestyle *changes* Jesus wants us to make in service to Him. If you're usually a person who keeps to themselves, or maybe you carry a bit of a cynical perspective, actually smile in order to bring a little joy into the life of another, and not because you think God will look favorably upon you, but because it feels good to be good. Our thoughts and actions should be congruent, and we should genuinely *want* to be better people. You should actually *want* to cuss less because it's the way Jesus wants us to represent ourselves, don't just swear less because *God said so*. In order to be better versions of ourselves, we need to **genuinely** want Jesus to show us where, in our own lives, we can improve ourselves through Him.

2 Peter 3:9, ERV

9 The Lord is not being slow in doing what he promised — the way some people understand slowness. But God is being patient with you. He doesn't want anyone to be lost. He wants everyone to change their ways and stop sinning.

Matthew 3:8, NLT

8 Prove by the way you live that you have repented of your sins and turned to God.

January 27
Not Everyone Will Go to Heaven

Matthew 7:21, ERV

21 "Not everyone who calls me Lord will enter God's kingdom. The only people who will enter are those who do what my Father in heaven wants."

Matthew 7:13-14, ICB

13 "Enter through the narrow gate. The road that leads to hell is a very easy road. And the gate to hell is very wide. **Many people enter through that gate.** 14 But the gate that opens the way to true life is very small. And the road to true life is very hard. **Only a few people find that road.**"

As wonderful as God's love through Jesus is, the path to eternal life is narrow, and not everyone will get to Heaven. Non-believers, people who do not repent, or change their sinful behavior will not make it, according to the Holy scripture, and Jesus' words. As Christ-followers who believe in God, we must also believe in the son of God, Jesus Christ. We must accept His position as the Messiah, who died for us all, love, trust, and follow Him. Through Jesus we are given the Holy Spirit, the invisible guide that lives inside of all those who accept Jesus into their hearts.

The decision to follow another is the biggest one we'll ever make. Belief is trust, and the only way we can trust Jesus is to read and understand the body of work He left behind, His teachings and His example of love. Fortunately, the bible is a chronological, historical transcript of the life and times of Jesus, before and after His lifetime here on Earth. This is meant to be our guide, all that we require to understand about Jesus. We cannot read some parts of the bible, and not others, we don't get God's whole message to us that way. Read the bible, and pray for trust and understanding if you're struggling with your faith. With our faith, as with anything, we begin where we *are*, and we don't look back.

John 14:6, ESV

6 Jesus said to him, "I am the way, and the truth, and the life. No one comes to the Father except through me."

Revelation 21:8, ERV

8 "But those who are cowards, those who refuse to believe, those who do terrible things, those who kill, those who sin sexually, those who do evil magic, those who worship idols, and those who tell lies—they will all have a place in the lake of burning sulfur. This is the second death."

January 28
Why Do We Need God?

Romans 6:23, ERV

23 When people sin, they earn what sin pays—death. But God gives His people a free gift—eternal life in Christ Jesus our Lord.

Jeremiah 29:11, ESV

11 "For I know the plans I have for you," declares the Lord, "plans for welfare and not for evil, to give you a future and a hope."

We all sin, we all know it, whether we admit it to ourselves or not. God knows this, and hopes we'll seek Him. If we all sin, none of us are in a very good position to determine fairness or judgement, for this is God's job (James 4:11-12). God only wants what's best for us, and hopes we'll follow Jesus in the attempt to get closer to Him. If we follow God, and pledge to give our life to following Jesus and abiding by Him in the Holy Spirit, we must accept that all control belongs to Him (Job 12:10). This will stop some believers right in their tracks, as many people like to make their own choices. Trusting our lives to Jesus also means trusting the life He has planned for us will please us, and not to make choices for ourselves. The bible assures us that God's plans are to give us hope and prosperity, what's wrong with that? He's given us a choice (Deuteronomy 30:19-20).

God's doctrine for humanity is the law, and we'll be punished if we don't abide. Even if we don't *believe* in God, that doesn't take away from this fact (Revelation 1:8). If we don't follow Jesus, change our behaviors and reset some of our priorities, we won't receive the help of the Holy Spirit. This means no growth or prosperity in Christ, no salvation, and certainly no Heaven. (Romans 6:23) Your soul dies as well, not basking in the glory of everlasting happiness in Christ, nothing is worth losing this. God's way is superior, and can't possibly compare to what we, as humans, are able to accomplish on our own. The good news includes the ability to repent any time, and receive forgiveness. It's never too late to start anew in Christ.

Ezekiel 12:25, ERV

25 "That's because I am the Lord, and if I say something will happen, it will happen! I will not wait any longer. Those troubles are coming soon—in your own lifetime. Hear me, you people who always refuse to obey! When I say something, I make it happen." This is what the Lord God said.

January 29

How God Wants Us to Live

Romans 12:9-13, ERV

9 Your love must be real. Hate what is evil. Do only what is good. 10 Love each other in a way that makes you feel close like brothers and sisters. And give each other more honor than you give your-self. 11 As you serve the Lord, work hard and don't be lazy. Be excited about serving him! 12 Be happy because of the hope you have. Be patient when you have troubles. Pray all the time. 13 Share with God's people who need help. Look for people who need help and welcome them.

Test everything, as not everything is from the Holy Spirit. Not everyone has pure intensions, and not everyone is an active Christ-follower. Some Christ-followers are content to pass judgement on others from their porches, not brave enough to change their ways for their own Lord. People live in ignorance that they are living good and pure lives, there is always room for improvement! We cuss, we lie sometimes, we deceive people to avoid unpleasant commitments or engagements, we are imperfect sinners. Many of us have more than a little contempt for our fellow man at times, and it takes very little irritation from others to set us off others. If we clean up our intensions, and focus on the Lord more than ourselves, we can unlearn the selfish arrogance the world has taught us. The world doesn't owe us any comforts (Job 41:11), we are all being tested by the Lord (Zechariah 13:9).

Jesus Christ is the good news! Our impatience, our frustration, even our con-tempt can be handed over to the Lord in prayer. We can always ask for a change of heart, to love a little deeper, have a little more grace toward others, and see the world with kinder eyes. We aren't ever going to be perfect (Romans 3:10), but we can improve ourselves each day. If we all improved just a little bit, think how different our environment would be. Know that some people will never change their behavior, and we are all at different stages in our relationship with Christ, and none of us is any better than the other. We must be tolerant and forgiving along with loving and patient, and that will take lots of time, practice, and patience! We are all works in progress, but the key word is *progress*.

Ephesians 4:29-32, CEB

29 Don't let any foul words come out of your mouth. Only say what is helpful when it is needed for building up the community so that it benefits those who hear what you say. 30 Don't make the Holy Spirit of God unhappy—you were sealed by him for the day of redemption. 31 Put aside all bitterness, losing your temper, anger, shouting, and slander, along with every other evil. 32 Be kind, compassion-ate, and forgiving to each other, in the same way God forgave you in Christ.

January 30
Redeemed

Acts 3:19, ESV

19 Repent therefore, **and turn again**, that your sins may be blotted out,

Revelation 3:19, ESV

19 "Those whom I love, I reprove and discipline, so be zealous and repent."

From our lack of control in our own lives, to the sins we must repent for, to the tests of faith we must endure, to the kindness and forgiveness we are called to give to our enemies, so many aspects of following Christ can dishearten us. Humans were designed to be incomplete without God, and many people struggle with this realization. Once we can accept the fact that we are all sinners, and will always have the propensity to sin, (Genesis 6:5) we can focus on repentance. Repentance is the process in which we ask the Lord to forgive us of our sins, and renew our vow to adhere to His commandments more astutely. Our sins show us where we need more righteousness, our inherent need for Christ's salvation, and bring us to a state of humility that is pleasing to the Lord. If we don't admit our sins, or feel badly that we've broken our vows with the Lord, then we should be praying for a purer heart. Jesus explains that it is from within our own human hearts that wicked desires are conceived (Mark 7:20-23).

As we learn to accept the sins we've committed we learn more about what we truly desire. Some people seek love and acceptance, but others have greedy, selfish desires of wealth, status, or privilege. From these secret desires of our hearts we form our priorities and goals, and often we're doing this without regard to Christ's plan for us. Following repentance for our wrongs, we should be resetting our priorities to reflect a purer heart in Christ Jesus. Even though we know we're going to sin again tomorrow, we shouldn't be comfortable, or passive about our sins. If we genuinely want a purer heart that is pleasing to the Lord, we would genuinely feel remorseful for breaking His covenant. We are called to love the Lord with all our heart, soul, mind and might (Deuteronomy 6:5-6, Matthew 22:38), and to love our neighbors as ourselves (Matthew 22:39). If we're gossiping, lying, hating, judging, arguing with, secretly lusting for or envying, jealous of, or in competition with others, we're not spreading love, but wickedness. Sinning just comes naturally to us, unfortunately, but we don't have to settle with that. We sin over and over again, so we must repent over and over again (Matthew 3:8). Only God can forgive our sins, and we must come to Him with humble, repentant hearts to receive Him. We need to know, and understand the scriptures, and pray for the understanding to incorporate them into our lives. We do this through prayer, reflection, and repentance. Pray, repent, repeat, brothers and sisters, and be clean in the name of our Lord and Savior. AMEN!

Isaiah 44:22, ERV

22 "Your sins were like a big cloud, but I wiped them all away. Your sins are gone, like a cloud that disappeared into thin air. **Return to me, for I have redeemed you.**"

January 31

Got God?

1 Samuel 12:14-15, ICB

14 You must honor the Lord and serve him. You must obey His commands. Both you and the king ruling over you must follow the Lord your God. If you do, it will be well with you. 15 But if you don't obey the Lord, and if you fight against His commands, he will be against you. He will do to you what he did to your ancestors.

Psalm 145:18-19, ESV

18 The Lord is near to all who call on him, to all who call on him in truth. 19 He fulfills the desire of those who fear him; he also hears their cry and saves them.

Without God, our souls either perish or are condemned to Hell (John 3:18, Romans 6:23). There's really nothing to be 'on the fence' about, here, we either do or don't serve God. Our quirks, habits, convictions, flaws, mistakes, lessons and gifts will all be used as a mosaic in God's great work when we decide to give our lives to God. Along with the rest of us misfit sinners, we who serve are part of the body of Christ in the ultimate battle of good versus evil. It's true. Serving is hard work, and we'll always be sinners, but we'll be sinners working for God, under Jesus and commanded by the Holy Spirit. We each play a role, offer a talent or gift, in the service of Christ (Romans 12:4-8).

Alternately, If you don't serve God, then you are *against* him and a big waste of talent. There are souls walking among us who fit this very bill, and some of them don't even know it. If we can show someone how to follow God more devoutly, pray a little more, read the bible a little more, then we've done our part in the fight against good and evil. Without God in our lives guiding our steps, we're lost sinners that continue to make poor decisions and bring undue hardships on ourselves. Only God knows our true and right path, and the more we try to ignore, or exclude God in our daily lives, decisions and choices, the farther we distance ourselves from His love and salvation (Zechariah 1:4). Life is tough enough, the smart choice is to align our hearts with God. No matter what we've done, our Heavenly Father is ready to forgive those who repent. Every sinner out there has something to offer, we only need help finding it. Search your heart, is God *your* first priority?

Romans 6:16, ICB

16 Surely you know that when you give yourselves like slaves to obey someone, then you are really slaves of that person. The person you obey is your master. You can follow sin, or obey God. **Sin brings spiritual death.** But obeying God makes you right with him.

Matthew 12:30, ERV

30 "Whoever is not with me is against me. And anyone who does not work with me is working against me."

February 1
Don't Misunderstand, Read Your Bible!

1 Timothy 6:3-7, ERV

3 Some people will teach what is false and will not agree with the true teaching of our Lord Jesus Christ. They will not accept the teaching that produces a life of devotion to God. 4 They are proud of what they know, but they understand nothing. They are sick with a love for arguing and fighting about words. And that brings jealousy, quarrels, insults, and evil mistrust. 5 They are always making trouble, because they are people whose thinking has been confused. They have lost their understanding of the truth. They think that devotion to God is a way to get rich. 6 Devotion to God is, in fact, a way for people to be very rich, but only if it makes them satisfied with what they have. 7 When we came into the world, we brought nothing. And when we die, we can take nothing out.

The bible uses both literal and figurative language among vivid symbolism to illustrate stories with layered morals, its written in many styles, and interpreted slightly differently depending on the minister, preacher, or priest. It's no wonder some people don't understand it, misinterpret it, or don't take the lessons and morals in full context. Some people never even *attempt* to read or understand the bible. If we are to live by Christ Jesus, we should want to understand His life, what happened leading up to the birth of Christ, His life and teachings, His ministry, His death and finally, His resurrection. If we *don't* read the bible in its entirety we aren't going to *understand* the bigger picture (Matthew 22:29).

It can be easy for some people to hyper-focus on a few specific scriptures, twist them out of context, and miss the greater meaning. It's important to remember the bible doesn't *exclude* anyone, 'all nations,' 'all mankind,' 'all humanity falls short,' are words and phrases used in the bible to illustrate that God's love, as well as His *rules* escape no one (Psalm 139,). The scriptures weren't left for us to interpret on our own, it was meant to be a guide on how to live the life we are called to as followers of Christ who live according to God. Not meant for a one-time read, the bible is meant to be a *daily guide* that we review over and over to derive guidance and support in our life journey to righteousness. If we only read certain *parts* of the bible, or just certain *verses* and not the whole story in its entirety, we're not really going to appreciate the full understanding and perspective intended. We should be honoring the work put into the scriptures, given to us by God to aid in our life journey, by actually *reading* them, *understanding* them, and *implementing* its teachings into our lives. Again, we are called to strength, persistence, and diligence in our pursuit of Holiness (Galatians 6:9). Read on, my brothers and sisters!

2 Timothy 3:16-17, ERV

16 All Scripture is given by God. And all Scripture is useful for teaching and for showing people what is wrong in their lives. It is useful for correcting faults and teaching the right way to live. 17 Using the Scriptures, those who serve God will be prepared and will have everything they need to do every good work.

February 2
Called to Action

John 14:21, ERV

21 (Jesus said) "Those who really love me are the ones who not only know my commands but also obey them. My Father will love such people, and I will love them. I will make myself known to them."

James 4:17, ESV

17 So whoever knows the right thing to do and fails to do it, for him it is sin.

Pray, repent, listen, and be righteous. God's instructions for our lives reads simply, but is far more difficult in practice. It's not enough to just love Him and believe in Him, it's not even enough to pray every day. God want's our souls; our attitudes, our passions, our dreams and fears every day, and forever. Through Christ Jesus, we are expected to pray our sins away, ask for forgiveness, and communicate everything else that is taking up residence in our minds. Jesus doesn't just want to know from us what we're thinking and feeling, but desires us to follow His plan for our lives (Psalm 32:8). In doing so, Jesus also wants to guide our interactions with others, what goals we set, and how we set out to achieve them.

As humans on Earth, we must abide by the laws of our civilization. Abiding by all laws is important, but as servants of our faith, we are called to abide in the covenant we have with our God. We abide in Christ by loving Him, by being thankful and humbled by His sacrifice and majesty, and by changing our hearts and lives to pattern His (Deuteronomy 13:4). Serving means a lot of different things, and this can be confusing Simply put, we serve Christ by making him a priority in our lives, and we put that into action by our good works (Matthew 5:16). "Works" meaning action of some kind, we are expected to give back to our communities and lead by example. After all, our lives will never change if we never change anything in our lives. Our good works and steadfast effort to follow Christ's example is how we honor Jesus and sustain our faith. Ask yourself, are you currently doing enough to sustain *your* faith?

Matthew 15:8-9, ERV

8 "'These people honor me with their words, but I am not really important to them. 9 Their worship of me is worthless. The things they teach are only human rules.'"

1 Peter 2:21, ESV

21 For to this you have been called, because Christ also suffered for you, leaving you an example, so that you might follow in His steps.

February 3
Temptation

1 John 2:16, ESV

16 For all that is in the world — the desires of the flesh and the desires of the eyes and pride of possessions — is not from the Father but is from the world.

James 1:13, ESV

13 Let no one say when he is tempted, "I am being tempted by God," for God cannot be tempted with evil, and he himself tempts no one.

Just because we're good Christ-follower's doesn't mean our lives have to be full of stern, boring, devout service void of joy or pleasure. Not losing our tempers on a regular basis, feeling assured and advocated for, and free lessons in how to be a better person are pretty awesome benefits of being a good Christ-follower. Doing the right thing is its own reward, but sometimes we just need to release a little positive energy. Laughter, theatre and dance, music, stories and fellowship are all pleasant distractions that don't require theft, swearing, competition or lude sexual acts. Keep in mind, people who *are* seeking these unwholesome activities are out there, walking among us, masquerading as good stewards of their faith. Temptation will find us all, no one is immune.

God never promises *not* to give us more than we can handle, but tests and humbles us to see what's truly in our hearts (Jeremiah 17:10, Isaiah 48:10, Zechariah 13:9). All the blessings in our lives, as well as the pain and tribulation, all come from God (Isaiah 45:7). When we stray too far from the Lord, He creates and lifts barriers in our lives to steer us back to Him. We don't always share God's faith in ourselves, and can become bitter and resentful when we don't understand God. Even here, though, when we struggle to understand our struggles, we must have faith that God is being fair, just, and loving. We can certainly feel challenged enough to make poor choices, we all do. We shouldn't be so tempted by outside appearances, unholy vices, or tempted to break our vows with another, our relationship with Jesus should be worth more than that to us. We will be tempted daily, and are expected to resist as Jesus did (Matthew 4:1-11). We are all *able* to resist temptations with Christ's help (Philippians 4:13). God wants us to fear Him, yet be strong in our faith to trust Him at all times, no matter what He puts us through! Brothers and sisters, we must continue to make wholesome choices in the footsteps of Jesus.

1 Corinthians 10:13, ERV

13 The only temptations that you have are the same temptations that all people have. But you can trust God. He will not let you be tempted more than you can bear. But when you are tempted, God will also give you a way to escape that temptation. Then you will be able to endure it.

February 4
Anger

Colossians 3:8, GW

8 Also get rid of your anger, hot tempers, hatred, cursing, obscene language, and all similar sins.

James 1:19-20, GW

19 Remember this, my dear brothers and sisters: Everyone should be quick to listen, slow to speak, and should not get angry easily. 20 An angry person doesn't do what God approves of.

We can get angry when we can't find something, or when we're pressed for time and feel we have too much to do. We can get angry when we feel we've been wronged, cheated, or deceived by another. We can get angry when someone we love or care about is wronged, cheated, or deceived by another. We can tell ourselves that getting angry is part of being human, that everyone experiences it, and that our feelings are justified. Any attempt to normalize anger is sinful, giving in to hate and the loss of self-control, forgiveness, and grace that God calls us to by example. We can't love our neighbor if we're angry with him, and Jesus tells us to love our neighbors as ourselves. Forgiveness cannot occur when we're trying to dole out our own version of justice after we've judged another sinner, because their sins offended us. Everyone sins, you sin, I sin, your brother, sister, cousin, friend, sins, our parents sinned. No one is better than anyone else, all humans fall short in the eyes of God, the bible explains (Romans 3:23).

God is the final judge, and determines everyone's fate by their heart, and will have final vengeance on the unrighteous (1 Samuel 16:7). We are only meant to serve God, and submit to His will for us, we aren't given the authority to judge one another. Aside from Jesus Himself, even the most righteous person is a sinner, because all are equal in the eyes of God. Anytime we take our focus off of God, focused on our anger, focused on getting back at someone, focused on what's been done to us, we're letting evil win over us. We need to pray when we're pressed, frustrated, hurt, or wronged. Praying when we're the most in need, emotionally and spiritually, is powerful and significant. When we pray at the height of our anger, asking for help, we are stopping the cycle of hate and turning to love instead. When we hand over our problems, worries, and concerns to the Lord, we're letting Him handle it. We're designed to need God, and when we actually turn to Him for our everyday frustrations, and more, we're showing our faith in Him. Not handling our anger in our own way is the key, stop, and pray through it instead (Proverbs 29:11). Removing ourselves from a situation until we've calmed down is a display of self-control, and relying on prayer to rid us of the hate is God's solution for human anger.

Romans 12:17, NASB

17 Never repay evil for evil to anyone. Respect what is right in the sight of all people.

Ephesians 4:32, ESV

32 Be kind to one another, tenderhearted, forgiving one another, as God in Christ forgave you..

February 5
Understanding Our Pain

Romans 5:3-4, ERV

3 And we are also happy with the troubles we have. Why are we happy with troubles? Because we know that these troubles make us more patient. 4 And this patience is proof that we are strong. And this proof gives us hope.

As humans we will all suffer, be reduced to tears over something lost, and feel intense moments of grief. But, why must we suffer? Is all of this pain life throws at us really necessary? God is our Heavenly Father, and as such, we are given discipline to help in our quest to be more Christ-like. When we stray from our righteous path, or need building up and strengthening, we are disciplined by the Lord. Some of us have lost loved ones or relationships, or been betrayed by someone we trusted. Some of us have experienced wrongs we feel are unjust, or just hurt because someone else we care about is suffering. Bad things happen to good people (Jerimiah 49:12a), and life just hurts sometimes. Who we turn to when we're suffering or in need is what God is looking at (Amos 4:6-12).

We can bring trouble into our lives with the poor decisions we make, not consulting the Lord first, and not gracious enough for what we have. We can quickly become impatient, distracted, irritated and focused on ourselves instead of others. Prayer to the Lord in times of strife is vital, and our comfort is assured by doing so (Psalm 50:15). However, the Lord works on His own timeline and in His own way. Perhaps His solution to your problem looks differently than the one you had in mind, but the Lord sees what we cannot. When we are comforted by the Holy Spirit, we have emerged from our pain having strengthened both our hope and our faith. What's more, when we've come through pain we have an understanding that we can now offer comfort to others going through similar pain, and that's what God's love is intended to do. We pray to Jesus, we pray for ourselves and for those we love who are also hurting, and then we rest patiently in our faith for Him to restore us (Isaiah 55:7).

2 Corinthians 1:4, ICB

4 He comforts us every time we have trouble, so that we can comfort others when they have trouble. We can comfort them with the same comfort that God gives us.

Job 5:17-18, ERV

17 You are fortunate when God corrects you. So don't complain when God All-Powerful punishes you. 18 God might injure you, but he will bandage those wounds. He might hurt you, but His hands also heal.

February 6
God's Discipline

Revelation 3:19, ERV

19 "I correct and punish the people I love. So show that nothing is more important to you than living right. Change your hearts and lives."

Hebrews 12:11, ERV

11 We don't enjoy discipline when we get it. It is painful. But later, after we have learned our lesson from it, we will enjoy the peace that comes from doing what is right.

From large problems to small irritations, pain and tribulation can come in many forms, from physical to emotional, to spiritual distress. No one of us is exempt from experiencing pain, and we shall endure pain all of our time here on Earth. Sometimes our own choices, mistakes, and actions can bring us pain, sometimes pain is a test of faith or endurance, but all pain is a lesson. No matter the source of our pain, nor circumstances, we mustn't forget that God is in charge of the bigger picture. In the bible we are told that the Lord knows our hearts (Psalm 44:21), and knows what we're going to do before we do it. All knowing, all seeing, there are no coincidences in God's master plan (Isaiah 46:10).

Although pain is something we all want to avoid, we cannot progress in our faith without it. We are meant to learn something in our suffering, as our pain is not a coincidence (Isaiah 45:7). We are asked to endure our pain with humility and patience, no easy feat. But in patiently enduring our suffering, open to the lesson being taught, we will gain grace, patience, hope, tolerance, forgiveness, and compassion. As we are all on our own individual spiritual journeys we learn different things at different times based on what the Lord thinks we need (Proverbs 2:6-8). We are promised to be given help in the Holy Spirit to help us understand why we are going through what we're going through (John 14:26). We are also told to pay heed to the Holy Spirit's instructions, and will be rewarded with righteous salvation in Christ.

Proverbs 13:18, ESV

18 Poverty and disgrace come to him who ignores instruction, but whoever heeds reproof is honored.

Psalm 119:75, ERV

75 Lord, I know that your decisions are fair, and you were right to punish me.

February 7
Cravings & Desires

James 1:13-15, ESV

13 Let no one say when he is tempted, "I am being tempted by God," for God cannot be tempted with evil, and he himself tempts no one. 14 But each person is tempted when he is lured and enticed by His own desire. 15 Then desire when it has conceived gives birth to sin, and sin when it is fully grown brings forth death.

Mark 7:20-23, ERV

20 And Jesus said, "The things that make people wrong are the things that come from the inside. 21 All these bad things begin inside a person, in the mind: bad thoughts, sexual sins, stealing, murder, 22 adultery, greed, doing bad things to people, lying, doing things that are morally wrong, jealousy, insulting people, proud talking, and foolish living. 23 These evil things come from inside a person. And these are the things that make people unacceptable to God."

Life is full of temptations. We can be tempted to take things that don't belong to us, to say unkind words to another, to lie to hide the truth, or infringe on another for our own gain. Humans have proved throughout History to be fallible, often giving into sinful temptations. Some people like to blame anyone but themselves for their sins, unable or unwilling to assume guilt for their own choices. Sinful temptations are seductive, and yield some sort of pleasure or gratification that is less than holy. Our wicked desires come from within our own hearts, and the devil likes to use them to trick, and tempt, us away from Christ's righteous light (Acts 5:3, John 13:2). God may be purifying our spirits through Jesus, but our sinful human nature will face continuous temptations on our Earthly exile (1 Pet 2:11).

How we handle trials and temptations show the essence and true character of our faith, and we must all endure this throughout our lives. Prayer is a Christ-followers secret weapon against daily temptation, and we ask the Lord for strength and self-control. Being strong in our faith is removing ourselves from an evil situation before we succumb to it, and substituting bad behavior with humble, service-oriented love for one another. Looking closely at the friends and colleagues, the music, the programs and apps which amplify the type of good or evil we're surrounding ourselves with daily, can reveal much about the temptations we bring on ourselves (2 Peter 3:17). Having a good, and righteous nature begins with our attitudes, thoughts and motivations, and will reflect in everything we do, which should represent Christ.

Matthew 26:41, ERV

41 Stay vigilant and pray for strength against temptation. Your spirit wants to do what is right, but your body is weak.

February 8
Wealth

Ecclesiastes 5:10, GW/ESV

10 Whoever loves money will never be satisfied with money. Whoever loves wealth will never be satisfied with more income. this is also vanity.

1 Timothy 6:17-19, GW

17 Tell those who have the riches of this world not to be arrogant and not to place their confidence in anything as uncertain as riches. Instead, they should place their confidence in God who richly provides us with everything to enjoy. 18 Tell them to do good, to do a lot of good things, to be generous, and to share. 19 By doing this they store up a treasure for themselves which is a good foundation for the future. In this way they take hold of what life really is.

Our world is run on a monetary system, money is required to purchase any, and all, supplies we need for our survival: Food, clothing, shelter, transportation, and medical care all cost money. We all need money to survive, and there never seems to be enough. Desiring wealth for better comfort, or for pride because we think we deserve more than we have, or because we long for power is vanity, greed, and wickedness. Wanting more, telling ourselves we *need* more so that we can provide better for our children, or because we don't think we have all that we need, is still sinful. We are assured in the bible, that God will provide all we need according to His will (Luke 12:24), but many are not satisfied with this.

What causes people to be so unsatisfied with their lives that more money is the only solution? Perhaps people are reluctant to place their trust in God because they've never met Him personally, and cannot truly accept what they cannot see. Or, perhaps, some people who believe in God don't really understand Him, and are content to live in ignorance for the pursuit of 'more.' (Matthew 6:19-21) Maybe people just want more than they're given, they blindly chase after the uncertainty of acquiring more wealth, often losing their soul along the way. Greed, power, ego, and vanity are common reasons to want to become wealthy, and most unholy. We have what we have because God allows it, rich or poor, and He's watching to see how we use what we're given. More isn't better, more is greed, greed is vanity, and vanity is self-idolatry. Being a child of God, following the life of Jesus into eternal life, isn't easy, but leads our spirits to the only salvation that lasts.

Matthew 19:23-24, ERV

23 Then Jesus said to His followers, "The truth is, it will be very hard for a rich person to enter God's kingdom. 24 Yes, I tell you, **it is easier for a camel to go through the eye of a needle than for a rich person to enter God's kingdom."**

February 9
Pain and Trust

Proverbs 17:3, DRA

3 As silver is tried by fire, and gold in the furnace: so the Lord trieth the hearts.

Proverbs 3:11-12, ICB

11 My child, do not reject the Lord's discipline. And don't become angry when he corrects you. 12 The Lord corrects those he loves, just as a father corrects the child that he delights in.

Life is full of suffering. If God loves us so much, why must we hurt? This is a question many of us ask at some point in our lives. We get frustrated in our work, and sometimes with our colleagues, our interpersonal relationships can be challenging when negative vibes collide, we can be misunderstood, mistreated, and say things we don't mean in anger. It is easy to be impatient waiting in lines, which seem to be everywhere, preventing us from being more efficient and productive during a busy day. We can change our minds, let our greed and vanity win, and let one another down. As humans, we can get so fed up with the different frustrating circumstances of our lives that we can lose sight of the vast help we have in the Holy Spirit. Jesus *wants* us to come to Him, to give Him all of our burdens, to trust that God will provide all that we need, and be patient with His timeline (Psalm 37:4-5). We shall endure because Christ endured, and He is our redeemer.

We must have a strong faith, and believe that all of our needs will be provided for, no matter what our emotions try to tell us. We must have faith that the pain we are experiencing will teach us something we can apply to bettering ourself through Christ. If we don't know why we are meant to suffer we must ask for wisdom and knowledge so that we may learn, and we do this by prayer. Change is scary, but if we are to better ourselves through Christ we must accept the changes He must make in our lives to get us to our true potential. We may not be privileged to knowing the end result of the ongoing changes the Holy Spirit is making in our lives, but our faith will sustain us through any tribulation as long as we are fully trusting in the Lord.

Proverbs 20:24, ICB

24 The Lord decides what a person does. So no one can understand what his life is all about.

James 1: 3-4, ERV

3 You know that when your faith is tested, you learn to be patient in suffering. 4 If you let that patience work in you, the end result will be good. You will be **mature and complete**. You will be all that God wants you to be.

February 10
Our Need for God

Romans 6:23, ESV

23 For the wages of sin is death, but the free gift of God is eternal life in Christ Jesus our Lord.

Ezekiel 12:25, ERV

25 "That's because I am the Lord, and if I say something will happen, it will happen! I will not wait any longer. Those troubles are coming soon—in your own lifetime. Hear me, you people who always refuse to obey! When I say something, I make it happen." This is what the Lord God said.

We all sin, and deep down we all know it, whether we can admit it to ourselves or not. God knows this, and hopes we'll seek Him. If we all sin, none of us are in a very good position to determine fairness or judgement, this is God's job. God only wants what's best for us, and hopes we'll follow Jesus in the attempt to get closer to Him. If we follow God, and pledge to give our life to following Jesus, abiding in Him by the Holy Spirit, we must give up control over our lives to Him (Titus 2:11-12). This will stop some believers right in their tracks, people like to have control over their own lives, and make their **own** choices. Trusting our lives to Jesus also means trusting the life He has planned for us over the one we would choose for ourselves. The bible assures us His plans are to give us prosperity and hope, what's wrong with that? He's given us a choice.

God's doctrine for humanity is the law, and we'll be punished, or severed from the Lord's herd if we don't abide (John 15:6). Even if we don't believe in God, that doesn't take away from this fact, God intends to sort each and every one of us. If we don't follow Jesus, change our behaviors and reset some of our priorities, we won't receive the help of the Holy Spirit. This means no growth or prosperity in Christ, no salvation, and certainly no Heaven. Your soul dies as well, not basking in the glory of everlasting happiness in Christ, nothing is worth losing this. God's way is superior, and can't possibly compare to what we, as humans, are able to accomplish on our own. The good news includes the ability to repent any time and receive forgiveness. It's never too late to start anew in Christ. Praise the Lord! Amen.

Acts 2:38, ICB

38 Peter said to them, "Change your hearts and lives and be baptized, each one of you, in the name of Jesus Christ for the forgiveness of your sins. And you will receive the gift of the Holy Spirit."

Jeremiah 29:11, NIV

11 "For I know the plans I have for you," declares the Lord, "plans to prosper you and not to harm you, plans to give you hope and a future."

February 11
Help from the Lord

Proverbs 16:33, ERV

33 People might throw lots to make a decision, but the answer always comes from the Lord.

Proverbs 3:26, ESV

26 for the Lord will be your confidence and will keep your foot from being caught.

The Lord will guide our steps, and He also decides how much discipline, or reward, we are given along the way. We all long to make our own choices, to succeed by them, and prove to ourselves and others we have something to offer the world. Making choices to suit our egos, or our physical needs, our own personal goals, or to give into sinful temptations takes our focus away from Christ (Romans 8:6). With each, sinful choice we make without Christ, we bring on more tribulation. Repentance is the only way back to Christ, and we must seek it humbly, with the honest desire to be cleansed, not just for self-preservation. If we pray for repentance, but never change our thoughts or behaviors, we're not showing the Lord we care enough about Him to change.

When we pray, we are using the Holy spirit to communicate with our Heavenly Hosts. When we pray, reflect, and revisit the choices we've made, we might see our indiscretions more clearly. When we make choices after repenting for something, we may pay closer attention to making the right ones. When we practice making better choices, the differences between righteous and unrighteous choices becomes clearer. This insight is given to us through the Holy Spirit, and it's prudent to follow it (Ezekiel 2:2). Every choice we make provides opportunities for a purer heart, but we must continue to make more wholesome choices through the help of the Holy Spirit in order to become righteous in the eyes of Christ. As humans, we will continue to make mistakes (James 3:2), but we have a choice in how to use this information. If we choose to learn from them and allow them to change us for the better, it *will* be painful and humbling, but commendable and pleasing in the eyes of our Lord and Savior. Win!

John 16:13, ERV

13 But when the Spirit of truth comes, he will lead you into all truth. He will not speak His own words. He will speak only what he hears and will tell you what will happen in the future.

Isaiah 41:10, ESV

10 "fear not, for I am with you; be not dismayed, for I am your God; I will strengthen you, I will help you, I will uphold you with my righteous right hand."

February 12
Confidence

Proverbs 3:26, ERV

26 for the Lord will be your confidence. He will not let you fall into harm.

Philippians 4:13, ESV

13 I can do all things through him who strengthens me.

Believing in yourself is great, but believing you're better than the homeless man panhandling on the street corner because you have a six-figure income, isn't great. No *one* human is made better than *another* by use of superior parts in the design, that is a ridiculous notion. Worldly pleasures like a nice home, expensive clothes, luxury cars and jewelry, and the adoration of others creates a competitive, and unrighteous environment. We can be deceived into thinking that the wealthy, attractive, movie star or successful business tycoon, or even people in our own personal inner circles, have more to offer than we do. Conversely, we may think we're a little smarter, or harder working than a homeless person who is begging for food and shelter.

You are the Lord's creation, and beautifully made. We *all* are. We may have made different choices with our lives, but that doesn't mean one person's life's contributions are more important to the Lord than another. As our heavenly Father, God wants to see us *all* prosper in Christ's love and direction (John 3:16). He has confidence and faith that we can fulfil our destinies if we follow His guidance in our lives, so we should also. If we aren't any better than anyone else, we certainly aren't any worse than anyone else either. If you're running low on confidence, pray, as the Lord will sustain you in all you do. Peace be with you, brothers and sisters.

Hebrews 13:6, ESV

6 So we can confidently say, "The Lord is my helper; I will not fear; what can man do to me?"

Hebrews 10:35-36, ESV

35 Therefore do not throw away your confidence, which has a great reward. 36 For you have need of endurance, so that when you have done the will of God you may receive what is promised.

February 13
Lost and Found

Ephesians 4:22-24, ICB

22 You were taught to leave your old self—to stop living the evil way you lived before. That old self becomes worse and worse because people are fooled by the evil things they want to do. 23 But you were taught to be made new in your hearts. 24 You were taught to become a new person. That new person is made to be like God—made to be truly good and holy.

Following Christ more closely is going to change us, this is inevitable. We may not be totally thrilled with our current version of ourselves, but what if we're not happy with the remodeling Christ is planning for us? Trusting the Lord takes time, He knows our hearts, and is patient and understanding with us. Long time habits we might be known for, our behavior, even our manner of speech and how we carry ourselves may look different to those who have known us after the Holy Spirit does His work (2 Corinthians 3:18). What if my family and friends don't like the changes, will they even recognize me? Jesus imparts upon us the importance of living a more righteous life, to be more wholesome. After all, we should be living to please the Lord, not people (Galatians 1:10).

When we allow the Holy Spirit to guide and direct our lives more closely we are following the teachings of Christ, allowing *tangible changes* to our lives. In our quest to be more righteous and holy, we exchange our pride for humility, our arrogance for modesty, and judgement for forgiveness, we fear God. Our actions, words, and behaviors should reflect the changes the Lord is making in us. Ultimately, we are seeking sanctuary and eternal respite in Jesus, so we shouldn't really give a hang what our family or friends think of the changes **He** is making in us. Our goal is to please God, not the world, not our family, and certainly not our friends (James 4:4). Getting to know our new selves is still change, and all change can be frightening. We know that our blueprints are approved by the highest source, and if we need help trusting the process all we need to do is pray. Forced love isn't really love, so it is up to us as individuals to accept or deny the changes the Holy Spirit wants to make in our lives. Choose wisely.

Matthew 10:39, ERV

39 "Those who try to keep the life they have will lose it. But those who give up their life for me will find true life."

Romans 12:2, ICB

2 Do not be shaped by this world. Instead be changed within by a new way of thinking. Then you will be able to decide what God wants for you. And you will be able to know what is good and pleasing to God and what is perfect.

February 14
Love

John 3:16, ESV

16 For God so loved the world, that he gave His only Son, that whoever believes in him should not perish but have eternal life.

Would you give your life for the one you love? Many of us would instinctively like to say, "Yes," without a drop of hesitation or fear. However, when actually faced with a life or death situation, none of us can really know just how we'll react. It would be safe to say that the people that know us the best are the ones closest to us, these are the ones we love. When we truly *love* someone we *want* to know them, and we want *them* to know us. We might even, occasionally, reveal things to those who know us the best, that we would never reveal to others. Many of us *say* we love God, we *love* Jesus, but how well do we truly *know* Him? If we say we love Jesus, how well do we remember His sermon on the mount? How many of us can truly say we understand what His message was, and have actually read (and re read) the scriptures enough to understand? In order to truly *show* that we love Jesus, we must want to get to know more about His ministry, and how we can apply it to our lives (James 1:22-25). If we're not doing this, actively and diligently, how are we reciprocating our love for God? Real, genuine, love is difficult to find, and is *always* reciprocated.

You are loved. Jesus Christ died so that *everyone's* spirit could live forever after our deaths, and nothing can take this offer off of the table for any of us. Christ did this out of God's love for *all* humankind, and this is the ultimate example of love to us from our creator. Reading the bible, in any form, learning the scriptures and trying to apply modesty, humility, service and prayer to our lives in more tangible ways are examples of how we can get to know Christ Jesus our Lord and Savior better. Over and over in the bible, Christ calls us to love one another as he has loved us (John 15:12, Matthew 22:37-40), but this is not an easy task. Some people are much more difficult to love than others, and some people don't appear that they *want* love from other people. We must *all* put down our egos, learn to forgive, accept a more humble attitude and perspective, and be open minded to sharing, fellowship, service, and love (Luke 6:37). We are called to lift up one another as Christ lifts us up, but most of us have more practice tearing down that building up. How can *you* lift someone up today?

1 John 4:19, ESV

19 We love because he first loved us.

1 Peter 4:8, ESV

8 Above all, keep loving one another earnestly, since love covers a multitude of sins.

February 15
Equally and Naturally Rotten

Mark 7:21-22, GNV/ESV

21 For from within, out of the heart of man, come evil thoughts, adulteries, fornications, murders, 22 thefts, all kind of craftiness whereby men profit themselves by other men's losses, covetousness, wickedness, deceit, uncleanness, sensuality, envy, slander, pride, foolishness. 23 All these evil things come from within, and defile a man.

Ecclesiastes 7:20, KJ21

20 For there is not a just man upon earth who doeth good and sinneth not.

Hiding among the world around us like the toy at the bottom of the cereal box, competitiveness, vanity, greed, power and the need for respect among one another whisper tauntingly to those with weak spirits. Contests, sports, social and academic arenas, and world governments can cause us to fight, argue, grow contempt, and pass judgement on one another. **The Bible tells us these behaviors are wrong, but the world keeps pulling us toward hate instead of love** (Matthew 5:38-42). Some of us have stopped trying to do good, or show more love toward others, frustrated with feeling like we're the only one trying. We all want to be loved, appreciated, and feel relevant in some way, but don't always seek this reassurance in the best ways. Even though we *know* the Lord provides all we need, and all we ever need to be proud of, we still fall for the temptation to satisfy our egos over the purity of our spirits.

God shows no favoritism (Romans 2:11, Acts 10:34-35), we are all rotten, and we are all going to be judged equally based on the lives we've lived (2 Corinthians 5:10, Revelation 22:12). We must accept this before we can even *begin* the road to righteousness. Our Lord calls upon us to be meek and humble (Colossians 3:12). If we are trying to tell ourselves we aren't sinful we are certainly being dishonest. One consolation is that we are *all* sinful and rotten, and not one more than another in the eyes of God. The *good news* is that Jesus came down as the perfect sacrifice, the only perfectly pure and righteous holy man. Dying for our sins, we can only find true righteousness in Jesus Christ (John 14:6). We continue our pursuit to live as He lived, learning about our weaknesses and sins, and finding peace and salvation through Him, *despite* our nature to be tempted by sin. This is how we remain true to our commitment to Jesus, with repeated repentance, and we also learn humility and patience while we strengthen our faith.

1 John 2:15-16, ESV

15 Do not love the world or the things in the world. If anyone loves the world, the love of the Father is not in him. 16 For all that is in the world—the desires of the flesh and the desires of the eyes and pride of life—is not from the Father but is from the world.

February 16
No Answer?

James 4:3, ESV

3 You ask and do not receive, because **you ask wrongly**, to spend it on your passions.

Matthew 21:22, ESV

22 "And whatever you ask in prayer, you will receive, **if you have faith.**"

It is comforting to know that we can communicate with our Lord and Savior through prayer. Just knowing we're heard brings a reassurance only God can provide in our lives. However, prayer is more complicated than some may think. Although we can speak our thoughts to the Lord easy enough, getting a response is more complicated. We may not get an answer to our prayers if we're hiding sin (Psalm 66:18), perhaps just not aware of them, or if we ask for the wrong things, or if we don't believe we'll receive what we've asked for. Even if we *say* all the right things, if our hearts are full of anger, contempt, impatience, or injustice, we may not be humble enough to be *heard* by God. Our state of mind can be complicated by our powerful emotions, they can certainly trip us up! We can easily feel justified in our outage, or contempt, when we feel we've been hurt or wronged. We're passing judgement in that justification, and passing judgement is a sin (James 4:11-12, Matthew 7:1).

If we've prayed, and received no answer we shouldn't assume that the mistake is God's. We are told that whatever we need we should ask for, and we'll receive it (Matthew 7:7), but it's not really as simple as it appears to be. If we ask for something to help us on our journey to being more righteous, we're more likely to get what we've asked for. We aren't going to get what we think we deserve, but what *God* thinks we deserve, and only after we've presented all our concerns to Him in prayer. Our emotions can play tricks on our logical thinking, and God is the only one who knows what is truly justified, and fair, in one's life. Just because we may *feel* outraged, wronged, disrespected, or treated unfairly doesn't mean what we're feeling is reality. We simply can't know all of the dynamics that went into a given situation, what someone else felt, prayed for, or endured. We also don't know what God has planned for our *own* future, we certainly can't know *another's* future. Clearly, we can't possibly know what the fairest, most righteous outcome should be in anyone's life. Only God knows what is best, and what each person should be enduring. This is faith. If we love God, if we're truly devoted to Him, we'll trust His judgement even when it hurts. We are all going through God's refining process, and we'll have to endure tests of faith, temptation, devotion, and endurance along the way. We must keep praying, reflecting on our decisions, and return again and again with increasing humility. Jesus warns us that not all will get to Heaven (Matthew 7:21), because if following was easy, everyone would be. Stay strong, be humble, and pray to the Lord for guidance, brothers and sisters!

Proverbs 15:29, ESV

29 The Lord is far from the wicked, but he hears the prayer of the righteous.

February 17
Children of God'

1 John 3:10, ESV

10 By this it is evident who are the children of God, and who are the children of the devil: whoever does not practice righteousness is not of God, nor is the one who does not love his brother.

Galatians 3:26, ESV

26 For in Christ Jesus you are all sons of God, through faith.

Over and over again, the bible refers to humanity as 'children' of God, as God is our creator, but it means more than that. As God's children, we've been given the position of power on the Earth, as rulers of all that inhabit it (Genesis 1:26). This is a heady role, as the dominate species, and quietly conjures up feelings of pride, control, and arrogance among many. Some would define our role on Earth as one of leadership, or domination. Yet, what God wants from us isn't congruent with the way humans actually perceive themselves. God doesn't want proud, arrogant, over-bearing control-freaks, the way the world would expect a leader to be. Instead, God calls us to be humble, naïve, approaching Him like a 'child' (Matthew 18:3). God wants us to approach Him with trusting and viridity, the appropriate amount of fear and wonder.

We are expected to come to God as children, because we are. Although we would all like to think we can reach a level of grace, sophistication or wisdom in our experience here on Earth, we often give ourselves more credit that we've earned. Many people forget Isaiah 45:7, that both the good, and bad in our world comes from God. Not only is God our creator, and final judge, but He is also in control of *every aspect* of our daily lives. We are all just following **His** master plan, not our own; some just closer than others. Full of ignorance and naivety, humans aren't capable of comprehending all that God intended, and know less than we think we do (Ecclesiastes 3:11). Only people who are living exclusively for themselves will be outraged to learn that God is in control, not us. Anyone who professes to love God, accepts their role as His child, and approaches with humility and repentance is considered a child of God. No matter what country, or religion someone was born into, no matter what sex they are, or identity they keep can determines someone's eligibility to be a child of God. Being a child of God is something we accept in our hearts and minds, and we don't have to prove that to anyone else but God.

John 1:12, ESV

12 But to **all** who did receive him, who believed in his name, he gave the right to become children of God.

February 18
All Suffering Is Fair?

1 Peter 4:1-2, ERV

1 Christ suffered while he was in His body. So you should strengthen yourselves with the same kind of thinking Christ had. The one who accepts suffering in this life has clearly decided to stop sinning. 2 Strengthen yourselves so that you will live your lives here on earth doing what God wants, not the evil things that people want to do.

Each life must endure pain and suffering, but not all suffering is viewed the same. We can all be fairly stern regarding our own, personal sense of justice, and can be most unsettled when we think that balance of justice has shifted. When some of us pray, we may not feel like we're being heard, as we don't always get what we've asked for. Many of us don't associate the many unrighteous choices we make to the pain and tribulation we suffer. When we fall into unrighteousness, or just to test our faith in Him, God sends us all pain, suffering and intermittent tribulations (Deuteronomy 8:2, Isaiah 48:10 Romans 3:5-6). Some of us have trouble forgiving others, or perhaps what we've asked for something in prayer that God had determined isn't in our best interest. Another reason our prayers may not be answered might be that our faith isn't strong enough, or maybe we're not repentant enough. We know that we must seek God with **all** of our hearts, in humility **and** repentance, and then He will hear us (Jeremiah 29:12-13).

When the entire crowd is partaking in sinful behavior, it is often extremely tempting to join them 'this one time.' Allowing ourselves to become innocent bystanders, and listening or 'overhearing,' while others around us are enjoying crude humor, or gossip, is still participation in the eyes of the Lord (Matthew 5:28). We must make sacrifices, *experience* hardship, annoyance, pain, injustice, grief in order to 'endure,' and this humbles us. Jesus endured more than any of us ever will, and if we want to earn a place in Heaven we will need to endure as He did. Some people bring God's justice into their lives by the sins they commit, others suffer to serve as an example of God's judgement. All suffering is a test of faith, for God always has a reason for what He does. Who are you calling out to in your time of need, a spouse, a friend, a lover, a family member? We are meant to need and rely on our Lord and Savior. Who else can offer what He can?

Luke 14:27, ERV

27 "Whoever will not carry the cross that is given to them when they follow me cannot be my follower."

Romans 5:3-5, ESV

3 Not only that, but we rejoice in our sufferings, knowing that suffering produces endurance, 4 and endurance produces character, and character produces hope, 5 and hope does not put us to shame, because God's love has been poured into our hearts through the Holy Spirit who has been given to us.

February 19
Just Stay Calm

Philippians 4:6-7, ESV

6 do not be anxious about anything, but in everything by prayer and supplication with thanksgiving let your requests be made known to God. 7 And the peace of God, which surpasses all understanding, will guard your hearts and your minds in Christ Jesus.

Exodus 14:14, ESV

14 The Lord will fight for you, and you have only to be silent.

Threats are an everyday consequence of life, and we all face them. Some of us are afraid of heights, tight or enclosed spaces, the dark, or flying on a plane. Other people are afraid they won't have all they think they need, and worry how they'll provide for their families. Fear is a part of our lives, but it doesn't have to hold our spirits captive. When we hand over these fears to Jesus in prayer, He vows to take care of it, and offers us reassurance that our specific concerns are being taken care of. Underneath that prayer we send off to our Lord is a strong hope and a deep faith. We have faith in the Lord that God will hear our prayers, and provide for us. What we all must remember is that God's ways are not our ways (Isaiah 55:8-9), and God's timeline is not like ours either (2 Peter 3:8). What better advocate to have on our side, but our Lord and Savior, and King of the universe? We should offer prayers of thanksgiving, and prayers of repentance along with our prayers of concern to Jesus. For blessed is the resolute guidance and steadfast love our Savior has for us (Jeremiah 31:3).

Just because we pray doesn't mean our troubles disappear like the wave of a magic wand, or with the snap of the fingers. What's important to realize is that we know our requests are being *heard* when we pray, and we can take *comfort* in that privilege. Waiting for God to work His miracles through us, and in our lives takes place on *His* timeline, not our own. God's work is far superior to our own, so we lean into our faith that tells us all of our needs will be provided for in just the right time, in just the right way, and all of our fears and anxieties will be calmed. We *trust* that this will happen, and rely on God to direct us through our difficulties. If we try to solve our own problems, coming up with our own mortal, short-sided solutions, we fail to let God manage them for us, let alone allow Him to direct our paths. So, like the scripture says, sit back, and let God do the driving. Peace be upon you, brothers and sisters.

John 16:33, ESV

33 "I have said these things to you, that in me you may have peace. **In the world you will have tribulation**. But take heart; I have overcome the world."

Isaiah 41:10, ESV

10 "Fear not, for I am with you; be not dismayed, for I am your God; I will strengthen you, I will help you, I will uphold you with my righteous right hand."

February 20
Not a Sprint, But a Marathon

James 1:6, ESV

6 But let him ask in faith, with no doubting, for the one who doubts is like a wave of the sea that is driven and tossed by the wind.

1 Corinthians 15:58, DLNT

58 So then my beloved brothers, be steadfast, immovable, always abounding in the work of the Lord, knowing that your labor is not empty in the Lord.

Imagine, if you will, this hypothetical scenario: You're going on a hike in the deep woods. You'll only know where to go when the light illuminates the path in front of you, and all that you'll need along the way will be provided for you. Sounds exciting right? Much like our walk with Jesus, we find ourselves needing things along a path, of which we know not the destination. Ask yourself, what do I need to become a better version of myself? Many of us might have different ideas about how we could improve ourselves, but the Lord's plan is the one that stands (Proverbs 16:9). If we love Christ then we're trying to follow His commandments to be more righteous and holy, and that takes a lot of lessons to get right. Many of us know where our deficiencies are, even if we keep them as camouflaged as we can. Some of us find ourselves needing more patience, some of us need direction, some need more self-control, still others need a deeper faith, and some don't think they need anything.

This isn't a short hike through the woods on a beautiful Summer morning, but a life-long journey of faith with pitfalls and booby traps along the way. The good news is that anything we think we may need to improve ourselves will be given to us, all we need to do is ask (John 14:13). If we'd like to be less angry and impatient, pray for that. If you'd like to be more organized and set firmer boundaries with others, then pray for that. Jesus is ready to give generously, as long as our motives are pure, and goals are humble. And, we must *not doubt* Jesus' ability to provide for us. It's not appropriate to pray for a windfall of money, that would be greedy and unrighteous, but we can pray for ways to make ends meet, or for opportunities for more income. We can pray for alternative solutions to our problems, we can pray to make better decisions, and for more willpower to deny the extras in our lives we don't need. When we ask, Jesus will provide what He thinks we deserve. We can all do a little bit more to be better than we were yesterday, what will *you* pray for?

James 1:5, ESV

5 "If any of you lacks wisdom, let him ask God, who gives generously to all without reproach, and it will be given him."

February 21
Renewal

1 John 1:9, ESV

9 If we confess our sins, he is faithful and just to forgive us our sins and to cleanse us from all unrighteousness.

Colossians 3:8-10, ESV

8 But now you must put them all away: anger, wrath, malice, slander, and obscene talk from your mouth. 9 Do not lie to one another, seeing that you have put off the old self with its practices 10 and have put on the new self, which is being renewed in knowledge after the image of its creator.

After a long day, nothing feels better than a cool dip the pool, or a soak in a bubbling jacuzzi, or relaxing deep tissue massage. Although many would argue that this is a great way to replenish our bodies, nothing feels better than the restoration and replenishment Christ's love and forgiveness provides us when we seek it. Just knowing that Jesus *hears* us makes us feel relevant, important and cared for (1 John 5:15). All of us could use a little more love in our lives. We know we make plenty of mistakes as sinning humans, wrong choices, contemptable thoughts, giving into worldly temptations, and not enough love for our fellow man are all weaknesses we succumb to. The bible explains that there is a difference between the desires we feel because of our bodies, and the desires we should be seeking in our spirits, and one is good while the other leads only to wickedness (1 John 2:16). Getting into fights, drunkenness, drug use, wild parties, lustful desires and fornication, adultery, rape, envy and jealously over what someone else has are all examples of where the desires of the flesh can lead a person (Galatians 5:19-21).

We commit sinful, glutinous, impure, unjust, and unholy acts daily, and these sins reflect the unrighteousness that our worldly, fleshy desires within us. Christ is holy, and if we're going to truly show we love Him we're going to want to try and be holy also. In Christ, we are forgiven but that doesn't give us carte blanche to sin with reckless disregard. We aren't really changing our negative, unrighteous behavior then, are we? Christ knows what is truly in our hearts, and if we really want to change or are just trying to get the benefits without any sacrifice to our worldly comforts. But, all is not lost! Our sins are forgiven by Christ, but he expects changed behavior in return. Now we consider ourselves followers of Christ, then we must consider ourselves vessels of His goodness.

Romans 6:15-16, ERV

15 So what should we do? Should we sin because we are under grace and not under law? Certainly not! 16 Surely you know that you become the slaves of whatever you give yourselves to. Anything or anyone you follow will be your master. You can follow sin, or you can obey God. Following sin brings spiritual death, but obeying God makes you right with him.

February 22
Relearning Good and Bad

Ecclesiastes 7:29, ERV

29 There is one other thing I have learned. God made people good, but they have found many ways to be bad.

Malachi 3:18, ERV

18 (The Lord said) "You people will come back to me, and you will learn the difference between good and evil. You will learn the difference between someone who follows God and someone who does not."

Life is full of choices that are either good or bad for us, and, unfortunately, the bad things are usually more enticing. We can sometimes fall prey to the bad things and partake in gossip, or lie to hide something we don't want discovered, or engage in worldly pleasures that are wrong in a moment of weakness. We are sinful, pleasure-seeking creatures who become easily distracted with the world's glittery, sinful temptations, and in doing so turn away from Jesus' servant-oriented righteousness. We cannot love what the world has to offer and Jesus Christ at the same time (James 4:4), and when we are distracted by the world we are turned *away* from the Lord. The thirst for money, physical pleasures, vengeance and spite toward one another are just a couple examples of the many sins that keep us distracted from applying the teachings of Jesus in our lives.

Our many repeated sins is precisely why we *need* Jesus, or we would destroy ourselves. We are all sinners, we cannot be judges, and are all in need of the Lord's mercy and grace. Jesus is a model to live our lives by, our savior and real life example to absorb our many sins. Jesus was tempted by the devil (Matthew 4:1-11), mocked (Matthew 27:27-31, Luke 22:64), beaten (Luke 22:63), whipped (John 19:1) and crucified on a cross (Luke 23:33, Mark 15:25) for our sins, making us all right with God (Romans 4:25). Jesus is an *amazing gift*, and we humans certainly need him! It's ok to acknowledge our mistakes, sins, and imperfections, but only to the extent that we know what to *repent* for, and repentance is vital to our eternal salvation in Jesus Christ. We shouldn't be using our sins to separate each other into categories with labels, or to compare our sins to each other's to see who is better. People will continue to make sinful, evil choices all around us, but, as followers of Christ we are expected to remain steadfast and strong while tempted. These are the daily trials and tribulations that test our faith, endurance, and resolve to love and honor our God by following Christ Jesus. Will you be strong enough to resist temptations in *your* day today?

2 Timothy 3:1-4, NIV

3 But mark this: There will be terrible times in the last days. 2 People will be lovers of themselves, lovers of money, boastful, proud, abusive, disobedient to their parents, ungrateful, unholy, 3 without love, unforgiving, slanderous, without self-control, brutal, not lovers of the good, 4 treacherous, rash, conceited, lovers of pleasure rather than lovers of God—.

February 23
As Righteous as We Can

Romans 6:17-18, ESV

17 But thanks be to God, that you who were once slaves of sin have become obedient from the heart to the standard of teaching to which you were committed, 18 and, having been set free from sin, have become **slaves of righteousness**.

1 John 3:10, ESV

10 By this it is evident who are the children of God, and who are the children of the devil: whoever does not practice righteousness is not of God, nor is the one who does not love His brother.

If we are good stewards of our faith, we are reading, and trying to understand, the bible as that was given to us for the teaching of God's word. For many people, the word 'slave' conjures up negative thoughts of merciless entrapment and unfair treatment, indeed wicked suppression. In the bible, the verse 'slaves of righteousness,' reflects our need to be constantly working to achieve the righteousness Jesus calls us to pursue (Proverbs 21:21). Additionally, the word 'practice in the verse from first John re-affirms we are never really free from the quest to be cleaner, holier people. We will always be learning, because it will always be in our first nature to sin.

Redemption is the way Jesus gave a sinful humanity a way to be free of our sin, but reminds us that it is up to us to continue to stay away from sinful behavior (John 5:14). Our Lord expects us to not only ask for forgiveness for our sins, but to learn them in order to avoid repeating them. When we make poor choices, when we sin, the Lord lets us suffer the consequences of our foolishness. When we repent, we are given an opportunity to learn from our mistakes, and prove to our Heavenly Father that we can change our behavior for Him. When we suffer tribulations, or discipline from the Lord, which are also tests of faith, we can either grow in righteousness, or we can grow bitter and resentful. (Lamentations 3:38-40) It might be *our* life, but we're *God's* creation and that's why His will is what is done, on Earth *and* in Heaven (Deuteronomy 10:14). The more we resist God's power and place in our lives, the more we suffer from missing out on salvation, forgiveness, redemption, and a pretty awesome eternal life in Heaven with God at the end of the journey. So we should upgrade our attitudes and hearts to a more humble place before God, repent, and show God we *can* be righteous!

Hebrews 12:11, ESV

11 For the moment all discipline seems painful rather than pleasant, but later it yields the peaceful fruit of righteousness to those who have been trained by it.

Matthew 5:6, ESV

6 (Jesus said) "Blessed are those who hunger and thirst for righteousness, for they shall be satisfied."

February 24
Worried About Other People, and We Shouldn't Be

Galatians 1:10, ICB

10 Do you think I am trying to make people accept me? No! God is the One I am trying to please. Am I trying to please men? If I wanted to please men, I would not be a servant of Christ.

Some people spend a lot of time wondering what others are thinking of them, we all do it, and sometimes without even realizing it. Humans are social creatures, and we all want to feel accepted, relevant, useful and important. We seek reassurances that we are doing the right things with our lives, in our work, and in our words and actions. It isn't unusual, or even unreasonable, to need reassurances like these to have more self-confidence. When we look to our worldly environment for the assurances we seek, the bible warns us that we are asking for trouble (Colossians 3:2, 1 John 5:19). We are all a work in progress, but we need to be careful to whom we're looking to for guarantees.

Jesus teaches us that we shouldn't fall prey to the trappings of worldly possessions or thoughts, and that our only focus should be on Him (Hebrews 3:1). Other human beings cannot offer us reliable, steadfast love, hope and guidance the way Jesus can, we are imperfect and will always disappoint one another. Jesus never disappoints, He remains the same forever (Hebrews 13:8). We must look to Jesus when we need reassurance that we're making the right choices in our lives, and repentance for our daily sins. Our environments are important, but only to the extent that we're helping one another, not comparing or judging. Ask Jesus, in prayer, to help you see your environment differently today.

Colossians 3:23-24, ESV

23 Whatever you do, work heartily, as **for the Lord and not for men**, 24 knowing that from the Lord you will receive the inheritance as your reward. **You are serving the Lord Christ.**

Proverbs 29:25, ICB

25 Being afraid of people can get you into trouble. But if you trust the Lord, you will be safe.

February 25
Allow Changes

Ephesians 4:22-24, GW/ESV

22 **You were taught to change** the way you were living. The person you used to be will ruin you through desires that deceive you. 23 However, you were taught to have **a new attitude**. 24 You were also taught to **become a new person**, created after the likeness of God in true righteousness and holiness.

Change is difficult. Fear of the unknown, unsure of the potential outcome, and uncertain where to find assurances are some reasons why people hesitate to embrace change. In our lives, change can mean anything from a slight shift in our daily responsibilities, to major modifications to our way of life. Accepting change as a follower of Christ means we defer our choices and decisions to the Lord, praying for His guidance through them, and listening to the Holy Spirit direct us. Loving, worshiping, and praising the Lord for all we have in our lives is terrific, but until we accept that we'll have to make some significant changes, we'll never really be *following* the Lord. If we never do anything differently, we're never going to progress and grow, in Christ Jesus (2 Corinthians 3:18). Change is hard, but trusting in the Lord is a special kind of challenge. Only through prayer, trial and error, repentance, and learning to listen to the Holy Spirit, can we understand how to follow the guidance of the Lord in our lives. A difficult, spiritual, and exigent concept for many of us, God is challenging us through change, to listen, and follow Him a little more closely.

The bible talks about the need for humans to change their hearts and minds, to ones that seek righteousness through Christ, instead of their desires (Jeremiah 24:7). When we allow the Holy Spirit to guide our decisions and choices, we're choosing God over our own goals and desires. How we set our goals and priorities, how we'll choose the jobs we'll ultimately take, how we spend our leisure time, how much we give to others, and how we treat other people are all decisions we should be including, and listening, to the Lord on. Just because we **can** make astute decisions on our own doesn't mean we **should** be. God is watching us all make our decisions, with and without Him, wondering who will actually seek Him. (Jeremiah 17:9-10) After all, God is the only one who knows everything that's happening, and why, so why *wouldn't* we want to consult Him more frequently? God is trying to purify us all, and the more we stubbornly fight Him the more we distance ourselves from His grace (2 Kings 17:14). If we let our own desires guide our goals, we're following wickedness, but if we submit to the Holy Spirit's guidance, we're choosing the Lord over ourselves. Listen carefully, and choose wisely brothers and sisters.

Ezekiel 36:26-27, ESV

26 "And I will give you a new heart, and a new spirit I will put within you. And I will remove the heart of stone from your flesh and give you a heart of flesh. 27 And I will put my Spirit within you, and cause you to walk in my statutes and be careful to obey my rules."

February 26
For the Outspoken & the Opinionated

Proverbs 18:2, ESV

2 A fool takes no pleasure in understanding, but only in expressing His opinion.

Philippians 2:3-4, ESV

3 Do nothing from selfish ambition or conceit, but in humility count others more significant than yourselves. 4 Let each of you look not only to His own interests, but also to the interests of others.

Many people have lost sight of what humility looks like according to what Jesus taught. Some people proclaim themselves as outspoken, or blunt, saying whatever they truly think without shame. Some people have positions of authority, and it's their job to come up with solutions, and delegate tasks to others. Other people have talents, privileges, or abilities that provide them with more opportunities than others. We all have confident and not-so-confident days, so how do we maintain a righteous balance between humility and self-importance? A modest person can be confident without believing they are better, or more important, than another. Modesty is knowing you're good at something but not bragging about it, or thinking you're better than others. Modesty is knowing you're intelligent, maybe even more than most, but not feeling you're superior to them. They key to understanding genuine modesty is in the gratitude toward God for the blessings in one's life, and not anything we could accomplish on our own. A conceited person believes their opinion is greater than someone else's, because they know they're right, and believes everyone should think the way they do. Conceited people have an elevated sense of intelligence, Influence or importance. Many of us can admit to knowing someone like this. (Romans 11:18)

As humans we naturally develop views, opinions, conclusions, and judgements as we are thinking, reasoning, social creatures. Unavoidable and yet dangerous, the opinions we form can sow the seeds of wicked thinking. When we use our formed conclusions and judgements to look down on someone because they think differently, or aren't as aware as we are, we are sinning. We cannot be loving our neighbor if we're looking down on them, or if we think we're better than they are, 'bless their hearts.' The bible teaches us that we should think of others above ourselves (Philippians 2:3), and shouldn't want people to seek our knowledge, but the knowledge in Christ Jesus. As followers of Christ, we don't want people to think the way *we* do, *we* aren't the way, the truth, or the life, but we are calling people to think the way *Jesus* taught. Jesus taught humility, modesty, self-control, forgiveness, and to love one another, placing others *above* ourselves, and calls us to do the same.

Romans 12:16, ERV

16 Live together in peace with each other. Don't be proud, but be willing to be friends with people who are not important to others. Don't think of yourself as smarter than everyone else.

February 27
Sin

Galatians 5:17-21a, GW

17 What your corrupt nature wants is contrary to what your spiritual nature wants, and what your spiritual nature wants is contrary to what your corrupt nature wants. They are opposed to each other. As a result, you don't always do what you intend to do. 18 If your spiritual nature is your guide, you are not subject to Moses' laws. 19 Now, the effects of the corrupt nature are obvious: illicit sex, perversion, promiscuity, 20 idolatry, drug use, hatred, rivalry, jealousy, angry outbursts, selfish ambition, conflict, factions, 21 envy, drunkenness, wild partying, and similar things.

Many of us have a basic understanding of right and wrong, but there is much gray in between that offers a breeding ground for sin and temptation. The bible explains that when Adam and Eve, the first humans, committed sin by disobeying God in the garden of Eden, they corrupted all of humanity. From that moment on, humanity was inherently prone to sin, secretly desiring to turn away from God's rules and re-inventing them from their own perspective (Genesis 6:5, Jeremiah 8:6). We all suffer because of this sin, and yes, it is our fault (Matthew 15:18-20). We are all made in God's image, but not one more valuable than the other. God sees us all as His humanity, His creation, and He looks upon us all as His species, that He loves more than we can ever understand. We came into this world individually, and shall undergo final judgement the same way.

When people go through difficulties, tragedies, or watch someone they love go through something terrible, we can wonder where God's compassion is. Sin is evil, and all around us, we all suffer and it's because of a number of things, most of which are due to humanities corruption and hardened heart toward God (Ecclesiastes 8:14). We don't know, or see what God sees, or what God knows, we don't see and understand all that God does. We cannot fully understand God's justice, or His mercy because we only have finite knowledge. However, we aren't *meant* to understand everything, we are called to put all our trust in Him (1 Peter 4:19). We don't get to accompany our loved ones to their final judgement so we can finally understand their life's tragedies in full context, and we don't get to see the final justice God administers to someone who might have committed a wrong against us, or someone we love. We also don't get to see the heart of a sinner who's repented and decided to turn their life around, and commit their life to God. Faith in God means we know we aren't always going to understand life, but we trust that God's will is just and merciful in the end.

Jeremiah 17:9-10, ERV

9 "Nothing can hide its evil as well as the human mind. It can be very sick, and no one really understands it. 10 But I am the Lord, and I can look into a person's heart. I can test a person's mind and decide what each one should have. I can give each person the right payment for what they do."

February 28
Don't Be a Spiritual Couch Potato

James 1:23, 2:26, ICB/ESV

23 A person who hears God's teaching and does nothing is like a man looking in a mirror. 24 He sees His face, then goes away and quickly forgets what he looked like. 25 But the truly happy person is the one who carefully studies God's perfect law that makes people free. He continues to study it. He listens to God's teaching and does not forget what he heard. Then he obeys what God's teaching says. When he does this, it makes him happy. 26 For as the body apart from the spirit is dead, so also faith apart from works is dead.

It's easy to get lazy. We all become impatient, frustrated, and fed up with our own households, our governments, and even ourselves at times. Not treating strangers like crap because we're irritated takes a great deal of self-control. After a busy day, hectic week, an argument, a personal set-back, or series of setbacks, we can easily become lazy in our righteousness. We may not think Jesus Christ has anything to do with that driver that cut us off, or that train that's going to make us late for an important appointment, or that co-worker that is treating us badly right now. We don't see all that our Lord, Jesus Christ, sees (Hebrews 4:13). We cannot know, from our own couches and perspectives, the bigger picture that He does. Maybe that co-worker just lost someone close to them, and they're hurting more than we are. Perhaps that train kept us from the drunk driver that blew a stop sign, and would've hit us had we been there.

Compassion for others who may be experiencing their own tribulations, gentleness in the way we speak to and treat one another, humility knowing we aren't the only one suffering, and patience with others' problems as well as our own is just what Christ calls us to do. We cannot become lazy in our faith, we will always be tested (1 Peter 1:7). Our actions and words toward others is an outward expression of our faith in Christ. We can't be couch potatoes in our faith and become lazy in our actions and words, especially when we're under pressure. Showing compassion with kindness, humility, gentleness and patience in the face of our own troubles is how we show Christ we're following Him closely.

Colossians 3:12, CJB

12 Therefore, as God's chosen people, holy and dearly loved, clothe yourselves with feelings of compassion and with kindness, humility, gentleness and patience.

March 1
Jesus as the Son of God

Luke 1:35, ERV

35 The angel said to Mary, "The Holy Spirit will come to you, and the power of the Most High God will cover you. The baby will be holy and will be called the Son of God."

John 1:14, GW

14 The Word **became human and lived among us**. We saw His glory. It was the glory that the Father shares with His only Son, a glory full of kindness and truth.

Some people have a difficult time accepting Jesus. Perhaps the fact that Jesus walked the earth as the only perfect human being leaves some people feeling jealous, or envious. Humans are clearly the dominant species on earth, as God has designed it this way, but humans are still a part of God's creation, and meant to serve Him along with the rest of His creation (Deuteronomy 6:5). The bible is quite clear on this, and once again we must examine the depth of our faith. Maybe we believe in a higher power, but the scope of our faith is limited to just this. Perhaps some are unaware that part of loving God is serving Him, and that *just believing* doesn't forward our faith (John 14:15, James 2:14-26) The bible is God's guide for us, and we can learn a great deal about God, and Jesus, in the reading of the scripture. If we desire the glory and rapture that awaits us in Heaven, we must understand the requirements for entry. We should *want to know* the **truth** of the word of God for ourselves.

Following Jesus will highlight our own imperfections, and many people have trouble with this. Focusing too sharply on our inadequacies can be painful, but not focusing on them enough, or in the wrong ways, can hinder our journey with Jesus. If we didn't know our sins, we couldn't repent for them. If we don't accept our sins, then we're not calling on Christ for the right things. Accepting our sins makes us humble, and that's an uncomfortable place for some people, but it's a step in the righteous direction! As humans we are ALL sinners in the eyes of God (Romans 3:23), each and every one of us, and we're all looked upon, and judged, **equally** by God. We are also all *loved, forgiven, and comforted by* the same by God (1 John 4:10), if we would only let go of our foolish pride and ask for it. Like a knight in shining armor, God sent a piece of Himself down to earth in the form of a man, Jesus Christ, as an offering for humanity. Believing in God means accepting the bible's word as God's word, and Jesus Christ as our Savior (1 John 4:14, Acts 4:12). If we are having trouble with any aspect of our faith, the Lord's comfort, guidance, grace and direction is only a prayer away.

Matthew 3:16-17, ESV

16 And when Jesus was baptized, immediately he went up from the water, and behold, the heavens were opened to him, and he saw the Spirit of God descending like a dove and coming to rest on him; 17 and behold, a voice from heaven said, "This is my beloved Son, with whom I am well pleased."

March 2
Our Gifts

1 Corinthians 12:1, 4-11, ERV

1 Now, brothers and sisters, I want you to understand about spiritual gifts. 4 There are different kinds of spiritual gifts, but they are all from the same Spirit. 5 There are different ways to serve, but we serve the same Lord. 6 And there are different ways that God works in people, but it is the same God who works in all of us to do everything. 7 Something from the Spirit can be seen in each person. The Spirit gives this to each one to help others. 8 The Spirit gives one person the ability to speak with wisdom. And the same Spirit gives another person the ability to speak with knowledge. 9 The same Spirit gives faith to one person and to another he gives gifts of healing. 10 The Spirit gives to one person the power to do miracles, to another the ability to prophesy, and to another the ability to judge what is from the Spirit and what is not. The Spirit gives one person the ability to speak in different kinds of languages, and to another the ability to interpret those languages. 11 One Spirit, the same Spirit, does all these things. The Spirit decides what to give each one.

As Christ-followers, we are always looking to deepen our faith, and searching for ways to act on our resolve to serve Christ. One way we can do that is in the discovery of our gifts, the special talent or calling unique to each of us. When we strengthen our relationship through the help of the Holy Spirit, we will be able to communicate through our spirits more efficiently, and our gifts will be made known to us (James 1:17). Maybe you already know what your gift is, or maybe you haven't, or didn't think *everyone* got one. If we are lost or confused in the quest to learn our gifts, we only need to pray for direction and knowledge.

Once we discover our gift; whether a healer, or a communicator, or a teacher, or a peacekeeper, we must use it in the service of spreading Christ's message (Matthew 28:19-20). Maybe this means a change in our lives, but if we are being led to it, we must consider it. All answers are found in prayer, and in the quiet listening we spend with Christ through prayer and devotion. We must allow the Holy Spirit to make changes in our lives, through the direction of our Lord, or we will never become worthy of our gifts we are intended to use in His service. We are given gifts to use to help one another, not to use in vain, or to hide up on top of a dusty shelf. Do you know what *your* gift is?

1 Peter 4:10, ESV

10 As each has received a gift, use it to serve one another, **as good stewards of God's varied grace.**

March 3
Calling All People to Service!

Acts 17:30, NKJV

30 Truly, these times of ignorance God overlooked, but now commands **all men everywhere to repent**.

Consider this: driving into town to run a long list of banal errands we see a haggard man on the corner holding a sign, asking for a helping hand. We may feel sorry for the man, but many of us turn our eyes away, trying to refocus on our own world, ignoring the suffering taking place before us. Perhaps we're telling ourselves that someone else will help them, and, therefore, we have no reason to feel guilty. We should all know better. It can be difficult to maintain a righteous spirit through temptations, trials, and uncertainty, especially in a world where wickedness and sin run unabated. Many of us have fallen victim to thinking that just doing our level best to keep from falling prey to the wickedness all around us is justification for not doing more to help our fellow man. This is wrong, as Jesus taught service to the poor, widows, and underserved as an example of loving our neighbors (Matthew 25:37-46). Many brothers and sisters in Christ suffer from homelessness, poverty, unsanitary, or abusive situations, have little or no medical care, food, or other resources. Just being a good person, avoiding gluttony, pride, lust, hate, gossip, and taking the Lord's name in vain is great, but isn't going to feed, clothe, or support our fellow brothers and sisters. Calling all believers! We can ALL be doing a little more…

Treating one another with love means helping one another in **any** way we can (Matthew 25:29). Some people are in need of resources like food or clothing, but others are in need of emotional or spiritual guidance. Recognizing what we can offer our brothers and sisters in need is the first step to loving another on the level that God calls us to. What can we do in our own communities to help the poor, homeless, hungry, and underserved? Volunteering time, special talents or services, donating food, clothing, financial donations are all ways we could be helping others in need. We can all donate a few items from our own households to help another with less; blankets, soap, non-perishable food, bottled water, books, and other items taking up space on our shelves could mean everything to the man holding the sign on the corner, begging for anyone to take kindness upon him. Put a small care package together, hand it to that homeless person on the side of the road holding a sign. Donating our time, food, services, or used clothing to a local homeless shelter or church can make all the difference in the life of someone who is struggling. A small act of service and love, one person at a time, we can change the world.

Colossians 3:23-25, NKJV

23 And whatever you do, do it heartily, as to the Lord and not to men, 24 knowing that from the Lord you will receive the reward of the inheritance; you serve the Lord Christ. 25 But he who does wrong will be repaid for what he has done, and there is no partiality.

March 4
Don't Pass Judgement

James 4:11-12, ERV

11 Brothers and sisters, don't say anything against each other. If you criticize your brother or sister in Christ or judge them, you are criticizing and judging the law they follow. And when you are judging the law, you are not a follower of the law. You have become a judge. 12 God is the one who gave us the law, and he is the Judge. He is the only one who can save and destroy. So it is not right for you to judge anyone.

What we, as a society, thinks as wicked may not be the same as God's view of wickedness. Without daily reading of the bible, routine prayers of repentance and supplication, we can fall away from our devotion to the one, true God. Understanding the bible is a time consuming endeavor, with words not commonly used today, and parable stories that can be open to interpretation. When people learn that wickedness according to God includes physical pleasures, pride, greed, stubbornness, loud opinions and crude humor, competition, deception, and wealth by example, people can become more than discouraged (Mark 7:20-23, Proverbs 6:16-19). Life is difficult with pain, tests of faith, and learning to walk the narrow path of righteousness, realizing that the pursuit of one's own pleasures is wrong in the eyes of God leaves many people discouraged with their faith.

Human judgement is naturally flawed, fueled by stereotypes, our own personal desires, powerful emotions, an unrighteous sense of justice, and individual prejudices. If we're focused on another person's business, we aren't really focused on our own. Some people have difficulty looking at, or admitting their sins, pride is the main stumbling block against humility. When we're humble, we can appreciate someone else above ourselves, like Jesus calls us to (1 Peter 3:8). When our hearts are ruled by evil and wickedness, we cannot understand God's justice, and feel a sense of injustice. Human pride, and arrogance fuels our over-inflated opinions, this prevents us from loving one another the way Jesus calls us to. Jesus doesn't need help deciding the fate of mankind, our opinion of others is usually misplaced, ignorant, and unwarranted. Forgiveness, humility, and love needs to replace our pride, arrogance, and judgement. Leaning closer into Jesus, asking for purer hearts, and repenting is the order of the day for those of us who still make the mistake of passing judgement.

Acts 10:42, ESV

42 And he commanded us to preach to the people and to testify that **he is the one appointed by God to be judge of the living and the dead.**

James 2:13, ESV

13 For judgment is without mercy to one who has shown no mercy. Mercy triumphs over judgment.

March 5
Non-Believers Beware!

John 5:38, GW

38 So you don't have the Father's message within you, because you don't believe in the person he has sent.

If we don't fully believe that Jesus walked on the Earth setting an example to live by, then died on the cross for our sins and was resurrected, we can't hear or feel the Holy Spirit.

Hebrews 3:12, GW

12 Be careful, brothers and sisters, that none of you ever develop a **wicked, unbelieving heart** that turns away from the living God.

We are all going to experience strife and affliction in our lives, but we can't let that make us angry or bitter at God. Through repeated prayer, repentance, and patience, we lean into the strength of our faith to sustain us through the rough times. We can never allow our hearts to doubt in the Lord.

Revelation 21:8, GNV

8 But the fearful and **unbelieving**, and the abominable and murderers, and whoremongers, and sorcerers, and idolaters, and all liars shall have their inheritance in the lake which burneth with fire and brimstone, which is the second death.

Although we'd like to believe that we'll *all* go to Heaven, the bible contradicts this. This is the fear of God.

John 16:8-10a, ERV

8 (Jesus said) "When the helper comes, he will show the people of the world how wrong they are about sin, about being right with God, and about judgment. 9 He will prove that they are guilty of sin, because they don't believe in me. 10 He will show them how wrong they are about how to be right with God."

Jesus knew that not everyone would accept Him, and He makes it clear that the Holy Spirit will continue to work on people's misguided confusion and doubt. Not accepting, and putting the Lord first in our lives is a sin, and we are assured that these people will be judged along with the rest of humanity.

John 3:36, ERV

36 Whoever believes in the Son has eternal life. But those who do not obey the Son will never have that life. They cannot get away from God's anger.

The belief in Jesus saves, and everyone is welcome. Humility and repentance is the road that will take us back to our salvation with God, but there is no everlasting life in Heaven for a non-believer.

March 6
Society

1 Peter 1:14, ESV

14 As obedient children, do not be conformed to the passions of your former ignorance.

Exodus 23:2a, GW

2a Never follow a crowd in doing wrong.

The latest trend, the newest technology, and the changing social norms can make the path to righteousness more difficult. Pressure to conform to those around us is part of human culture, and a major stumbling block for many people throughout History. Humans are social creatures, and can either provide comfort and support to one another, or competition, envy and deceit. Even if the world appears to be spreading hate, dissention, and highlights our differences and iniquities, God calls us to be loving, humble, and forgiving of one another (Ephesians 4:2). Foul language, disrespecting one another, judging, and insulting people are celebrated as common behavior, along with loud, obnoxious, opinionated personalities. Leaders of nations are often revealed to be untrustworthy, full of deceit, and forming unhealthy alliances behind closed doors. Somehow, the opposite of what God intended has become the accepted behavioral norm (James 4:4).

God tells us what is righteous in His eyes, as well as what He despises, all through the bible scriptures (Proverbs 6:16-19). We may not see, or hear, God as easily as the sin around us, but He is still watching, and we will all be held accountable for our choices (Matthew 12:36). We must have strong integrity to prevent societies wickedness from infecting our quest to righteousness. Making the right choices, saying no to gossip, foul language, comparing and judging people, turning away from our pride in exchange for humility is what God calls us to do, and to avoid committing these sins. All must conform to the creator, not the creation, so what we want is less important than what God wants for us. So, even when we feel like we're the struggling minority against a much greater problem, we must remain steadfast in our faith. Taking the sinful, easy way out, being lazy in our faith, this is how sin slowly creeps back into our lives. Stay strong, brothers and sisters!

Matthew 24:12, ERV

12 There will be so much more evil in the world that the love of most believers will grow cold.

Isaiah 10: 1-3a, ERV

10 Just look at those lawmakers who write evil laws and make life hard for the people. 2 They are not fair to the poor. They take away the rights of the poor and allow people to steal from widows and orphans. 3 Lawmakers, you will have to explain what you have done. What will you do then?

March 7
No Sin too Great?

Matthew 12:31-32, NASB

31 (Jesus said)"Therefore I say to you, **every sin and blasphemy shall be forgiven** people, but blasphemy against the Spirit shall not be forgiven. 32 And whoever speaks a word against the Son of Man, it shall be forgiven him; but whoever speaks against the Holy Spirit, **it shall not be forgiven him,** either in this age or in the age to come.

The bible tells us that all humans sin, and therefore all fall short in the eyes of God (Romans 3:23). We will make mistakes all our lives as humans, we will sin again and again. As humans we are imperfect in our hearts, and living among sin and wickedness on the Earth. Only the people who are chasing after Jesus' righteousness, and emulating His holiness are improving the way God delights in. If you think your faith is so strong and special that it alone is enough, and that you don't have to change anything, you are wrong, according to Jesus (Luke 13:2-3). If you think your sins are so bad, too many, or too frequent, or that you aren't figuring this new righteous thing out fast enough for Jesus, you are mistaken according to His words. Dying for us all, Jesus has redeemed everyone who believes in Him and seeks Him. Jesus is awesome.

According to the bible, God wants everyone to return to Him through redemption (Romans 2:4), as He wants to spend eternity in the Heavens He's created with all of us. The bible assures us that God forgives us 'generously' (Isaiah 55: 7), and loves us all equally (Deuteronomy 10:17). God knows our hearts, and if we are genuinely seeking repentance and change, or just a guilt-free conscience to continue doing our own will. To understand that God sent a part of Himself to Earth in the form of a man to die for the entire sinful lot of humanity is to understand the love God has for us (Romans 5:8). When we accept Jesus into our hearts, and when we seek to model our lives after His, we receive redemption and the map to a more righteous soul worthy of the kingdom of Heaven. This offer is for everyone, every day, forever, and it cannot be changed, misinterpreted or modified. No one can take this away from us, as Jesus has already paid for it. We *should* feel guilty about our sins, we wouldn't harbor the desire to change, learn, grow, or improve without it. Consequently, there is no righteous reason for avoiding repenting to the Lord for them. Pray to the Lord, brothers and sisters, embrace humility, and adopt a more honest mindset, redemption awaits the faithful! Praise God, in Jesus' name, AMEN!

1 John 4:9, NASB

9 By this the love of God was revealed in us, that God has sent His only Son into the world so that we may live through Him.

Jeremiah 24:7, ESV

7 I will give them a heart to know that I am the Lord, and they shall be my people and I will be their God, for they shall return to me with their whole heart.

March 8
Unique in Christ

Romans 12: 4-6, ESV

4 For as in one body we have many members, and the members do not all have the same function, 5 so we, though many, are one body in Christ, and individually members one of another. 6 Having gifts that differ according to the grace given to us, let us use them: if prophecy, in proportion to our faith.

School children often compare their grades and academic achievements to one another, as well as their clothing styles, and friend choices. As adults, we compare neighborhoods, cars, jobs, and the successes of our children. As humans, we share a great deal, and can't prevent the natural instinct to evaluate our own successes and failures based on what we see around us. Comparing ourselves to others is a slippery slope that usually leads to sin. We really are comparing apples and oranges any time we compare ourselves to others, for *any* reason. Although we are all sinners who need to be purified in Christ, we have different experiences, different pain and lessons learned, and different gifts. We cannot take anyone with us when Christ judges us in the end, so comparing journeys is non-sensical. We should be modeling our lives after Jesus anyway, not other people, so our focus should be on Him (2 Corinthians 10:12).

We are all on different places in our spiritual journeys, each given a unique set of skills and talents that we are meant to use among one another to serve the Lord (1 Peter 4:10). There is a reason for each painful experience and lesson we have learned (Daniel 12:10, Hebrews 12:5), all in accordance with who you are meant to be in Christ. God knows we are going to make mistakes, but desires us all to come back to Him in repentance. Each time we stray from the path to righteousness, the Lord redirects us. We all must decide for ourselves how closely we intend to follow Christ. If we decide to give our life in service, to follow Him in all we do, God won't forget us or abandon us (Psalm 9:10). Jesus came to heal the broken, so the cracks in our spirit allow His light to get in, and to mend us (2 Corinthians 12:8-10). No one can be you just the way *you* are, and the Lord is counting on that! Pretty neat

Isaiah 64:8, ERV

8 But, Lord, you are our father. We are like clay, and you are the potter. Your hands made us all.

Matthew 6:31-33, ESV

31 "Don't worry and say, 'What will we eat?' or 'What will we drink?' or 'What will we wear?' 32 That's what those people who don't know God are always thinking about. Don't worry, because your Father in heaven knows that you need all these things. 33 But seek first the kingdom of God and His righteousness, and all these things will be added to you."

March 9
Not the Judge

Zephaniah 3:8, NIV

8 Therefore wait for me," declares the Lord, "for the day I will stand up to testify. I have decided to assemble the nations, to gather the kingdoms and to pour out my wrath on them— all my fierce anger. The whole world will be consumed by the fire of my jealous anger."

Romans 2:16, ESV

16 on that day when, according to my gospel, **God judges** the secrets of men *by Christ Jesus*.

It's difficult to keep track of the sins we commit sometimes. Once in a while we do something that we *know* is wrong from the outset, but often our mistakes are hidden among the many different moments we experience throughout our days (Psalm 90:8). Traveling among other humans, we can be made aware of others' mistakes, and can be quick to form a judgement, or opinion, on the sins of others. Trying to focus on our own faults and fails while distracted by another's, we can form unfounded judgements subconsciously. Prejudice, stereotypes, hate, and division are the result when we are easily distracted by this viscous cycle of judgement toward one another. You can't be following Christ when you're too busy judging. Forming an opinion about another assumes more knowledge than we actually have, since no one but God knows what's in the heart of another (1 Kings 8:39).

Only the Lord has the right to pass judgement, so we really shouldn't be assuming that role for ourselves. Society has made comparing ourselves to one another a very marketable, yet dangerous, and easily distracting sin we are all tempted by. We are all interestingly different, but no one of us is better than anyone else (Romans 2:11). If we truly believe that, then there isn't anything *to* compare, we're not qualified to compare anything anyway. We are only responsible for being aware, and being obedient to God through Christ. We aren't treating one another fairly when we pass judgement on each other, as none of us are *qualified* to pass judgement. Additionally, we aren't 'loving' one another in Christ when we judge.

1 Corinthians 4:5, CEB

5 So don't judge anything before the right time—wait until the Lord comes. He will bring things that are hidden in the dark to light, and he will make people's motivations public. Then **there will be recognition for each person from God**.

Romans 14:13, CJB

13 Therefore, let's stop passing judgment on each other! Instead, make this one judgment — not to put a stumbling block or a snare in a brother's way.

March 10

Don't Get Sucked In

Colossians 2:8, ICB

8 Be sure that no one leads you away with false ideas and words that mean nothing. Those ideas come from men. They are the worthless ideas of this world. They are not from Christ.

1 Thessalonians 5 : 19-22, ERV

19 Don't stop the work of the Holy Spirit. 20 Don't treat prophecy like something that is not important. 21 But test everything. Keep what is good, 22 and stay away from everything that is evil.

Your good friend, family member, or colleague may be fun to be around, but they may not be living to their full potential in Christ. Maybe they are one of those non-acting believers who think that just going to church and praying once in a while is enough to secure their spot in heaven, and don't want to change too much about their current lifestyles. We must be steadfast in *our* faith journeys, and not let those around us who *do* allow themselves to succumb to unholy temptations, suck us into the same. The devil's trickery is afoot everywhere (1 Peter 5:8), and worldly pleasures, quick and less holy solutions to our problems, are always under our noses, tempting us to make poor choices.

According to Jesus, the only life worth living is a wholesome one (Matthew 10:39). We can see people's beliefs by their actions, are they kind and forgiving? Are they in a hurry, unbothered by having to step on someone else's morals or feelings to accomplish their worldly goals? We must be cautious with whom we associate for leisure, and stay away from those who are spreading hate and evil. Tricks and temptations can come in different forms, and we must be wary and vigilant. We only want to be following the light of the Lord's teachings, so reading our bibles is paramount in arming ourselves with the truth. People who are ignorant, unaware that their ways are still unholy, still pose a danger to our salvation. They may lead us astray inadvertently, which is another form of the devil's trickery (2 Corinthians 4:4). Although we should be showing kindness to everyone, we should be mindful of what our spirits are absorbing from those around us. We must pray that we are always aware of the things that are **not** from Christ, and we must listen to the Holy Spirit on this. Staying true to our faith means always representing our walk with Jesus through our actions, behaviors toward others, and our words, with the righteousness expected from a dutiful follower of Christ.

2 Corinthians 6:14, ERV

14 You are not the same as those who don't believe. So **don't join yourselves to them**. Good and evil don't belong together. Light and darkness cannot share the same room.

March 11
Perseverance

Galatians 6:9, ICB

9 We must not become tired of doing good. We will receive our harvest of eternal life at the right time. We must not give up!

James 1:12, ESV

12 Blessed is the man who remains steadfast under trial, for when he has stood the test he will receive the crown of life, which God has promised to those who love him.

After waiting in a long line, the last thing we want is another delay in getting us on our way. We seem to have an internal agenda, and don't like anything to interrupt our progress as we move along in our individual itineraries. Sometimes we just get fed up, frustrated, and annoyed at the circumstances of our lives. We can all lose our patience with doing the right thing. We shouldn't beat ourselves up for moments like these, but we should recognize when they are happening. These are opportunities to pray for patience and grace to get us through trying, and exasperating moments that would normally tempt us to lose our cool. Getting angry, honking our car horns, yelling and cussing at one another will only bring us more challenges (1 Thessalonians 5:15). Negativity breeds negativity. Break the cycle of negativity, stop before you lose your cool and say a quick prayer. It'll change everything, if you let it.

Being strong in our pursuit of being a better human being requires patience and diligence, and it's alright if we need extra help with those things. Jesus tells us that the more good we do in our lives, the better we'll feel about ourselves and the world around us, and the more good works we'll *want* to do (Luke 6:35-36). Stopping ourselves before our minor annoyances become larger irritations, and praying for support through them, is the key to breaking the cycle of negativity. Pray for the wisdom to know your triggers, the patience to understand that change takes time, and the perseverance to try harder the next day. Living a more righteous life takes strength, patience, perseverance, good communication with the Holy Spirit, and a willingness to allow changes in our lives.

Philippians 2:13, ERV

13 Yes, it is God who is working in you. He helps you want to do what pleases him, and he gives you the power to do it.

Matthew 24:13, ESV

13 But the one who endures to the end will be saved.

March 12
Self-Care

Mark 6:31, ERV

31 Jesus and His followers were in a very busy place. There were so many people that he and His followers did not even have time to eat. He said to them, "Come with me. We will go to a quiet place to be alone. There we will get some rest."

We've all heard the phrase, 'you can't pour from an empty cup,' but what does that mean, exactly? Following Jesus' footsteps is more of a challenge than we may initially realize, but this work is God's desire for us, and worthwhile. Trying to make better choices in our lives while being challenged by the world's distractions puts stress on our spirits, and this can affect our attitudes. We can get discouraged, disheartened, feel hopelessness, loneliness and despair as humans, and it can be hard to face another challenge when we're always looking around the corner for the next one (Matthew 6:34). After your day is done, the house or apartment is locked up for the night, and the sun sets on the days responsibilities, what kind of quality time are we actually spending with ourselves? Taking care to safeguard the peace in our hearts and minds, the bible once again tells us to put all of our worries and requests in prayer (Philippians 4:6-7).

No cellphone, no television, no Netflix, no TikTok, no social media sounds like a nightmare, or a power outage for some of us. Peace and quiet looks, and feels, different to each of us, we all like to relax in different ways. If we don't take a few minutes to ourselves *each day* to renew our spirits, we won't have what we need to face the next day's challenges. What's important to remember when taking time to ourselves to recharge our spiritual batteries is to be in a place where we can be at peace, with no outside distractions, causing a tug or pull on our emotions. When we decompress, we need to be one with our thoughts and feelings, and in a state of peace. This is when we can really feel what might be unbalanced inside of us, and anything we find should be given to Jesus in prayer. We can't really be in a peaceful state with music blaring, or the television on, while checking the stocks, or while checking our social media on our phones. Set down the phone, turn off all the outside distractions, and focus on *you* for a few minutes each day- then pray your findings to your Savior. If we're not devoting some time at the end, and beginning of our day to the Lord, what kind of relationship can we say we really have?

Matthew 11:28-30, ICB

28 "Come to me, all of you who are tired and have heavy loads. I will give you rest. 29 Accept my work and learn from me. I am gentle and humble in spirit. And you will find rest for your souls. 30 The work that I ask you to accept is easy. The load I give you to carry is not heavy.

Proverbs 4:23, NIV

23 Above all else, guard your heart, **for everything you do flows from it.**

March 13
Handling Our Own Problems

Proverbs 3:5-6, ICB

5 Trust the Lord with all your heart. Don't depend on your own understanding. 6 Remember the Lord in everything you do. And he will give you success.

Lamentations 3:22-24, ESV

22 The steadfast love of the Lord never ceases; His mercies never come to an end; 23 they are new every morning; great is your faithfulness. 24 "The Lord is my portion," says my soul, "therefore I will hope in him."

Bills pilling up, too many social obligations pulling you in different directions, family stress over choices the children are making, these are examples of things we all deal with daily that can weigh our spirits down. Add an argument with the spouse, family member or close co-worker and our emotions can be pushed to the breaking point. We can all relate to this type of stress. Sometimes it feels like we have more on our plate than we can handle, and it's easy to become overwhelmed. Through it all, we keep plugging along, choosing our battles, leaving the one's not fought to fester for another day. All of that stress can compound inside of us, adding even more pressure to our weak souls.

We aren't meant to deal with our troubles and emotional burdens on our own. We are meant to rely on Christ Jesus to sustain us, to provide *all* that we need, no matter how large or small the need. Sometimes we need a little reassurance, a little extra patience, or both! Perhaps we need help with our work life balance, or help understanding how to give ourselves more freely to God. Wherever we are in our walk with Jesus, no matter what we have on our plates, help is only a heartfelt prayer away. That's it, prayer. Only, when we're upset, hurt, or irritated it's difficult to find the calm grace needed to offer a respectful prayer. Keep prayers short and simple if necessary, but asking for help to deal with our everyday issues before they become larger issues is vital. It's important not to underestimate the power of an earnest prayer. Merciful Christ, sustain us in our hour of need, for we depend solely on you, AMEN.

Psalm 118:5-6, ESV

5 Out of my distress I called on the Lord; the Lord answered me and set me free. 6 The Lord is on my side; I will not fear. What can man do to me?

Psalm 55:22, ESV

22 Place your burden on the Lord, and he will support you. He will never allow the righteous to be moved.

March 14
Free Will

Proverbs 16:9, ERV

9 People can plan what they want to do, but it is the Lord who guides their steps.

Romans 6:23, ESV

23 For the wages of sin is death, but the free gift of God is eternal life in Christ Jesus our Lord.

We make all sorts of choices in our lives from where we will live, who we will live with, if we'll raise children, to what we'll do for a living. Some people are called to be healers, growing up all their lives wanting to help make the sick well, and assist the injured. Others dream of being a chef, cooking for the masses, and still others know from a very early age they will be peacekeepers or lawmakers. Not all of us feel a strong calling, and usually find something that suits our personality or abilities. The bible encourages work to sustain us, and so we won't be dependent on others for survival (1 Thessalonians 4:11-12), but the soul needs something more than just our careers to guide it. Our spirits can grow, but can only be nourished properly by Christ (John 6:35). We live with the choices we make, for better or worse.

Sometimes our choices come back to bite us. When we make choices based on our own understanding, we will typically bring on more trouble. We are designed to need God to make wholesome choices with our lives, and when we deviate from that we suffer consequences of those choices (Proverbs 1:23-25). Getting to know how the Holy spirit works and communicates through us can be difficult and confusing. Thoughtful requests, questions, and supplications can be presented to God in prayer through Jesus. Careful consideration, and internal reflection after praying is essential, for God isn't going to put our answer on a billboard, lit up in a thousand little blinking lights so there isn't any misinterpretation. We must learn by trial and error, by diligence and persistence, by faith. If we continue to make choices without regard to God in prayer, we risk cursing certain aspects of our life (Jeremiah 17:5). Choose wisely, brothers and sisters.

Deuteronomy 30:19-20a, ERV

19 "**Today I am giving you a choice** of two ways. And I ask heaven and earth to be witnesses of your choice. You can choose life or death. The first **choice** will bring a blessing. The other **choice** will bring a curse. **So choose life!** Then you and your children will live. 20a You must love the Lord your God and obey him. Never leave him, because he is your life."

John 1:11-13, CEB

11 The light came to His own people, and His own people didn't welcome him. 12 **Yet to all who did receive him, to those who believed in His name, he gave the right to become children of God**—13 born not from blood nor from human desire or passion, but born from God.

March 15
Pray First

Psalm 16:5, ESV

5 The Lord is my chosen portion and my cup; you hold my lot.

Isaiah 66:2, ESV

2 "All these things my hand has made, and so all these things came to be," declares the Lord. "But This is the one to whom I will look: he who is humble and **contrite in spirit** and trembles at my word."

Past mistakes, poor choices, and bad decisions, we've all made them. When our circumstances become more than we think we can handle, most of us turn to the Lord in prayer. This is never the wrong thing to do, as Jesus teaches us how to pray in the bible (Matthew 6:9-13). When we make choices and decisions based on our *own* thinking and reasoning, we will most likely come up short. Where was the Lord in this decision making process? We sometimes bypass the Lord when it comes to the choices we make in our lives, thinking we can handle making some decisions on our own. Before you know it, we're knee deep in more than we can handle, unmet expectations, pain and disappointment. We then pray to our Lord to save us from the poor choices *we've* made, and the consequences we've brought on ourselves.

Life's choices in our own hands just leads to more bad choices. The bible instructs us to put all our concerns and anxieties in prayer and supplication, as the Lord guides our steps (Proverbs 3:5-6). When we submit to Christ's plan for us, when we choose righteousness over our sins, we do this through each choice and decision make. We are turning away from sin, and toward the light Christ shines for us all when*ever* we rely on Him. Our lives will always bring forth challenges, but to put our lives in the hands of our Savior Jesus Christ is the safest, best thing we can do for our souls salvation. When we think about it, if we are following our own desires and choices, we *aren't* following Jesus. Who are *you* going to leave in charge of *your* salvation?

Proverbs 16:9, ESV

9 The heart of man plans His way, but the Lord establishes His steps.

Psalm 37:23, ESV

23 The steps of a man are established by the Lord, when he delights in His way.

March 16
If We Can Follow

John 8:12, ESV

12 Again Jesus spoke to them, saying, "I am the light of the world. Whoever follows me will not walk in darkness, but will have the light of life."

Luke 14:33, ESV

33 Jesus said to them, "So therefore, any one of you who does not renounce all that he has cannot be my disciple."

If Jesus were alive and on the Earth right now doing His ministry, and He called you to give up all your possessions, leave your family and follow Him, would you? Leaving everything behind may not have been a metaphor in 28 A.D. when Jesus was alive and walking the Earth, but does pose an interesting question. We must ask ourselves if we're able to give up certain aspects of our current lifestyle, and personality, in exchange for a closer relationship to Jesus, because that's what He's asking us. He's asking us to love Him more than anything else. Can we? Do we? The path to righteousness, and everlasting spiritual life, is narrow, as Jesus describes, and 'few' will be able to undertake it (Matthew 7:13-14).

When we make errors in choice or judgement, God lets us know through the changes in our life circumstances, by trials, suffering and tribulations (Revelation 3:19). Holy in *all* our conduct sounds impossible, because it is. Some of us are going to try harder than others to clean up our lives and our hearts, and this is what God is looking for (Psalm 14:2). Humans are naturally sinful creatures, God points out as early as the book of Genesis (6:5). this journey is **purposely** difficult, causing us to look deeper into ourselves, but not just to see and understand the sins we commit, but to purify our hearts to be more like Jesus. Only through deep introspection can we learn the faults and deficiencies of our hearts, then we will know what to repent, and pray for. Jesus is the strength to our weaknesses, but we can't fill those holes with His divine Spirit if we don't know where the holes are. Obedience is a word that causes some people to recoil, not wanting to submit to anyone or anything but our own will and design. Our pride gets in the way of the humility we require to submit to abiding by Christ. We cannot serve two masters (Matthew 6:24); we cannot serve ourselves *and* Christ. If we want to be more devoted to Christ, we can put this to Him in a prayer request, along with a deeper understanding of what's Holy, and a deeper trust in Him.

Luke 14:25-26, ERV

25 Many people were traveling with Jesus. He said to them, 26 "If you come to me but will not leave your family, you cannot be my follower. You must love me more than your father, mother, wife, children, brothers, and sisters—even more than your own life!"

March 17
A Trust Walk

Proverbs 4:25-27, ERV

25 Keep your eyes on the path, and look straight ahead. 26 Make sure you are going the right way, and nothing will make you fall. 27 Don't go to the right or to the left, and you will stay away from evil.

Isaiah 30:21, ERV

21 If you wander from the right path, either to the right or to the left, you will hear a voice behind you saying, "You should go this way. Here is the right way."

Trust is elusive, and with some people, it can be downright impossible to achieve and maintain. People are fallible, and will always carry the potential to disappoint. The bible assures us that through God's perfect love for us, Jesus' ultimate sacrifice, we will never be let down or forgotten (Isaiah 41:10). God is not of this world and it's sinful pleasures, and desires for us all to repent and seek Him through Christ Jesus over and over again. From us, God wants a softer heart, a more wholesome spirit, and complete devotion (1 Timothy 1:5). God calls upon us to love Him with all of our hearts, souls, strength, and mind. He's calling on us to *trust* Him.

When we place our complete trust in God, we are essentially blindfolded and being led through life by something larger than ourselves. On one hand it can be scary not knowing what to expect, what will happen to us, or how our needs will be fulfilled. On the other hand, it's nice not having to worry or concern ourselves with planning our lives, knowing that the Lord sees to our needs, and provides all that we will require (Matthew 6:31-33). We must be content with less, as the world often leads us to believe we need more in our lives to be happy. Jesus teaches us that the humble, the meek, the gentle soul is the example of Holiness (Matthew 5:2-10). Nothing in the world today can offer the grace, the wisdom, and the salvation that comes from following Jesus Christ. Flashy jewelry, toned physique of young, beautiful, perfect-looking people of power, wealth and fame can be very distracting to some people who long for the sinful pleasures of conceit, lust and greed. When we are looking at ourselves, or others, or what the world has to offer us, we are turned away from the Lord (Isaiah 59:2). We can always pray to the Lord for a deeper faith, to trust Him more, if we feel unsure.

Psalm 32:8, ERV

8 The Lord says, "I will teach you and guide you in the way you should live. I will watch over you and be your guide."

2 Corinthians 5:7, GW

7 Indeed, our lives are guided by faith, not by sight.

March 18
All of God's Rules Count

Luke 16:17, ERV

17 (Jesus said) "But even the smallest part of a letter in the law cannot be changed. It would be easier for heaven and earth to pass away."

James 2:10, ERV

10 You might follow all of God's law. But if you fail to obey only one command, you are guilty of breaking all the commands in that law.

Following God's rules aren't going to be easy, because sinful people are happier when they're allowed to sin, and God requires we avoid the temptation to commit sins. Some of us try, ignoring some of the rules while following others that might be easier. It is easy to ignore the man asking for handouts on the corner, but a friend in Christ would give them food, drink, clothing, or some other type of assistance. Outraged at an injustice, our first instinct might be to yell back when someone lashes out at us, but we should turn the other cheek and pray for them (Matthew 5:44). Instead of competing with an envious co-worker, compliment them and restrain from judging them (Luke 6:31). For some people, this can be too difficult, and many give up. For others, being ignorant to God's laws, taking them out of context, or not fully understanding them is not an acceptable excuse (Acts 17:30).

We have been given the assistance of the Holy bible, now available in a translation we can all understand, to better understand our ongoing relationship with God. Losing any meaning that could be lost by translation is minor compared to the ignorance of not reading the bible at all. We have also been given the help of the Holy spirit through Christ Jesus (Acts 2:38), that some people never learn to use, or comprehend. There is no reason *not* to launch a better individual understanding of the bible, as there are free websites and resources available to people of all levels of understanding. Research the commandments and laws, take time at the end of the day to reflect on them as well as our own, individual lives. Praying, talking with our partners or spouses, meditating or spending quiet time daily to look inward we can find peace in our hearts, as well as hear the Holy Spirit guiding us. The more we learn about righteousness, and how to achieve it through Christ, and the more we apply this to our lives, the more knowledge we acquire. As we trim and cultivate our lives in this way, we convert our souls into the righteousness the Lord seeks in us.

Psalm 19:7-9, KJ21

7 The law of the Lord is perfect, converting the soul; the testimony of the Lord is sure, **making wise the simple**. 8 The statutes of the Lord are right, rejoicing the heart; the commandment of the Lord is pure, enlightening the eyes. 9 The fear of the Lord is clean, enduring forever; the judgments of the Lord are true and righteous altogether.

March 19
Competition

Romans 10:12-13, ICB

12 That Scripture says "anyone" because there is no difference between Jew and non-Jew. The same Lord is the Lord of **all** and gives many blessings to **all who trust in him**. 13 The Scripture says, "**Anyone** who asks the Lord for help will be saved."

Famous people are fun to watch, we read about them, watch their movies, music, and shows, and follow their work with interest. We can become discouraged when measuring our lives' accomplishments to others who appear to have more than we do. It's true that there will always be someone else who is wealthier, taller, better looking, smarter or more successful. However, this is only true if we allow ourselves to get caught up in comparing ourselves to others. It's made clear in the bible, Jesus sees us all the same (Acts 10:34). No one person is better in the eyes of God than another, so why do we humans fall prey to the vicious, and pointless, cycle of comparing ourselves to one another. In fact, only Jesus can offer the reassurances we all search for. We all are born with the same capabilities to love, and serve God equally, and we're all given free will to choose (Deuteronomy 30:19), and each given different gifts by the Holy Spirit (1 Corinthians 12:10-11).

In our individual life journeys we should be directly focused on our relationship with Jesus, emulating **His** holiness, not one another. It can be hard *not* to compare ourselves with others when we interact and commune so closely on a daily basis. Jesus isn't comparing our triumphs and failures to one another, but to His own righteousness and purity of heart, so we shouldn't be comparing one another either. If we compare ourselves to our environment, what happens when that environment changes or disappears? Instead of comparing ourselves to someone else, who is likely sinning also, just *differently*, compare instead to an earlier version of ourselves. This is how we improve. Speak to Jesus in prayer today about where you'd really like to be on your journey with Him, *and* yourself. Also, pray for opportunities to build up another person, instead of comparing yourself to them, or trying to outdo one another.

Philippians 2:3-4, ESV

3 Do nothing from rivalry or conceit, **but in humility count others more significant than yourselves**. 4 Let each of you look not only to His own interests, but also to the interests of others.

Galatians 3:28, ERV

28 Now, in Christ, it doesn't matter if you are a Jew or a Greek, a slave or free, male or female. You are all the same in Christ Jesus.

March 20
The Devil Lurks

Matthew 13:19-22, ESV

19 "When anyone hears the word of the kingdom and does not understand it, the evil one comes and snatches away what has been sown in His heart. This is what was sown along the path. 20 As for what was sown on rocky ground, this is the one who hears the word and immediately receives it with joy, 21 yet he has no root in himself, but endures for a while, and when tribulation or persecution arises on account of the word, immediately he falls away. 22 As for what was sown among thorns, this is the one who hears the word, but the cares of the world and the deceitfulness of riches choke the word, and it proves unfruitful."

Mired in bills, appointments, or deadlines, concerned with the choices our children are making, there never seems to be enough time to get everything on our itineraries done, let alone get a minute to collect our thoughts and relax. To many, this sounds all too familiar, and the last thing we might be thinking about is, 'Have I prayed today?' Life is pretty distracting, and the salvation of our eternal spirits, or souls, isn't usually the first thing that crosses our minds on a daily basis. It's no surprise then, to learn that we're not as far along on our path to righteousness as we could be. God is our source of life, our salvation, and eternal rest at the end of a life He hopes we'll devote to Him (1 Kings 8:61). It is through this devotion that we derive our strength to ward off temptation, to endure tribulations, and summon tools we can use to stand against the devil.

Our lifeline to God is Jesus (John 14:6), and He is a prayer away, but we need to take the time to do that. If we are putting Jesus first in our lives we should be automatically seeking Him through prayer at least daily. We will be tempted to sin every day, and most of us will lose that battle. Only God has the omnipresent power to know our thoughts, our true heart's desire. Many things threaten to distract us, mislead us, blind us from the truth, or tempt us away from Christ that we aren't aware of, or are able to recognize, that are all controlled by the devil (2 Corinthians 4:4, 11:14). In this way, God is able to determine which souls diligently and earnestly pursue Him in love and true faith, and which souls turn away from Him. We are all susceptible to the devil's trickery and deceit while here on Earth, but we don't have to let it pull us off our path. If we seek Jesus when we are being tempted, or when we are feeling wronged or slighted, every time we need a little more strength, those tribulations can actually *help* to build up the strength we have in our faith.

James 4:7, ERV

7 So give yourselves to God. Stand against the devil, and he will run away from you.

March 21
Prejudice

1 John 2:2, ESV

2 He is the propitiation for our sins, and not for ours only but also for the sins of **the whole world**.

Colossians 3:11, ESV

11 Here there is not Greek and Jew, circumcised and uncircumcised, barbarian, Scythian, slave, free; but **Christ is all, and in all**.

Looking for a sense of normalcy, that we're doing things correctly in relation to those around us, and that we're not missing out on anything in life would be considered a justifiable status quo by most people. Many would even agree that seeking a degree of acceptance, love, and sense of belonging and success amongst our peers is healthy, and ordinary. For those that are also hoping to find Jesus welcoming us with open arms in Heaven, we will never find the love, acceptance, and fulfillment our hearts seek through *anything* we achieve on Earth (1 John 2:15-17). Not the success of our careers, nor the great works we leave, or even in the growth and health of our families can produce the divine salvation found in a relationship with Christ Jesus. Those things can make life on Earth worth the exile, but the fulfillment our spirits and souls seek can only be found through the truth that is Jesus Christ. Spiritual salvation can only be achieved through a life devoted to following Christ Jesus (Acts 4:12), and sharing and passing that love onto our brothers and sisters.

Seemingly innocent conversation about someone else's love or romantic life, or relationship status, or how much someone is making, or what they are spending it on, or someone's reputation isn't really innocent. Discussing world peace, and what the leaders *should* be doing, even for the advocacy of humankind is wrong, because it involves forming a preconceived conclusion or ideas about someone. People spend a great deal of time thinking and talking about others, worrying about what they'll think or how they'll fit in. Although friends, family, gossip and sinful worldly distractions can produce mild amounts of pleasure, true happiness in our soul can only come from righteousness through Christ Jesus. Trying to follow along Christ's narrow path of Holy righteousness is tough enough on our own without focusing unduly on those around us and what they are thinking, an evil distraction at best! No one accompanies us to our judgements before Christ (1 Timothy 6:7), so their opinions should be taken with a degree of skepticism. Unless our words are used for the intention to assist spiritually in prayer, or praise, or to partake in righteous fellowship, or to build another up, they are worthless (Matthew 12:36). Christ accepted all sinners regardless of their sex, their sin, or their heritage, or their pasts into His kingdom. Why then, do we still judge one another on these things?

Matthew 7:1-2, ERV

1 "Don't judge others. 2 If you judge others, you will be judged the same way you judge them. God will treat you the same way you treat others."

March 22
Pious Pretenders

Galatians 3:26-27, 29, ICB

26-27 You were all baptized into Christ, and so you were all clothed with Christ. This shows that you are all children of God through faith in Christ Jesus. 29 You belong to Christ. So you are Abraham's descendants. You get all of God's blessings because of the promise that God made to Abraham.

Some may believe that because someone has a criminal record, has a gambling or addiction problem, is living an alternative lifestyle, has a learning disability, or dresses or expresses themselves differently, that they cannot love or understand God. If we are *all the same* in Christ because of our belief in Him, we should be more accepting of other sinners, not prejudice or exclusionary (Luke 18:9-14). Some people will never be able to accept God, but that doesn't make those of us better because we do (Philippians 2:3).

People can often reject things because of pre-conceived ideas, unpleasant previous encounters, and other beliefs. We all learn and grow differently, and shouldn't reject anyone, because rejecting another is rejecting someone Christ died for. The bible confuses us at times with strange laws, apparent contradictions (1 John 5:18, 1 John 1:8), and symbolism that is difficult for some to interpret (Revelation 17:3-4). Many people come out of reading the old testament, having read all of the specific rules and laws, and rest their conclusions about faith solely based on their opinions of those laws. God realized His humans wouldn't *automatically* love, and be faithful to Him in return (Gen 6:5), so He had to find another way to sort the faithful from the unfaithful (Matthew 13:47-50). What some people forget, or perhaps don't realize, is that no human can be made right with God by their own efforts (Romans 3:20). As confusing as all the laws, commandments and rules are, there are really only two (Matthew 22:36-40).

If we had more love for one another in our hearts, we wouldn't be committing any sins against one another. All humanity is sinful because of what happened in the Garden of Eden (Romans 5:12), and since we're all guilty there's no reason to blame, or point fingers at one another. We are only to know about our iniquities to highlight our need for God, because He wishes for us to turn to Him so He can heal us. God sent Jesus by way of natural, human birth, the only man with God **in Him**. The perfect mix of divinity within a mortal body, Jesus is a divine example of a human who was able to live without sinning: the perfect sacrifice for God's sinful creation. If we think we are more morally conscious than anyone else, **we are hypocrites**, because all humanity has proved to be corrupt. May we all keep open minds, and hearts, in Christ Jesus, our Lord. Amen.

Romans 3:28, ERV

28 I mean we are made right with God through faith, not through what we have done to follow the law. This is what we believe.

March 23
Modesty and Humility

1 Peter 5: 6, ESV

6 Humble yourselves, therefore, under the mighty hand of God so that at the proper time he may exalt you.

It is hard to convince people we're humble when we're blasting our opinions to anyone who'll listen, have boisterous behaviors, dress obnoxiously with loud jewelry, wear expensive clothes, and sport elaborate hairstyles. What's more, it's difficult to practice humility when we judge, or categorize, or make assumptions about other people then tell ourselves that we're just 'observant,' or 'analytical in nature.' (Proverbs 16:5, 16:18, Romans 14:19) Additionally, it's near impossible to identify as humble, when we find ourselves feeling proud, secretly arrogant *really*, while we try to tell ourselves we just have a 'healthy self-esteem,' or tell ourselves we're just 'self-confident,' or 'blessed,' when we're secretly proud of the ego, or reputation we've developed. (Proverbs 31:30) Some people brag about how much alcohol they can drink and still survive, while others are proud of the many extra-marital affairs they have consummated. Still others are secretly proud of the business they've created, awards they've earned, or work they've amassed, finding themselves secretly more gifted, talented, or blessed than another. Some people think they have the ideal family life, and brag to others about the success of their children, or the awards their family member has received, quietly thinking they've made superior choices to another. Hey! We all may have different gifts, but not one of us are any better (or worse) than another. We can't take our awards, accomplishments, or even our really awesome family with us when we face God at our final judgement. We all just have a limited time, so, what are we trying to *accomplish* here? Life isn't about **us and other people**, it's supposed to be about us, as individuals, and our relationships with God. We need to take an honest look at ourselves, spiritually, because God is.

Pride and bragging-how much we can drink, how many restaurants we've been to, how many people want to sleep with us, our athletic prowess or awards, how intelligent we think we are, family success-All of these are either sinful or *irrelevant*. Kindness, simplicity and restraint, sincerity and genuineness, generousness, *spiritual maturity*, discipline and self-control are the model of righteousness. These are all examples of the holiness we are to emulate, as Christ was holy (1 Peter 1:16). Pride and humility are opposites of one another, one cannot be proud and humble at the same time. We are all 'blessed,' since Jesus died for all of us. Jesus is the example of what to model our lives by, and He is who we should all be focused on, not one another. When we follow the model Jesus left, and when truly sought after, this is the gifts of God, pulling us closer to Him through the blood of Christ. Thanks be to God, blessed and Holy is He, AMEN!

1 John 2:16, ESV

16 For all that is in the world — the desires of the flesh and the desires of the eyes and pride of possessions-is not from the Father but is from the world.

March 24
Self-Control

2 Peter 1:5-8, ERV

5 Because you have these blessings, do all you can to add to your life these things: to your faith add goodness; to your goodness add knowledge; 6 to your knowledge add self-control; to your self-control add patience; to your patience add devotion to God; 7 to your devotion add kindness toward your brothers and sisters in Christ, and to this kindness add love. 8 If all these things are in you and growing, you will never fail to be useful to God. You will produce the kind of fruit that should come from your knowledge of our Lord Jesus Christ.

It can be easy to find ourselves impatient, frustrated or even angry when driving, as many people are in a hurry, or just not paying attention. Some people honk their horn, yell and shout, or even offer profane gestures to drivers that produce their wrath. Not everyone holds the elevator door open for the one person who is rushing to catch it, people are often focused on themselves and not necessarily their fellow brothers and sisters. We all come from the same God, a God assures that us that when we seek Him we'll find all we need (Jeremiah 29:13), a God who calls us to love one another and leave final judgement to Him. It seems like we're all too busy in search of more, more money, more respect, more time, more respite, more security, to trust any of our needs to God. Most of the time what people really need more of is less. We need less anger, less anxiety, less judgement, less planning and more trust in God.

Some of us know of someone who brags about saying whatever comes into their mind, and those people are usually pretty proud of their unfiltered, obnoxious ignorance and disgrace. When we let our emotions take over; anger, lust, worry, vengeance, pride, only dissention, sexual impurity, strife, war and boasting result. Giving in to human emotions without prudent self-control and righteous guidance is irrational foolishness according to the bible (Proverbs 16:32, Colossians 3:2, James 1:20). How are we to discern the tricks of the wicked, and how are we to avoid sin when we race through our incoming thoughts, sprinting to a reaction without pause for sensible consideration? How are we to truly understand *anything* when our thought to reaction time is less than ten seconds? We are called to think before we speak, pray before we decide anything, and remember that, as followers of the one true Christ, we want to project Jesus' example as we interact with others. Discipline and self-control can be difficult in a sinful, dynamic, disruptive world full of temptations, traps, vices and tests of faith. Those of us who really want to *show* God we can love and obey Him as we're called to must consider the practice of appropriate restraint a delightful test of faith from which our strength, discipline and self-control can mature in our faith through Jesus Christ. We pray, usually more than once, when we need extra strength, willpower, encouragement and guidance during the many tribulations we will all face throughout our lives.

Proverbs 21:23, ESV

23 Whoever keeps His mouth, and His tongue keeps himself out of trouble.

Philippians 4:7, ESV

7 And the peace of God, which surpasses all understanding, will guard your hearts and your minds in Christ Jesus.

March 25
This is My Way, Walk in It

Proverbs 3:7, ESV

7 Be not wise in your own eyes; fear the Lord, and turn away from evil.

James 1:21, ICB

21 So put out of your life every evil thing and every kind of wrong you do. Don't be proud but accept God's teaching that is planted in your hearts. This teaching can save your souls.

Humans like to complicate things by making their own choices. We all want to be independent, and believe we will only be *truly* satisfied in life if *we* are the masters of our own destinies. We like to tell ourselves that with either success or failure we'll be able to live with ourselves if we were the *only* ones in control of our lives. We are deceived. Humans are limited in their understanding, and corrupted by sin and wickedness all around them. Humans aren't capable of interpreting everything that happens to them correctly, and therefore, need to be able to trust in God's direction (Jeremiah 16:17, Jeremiah 23:24). God's will is going to be done, no matter what we try and do on our own, for He sees all and has power over all. When we try to make our own choices and decisions, we are acting on inaccurate and incomplete knowledge, and turning away from God in the process, and this will only bring on more strife (Isaiah 53:6).

We are called to listen to the Holy Spirit guiding our thoughts, morals, and standards instead of giving into the whim of our own desires (Matthew 16:24). The bible teaches us that the scripture is to be used for directions on how to lead a more righteous life, and how to pursue Holiness through Christ Jesus (2 Timothy 3:16-17). God gives us strife to learn from our mistakes and come back to His guidance. Submitting to God is a reflection of the loving relationship between God and His humanity; it's accepting our role as children of our creator, it's us submitting to His teaching, and it's Him telling us we're forgiven. God has a plan for our lives, and intends to see it all the way through *despite* our efforts to sidetrack His rightful place as our Heavenly Father, and creator. We can show God we love Him by submitting to Him in every aspect of our lives. Stay humble, and praise the Lord, brothers and sisters.

1 John 5:3, NASB

3 For this is the love of God, that we keep His commandments; and His commandments are not burdensome.

Isaiah 30:21, ESV

21 And your ears shall hear a word behind you, saying, "this is the way, walk in it," when you turn to the right or when you turn to the left.

March 26
Kingdom of Opposites

Matthew 23:12, ESV

12 Whoever exalts himself will be humbled, and whoever humbles himself will be exalted.

1 John 2:15-161, ERV

15 Don't love this evil world or the things in it. If you love the world, you do not have the love of the Father in you. 16 This is all there is in the world: wanting to please our sinful selves, wanting the sinful things we see, and being too proud of what we have. But none of these comes from the Father. They come from the world.

If you asked the average person how they measure success you might hear wealth, social or economic status, or by the amount of philanthropic donations made. It can be easy to boast to our friends about our accomplishments, academic achievements, or awards. We are proud of ourselves when we accomplish something we have set out to achieve or master, what's wrong with that? According to the bible, and the gospel, everything. Pride is a negative emotion, brought on by the need to be valued greater than those around us.

Our competitive, capitalistic nature is really a *negative* quality, and completely *opposite* of what the bible teaches as behavior to seek when following Christ (Mat 20:25-28). Our society is run by money, and many people chase after the ghost of financial security when Christ warns us against this (Matthew 19:24). All we need will be provided for, so when we go after more we are pursuing this for our own pride, selfishness, and vanity (Luke 12:15). The gospel echoes the importance of humility, and love for one another, mimicking the love Jesus showed for all of us. Opposing our evil, capitalistic drive to acquire as much as we can in this world, Jesus taught to be humble, to forgive our enemies, and that true wealth was achieved by giving. Not many of us see the benefits of giving our hard-earned money, time and efforts to anything that doesn't serve ourselves. Pride is a selfish, greedy, common human quality, isn't loving our neighbor, evil, and, and comes in many hidden forms. Lord, build us up in humility, and protect us from our sinful pride. AMEN.

Jeremiah 9:24, ERV

24 The Lord said, "But if someone wants to brag, then let them brag about this: Let them brag that they learned to know me. Let them brag that they understand that I am the Lord, that I am kind and fair, and that I do good things on earth. I love this kind of bragging."

March 27
All Will Be Humbled

Luke 14:11, ESV

11 "For all those who exalt themselves will be humbled, and those who humble themselves will be exalted."

Humility is an important quality to God, and the bible represents this through a repeated theme throughout the old and new testaments. Pride is the opposite of humility, so the two cannot co-exist. Many people would say they are proud of theirs or their children's accomplishments, or the number of grandchildren they have, or even their physical appearance. Since all things, both good and bad, come from the Lord (Isaiah 45:7), what are **we** so proud of? All of our blessings, wisdom, and good fortune come from the Lord (James 1:17). We all have forgiveness and grace through salvation because God is all-powerful and loving, not because **we're** all so amazing. As a matter of fact, the only bragging the Lord *doesn't* mind is the kind that praises Him (Jeremiah 9:24). When we become proud, of anything in our lives, we turn away from God and toward the mirror. We are all God's creation, and when we turn from Him, in *any* way, He is displeased. For the same reason, when we fail to give Him proper praise for the good things in our lives, God is also displeased. Some of us don't even know that they've turned away from God, focused on the minutia of our lives or of those around them. What we don't know about God's world, His word, and our place in it can only be our own fault. Understanding our place in this world God created is much easier when one studies the bible.

The ultimate fate of our souls is up to God, whether we enjoy the fruits of everlasting life in Heaven with our creator, or suffer eternally in the lake of sulfur is completely up to His final judgement (Rev. 20:15). We have all been given ample warning to repent and seek God in all we do, but some of us pretend this command has an expiration date (Mat. 24:35). Still others like to think they only have to follow the scriptures **they** believe in, and this is another man-made, made up rule. When we modify the scriptures to suit our own beliefs and prejudices, we are turning away from God and worshiping our own laws instead of God's (Mat. 5:18). The holy path of righteousness, is servitude to our Heavenly Father, and isn't supposed to be an easy life, but one devoted to our God. If we don't all come to realize our place in God's world, and humble ourselves before Him, He will. In His way, and in His timing, God will humble us all.

Isaiah 45:23, ERV

23 "When I make a promise, that promise is true. It will happen. And I swear by my own power that everyone will bow before me and will take an oath to obey me."

Isaiah 5:15-16, ERV

15 Everyone, common people and leaders alike, will be humbled. Those who are now so proud will bow their heads in shame. 16 The Lord All-Powerful will judge fairly, and people will honor him. They will respect the Holy God when he brings justice.

March 28
Not a Cake Walk

Matthew 10:34-39, GW

34 "Don't think that I came to bring peace to earth. I didn't come to bring peace but conflict. 35 I came to turn a man against His father, a daughter against her mother, a daughter-in-law against her mother-in-law. 36 A person's enemies will be the members of His own family. 37 The person who loves His father or mother more than me does not deserve to be my disciple. The person who loves a son or daughter more than me does not deserve to be my disciple. 38 Whoever doesn't take up His cross and follow me doesn't deserve to be my disciple."

Matthew 19:25-26, GW

25 He amazed His disciples more than ever when they heard this. "Then who can be saved?" they asked. 26 Jesus looked at them and said, "It is impossible for people to save themselves, but everything is possible for God."

Humans are creatures of habit, following predictable patterns and each having our own, comfortable routines. We set our routines by our responsibilities, our duty to our family, and our personal desires and goals. Most people would admit that they have a closer relationship with members of their family, or close friends, than with their Savior. Many people wouldn't see anything wrong with this, perhaps because they interact with them more than they do Jesus? Some people think that because they believe in, and love Jesus, they don't need to restructure their whole lives for Him. WRONG (John 14:15, Matthew 16:24). Our priorities say a great deal about what is in our hearts, and humans are notoriously selfish and stubborn when it comes to prioritizing God.

As humans, it is important to understand that any preconceived notions about God is ignorance without knowledge of His word. Many people assume that because God is loving that He wouldn't bring anything to our lives but blessings, never-ending happiness, and success. When they feel pain, tribulation, suffering, hardship or conflict their first instinct is to feel a sense of indignation. Jesus makes it clear in the above passages that following Him isn't going to be sunshine and roses, but full of conflict. Additionally, if we are to remain **loyal** to God, He must be the priority in our lives above *everyone* else. This means that God should get more regular devotion, more praise, and more respect than we're probably giving Him, currently. For example, before we make a choice in our lives, we consult God in prayer. When we make mistakes, we repent to God, and when things go well in our lives we are to praise God (James 5:13). If our faith comes into conflict with our family or friends, who might be making less than righteous choices, Jesus calls us to choose Him over *everyone* else. What might seem impossible to us isn't supposed to deter us from being more contrite followers of Christ, but is intended to show God who is earnest about actually trying.

March 29
Trust

Isaiah 53:6, GW

6 We have all strayed like sheep. Each one of us has turned to go His own way, and the Lord has laid all our sins on him.

Jeremiah 17:5-6, ESV

5 Thus says the Lord: "**Cursed is the man who trusts in man** and makes flesh His strength, whose heart turns away from the Lord. 6 He is like a shrub in the desert, and shall not see any good come. He shall dwell in the parched places of the wilderness, in an uninhabited salt land."

Contrary to all of the self-proclaimed perfectionists out there, the bible informs us that humans were designed to be flawed, Ecclesiastes 7:20 'Surely there is not a righteous man on earth who does good and never sins.' We are designed to need our loving God and creator in our everyday lives, for His word, His grace, His guidance and direction, and His forgiveness. Complicated and full of double, and hidden meanings, the bible can be easily misunderstood (Matthew 22:29). Learning what happened before us, what God wants from us, and how we fit into the lessons of the scripture is something we must pursue in order to grasp how we all fit in to the bigger picture. Trust is the belief that we can count on someone or something's reliability, and this can be like catching the wind.

Human beings will always carry the potential to disappoint, but our Lord is the same now as He was yesterday, He will be the same tomorrow, and forever (Hebrews 13:8). Knowing we need God, and knowing He'll never change even though our environments change, why don't we place more faith in Him? When we trust in our friends, our environment, our society, our governments, we can all face disappointment and unmet expectations. When we trust in the Lord, however, we are reinforcing our faith, knowing that He won't abandon us. God calls us to repent, and to seek Him, but we can't do that when we're focused on ourselves, our problems, our unanswered prayers, or other people's lives.

Psalm 9:10, ESV

10 And those who know your name put their trust in you, for you, O Lord, have not forsaken those who seek you.

Isaiah 2:22, ERV

22 Stop trusting other people to save you. Do not think too highly of them; they are only humans who have not stopped breathing yet.

March 30
Comfort Eternal

Romans 8:20-21, 23-24a, CEV/ICB

20 Meanwhile, creation is confused, but not because it wants to be confused. God made it this way in the hope 21 **that everything God made would be set free from ruin. There was hope that everything God made would have the freedom and glory that belong to God's children.** 23 The Spirit makes us sure about what we will be in the future. But now we groan silently, while we wait for God to show that we are his children. This means that our bodies will also be set free. 24 **And this hope is what saves us.**

Suffering is all around us, and it doesn't feel fair. People we love suffer horrible diseases while corrupt people seem to flourish unscathed. Rest assured, we aren't seeing everything that goes on in another's life, or how God is working in it. What's more, nowhere is it written that life was going to be fair (Ecclesiastes 8:14). The path to righteousness is narrow, difficult, and will require some uncomfortable sacrifices. But why must everything be such a struggle? Here on Earth, the devil reigns while God's kingdom is in Heaven. We must go through hell on Earth to prove we're worthy of God's everlasting life in Heaven (2 Thessalonians 1:5). Know that God doesn't accept just anyone, either (Jeremiah 30:21).

When Jesus died for us, he died for the sins of all mankind. This gave all of us access to eternal life, instead of paying for our sinful lives with death. However, the caveat is that we must accept Jesus into our hearts. This means more than simply believing in Jesus as our Savior, we must endeavor to live a lifestyle more Holy, and renounce sinful choices (Psalm 37:27). Life will be difficult while here on Earth, but those who remain steadfast in their quest for righteousness through Christ Jesus will have eternal rest in Heaven for their souls. So if we want utopia in Heaven after we die, we must earn it in this *life* as a human surrounded by sin and temptation. How bad do *you* want eternal life, enough to endure suffering and change your life for Jesus?

John 16:33, ERV

33 "I have told you these things so that you can have peace in me. **In this world you will have troubles.** But be brave! I have defeated the world!"

Isaiah 25:7-8, ERV

7 But now there is a veil covering all nations and people. This veil is called "death." 8 But death will be destroyed forever. And the **Lord God will wipe away every tear from every face**. In the past, **all of His people were sad**, but God will take away that sadness from the earth. All of this will happen because the Lord said it would.

March 31
God is in Control

Proverbs 19:21, ESV

21 Many are the plans in the mind of a man, but it is the purpose of the Lord that will stand.

No matter what plans we may have made for our own lives, God's will is what will be done. Fighting God's will only bring on more trouble, but accepting our place in our relationship with God is difficult for many to understand. We are called to let go of our need for autonomy in our lives, and submit to God. He assures us that His way is better, and that we only need to trust Him a little deeper.

James 4:14-15, ESV

14 yet you do not know what tomorrow will bring. What is your life? For you are a mist that appears for a little time and then vanishes. 15 Instead you ought to say, "If the Lord wills, we will live and do this or that."

We're not supposed to know what's coming next, nor are we to plan ahead for any possible scenario, we are called to accept God's will and put all of our trust in Him. How we handle our helplessness, as well as our mistakes, tells God what He needs to know about what is really in our hearts.

Philippians 4:6-7, ESV

6 do not be anxious about anything, but in everything by prayer and supplication with thanksgiving let your requests be made known to God. 7 And the peace of God, which surpasses all understanding, will guard your hearts and your minds in Christ Jesus.

Whatever we need, we pray to God for. Likewise, whatever we are concerned with, or worried about, no matter how big or small, we are called to tell God in prayer. When we do this, we are letting God handle it, and placing our full trust in Him, not forming plans and solutions on our own in case God doesn't respond the way we want. Placing our worries onto Him means allowing Him to settle, solve, and supplement us as His will ordains, and not by our own.

Luke 1:37, ESV

37 For nothing will be impossible with God.

God is all powerful, Almighty, and holy. God is fair, just, and loving. God is capable of giving and taking away life. Humans are God's creation, and totally fallible. We should not only believe in God, but trust in Him. Enough said. AMEN.

April 1
Consequences

Isaiah 59:2, ICB

2 It is your evil that has separated you from your God. Your sins cause him to turn away from you. And then he does not hear you.

Titus 1:15-16, ERV

15 To people who are pure, everything is pure. But to those who are full of sin and don't believe, nothing is pure. Really, their thinking has become evil, and their consciences have been ruined. 16 They say they know God, but the evil things they do show that they don't accept him. They are disgusting. They refuse to obey God and are not capable of doing anything good.

God's rules to live righteous and holy lives can feel pretty strict for humans that sin by nature. Additionally, some people may not want to submit control of their lives, their personality, habits and lifestyle to the judgement of God. Just an FYI, for anyone who doesn't know already, God is in control of every life (Proverbs 16:33, Job 12:10 Isaiah 41:4, John 15:5). Still others assume their belief in God and Jesus alone is enough to sustain their good graces, and don't think changing themselves or their already complicated lives for words that were written three thousand years ago is necessary (Matthew 24:35). We always have a choice (Deuteronomy 30:19). If we do not change our lives for God, it is the same as living against God. Yikes!

God always gives us a choice, and hopes we'll choose redemption, and return to our faith in Him. We can go our own way, make our own choices based on our own desires and live with the consequences good or bad on our own merits and judgements, but the bible is pretty clear on the ramifications of this (Jeremiah 8:6, Zechariah 7:13, Luke 11:23). Righteousness can't exist in our lives without humility and change. Choosing a life without adhering to God's commands may seem like the easier choice to some, but without the Lord's love, and grace, is spiritual death. To those of us who find following the Lord the natural choice, will discover it couldn't be more difficult. Living a holy lifestyle means everything from the music you listen to, to the shows and programs you watch, how you attend church (if at all), how you speak to others, the people you associate with, how you raise your family, and how you shape your priorities. No easy feat, but that's why the path to Heaven is narrow, while the path to hell is wide (Matthew 7:13-14). Choose wisely, brothers and sisters.

Mark 12:24, ESV

24 Jesus said to them, "Is this not the reason you are wrong, because you know neither the Scriptures nor the power of God?"

April 2
Hell on Earth?

John 16:33, ESV

33 I have said these things to you, that in me you may have peace. In the world you will have tribulation. But take heart; I have overcome the world."

Violence, pride, greed, envy, revenge, sexual promiscuity, drunkenness, lies, are all words that could accurately describe the world we currently live in. These are also words the bible uses to describe unholy, evil traits inherent of the human race. Our world is driven by greed and selfishness, and reveres people with power and influence over kindness and service-oriented leadership. Loud opinions, wealth, power and respect drive many people in today's society, and the bible describes this as sinful wickedness. This has been the way of humanity since the dawn of man (Genesis 6:5, Romans 5:12). It should be no surprise, then, to learn that the world under the power of the devil. Some people may ask, why would God allow the devil to wreak such havoc on His human race? If we never went through difficulty, we wouldn't be able to prove that we would actually seek the Lord's guidance just by our faith in Him. (Isaiah 48:10, Jeremiah 9:7).

When transgression, immorality and temptation surround us the odds to commit sin seem to be stacked against us. We can't throw our hands up in defeat, proclaiming, "Why bother trying, I might as well get as much as I can and indulge then!" We pray through temptation, for Jesus to give us the strength and self-control to make the righteous choice. We can still save our lost souls by repenting to Christ in prayer, we can ask God to change our hardened, greedy, selfish hearts into one's that love other's more freely. Jesus doesn't want us to look upon one another with contempt and hate, but with love and generosity and forgiveness. Jesus led by example, by forgiving His enemies, by loving them, by dying for them. Honor is achieved by Heavenly requirements, in serving others out of love for one another, not by expecting to *be served* (1 Peter 4:10). Jesus taught that true wealth was achieved by giving, not by acquiring (Mark 10:45). This is difficult, especially when you sometimes feel like you are the only one trying. Jesus knew this road would be difficult, and is always a prayer away for guidance and support. We may live in a hell on Earth, but it doesn't have to live inside of us. Don't give up the good fight when there is so much at stake!

Deuteronomy 8:2, ESV

2 And you shall remember the whole way that the Lord your God has led you these forty years in the wilderness, that he might humble you, testing you to know what was in your heart, whether you would keep His commandments or not.

1 John 5:19, ESV

19 We know that we are from God, and the whole world lies in the power of the evil one.

April 3
All Are Evil

Romans 3:10, NASB

10 As it is written: "There is no righteous person, not even one;

Genesis 6:5, ESV

5 The Lord saw that the wickedness of man was great in the earth, and that every intention of the thoughts of His heart was only **evil continually**.

Those who aren't reading their bibles may not be aware that they've inherited a propensity for sin and wickedness, as a member of the human race (Romans 5:12). Some of the reasons we struggle as sinners trying to follow Christ is because God is trying to teach us something, or we are paying a penance for a poor choice through His divine justice. Another reason we struggle is that we are inherently corrupt as humans, seeking our own solutions, forming our own opinions of justice outside of the Lord, making decisions in the absence of the Lord, and giving in to selfish pleasures. The bible warns us that the 'evil one' controls the whole world (1 John 5:19), and most of us wouldn't be surprised to learn this. We encounter anger, contempt, gossip, greed and deceit on a daily basis in our lives, all the result of evil at work in our world. In a way, we are living a *certain kind* of 'hell on Earth,' right now. Our impatience stems from our arrogance, and when our personal sense of injustice has been threatened we are taking God's place as the judge (James 4:11-12). Our world doesn't owe us anything, we were meant to serve God, our creator.

Jesus encourages us, through the warning of His disciples, to resist temptation and evil, which indicates we have a choice. Our lives will always be fraught with the dark spirits' trickery and evil temptations hiding in unlikely places. The devil also blinds those who won't repent, causing them to be ignorant to the teachings of Jesus (2 Corinthians 4:3-4). As Christ-followers, we are expected to remain steadfast in our faith, resolute in learning Jesus' teachings and adapting our lives to them, and show this light to others. We are expected to fail, but to get right back up, repent, and try a little harder the next time. Through prayer we can derive strength, resolve, and wisdom from Christ and the Holy Spirit. Our world doesn't serve us, but offers us a distracting minefield of opportunities to infiltrate our journey to righteousness, we must steer clear of by remaining focused on Jesus. Stand strong, brothers and sisters!

Ecclesiastes 7:20, ESV

20 Surely there is no one on earth who always does good and never sins.

Romans 6:12, ERV

12 But don't let sin control your life here on earth. You must not be ruled by the things your sinful self makes you want to do.

April 4
Choosing Our Friends?

1 Corinthians 15:33, ESV

33 Do not be deceived: "Bad company ruins good morals."

1 Corinthians 5:11, ESV

11 But now I am writing to you not to associate with anyone who bears the name of brother if he is guilty of sexual immorality or greed, or is an idolater, reviler, drunkard, or swindler—not even to eat with such a one.

We encounter many kinds of people in our daily lives, and we tend to make friends with those whose morals and lifestyle clique with our own. Other people we meet are a distraction, at best, and still others we could do without all together. Some people make jokes at the expense of another, but think it's alright because the subject of their ridicule isn't present. This is still wrong. The crude guy making jokes on our lunch hour is clearly sinful, but is also funny, so what's the harm in partaking in His company for the moment and not taking His example to heart? Plenty, according to the bible. The bible warns us about associating with people who readily choose wickedness, (Proverbs 20:19, 22:24, 23:20, 24:21), because we tend to take on the habits, attitudes, behaviors, and even the beliefs of those we closely associate with.

Some people manipulate others to get what they want, and the Lord makes it clear that this is frowned upon (Matthew 7:15, 24:4). We may not think our behavior as harming to anyone, but morally corrupt behavior is not of Christ, even in jest or levity, and it's something we need to hold ourselves more accountable for. It's not enough to simply avoid these attitudes and behaviors, but God expects us to completely eliminate them from our thoughts (1 Peter 2:1). Completely purging ourselves of all sin in our hearts isn't an easy task for a bunch of sinful rebels. It can be a struggle to maintain our budding young holiness in a world made up of sinners, some of whom don't have a clue, and others who will never care enough about the Lord to change. Our goal should be Jesus; to be more like Him, to submit to new attitudes and behaviors that please Him, and to eventually join Him in Heaven one day. Some people can help us *grow* in our faith, others offer an example of what *not* to do, and others can be stumbling blocks if we *allow* them, but all people have a purpose. Humans naturally assimilate to their surroundings, we must closely guard who we're allowing our spirits to integrate with.

Proverbs 12:26, ERV

26 Good people are careful about choosing their friends, but evil people always choose the wrong ones.

Psalm 1:1, GW

1 Blessed is the person who does not follow the advice of wicked people, take the path of sinners, or join the company of mockers.

April 5
Let Jesus Change You

Ephesians 4:22-24, ERV

22 You were taught to leave your old self. This means that you must stop living the evil way you lived before. That old self gets worse and worse, because people are fooled by the evil they want to do. 23 You must be made new in your hearts and in your thinking. 24 **Be that new person** who was made to be like God, truly good and pleasing to him.

Fellow followers of Christ, imagine if you will, this scenario: Two people are waiting in a long line. One is muttering cuss words under their breath and shifting their weight back and forth while looking impatiently at their watch, while the other is calmly smiling and talking to the people in line behind them pleasantly. Just the description of these two people highlight the differences in their grace, not to mention their attitudes, and subsequent behaviors. Impatient people are irritated when their pace is slowed by another, as if to *expect* a clear path whenever they think they deserve it. Impatience is an example of arrogance, like cynicism and sarcasm, which stem from preconceived expectations formed by an abundance of sinful pride (Psalm 37:7). When we walk in the light of Jesus, our actions, words, attitudes and behaviors will be different than that of our old selves, and they *should* be! We should *want* to follow Jesus to show our love for Him, for God, and to demonstrate our growing faith, and the results will have tangible results in our everyday lives (Psalm 51:10). How would Jesus view us based on our actions today?

Walking in righteousness looks and sounds different than the behavior of the average human who is often in a hurry, or frustrated, or oblivious to the plight of their neighbor. While some people are focused on what is pleasing to themselves and others around them, Christ-followers are *only* focused on what is pleasing to God, and that looks different on people. A Christ-follower tries to carry a calm, quiet demeanor, speaking only when necessary and keeping in kindness always, as opposed to the frantic, rushed, opinionated rants of a judgmental, corrupt, sinner who creates hate and division. A forgiving, humble, gentle, and service-oriented nature looks and sounds very different than the spiteful, prideful, aggressive, and greedy (1 Peter 3:3-4, 1 John 2:16). Impatience, cynicism, sarcasm, pride and arrogance will slowly be replaced by patience, faith, grace, humility, forgiveness, and love. This is what righteousness looks like. Praise Jesus! AMEN.

Ezekiel 36:26, ESV

26 "And I will give you a new heart, and a new spirit I will put within you. And I will remove the heart of stone from your flesh and give you a heart of flesh."

April 6
Where Unrighteousness Hides

Ephesians 4:31-32, CEB

31 Put aside all bitterness, losing your temper, anger, shouting, and slander, along with every other evil. 32 Be kind, compassionate, and forgiving to each other, in the same way God forgave you in Christ.

Being compassionate and forgiving to the person who cut us off on the way to work, stole our promotion, spread a rumor about us at work instead holding a grudge, or submitting to revenge are examples righteousness. Our example is Christ Jesus, difficult for all of us, but not impossible.

Jeremiah 8:4-6, CEB

4 Say to them, The Lord proclaims: When people fall down, don't they get up? When they turn aside, don't they turn back? 5 Why then does this people, rebellious Jerusalem, persistently turn away from me? They cling to deceit and refuse to return. 6 I have listened carefully but haven't heard a word of truth from them. No one regrets their wrongdoing; no one says, "What have I done?" **Everyone turns to their own course**, like a stallion dashing into the thick of battle."

We're all going to sin, this shouldn't really be a 'news flash.' When we sin, we need to humble ourselves, and actually allow ourselves to feel bad about sinning against God. It's from this remorse that we pray for repentance, when we *genuinely* want to do better by Him. No matter what we've done, God just wants us to come back to Him.

Psalm 50:16-20, ERV

16 But God says to the wicked, "Stop quoting my laws! Stop talking about my agreement! 17 You hate for me to tell you what to do. You ignore what I say. 18 You see a thief and run to join him. You jump into bed with those who commit adultery. 19 You say evil things and tell lies. 20 You sit around talking about people, finding fault with your own brothers."

As tempting, and as natural as it may feel, forming judgements and opinions about one another is wrong. Leading only to gossip, envy, deceit, hatred, and dissention, finding fault with one another is sin. Replace that pride and arrogance with love, humility, and forgiveness in Christ's name. AMEN!

April 7
We Need Armor?

Ephesians 6:11-12, ERV

11 Wear the full armor of God. Wear God's armor so that you can fight against the devil's clever tricks. 12 Our fight is not against people on earth. We are fighting against the rulers and authorities and the powers of this world's darkness. We are fighting against the spiritual powers of evil in the heavenly places.

Silent forces of good and evil afoot among us almost sounds like the theme of a scary movie more than the current state of humanity. The devil, or Satan, was an angel in Heaven before he was kicked out for exalting himself above God in His heart (Isaiah 14:12-15), and has power here on earth (Job 1:7, Matthew 4:8-9). The spirits of those who have passed away, are sleeping, according to the bible (Daniel 12:2, John 11:11-14). Ghosts, apparitions, and unembodied spirits aren't from those who have passed, then, they are far more sinister. The devil employs the use of demon spirits to aid him, and the bible warns of these dark and evil spirits on Earth, trying to separate man from His true relationship with God (Mark 16:9, Luke 8:30, Luke 7:21). Masquerading as an angel of light, Satan deceives us into thinking unholy thoughts, wanting sinful things, and spreading hate and suspicion among us (2 Corinthians 11:14). Playing on our insecurities and vulnerabilities, evil preys on our desire to be exalted by making us desire to be more, and have more than our neighbors.

Spiritual powers of darkness have corrupted many people on Earth through war, murder, violence, hatred, prejudice, fear, contempt, conceit and lust. Any of these can be found in the music people listen to, the movies and shows people watch, the language they use toward one another, and on the lips of the leaders of Nations. Some people who actually believe in God are under the power of dark spirits and may not even know about it. Search your heart, do you still have suspicions and fears? If we fully trust in the Lord our God, we don't fear anything but Him, and our salvation in Him, and we rest in that faith instead of worldly anxieties. Praying to Jesus in prayer is a much better solution than anything sinful or corrupt we could come up with on our own (Jeremiah 17:5). Following Jesus more closely, studying the bible more thoroughly in the true context the stories were written, and praying devoutly, and regularly, is always going to be the best 'armor' to guard against being corrupted by the devil's temptations, and our propensity to sin.

1 John 4:2-4, ESV

2 By this you know the Spirit of God: every spirit that confesses that Jesus Christ has come in the flesh is from God, 3 and every spirit that does not confess Jesus is not from God. This is the spirit of the antichrist, which you heard was coming and now is in the world already. 4 Little children, you are from God and have overcome them, for he who is in you is greater than he who is in the world.

April 8
Unanswered Prayers?

Proverbs 28:9, ERV

9 When people do not listen to God's teachings, he does not listen to their prayers.

It can be frustrating when you pray and pray, and still feel like your prayers aren't being answered. As humans, we cannot fully grasp God's omniscient power and knowledge for mankind, and not understanding can *really* test our faith (Isaiah 55:8-9). The bible directs us once again here, and gives us reasons why, because it *is* true that some prayers *aren't* answered. Either you're not listening, or what you're asking for isn't in your best interest, or you aren't holy enough right now to hear and receive the Holy Spirit (James 4:3, *below*, Isaiah 59:2, Proverbs 28:9). Still another reason could be that you're not praying *correctly* (Matthew 6:7-15). Remember we call Jesus 'Lord' for a reason, and should put humility into practice when we pray.

We're an impatient species, we want everything without waiting for any amount of time. In our thirst for more, to be better, faster, and more efficient at multi-task-ing we lose sight of the Holy Spirit who directs *and advocates* for us. We must be calm, *patient* and humble to receive the Holy Spirit, and not just for a few minutes when it's convenient for us and simply to communicate our needs, but *steadfastly* in our everyday lives. We shouldn't be praying like we're ordering a sandwich from the local deli; "Yeah, gimme some help with a rent payment, with a side of car payment, and a grocery supply for the next three months." Not appropriate. Bottom line here is, no answer to a prayer is still an answer; 'Father knows best.'

We must *want to be* a calmer, more patient, humble person, and should seek the Holy Spirit's guidance through prayer if we're struggling with this (Psalm 51:10). The Holy Spirit will show us our faults so we can *repent them in prayer to Jesus*, not so we can feel like we're being constantly punished by God, or to compare them to the sins of other humans. This knowledge about our sins is really a gift, because when we *know* what we've done wrong we can pray it away, forever. It's also through learning what sins we commit that the Lord shows us the areas in which we need improving. When we're in this position of *righteousness*, the Lord's direction will be made clear to us by the Holy Spirit (Ezekiel 36:26-27). When we *do* receive the knowledge of the Holy Spirit, guiding our path and answering our requests, know that it may not be what we asked for (Proverbs 16:9). How deep is *your* faith?

James 4:3, ERV

3 Or when you ask, you don't receive anything, because the reason you ask is wrong. You only want to use it for your own pleasure.

Romans 8:25, NIV

25 But if we hope for what we do not yet have, we wait for it patiently

April 9
Right and Wrong, Seen and Unseen

Proverbs 16:4, ESV

4 The Lord has made everything for its purpose, even the wicked for the day of trouble.

Choosing righteousness over unrighteousness isn't like choosing between whether to have chicken or fish for dinner. Righteousness comes from a lifetime of discipline, of a willingness to change every aspect of our lives, from a longing within the heart to be more like Christ, and the desire to show God our love and devotion to Him. Our heart decides what it wants, and our minds find a way to obtain it, that's just human nature. Many of us might be under the false impression that humans cannot have a change of heart, that we are the way we are. The bible is full of God pleading to humanity to repent and come back to Him in faith, asking us to have a change of heart (Jeremiah 24:7, Ezekiel 11:19, 18:31-32, Malachi 3:7, Joel 2:12). God wants us to have hearts that are devoted to Him, and His word, not one that seeks independence, and spiritual autonomy from the Lord's rules. Some people commit sins they think are less severe that other people, and stumble through their lives by their own consequence never attaching blame to any of their decisions, actions, behaviors or words. All sin is wicked (1 John 5:17). All humans sin (Romans 3:23). We should all be more thankful that Jesus gave us an opportunity at redemption.

Wicked people in the bible are described as people whose heart's desires are of things only the world can give them, money and wealth, fame and respect, possessions and positions of power. None of these will lead to salvation. As a matter of fact, these are sinful goals that reflect a wicked heart in love with the devil's world here on Earth. (1 John 2:15, James 4:4) The bible covers this at length, and teaches 'moral' stories that many people don't read, or ever truly understand, that are designed to get people thinking about the direction of their *own* moral compass (Seed Parable Matthew 13: 1-23, The 10 Bridesmaid's Matthew 25: 1-13, The Prodigal Son Luke 15:11-32, and The Good Samaritan Luke 10:25-37). When we ask for things for the wrong *reasons*, or we ask for the wrong *things*, our prayers may seem unanswered. We need to seek God through Jesus, and only through a more righteous soul will we be able to follow Jesus. Only reading and understanding the bible **first hand** can an individual grasp the true meaning behind the spiritual quest Jesus calls us to. While we're here on a tangible, wicked Earth our mission is to avoid all the distractions and temptations it offers, in order to get closer to an invisible, far more powerful, spiritual God. Are you going to be one of the wicked who challenge the struggling righteous, or are you going to be a righteous survivor of a once wicked human in Christ?

James 4:1-22, ESV

1 What causes quarrels and what causes fights among you? Is it not this, that your passions are at war within you? 2 You desire and do not have, so you murder. You covet and cannot obtain, so you fight and quarrel. You do not have, because you do not ask.

April 10
Keep Trying

Exodus 20:6, ERV

6 The Lord said, "But I will be very kind to people who love me and obey my commands. I will be kind to their families for thousands of generations."

2 Timothy 4:7, KJ21

7 I have fought a good fight; I have finished my course; I have kept the faith.

If all of humanity is eternally rotten and sinful, why bother trying *to change,* if we're just going to be forgiven anyway? Just because we're always going to be *prone* to sin doesn't mean we should rationally *cozy up to* sin, or *inauthentically* ask for forgiveness when we've sinned. God see's our hearts, and knows if they're **genuinely earnest and humble** toward Him, or if we harbor contempt with the desire to seize autonomy for ourselves (Jeremiah 17:10). When we submit ourselves before Christ with humility we are choosing righteous behavior. When we turn the other cheek in an argument instead of yelling back or becoming angry, or when we walk away from gossip we are choosing to be Holy. We learn this through our relationship with Christ, by learning from our past mistakes, and by studying the bible and Christ's ministry. To know someone is to love them, and to know Christ and what He desires from us is how we show Him we love Him. We cannot do this by just simply believing (John 14:15).

The bible teaches us that faith without actually doing good works or changing our sinful behavior isn't being a good steward of our faith (James 2:26). Even though we can never attain righteousness the way Jesus was able to doesn't mean He isn't expecting us to try. Just like we cannot derive the knowledge of the bible simply by putting our hand on the cover, we cannot expect to become better versions of our true selves without change, repentance, prayer and tribulations. After all, if we're going to consent to a righteous quest through Christ our Lord, we have to expect things about ourselves to change as we begin to make different choices. Jesus set the example for the righteousness and Holiness that we need to emulate to earn our seat at the Heavenly table. God knows our hearts, and it's in our dogged pursuit that proves our convictions.

2 Corinthians 4:16-18, ERV

16 That is why we never give up. Our physical body is becoming older and weaker, but our spirit inside us is made new every day. 17 We have small troubles for a while now, but these troubles are helping us gain an eternal glory. That eternal glory is much greater than our troubles. 18 So we think about what we cannot see, not what we see. What we see lasts only a short time, and what we cannot see will last forever.

April 11
Break the Cycle

Matthew 12:35, ERV

35 Those who are good have good things saved in their hearts. That's why they say good things. But those who are evil have hearts full of evil, and that's why they say things that are evil.

1 Peter 3:9, ESV

9 Do not repay evil for evil or reviling for reviling, but on the contrary, bless, for to this you were called, that you may obtain a blessing.

On the way to work someone pulls out in front of us, at the newsstand someone in front of us takes the last copy of the paper we looked forward to reading, and someone else took the last good parking space in the lot. Our days can provide plenty of stress, frustration, and aggravation to produce ready potential for losing our composure. It can be easy to pass this aggravation, stress, and frustration onto someone else when we're feeling raw and vulnerable. Instead of snapping at our colleagues, or being short because we're having a bad day, put on the face of kindness and humility instead. We can feel outraged when we're treated poorer than *we* would treat people, but we have an opportunity to break the cycle of wickedness many people don't realize (Luke 6:27-37, James 4:7).

Bad attitudes and behavior only begets more bad attitudes, for two wrongs never make a right, ethically. Many people are misled by what courage and strength looks like, impressed by foul-mouthed, violent, or confrontational people with large egos and even larger mouths. Powerful people like to flaunt their clout, the strong like to prove it by oppressing the weak, and the wealthy like to flaunt their cars, clothes and jewels. These are all examples of the hearts of the wicked, capturing the attention and adoration of those that court wickedness and sin. *True* power is the ability to remain graceful when provoked, to show restraint when wronged, to turn the other cheek when everything inside wants to avenge (Matthew 5:38-39). What's more, it takes a righteous amount of grace to serve others instead of being served *by* others. It takes an incredible amount of self-control to offer kindness in the face of anger, outrage, disappointment, or fear. Break the cycle of sin and wickedness in your own lives, brothers and sisters, and derive strength from Christ Jesus.

Romans 12:21, ESV

21 Do not be overcome by evil, but overcome evil with good.

Psalm 37:23-24, ESV

23 The steps of a man are established by the Lord, when he delights in His way; 24 though he fall, he shall not be cast headlong, for the Lord upholds His hand.

April 12
Don't Chastise Yourself, That's the Lord's Job

1 Corinthians 11:32, ERV

32 But when the Lord judges us, he punishes us to show us the right way. He does this so that we will not be condemned with the world.

Proverbs 2:6, ESV

6 For the Lord gives wisdom; from His mouth come knowledge and understanding.

Life brings joy, pain, suffering, triumph and uncertainty to each of us. No matter how deep our faith in God, we will *all* still experience tribulations in our lives. Some of us go through painful experiences, either large or small, and wonder what God's role is in it all. Why *do* we suffer? Sometimes, we make a choice, say the words, even though we know in our hearts it isn't very holy or righteous. After all, not everyone is thinking before they speak or act. Through the same conduit of prayer that repentance allows, we can practice listening more closely to that little 'voice' in our heads trying to steer us toward what's right. Sometimes warning us of a pending bad decision, or a type of vibe that tells us to be wary of someone or something, or something that points us in a specific direction when we're making a decision, we all have something deeper within that is trying to guide us. When we make a poor choice, think or say something curt or condemning about another, we will be corrected by our Father in Heaven. Omnipresent and ruler of the universe, God's will is to be done on Earth as it is in Heaven, as the bible explains (Isaiah 46:10). So, God has the final say in what ultimately happens to us, and when we stray from this we require redirection.

As much as we'd all like to congratulate ourselves on being the masters of our own intelligence and wisdom, the bible explains that *all* knowledge is granted by God. Put simply, we may have to do the work, but God allows us to know only what He thinks we need by His opportunities granted to us. We shouldn't feel badly about making mistakes, God created us to need Him, so we're going to make them. It's only when we begin to think we can do things on our mortal own that His correction seems like suffering, tribulation, pain, or perpetual bad luck. We suffer so that we are forced to look deeper inside ourselves, to understand the discord occurring within us, and this is to learn what our role was in the mistake we made. We are meant to learn what our mistakes are so we can *repent* for them, and know what behavior the Lord does *not* wish us to repeat. We also suffer so that God can be assured that *He* is the primary source of comfort and direction we seek (Jeremiah 29:13, Psalm 14:2). Before we speak, before we choose, we should remind ourselves that we're Christ-followers, children of the Almighty God, walking in the footsteps of Jesus; We should behave accordingly.

Hebrews 12:11, ERV

11 We don't enjoy discipline when we get it. It is painful. But later, after we have learned our lesson from it, we will enjoy the peace that comes from doing what is right.

April 13
Listen to Your Father

John 14:15, ESV

15 "If you love me, you will keep my commandments."

James 2:14-17, ERV

14 My brothers and sisters, if a person claims to have faith but does nothing, that faith is worth nothing. Faith like that cannot save anyone. 15 Suppose a brother or sister in Christ comes to you in need of clothes or something to eat. 16 And you say to them, "God be with you! I hope you stay warm and get plenty to eat," but you don't give them the things they need. If you don't help them, your words are worthless. 17 It is the same with faith. If it is just faith and nothing more—if it doesn't do anything—it is dead.

Many people can admit they believe in God, and that's great! However, simply believing isn't really enough. God wants us to *live* the right way, by Jesus' example. Going to church, praying occasionally and perhaps before a meal, a crucifix hanging on the wall in your home are all wonderful ways of loving God, but are all really just platitudes. Trying to live a better life, being a better person, one action at a time is what God desires from us. Our heavenly Father knows we are sinners, and need all the help we can get so we have the bible as a guide, and the Holy Spirit to help us communicate with Jesus throughout our journey. All of that help, and yet we still fall short of our true potential in our relationship with Christ Jesus.

Not everyone who believes in God will be willing to follow Him. Repentance means we're truly wanting to learn from our mistakes, and improve ourselves through Christ's mercy and grace. If we say we love God, but do nothing to try and improve ourselves, we aren't truly repentant. Maybe we can take this in baby steps, one sin at a time, but the important thing is to *take* a step in the right direction. Today. Now. Think for a moment about the day, and all of the interactions we take part in; our words, expressions, tone of voice and behaviors, are they relevant, forgiving, and kind? We must decide for ourselves, if we're going to listen to the commands of our Heavenly Father, and 'clean up' our attitudes toward ourselves, God, and other people. Taking our example from Jesus, we should be treating people better than ourselves (Matthew 7:12, Philippians 2:3). We must ask ourselves, 'Do we try to live as close to Jesus' example as possible? Think about that for a moment, because not all believers are followers. How true is *your* obedience to God?

Matthew 7:21, ESV

21 "Not everyone who says, 'You are my Lord' will enter the kingdom of heaven, **but he who does the will of My Father** who is in heaven will enter."

April 14
Passover

Exodus 12:7, 11b-14, ESV

7 God said to Moses, "Then they shall take some of the blood and put it on the two doorposts and the lintel of the houses in which they eat it." 11b God said to Moses, "For, it is the Lord's Passover. 12 I will pass through the land that night, and I will strike all the firstborn in the land, both man and beast; and on all the gods I will execute judgments: **I am** the Lord. 13 The blood shall be a sign for you, on the houses where you are. And when I see the blood, I will **pass over** you, and no plague will befall you to destroy you, when I strike the land. 14 This day shall be for you a memorial day, and you shall keep it as a feast to the Lord; throughout your generations, as a statute forever, you shall keep it as a feast."

God's love for us is illustrated through His many relationships with the characters in the bible using many colorful stories, poems, and prayers. Over and over, God allows His people to come back to Him, often with specific instructions on just how to do that. We are called to repent, to *come back* to God after sinning, and promise Him we'll follow more closely (Isaiah 44:22, Ezekiel 18:32). This is a love affair between God and His humanity, us, and we're called to be faithful to Him. Passover is a time of celebration, of God's deliverance of His people from slavery and oppression, a promise He made in Genesis (Genesis 12:1-4). People may celebrate this joyous commemoration in slightly different ways, but the bottom line is that **God keeps His promises.**

On the last night of His time on earth, the 'last supper,' Jesus assembled His disciples to celebrate Passover. It was on this occasion that Jesus initiated communion by breaking bread and telling His disciples to 'eat' of His 'body,' in remembrance of Him (Matthew 26:26-28). By partaking in communion, we're essentially putting Christ 'in' us, taking His Holy Spirit into our souls. We are symbolically re-affirming our faith in Jesus, and honoring His sacrifice for us by putting Him first, and vowing to be more *like* Him in our own lives. It is through this re-affirmation of our faith that we show our devotion to God, and the love story continues. Brothers and sisters, praise God through Christ our Lord, King of the Universe, now and forever! AMEN.

Exodus 12:8, ESV

8 They shall eat the flesh that night, roasted on the fire; with unleavened bread and bitter herbs they shall eat it.

1 Corinthians 5:8, ESV

8 Let us therefore celebrate the festival, not with the old leaven, the leaven of malice and evil, but with **the unleavened bread of sincerity and truth.**

April 15
Keeping Up with the Jones'

1 Samuel 2:3, ESV

3 Talk no more so very proudly, let not arrogance come from your mouth; for the Lord is a God of knowledge, and by him actions are weighed.

Sporting events, political rivalries, and social conflicts all involve competitiveness, and our world is full of many different kinds of competitions. Cooking competitions, beauty pageants, sporting events, all pit one person or persons against others in order to see who is more skilled, talented, or gifted. Many people would say that a competitive nature means someone is determined or tenacious, and consider this a positive quality in a person. What is considered positive in *our* world isn't necessarily considered positive by God's standards, however. This might be unpleasant for all of those stubbornly arrogant people who are quietly proud of their stubbornness. When we compare our successes by the successes of other people, we are focused on the wrong things, the bible tells us (John 8:54, James 3:16). The bible explains that we are *all* imperfect, *sinners* (Romans 3:23), and are judged individually at the end of our life, by Christ (John 5:22). Consequently, our superficial contests are just that, and will only ever prove that we all have *different* skills, gifts, and talents.

The purpose of our individual talents are to use them to help one another, serving God, all parts of a bigger whole in Jesus. We can only strive to be better versions of our *own selves* and not someone else, as we will never be anyone else. Jesus Christ is the model to live our lives by, not our neighbors, friends, colleagues, our religious or political leaders, or professional entertainers. The need to prove one is better, stronger, faster, smarter, prettier, or more successful are just some of the ways people get distracted, turning away from the teachings of Christ. What's more, judging one another on our differences or sins distracts, divides, and spreads unrighteousness through arrogance, pride, greed, envy and jealousy. When we focus on our *differences*, or *compete* with one another, we are turning away from Jesus, who tells us to love one another as ourselves and put others above ourselves in service. Hey, there is no perfect life, we are all just a bunch of sinners in a perpetual state of potential. We wouldn't want someone else to interfere, or hinder, our own progress, so we shouldn't create barriers to another's success either. Building one another up through prayer, encouragement, generosity and fellowship instead of competition, judgement, envy and individualism is the way to salvation through Christ. Stay strong brothers and sisters, don't lose focus! AMEN.

Galatians 5:26, ESV

26 Let us not become conceited, provoking one another, envying one another.

Proverbs 13:10, ERV/ESV

10 Pride causes arguments, but with those who take advice is wisdom.

April 16
All Are Welcome

Acts 10:34, ERV

34 Peter began to speak: "I really understand now that God does not consider some people to be better than others. 35 **He accepts anyone who worships him and does what is right. It is not important what nation they come from.** 36 God has spoken to the people of Israel. He sent them the Good News that peace has come through Jesus Christ, the Lord of **all** people."

Sometimes the differences we see in people cause us to speculate unfairly, applying stereotypes and sowing the seeds of prejudice. Just because someone is a different race, sex, or comes from a different culture or religion doesn't warrant negative preconceptions of a person, or group of people. Jesus taught us to treat one another the way we would want to be treated, and love others as ourselves (Mark 12:29-31). Developing negative preconceptions of people isn't loving one another, or treating people the way our Lord and Savior taught us. Besides, we shouldn't *assume* we know and understand someone else's spiritual journey, or sins (James 2:8-12). The problem with this pattern of thinking is that we shouldn't be interpreting, judging, categorizing, or assuming *anything*, but obeying. God's law is sound, just, compassionate and fair. When we leave the decisions and judgements to God, we acknowledge that **He** is in control. However, when we make decisions and judgements on our own, we take the judges seat and power away from God, and take it onto ourselves. God's law is difficult, and not everyone will follow him (Luke 14:25-27, John 6:64). Those that do follow, exhibit the love of God and commitment to faith that He's looking for, no matter the nation they come from, no matter their lineage, no matter what they've done, and that's the whole point.

God can protect us from the evil that threatens to corrupt us, but we need to continuously seek Him. Praying for guidance, praying for strength in our faith, and praying for self-control will help us fight off the temptations that can hijack our hard-earned righteousness. We need to meet God half way though, and make a significant effort to make better choices, and to stop ourselves before we give in to temptation. Life is brutal and unforgiving, evil looks to undo us because we belong to God (Matthew 10:22). If we are naïve enough to disbelieve this, when its written in the bible, than the devil has already corrupted our faith. Repentance is our only salvation from the spiritual death the sins bring upon us. Salvation and forgiveness is a gift, not anything we could ever have earned, and it is from God. Stay strong in your faith, brothers and sisters. Praise God! AMEN.

Isaiah 55:7, NASB

7 Let the wicked abandon his way, and the unrighteous person his thoughts; and let him return to the Lord, and he will have compassion on him, and to our God, For he will abundantly pardon.

April 17
A Deeper Faith

Hebrews 11:6, ESV

6 And without faith it is impossible to please him, for whoever would draw near to God must believe that he exists and that he rewards those who seek him.

Romans 10:17, ESV

17 So faith comes from hearing, and hearing through the word of Christ.

Faith is about trust, relying on an invisible God we cannot hear to guide us and provide all we need. Many of us don't stop to think about what's guiding the direction we are going, we just know we need more money, more time, and better world conditions. Some of us never come to understand that God's will is what is going to happen, to you, to me, to all of humanity (Lamentations 3:37-38). We don't get what we want just because we pray for it, some things we pray for aren't in our best interests, and only God knows what we truly need. If we need strength to get through a temptation, or wisdom to understand a lesson He's trying to teach us, or comfort during a time of pain, or help learning how to be more humble or forgiving, we're more likely to have these types of prayers answered.

After you pray, if we're thinking to ourselves 'well, we'll see,' or, 'we'll hope for the best,' our faith isn't strong enough. When we pray for strength, or patience, or humility, or understanding, or compassion, or for more love for our fellow man we believe we will get it. As stewards of our faith in God, we pray to Jesus to help us understand how to reset our sinful, wicked human hearts on a course of righteousness through Him. Our faith tells us we will get what we asked for, but in God's way and in God's timeframe and not our own (Ecclesiastes 3:1,11). This is where many people misunderstand, God's will is still God's will even if we think we make our own choices. Creating certain opportunities while eliminating others, applying tribulation, blessing us with good fortune, or plaguing us with strife, the hidden template that shapes our lives is fashioned by God. Like righteousness, faith itself is something we should always be pruning, cultivating and nourishing, all throughout our lives. As we learn more, we are enlightened more by our deepening faith and understanding of our Lord. All the while, our hearts become more obedient toward Him, softening, as we grow in Christ Jesus.

Matthew 21:21-22, ESV

21 And Jesus answered them, "Truly, I say to you, if you have faith and do not doubt, you will not only do what has been done to the fig tree, but even if you say to this mountain, 'Be taken up and thrown into the sea,' it will happen. 22 And whatever you ask in prayer, you will receive, if you have faith."

April 18

Doers of the Word

James 1:21-22, NIV

21 Therefore, get rid of all moral filth and the evil that is so prevalent and humbly accept the word planted in you, which can save you.22 **Do not merely listen to the word, and so deceive yourselves. Do what it says.**

Luke 11:28, ERV

28 But Jesus said, "The people who hear the teaching of God **and obey it** — they are the ones who have God's blessing."

Romans 2:13, ESV

13 For it is not the hearers of the law who are righteous before God, but the **doers** of the law **who will be justified**.

In the bible, good works are usually ways of helping the needy, by way of food, or clothing, or shelter, aid of some kind. Aside from a measly offering at church, or a large tip at a restaurant, most of us leave taking care of the less fortunate to bigger organizations like the Red Cross, government programs and homeless shelters. Some of us pretend we don't see the man begging on the street corner hoping for an ounce of kindness, or the small group of ragged people shivering, huddling around the burning trash barrel trying to ward off the cold. **Is it because we think others will do more, or maybe we just don't care, that we ignore the plight of our fellow man?** Perhaps we just don't think someone else's needs or plight is our responsibility, and we tell ourselves we don't *have* to care. Jesus calls us to help those in need, to love our neighbors, and in saying this placed the responsibility onto us (Deuteronomy 15:7, Proverbs 19:17, Matthew 5:42).

We could all be doing more to help those in need, but also, we are *asked* to by our Lord and Savior (Luke 14:13-14). We don't all have extra money in our bank accounts to help those larger agencies helping those less fortunate, but we all have local churches and food banks that need support. Why not donate unused clothing to your local church, or donate those extra items cluttering your pantry to a local food bank? Why not volunteer your time? Take a small bag of fruit or bottled water with you the next time you are running errands, and give it to someone begging on the side of the road, as there are plenty of them out there! Buy an extra meal when your ordering at a drive-thru for the homeless man on the corner who is always holding up a sign in need of help. If we each did just *one* of these things, imagine the **force of change** we could generate?

Matthew 25:40, CSB

40 "And the King will answer them, 'Truly I tell you, whatever you did for one of the least of these brothers and sisters of mine, you did for me.'

April 19
Watch Your Mouth!

Colossians 3:8, ICB

8 But now put these things out of your life: anger, bad temper, doing or saying things to hurt others, and using evil words when you talk.

Proverbs 17:27, ICB

27 The person who has knowledge **says** very little. And a person with understanding stays calm.

Words are powerful. How we use them is another reflection of our righteousness, or unrighteousness, as the case may be. We have all said things we don't mean on occasion, and we all have our emotional limits. When acting out of strong emotions like anger, hurt, confusion or pride, we can be careless with our words. We should be thinking about our words before we speak them, and we should always exhibit self-control when we use them. Hey, there is a reason why we have two ears and one mouth! The Lord calls us to mind our words, pray and run all of our decisions by the Holy Spirit and wait patiently for His response (Romans 8:14, Psalm 27:14). That process takes time, and we should be silent in the waiting. Here though, we're not just watching *what* we say, but how *much* we say, and *how* we say it.

Our words have the capacity to inspire, heal, rebuild, educate, minister and comfort one another. The right words at just the right time can prevent someone from taking their life, or cause them to want to. Think about how many times you speak to other people in your day, probably too many occasions to count! In all we do *and* say we represent the Lord, and he doesn't want uncouth, unholy reprobates swearing, lying, boasting and criticizing each other (Matthew 12:37). We all have the capacity to think ugly, unkind thoughts, we should keep them silent while we pray for the Lord to replace them with more righteous ones. We should offer a compliment to someone we don't usually talk to, smile at a stranger, and genuinely want to help rebuild the lost. This is how we become more righteous in Christ. Speak less, and with careful intention. Practice the pause before speaking, is it relevant, is it kind, is it necessary?

Ephesians 4:29, ESV

29 **Let no corrupting talk come out of your mouths**, but only such as is good for building up, as fits the occasion, that it may give grace to those who hear.

Proverbs 18:21, ERV

21 The tongue can speak words that bring life or death. Those who love to talk must be ready to accept what it brings.

April 20
Less Is More

Matthew 5:5-8, ESV

5 Jesus said, "Blessed are the **meek**, for they shall inherit the earth. 6 Blessed are those who hunger and thirst for righteousness, for they shall be satisfied. 7 Blessed are the **merciful**, for they shall receive mercy. 8 Blessed are the **pure in heart**, for they shall see God."

Proverbs 29:11, ESV

11 A fool gives full vent to His spirit, but a wise man **quietly holds it back**.

From our speech, attitude and the way we present or carry ourselves, to the way we dress, to the way we live: Less is more. The more we learn from the bible, the more we begin to develop a picture of the righteous person. Slow to anger, meek and humble, loving their neighbor, not arguing and being courteous to all are examples the bible gives as true righteous character (James 1:19, 1 Peter 3:8-9). Most of us don't live up to all of those characteristics, unfortunately. We must ask ourselves, why? Jesus tells us we all get what we deserve in the end, as He is the final judge. We must ask ourselves just how staunchly did we try to improve our lives, how closely did we follow the Holy Spirit, and just how deeply did we pursue Christ on our life journey?

What our hearts and minds desire usually gets in our way of a more righteous lifestyle, most of us have difficulty either resisting temptations or recognizing them for what they really are. We are never without Christ, as He lives within us through the Holy Spirit when we renew our spirits through Him (Titus 3:5). Alone, naked and in the dark Christ still remains with us. Our faith is like our 'wi-fi' connection to Christ, prayer and the Holy Spirit keeps the connection strong. It's in our strong connection to Christ that we derive strength to recognize and fight off temptation, gain guidance and knowledge, and forgiveness for our sins. Many people wouldn't relish describing themselves as meek, or humble, and that's just the problem. Society doesn't respect the meek, but heralds the proud and assertive. If the bible's description of righteousness looks far and away different from the person we've become, we must believe the good news and repent to Christ Jesus. Begin today to turn your sinful heart around, Jesus accepts everyone who truly wants forgiveness and change (1 John 2:2). *More* prayer and repentance brings *less* sin and wickedness, brothers and sisters!

Titus 3:2, ESV

2 to speak evil of no one, to avoid quarreling, to be gentle, and to show perfect courtesy toward all people.

John 3:30, KJV

30 He must increase, but I must decrease.

April 21
Don't Be Crude

Ephesians 5: 4, ESV

4 Let there be no filthiness nor foolish talk nor crude joking, which are out of place, but instead let there be thanksgiving.

James 3:10-11, ESV

10 From the same mouth come blessing and cursing. My brothers and sisters, these things ought not to be so. 11 Does a spring pour forth from the same opening both fresh and salt water?

Many people describe themselves as having a 'crude' sense of humor, or being boldly opinionated, and they can be distracting at times, but not always in a good way. Humans will always find something to disagree on, and some people aren't afraid to offend people who have different convictions. Poking fun at our differences can be a harmless distraction from life's daily struggles and pressures. We may think there is nothing wrong with a crude sense of humor, that humor itself is a positive quality. All things, even good things, need to be experienced congruent with what is righteous and appropriate (James 3:13, Romans 13:13-14). Forgiveness and understanding can't really happen if we're looking for the differences in one another. Opinions don't have to be damaging, if humans could only master the art of self-control. Humor is wonderful, as long as it's not at the expense of one's righteousness or dignity. In our words, our actions, and our behaviors we represent Christ, as His followers. So, even in our humor we must consider what is appropriate, always display self-control, and behave in a way that is respectable to Christ.

Crude, obnoxious, insulting, or pithy humor may be revered in society, but is wrong in the eyes of God, as much as is lust and adultery. The bible tells us that even if we're simply thinking wicked or impure thoughts we are committing a sin, and this is just as wrong as committing the act itself (Matthew 5:27-28). Again, what motivates you? Coveting, or wanting something that someone else has is also impure and unrighteous. Wanting more; more money, more respect, more recognition, is also wrong and considered idolatry in the eyes of God (Philippians 3:19). The only thing we should want to seek more of is Christ, and nothing for selfish gain. Sharing uplifting stories, listening to praise music, fellowship and worship together, enjoying nature with our family, reading wholesome books, and participating in humor that isn't unrighteous are all rewarding ways of enjoying life without wickedness. It's time to reset our internal compasses to what's righteous but elusive, instead of what's crude, yet accepted.

Colossians 4:6, ESV

6 Let your speech **always be gracious**, seasoned with salt, Then you will be able to answer everyone in the way you should.

Ephesians 4:29, ERV

29 When you talk, don't say anything unwholesome. But say the good things that people need — whatever will help them grow stronger. Then what you say will be a blessing to those who hear you.

April 22
Be Careful What You Wish For

Luke 16:13b, GW

13b "You cannot serve God and wealth."

Mark 10:25, ESV

25 "It is easier for a camel to go through the eye of a needle than for a rich person to enter the kingdom of God."

Money makes the world function, we buy our residences, food, education, health care, and transportation with money. Money itself is simply harmless, dirty, paper, but the desire we can develop to have more of it is the real danger. If we truly trust that the Lord will provide all that we need, why do we think we need more? Perhaps some people aren't fully aware that God provides all their needs (Genesis 9:3), or don't trust that all their desires will be met with God (Psalm 37:4). When we pray to God with our concerns and trust that He will make sure we have what we need, we are being faithful servants to Him. However, when we focus on money, and how we can get more of it, we are serving ourselves instead of God. Serving ourselves is vanity (Ecclesiastes 4:4) or self-exaltation, and indicates a lack of faith and gratitude toward what God has provided for us.

Fine jewelry, an exotic vacation, an opulent home, brand name clothing, a luxury automobile, a robust stock portfolio, the best education money can buy, these are the dreams and goals of many people. As coveted as these items are, none of these things will bring one closer to God's salvation. In fact, these expensive possessions carry with them the risk of separating us from our covenant with God. When we have more than another, we may be tempted to think we are smarter, more sophisticated or harder-working than another. If we're surrounded by the best of everything, we might grow more fearful of others taking it from us and resort to deceit to keep it. Greed, arrogance, pride, and deceit are more likely to emerge in someone whose fixated on their financial security. We were created to serve God (Ephesians 2:10, Rev. 4:11), and when we try to accumulate wealth beyond what the Lord has provided for us, we are serving our vanity. When we have success, we should praise God for providing, and help those who have less, or are struggling. Likewise, when we suffer, we repent and pray for God's mercy, and remain confident that we won't be forsaken. Either way, we are under God's plan, not our own (Jeremiah 10:23). Worldly comforts are deceptively pleasant, but God's grace and approval should be worth more to us.

Ecclesiastes 5:10, ERV

10 Those who love money will never be satisfied with the money they have. Those who love wealth will not be satisfied when they get more and more. This is also senseless.

Mark 8:36, ESV

36 For what does it profit a man to gain the whole world and forfeit his soul?

April 23
Repeating Mistakes

Daniel 12:10, ERV

10 Many people will be made pure—they will make themselves clean. But evil people will continue to be evil. And those wicked people will not understand these things, but the wise people will understand them.

When we slip in our faith we may tell ourselves, "Oh well, we're trying, and that's what really matters." But, are we really? Even the most faithful Christ-followers can become stuck in their walk with Jesus. We can't move on to the next lesson before we master the one before us, and that's confusing to most of us. Our mistakes are sins, pride, greed, lust, hate, envy, just to name a few. In our suffering we are meant to learn and understand our mistakes. When we know what we're doing wrong we can repent for that mistake (Psalm 119:71). If we continually beat ourselves up for making mistakes we are judging and condemning ourselves, and that's a job only meant for God (Psalm 75:7). If we're constantly losing our tempers we are in need of patience and forgiveness, and we must seek that through the Lord. If we tell ourselves we couldn't possibly have sinned, we're lying to ourselves (1 John 1:8), and should check for an excess of pride. We can learn what sins we're committing by comparing our actions, words, and behaviors to the teachings Jesus and His disciples spoke about in the bible. When we learn what sins we're committing, we can pray for strength in the area we are deficient, and we rely on the Lord (2 Corinthians 12:9).

If we, as followers of Christ, keep our eyes focused on the Lord He will show us our mistakes and errors. We must study Christ's teachings, His behaviors and motives and mimic them in our own lives. As we keep our focus on Christ, we will eventually be able to clearly see our sins. Perhaps we have been covetous of someone in our life, need to change a thought or behavior, or forgive someone. When we know what our sins are we need to repent, and then move on. We are told that looking back at our mistakes is not what we're directed to do, and is a trick the devil plays on our limited minds (1 Chronicles 21:1, Acts 5:3). We understand, we repent, and in doing so give it all our negative issues to Jesus. Jesus looks into our hearts and forgives us, He corrects until He thinks we're ready, and then we move forward in our faith. Don't look back, look to Jesus.

Proverbs 26:11-12, ERV

11 Like a dog that returns to its vomit, a fool does the same foolish things again and again. 12 People who think they are wise when they are not are worse than fools.

Philippians 3:13, ERV

13 Brothers and sisters, I know that I still have a long way to go. But there is one thing I do: I forget what is in the past and try as hard as I can to reach the goal before me.

April 24
Reproof

Hebrews 12:11, ESV

11 For the moment all discipline seems painful rather than pleasant, but later it yields the peaceful fruit of righteousness to those who have been trained by it.

Sometimes even our most well thought out plans fail, people disappoint us, and good people suffer wrongly every now and then, but our God loves us. Many of us assume that if our God loves us He wouldn't let anyone suffer, but this is, again, an assumption (Isaiah 45:7, Proverbs 16:4). As humans we cannot see how our individual lives fit into the grand plan God has for all humanity, nor can we see what causes other humans to commit the particular sins they do. As we cannot see everything, we cannot assume to know if God is punishing someone, or if He's letting them suffer the consequences of their own actions or motives. What's more, we all sin, so we cannot compare and weigh one another's 'presumed' sins in secret, or we're taking away from God's final judgement. When we judge others we're pushing God out of the judges seat, and sitting in it ourselves.

If we want to continue to grow in Christ Jesus, learning to be more righteous, we are going to have to submit to correction (Hebrews 12:6). For it is in correction through humility that we find positive change, not through condemnation, conquest, or pride. We need to be able to accept criticism, correction, failure and strife from whatever source God sees fit to show us. If we are always in a state of acceptance with regard to correction, we won't see it as condemnation, but another stepping stone to improvement. In order to be able to place our strife and shortcomings as building blocks we must first submit to the Lord, repent, and adhere to a holier life-style from within. Another vital component of faith is forgiveness of ourselves, as well as those against us, and full trust in the Lord Jesus to guide us and provide all we need.

Zechariah 7:11-12, NIV

11 But they refused to pay attention; stubbornly they turned their backs and covered their ears. 12 They made their hearts as hard as flint and would not listen to the law or to the words that the Lord Almighty had sent by His Spirit through the earlier prophets. So the Lord Almighty was very angry.

Proverbs 10:17, ESV

17 Whoever heeds instruction is on the path to life, but he who rejects reproof leads others astray.

April 25
Wrath

Psalm 37:8, ESV

8 Refrain from anger, and forsake wrath! Fret not yourself; it tends only to evil.

We all get angry, it happens to all of us, and more often that we'd like. Waiting in lines can test our patience, but being lied to or wronged in any way can produce stronger feelings of ire. We all have our emotional limits, and need to be aware of these limits as we interact with others. Being angry, getting mad, really any sort of discord can tempt us to sin. We can only approach God with humility, and when we're angry we are far from humility. In fact, when we feel wronged we've had to have passed some sort of judgement to reach the conclusion that an injustice has been committed against us (James 4:11-12). When we are insulted we can become outraged, but Jesus calls us to turn the other cheek (Matthew 5:38-39). If we are too proud we can become insulted when our expectations disappoint us, but are here **not** to be served, but to serve (Matthew 20:27-28).

Getting a few minutes to ourselves to calm down isn't always possible, so what is there to keep us from completely losing our cool? Prayer and patience. We must be calm to accept or receive anything from the Holy Spirit (Isaiah 66:2), and anger prevents us from moving forward spiritually. We must learn what triggers our tempers, and learn ways to intercept our thoughts before they carry us away. God wants us to approach our lives with more patience and grace, and be slow to anger. Sometimes that is easier said than done. As humans, our temperament will be tested again and again. We must remain steadfast in our grace and patience, and not let our anger get the better of us. Finding ways to focus on simple tasks, exercising or taking a walk, reading scripture, or journaling are ways to calm the mind down when angry. Keep prayers when we're upset to a minimum, and always in a way that honors and respects God. We must remember that when we lose our tempers we lose our perspective, our grace, and our self-control, we lose our mind's for a moment. When we're faced with a challenge like anger, we must lean on Christ and the Holy Spirit to guide us back to the proper perspective. By praying to the Lord in our time of anger, we put the control of the situation back into God's hands, where it rightfully belongs.

Matthew 5:44-45, ESV

44 But I say to you, Love your enemies and pray for those who persecute you, 45 so that you may be sons of your Father who is in heaven. For he makes His sun rise on the evil and on the good, and sends rain on the just and on the unjust.

James 1:19-20, ICB

19 My dear brothers, always be willing to listen and slow to speak. Do not become angry easily. 20 Anger will not help you live a good life as God wants.

April 26
Dealing with Conflict

Luke 6:27-28, ICB

27 "I say to you who are listening to me, love your enemies. Do good to those who hate you. 28 Ask God to bless those who say bad things to you. Pray for those who are cruel to you."

We have all been part of an argument or disagreement with another. As constantly sinning humans, we can say and do hurtful things to one another. Be nice to our enemies? That may sound like a lot to ask, but that's just what Jesus did, and just what He's asking us to do (Romans 12:14). We can lash out verbally, harbor grudges against one another, and even bring physical harm to one another. We may see an angry face yelling back at us, but what we're not seeing is another brother or sister in pain. Maybe someone has been fed false information, is afraid to be hurt again, or needs help with direction, or has undealt with pain and is lashing out as a result. We cannot know what our brothers and sisters in Christ are burdened with. No matter what people may be going through, when we treat them with patience, grace, and understanding, we are showing love to our fellow man. This sort of behavior is pleasing to the Lord.

As Christ-followers, we search for ways to be more virtuous in our thoughts, actions, and words. We all carry different views and perspectives that can bump and collide in the most unfriendliest of ways. Not all of us deal with our troubles in a healthy manner. Some of us push our troubles down and suppress them, not wanting to deal with them at all. Others deal with their troubles by complaining to everyone who'll listen, but aren't interested in changing any of their behavior. Not everyone is going to be in the same spiritual place you are, and not everyone is following Christ. We can pray for those who need direction, and for those who need help getting through their pain. With our different perspectives, experiences, choices, opinions and styles, we have a lot to offer one another, but that isn't always easy to see or remember in an argument. We can use our differences to learn and grow from others, and work harder to avoid scrutinizing or criticizing other people. We may not know what's in the heart or mind of another, but we can always offer patience and support instead of criticism and scrutiny. The next time you're in a tense situation with someone ask yourself, what would Jesus do?

Matthew 18:21-22, NIV

21 Then Peter came to Jesus and asked, "Lord, how many times shall I forgive my brother or sister who sins against me? Up to seven times?" 22 Jesus answered, "I tell you, not seven times, but seventy-seven times."

1 Peter 3:9, ICB

9 Do not do wrong to a person to pay him back for doing wrong to you. Or do not insult someone to pay him back for insulting you. But ask God to bless that person. Do this because you yourselves were called to receive a blessing.

April 27
Grace

2 Peter 1:5-7, ERV

5 Because you have these blessings, do all you can to add to your life these things: to your faith add goodness; to your goodness add knowledge; 6 to your knowledge add self-control; to your self-control add patience; to your patience add devotion to God; 7 to your devotion add kindness toward your brothers and sisters in Christ, and to this kindness add love.

Grace is a word that means many things, can be complicated to understand fully, and is difficult to achieve and maintain. To carry oneself with grace is to be patient, soft-spoken and not quick to anger, loving and humble, that is, according to the bible (James 1:19-20). We are challenged in our daily lives with minor nuisances and annoyances, which can make carrying ourselves with grace nearly impossible. Nothing is more irritating than someone who refuses to look up from their cell phone when you're talking to them, or someone who takes the last parking spot, or when someone refuses to stand to the side on an escalator. No matter what we're challenged with in our daily lives, a little more patience, forgiveness and understanding will help us handle ourselves with more *grace*. No one wants to be cut off while driving, but do you *really* want to be that person who honks and acts like a jackass waving their fist at a stranger who doesn't care that you're upset with them? If we're running a little low on patience, we simply pray for what we need. We need to stop, and focus more on Jesus, not ourselves or one another.

Grace is powerful, and can spread like an infectious smile from one to another. A display of patience and grace by one should encourage *all* of us to practice more patience and compassion toward one another. Instead of yelling at someone in anger we can show restraint, "I wish you better treatment than you've given me," is better than shouting insults, or swearing at people. We need to let go of the need to be first in line, the need to feel proud, the greedy thirst to acquire 'more' than another, to view this life and the world we live in as a race, or competition. Life *isn't* a competition, that's not what we're doing here. To view life as a competition of *any* sort is equivalent to thinking the world is flat. We are all God's creation, equally prone to sin, and none better than another. We are here to *prove to Jesus that* we're worthy of ever-lasting life and rapture in heaven, and we do this facing our challenges with grace. We do that by our restraint, self-control, kindness toward one another, by our patience, understanding, and love. So take a little more patience with you today, and let a little more humility lead you to the Lord's grace.

Titus 2:11-12, ESV

11 For the grace of God has appeared, bringing salvation for all people, 12 training us to renounce ungodliness and worldly passions, and to live self-controlled, upright, and godly lives in the present age.

April 28
Equal and Abundant in Christ

Ephesians 3:20, GW

20 Glory belongs to God, whose power is at work in us. By this power he can do infinitely more than we can ask or imagine.

Psalm 16:5, GW

5 The Lord is my inheritance and my cup. You are the one who determines my destiny.

Christ has enough love for all, and all are equal in the eyes of the Lord. (Galatians 3:28, Acts 10:34) The scripture tells us this, and we can rest assured in Christ's vast grace. We don't read anywhere that first come, first served when it comes to our salvation. We don't read that whoever makes the most money, or does the most good deeds, or whoever is the most loved gets more somehow. What God values in a person is grace, humility, love, and self-control, while the world salutes arrogance, pride, power, and wealth. Salvation is a personal quest within ourselves, to rid ourselves of sin, and to live a more righteous life where sin doesn't have control over us. The bible assures us that life isn't a competition to see who can be the most accomplished (Galatians 6:4), but an attempt to purify the sins of humanity in preparation for eternal life in Heaven (Jeremiah 17:10, Isaiah 48:10,17). We all get what we deserve in the eyes of God, and he shows no favorites.

Scripture tells us not to get caught up in worldly sins, or to be in competition and comparison among each other (Luke 16:15). We aren't going to get into the Lord's graces when we're focused on our surroundings, and how we fit into the world. God wants us to be focused on Him, the creator, not His creation. We're built to seek the Lord and His grace, His knowledge, to follow His behavior and re-shape our convictions to His. Each day is an opportunity to see who you can help instead of compare yourself to, an opportunity to share the Lord's teachings and set a better example than you did yesterday. We can't allow the distractions of the world to let us be fooled into comparing ourselves to others, but need to look inward instead. We are all God's creation, brothers and sisters in Christ Jesus, and there is enough love and forgiveness for all of us. Peace be with you.

John 15:5, GW

5 "I am the vine. You are the branches. Those who live in me while I live in them will produce a lot of fruit. But you can't produce anything without me."

1 Peter 1:17, CEV

17 You say that God is your Father, but **God doesn't have favorites! He judges all people by what they do.** So you must honor God while you live as strangers here on earth.

April 29
Just Leave It to God

Proverbs 15:3, ESV

3 The eyes of the Lord are in every place, keeping watch on the evil and the good.

Ecclesiastes 7:20, NASB

20 Indeed, there is not a righteous man on earth who continually does good and who never sins.

Many of us think that if *we* think we're a pretty good person, despite our occasional mistakes, then *God* will too. This is a dangerous assumption, as we are assuming we understand how God renders judgement when we couldn't possibly. The bible tells us that humankind is corrupt in their hearts, prone to sin and deceit, that we are *all* sinful, and God calls us all to repent (Gen. 6:5, Romans 3:23, Acts 17:30). Humans may pass judgement, but we will always disappoint and fall short, and one never really knows what's in another's heart. Only God knows what's in our hearts. Humans have had trouble understanding God, how He loves, and why He disciplines. The mysterious, gentle, yet stern nature of God's correction and redirection in our lives leaves many us with pain, tribulation, and questions.

As lovely as it would be to think that God accepts all of us, all of the time, the bible assures us this isn't true (1 Samuel 16:7). God calls us to repent, to turn away from our sinful ways, and follow the righteous teachings of Jesus. If all humans are prone to sin, and all fall short in the eyes of God, then we *need* God to weigh our final, and fair judgement. Human judgement is clouded by bias, and an inability to see the big picture that is God's plan, while God's judgement remains steadfast, generous, and true. Humans shouldn't be judging anything, because none of us are capable. Humans may always have a difficult time understanding God due to all of the deceit and wickedness blinding many people to the truth. Some people don't want to accept that they *need* God, they feel superior to others, and don't want to consider themselves less than anyone, including God (Jeremiah 8:6). In the end, **God's judgement** will certainly be more **fair and just** that what the world considers fair and just.

Psalm 14:2, CSB

2 The Lord looks down from heaven on the human race to see if there is one who is wise, **one who seeks God**.

Isaiah 55:8-9, ESV

8 "For my thoughts are not your thoughts, neither are your ways my ways," declares the Lord. 9 "For as the heavens are higher than the earth, so are my ways higher than your ways, and my thoughts than your thoughts."

April 30
Got Jesus?

John 14:6, ESV

6 Jesus said to him, "I am the way, and the truth, and the life. No one comes to the Father except through me."

Luke 12:8-9, ERV

8 Jesus said, "I tell you, if you stand before others and are willing to say you believe in me, then I will say that you belong to me. I will say this in the presence of God's angels. 9 But if you stand before others and say you do not believe in me, then I will say that you do not belong to me. I will say this in the presence of God's angels."

Jesus is the human embodiment of God, and our Savior (John 10:30). He died on the cross so that our sins could be forgiven, and our spirits would have everlasting life in heaven. It is clear that whoever *believes* in Jesus, will have access to this everlasting rapture awaiting them in heaven. However, not everyone walking among us truly believes in Jesus. Even others that *do* believe don't do anything more than that. Unbelievers and believers who aren't serving the Lord can provide a breeding ground for a lack of faith. We all suffer because Jesus suffered. When we suffer as good stewards of our faith, we learn and grow, and the pain we felt is transformed into a lesson used to improve ourselves. When we suffer as non-believers, we just suffer (1 Peter 3:17).

Trust is complicated, and not all of us are ready to trust in the Lord. When we understand that everything is in the Lord's control, and not our own, we are humbled (Proverbs 20:24). This is how we fear and respect Him, as He can take anything from us at any time (Job 1:21). We must pray to be able to see with unbiased eyes, and think with non-judgmental minds the glory and significance that is Jesus Christ. Everyone is welcome who believes and repents (Romans 10:9, Mark 1:15), and all who repent will be forgiven (Acts 3:19. We all have an equal opportunity to discover Christ's miracles, read about His teachings, and choose for ourselves. We shouldn't let past experiences, grudges or pride keep us from discovering what we are truly capable of. Only God's power can create miracles in our lives, and only Jesus can bring out our *true* potential. No fear, no challenge, no indiscretion can keep Jesus' love from us, we only need to let Him into our hearts. Search your heart for Jesus, how deeply is He ingrained in *you*?

2 Thessalonians 1:8-9, ERV

8 He will come with burning fire to punish those who don't know God—those who refuse to accept the Good News about our Lord Jesus. 9 They will be punished with a destruction that never ends. They will not be allowed to be with the Lord but will be kept away from His great power.

May 1
Maintenance For Our Souls

Matthew 11:28-30, ESV

28 "Come to me, all who labor and are heavy laden, and **I will give you rest**. 29 Take my yoke upon you, and learn from me, for **I am gentle and lowly in heart, and you will find rest for your souls**. 30 For my yoke is easy, and my burden is light."

Work and career pressures, raising a healthy family in a toxic world, and responsibilities we pile on ourselves, stress is a part of the human experience. Let's be honest, no amount of sleep can reduce the load of stress that accumulates in our lives. Taking care of ourselves is a priority, but we don't come by this ability naturally. We want more; more money, more time, more opportunities, and we don't usually allow ourselves to go with less (Proverbs 27:20). Sometimes less is just what we need; less schedules to adhere to, less peer pressure trying to persuade us to make unwholesome choices, and less opinions shouting at us from opposing directions. Peace comes with simplicity, and less is often more when considering the counsel of our spiritual well-being (John 3:30). As horrifying as it sounds, turning off our devices, and closing our doors to foster some personal time is something we should all be incorporating into our lives. Daily prayer is useless if we're not taking the time to *listen*. We need to love ourselves enough to take personal time when we need it, and that might mean sacrificing extra work hours, or social time, on occasion.

It's often only after something has broken, that we give attention to something that desperately needs it. Our own spiritual well-being is no different. When we deny ourselves the time to ourselves to decompress, and destress, we have less strength to defend against sin and temptation. When we're under pressure, we see less, and we have a greater tendency to react badly to challenges in our day. Whether it's indulging in a deep tissue massage, a picnic with your favorite person, or a personal day off at home to tinker around the house, we all need a day to recharge our inner batteries. Our bodies need rest, our hearts needs peace and love, and our spirits need Christ's grace. We cannot deprive ourselves of the time needed to replace what is lost in our day, we expend mental, emotional, and spiritual energy throughout the day. After all, one cannot pour from an empty cup. How are **you** filling up?

Ephesians 5:29, ESV

29 For no one ever hated his own flesh, **but nourishes and cherishes it**, just as Christ does the church.

Genesis 2:2, ESV

2 And on the seventh day God finished his work that he had done, **and he rested** on the seventh day from all his work that he had done.

May 2
The Devil's Purpose

Isaiah 45:7, GNV

7 "I form the light, and create darkness: **I make peace, and create evil: I the Lord do all these things.**"

The battle between the forces of evil and the forces of light sound like a tagline for the latest science-fiction fantasy. Many people take more stock in reality, and roll their eyes at such tales of far-fetched capriciousness. We might want to give that far-fetched, 3000 year old, religious 'fantasy' a little more thought, since we're all in it. We are **all God's humanity**, and everything in the bible pertains to each, and every one of us. The bible, God's word, has no expiration date, and has prophesies that have not occurred yet. In the bible, the devil tempts, deceives, tricks, and is even allowed to test people (Job 1:12). The devil even has followers, and pulls people away from God by playing upon an individual's weaknesses and desires (Revelation 12:9). We will all be under pressure, tempted, broken down, and deceived in our lives. This pain and negativity, personified by the devil, serves a purpose. Sometimes, people are so lost they don't realize this, and wonder why God *allows* pain. People who think God is unfair are treating **Him** unfairly, by expecting things to always be the way *they* think it should be, and not trusting, or turning to Him when He crashes their world down upon them. We are to recognize, and praise the constant force of love that is perfectly balanced with the divine justice that is God, the creator of our universe. God knows that not everyone will love Him in return, these are the devil's children (1 John 3:10).

It's in our humility that we can truly see the power of God in our lives, but the forces of evil are very good at playing our greed, vanity, pride, and arrogance against one another. When we judge one another because someone else may sin differently, or when we're secretly envious or lustful of another, or we deny someone forgiveness, evil wins. When we turn the other cheek, compliment another instead of judging them, forgive or pray for an enemy, or walk away from others that are participating in wickedness, righteousness wins. The devil blinds people from understanding the power of God's word, which can truly transform a person's soul when taken in and understood (Matthew 13:19). We must arm ourselves with the knowledge that is in Christ Jesus, while remaining savvy to the spiritual forces at work within us all. We all have souls, the invisible part of us that makes us individuals-that's what God is fighting to keep, and the devil's trying to corrupt. We're either going to submit to the forces of good, or the forces of evil, because we're only the dominant species in the *animal* kingdom. Ignorance, stubbornness, and disbelief are all part of the devil's deception. We are either chosen as one of God's people (John 6:44), or we're left for the devil (Revelation 20:15). We may not **want** to believe that we're in an invisible battle between good and evil or not, but we are, and our time is ticking…

2 Timothy 2:26, ESV

26 and they may come to their senses and escape from the snare of the devil, after being captured by him to do His will.

May 3
Avoid Pleasure-Seeking

1 Corinthians 7:8-9, ESV

8 To the unmarried and the widows I say that it is good for them to remain single, as I am. 9 But if they cannot exercise self-control, they should marry. For it is better to marry than to burn with passion.

Hebrews 13:4, KJ21

4 Marriage is honorable in all, and the bed undefiled; but whoremongers and adulterers God will judge.

Physical desires come naturally to humans, and we all seek it one way or another to satisfy those yearnings. Humanity ranges from people that handle their physical urges with patience and integrity to people that take what they want by force without regard to others. The bible is very clear that the type of person who claims to be a follower of Jesus will exhibit self-control, and behave in a morally upright manor, both spiritually and physically. We're going to have desires, there is no way around that, and the physical pleasures of this world are not only tempting, but readily available, and all around us.

The bible teaches us that marriage is the vessel that allows physical pleasure and gratification through one another, but in a dignified, loving, respectful way. In a righteous marriage both parties mutually benefit from a shared physical love, and this love is a blessing from God (Genesis 2:24). In the bible, we understand that the importance of the message is regarding the integrity and pureness of the love, and keeping all sexual relations *within* that marriage to maintain righteousness.

However, anything that is done, wished about, or lusted for **outside of** this **marriage** is considered giving into temptations, adulterous and evil. Even simply *thinking* a sinful thought is as bad as committing the act (Matthew 5:28), and, as the bible also stresses, one evil act often leads to another (Psalm 7:14). If, at first, we give into lust, then we're more prone to adultery and then comes deceit, drunkenness, and anger. Like eating potato chips, one evil temptation leads to another evil temptation, you're never going to be satisfied with just one. When we let our temptations *conquer* us we become impure, immoral, and we lose our integrity in Christ Jesus. No physical pleasure on Earth should be worth losing our righteousness, what we've worked so diligently to learn, acquire and maintain (Luke 9:25). Keep your desires under your own roof, and repent when your thoughts or actions are impure!

Galatians 5:19-21, ESV

19 Now the works of the flesh are evident: sexual immorality, impurity, sensuality, 20 idolatry, sorcery, enmity, strife, jealousy, fits of anger, rivalries, dissensions, divisions, 21 envy, drunkenness, orgies, and things like these. I warn you, as I warned you before, that those who do such things will not inherit the kingdom of God.

May 4
Words

2 Timothy 2:16, ERV

16 But avoid irreverent babble, stay away from people who talk about useless things that are not from God. That kind of talk will lead a person more and more against God.

James 1:26, ERV

26 You might think you are a very religious person. But **if your tongue is out of control, you are fooling yourself.** Your careless talk makes your offerings to God worthless.

What kind of person cusses at and flips off another driver in anger and disdain? Hopefully not a fellow follower of Christ. Words are powerful, what we say, and mean can lift up, or tear down another. As followers of Christ, how we speak, what we say, and how we carry ourselves represents our Lord, and Savior, in Jesus. Restraining our words, filtering our thoughts to what is useful, relevant, and kind is difficult. Self-control is a challenge because our emotions can signal us in ways that test our righteousness, often making situations feel worse than they really are. When we're at odds with another, under pressure, it can be difficult not to want to put our need for emotional balance before our salvation (Prov. 3:5). Life can be so discouraging, so humbling, so painful that we seek pleasure and respite from the harsh world in its sinful distractions. Not giving into gluttony, revenge, deceit, adultery or slander when we're at the height of our disdain can feel impossible sometimes. We must consider how much we really *want* to model our lives after Jesus' when temptation to lose our pious integrity and self-control descends on us.

We must carry ourselves with patience, trusting in the Lord and be slow to anger (Proverbs 29:11). Whatever injustice we think we're suffering, any pain we endure, will be reconciled by Christ Jesus in the end, so what life does to us shouldn't matter (Hebrews 13:6). We must be careful not to pass judgement on what *we* think is fair and just, because we are expected to trust that God will deal with everything with **His** divine justice. What matters is how we react to our suffering, and that we call upon Jesus through the Holy Spirit for the comfort and guidance we need. Our words should direct people to the love, forgiveness, and salvation in Christ Jesus, anything else should be considered a waste of our words. We were given two ears and only one mouth, as such we should be listening more than we speak. The Word of God is where our spirits get their life, and light, we should not only know it, but our lives should be a reflection of it.

Matthew 4:4, GW

4 Jesus answered, "Scripture says, 'A person cannot live on bread alone but on **every word that God speaks.**' "

Proverbs 17:27, ESV

27 Whoever restrains His words has knowledge, and he who has a cool spirit is a man of understanding.

May 5

Things Jesus Never Said:

"Follow your heart/dreams"-

> Jeremiah 17:9, KJV
>
> 9 The heart is deceitful above all things, and desperately wicked: who can know it?

"Be true to yourself"-

> Matthew 16:24, ERV
>
> 24 Then Jesus said to His followers, "If any of you want to be my follower, you must stop thinking about yourself and what you want. You must be willing to carry the cross that is given to you for following me."

"Go with your gut"-

> Proverbs 3:5, ESV
>
> 5 Trust in the Lord with all your heart, and do not lean on your own understanding.

"As long as you're happy"-

> 1 Peter 1:14-16, ESV
>
> 14 As obedient children, do not be conformed to the passions of your former ignorance, 15 but as he who called you is holy, you also be holy in all your conduct, 16 since it is written, "You shall be holy, for I am holy."

We can say a lot of things to each other under the guise of encouragement, hope, help and support when we want to assist someone we care about. Good intensions, no matter how sincere, don't always result in righteous advice. **God's word** is designed to inspire righteous, holy, loving behavior from more compassionate hearts, and we can derive strength, grace, and wisdom from them, but **we must listen** to what He says (Matthew 22:29). As much as we want to guide our own destinies, make our worldly dreams come true, fix our own problems and mistakes, we get what **God** allows (Ezekiel 3:10). If we truly love God, we should be following His example in Christ Jesus, not our *own* desires. We were made imperfect, and created in the image of our God, *to be fulfilled by Him.*

Humanity has a heart that has a penchant for sinful behavior. Hiding in everyday places, our judgement of one another, our anger, our impatience, our imperviousness to the plight of our neighbors, our greed, our pride, our insults, the crimes we commit against one another, render us sinful. Anything that tells us not to listen to God's call for our repentance in order to receive His glory in eternal salvation should be considered wicked, and not of God. Don't follow your dreams, or go with your gut, or be true to yourself, but pray on, brothers and sisters, and let's **follow Christ Jesus** as closely as we can.

May 6
Forgiveness, Correction, and Punishment

Jeremiah 17:10, GW

10 "I, the Lord, search minds and test hearts. I will reward each person for what he has done. I will reward him for the results of His actions."

Jeremiah 23:23-24, GW

23 "I am a God who is near. I am also a God who is far away," declares the Lord. 24 "No one can hide so that I can't see him," declares the Lord. "I fill heaven and earth!" declares the Lord.

Our God in Heaven has His finger on the pulse of humanity, each one of us is completely transparent to Him. When we assume more control over our lives than we actually have, we are arrogant. God's agenda includes reforming, reshaping, and retooling the human heart to be more devoted and faithful to Him. Through correction, at first, and if we're still too stubborn and proud to humble ourselves before God, He disciplines us (Job 5:17). We are to follow His commandments, obey His will in our lives, and follow Jesus' example. When we don't do this, when we lean on our own understanding, our own choices, our own solutions to our problems, we are living for ourselves and not for God. We are told to come to our Lord in prayer, for **all** that we need, and to place at His feet **all** that we're worried about (1 Peter 5:7).

We are all under pressure, we are all being refined by God's divine process. For some, unfortunate people, the devil has clouded their understanding and they have become bitter and resentful to God, preventing them from truly understanding God's grace (2 Corinthians 4:4). We can all be deceived, and should not judge others by their sins, especially since we **all** commit them! As followers of Christ, we shouldn't be resentful, or fearful, or hesitant, or doubtful, but full of faith and trust in God. No one *likes* discipline, but our arrogance can cause some people become indignant to God as a result. When we give God the proper respect and praise, by remaining humble, we put ourselves in the best position to receive God's mercy and grace. Instead of thinking everything is NOT fair, that good things aren't made for us, trust that God will never forsake those that rest on their faith in Him (Ezekiel 33:17-20). Trust in God's plan for us, and not rely on our own knowledge, but submit to God's will for us. Enhancing, polishing, improving, cleansing us, God is *trying* to make us holy. Shine on, and stay strong, brothers and sisters! Praise the Lord, and His Almighty grace. AMEN.

Jeremiah 32:33, ERV

33 "They should have come to me for help, but they turned their backs to me. I tried to teach them again and again, but **they would not listen** to me. I tried to correct them, but they would not listen."

Hebrews 12:11, NIV

11 No discipline seems pleasant at the time, but painful. Later on, however, it produces a harvest of righteousness and peace for those who have been trained by it.

Matthew 5:22, ESV

22 "But I say to you that everyone who is angry with His brother will be liable to judgment; whoever insults His brother will be liable to the council; and whoever says, 'You fool!' will be liable to the hell of fire."

Psalm 37:8, ESV

8 Refrain from anger, and forsake wrath! Fret not yourself; it tends only to evil.

James 1:20, ESV

20 For the anger of man does not produce the righteousness of God.

Frustrated with our bodies, our jobs, our spouses, and sometimes, our whole lives can seem like the same old fight over and over again. Peace of mind often seems to allude us, as we can get bogged down with schedules, responsibilities, and unmet expectations. God isn't appearing on mountain tops, or talking to people from bushes, and it's been more than two thousand years since Jesus was crucified. Sometimes, it seems like humanity has forgotten God. Humanities relationship with our creator has gone on for thousands of years, we may be late-comers but we're not immune to the message of the bible (1 Peter 1:24-25). God wants us to be holy, like Him, so we can all enjoy eternal life together, and it's apparently an exclusive ticket (Matthew 7:14). In order to be more holy, we're going to have to exhibit self-control and grace.

Many of us walk around, allowing ourselves to be distracted from His narrow path. Righteousness is allusive enough on its own for a race of sinful humans, but when God's discipline is unleashed in our lives, we can become discouraged to the point of frustration or despair. One too many bad choices, sinful words or thoughts, can compile on some of us who aren't paying attention. It isn't enough for us to just believe, God wants us to *want* to be more like Him, and to seek Him. Some of us can even become so misunderstood, confused, tricked or deceived that we can develop an anger toward God for putting us through the pain and sadness He has. It takes humility to go from anger to acceptance of God's will, and turn to Him for comfort and direction instead of being outraged that something negative has happened. We may all suffer differently, but we all suffer. Instead of becoming angry at the only one who can help, we should ask Him for direction, comfort, and mercy instead.

Ephesians 4:31-32, ESV

31 Let all bitterness and wrath and anger and clamor and slander be put away from you, along with all malice. 32 Be kind to one another, tenderhearted, forgiving one another, as God in Christ forgave you.

May 8
Sin Brings Ruin and Shame

Ephesians 6:12, ESV

12 For we do not wrestle against flesh and blood, but against the rulers, against the authorities, against the cosmic powers over this present darkness, against the spiritual forces of evil in the heavenly places.

Proverbs 18:3, ESV

3 When wickedness comes, contempt comes also, and with dishonor comes disgrace.

Picture this: You're on your way home from a bad day at work, a little aggravated. Stopping at the grocery store, in a hurry, you rush to grab the last box of dinner rolls on special before an older woman could reach for them. In the car on the way home someone cuts you off at a stop sign and nearly hits you, you cuss at them from the confidence of your own car. Before dinner, that same night, you pray, thanking God for your meal and your health. It doesn't take much for a bad day to get worse, and with it, our attitudes and behaviors. As humans, we all have our limits, and as perpetual sinners we will always face suffering and strife (Matthew 6:34, John 16:33). We have a choice, though, in how we act, behave and speak to one another. The dark forces the bible warns about lurk among each of us daily, in the form of impatience, frustration, intolerance, pride, judgement and greed.

It can be incredibly tempting to lose our tempers when we become impatient and frustrated, or when we feel we've been wronged or treated unfairly. In our rush to be offended, or form a judgement, we forget our place. God is in charge, not us, and He decides both punishment and reward (Psalm 75:7). Arrogance, pride, and greed are unrighteous and wicked according to the bible, and will only create more sin and wickedness. We must be mindful that we are Christ-followers, and, therefore, servants that represent the *servant Savior* (Philippians 2:5-8) by our good works. So, no matter how much pressure the world puts on us; in our jobs, in our homes, in our cars on the road, in the doctor's office waiting room, at the grocery store, we should be treating one another with love, patience, and forgiveness. As a matter of fact, just when the pressure surrounding us feels like too much, we need to be even *more* mindful of dark forces preying upon us. We all need God, but the dark forces like to fuel our sinful pride, causing us to think we don't need God, that He is more of a hinderance than a help to us. Our sin brings us ruin and shame before the Lord, and our repentance to Christ is how we purge ourselves of this wickedness. To pray in repentance we must give up our pride, this will best position us to receive the grace we need from God. That patience, along with the grace and strength through Christ our Lord will keep us from acting like evil, wicked wretches who don't belong to Jesus Christ in those most difficult moments.

Psalm 10:3-4, ERV

3 Those greedy people brag about the things they want to get. They curse the Lord and show that they hate him. 4 **The wicked are too proud to ask God for help. He does not fit into their plans.**

May 9
Control

Philippians 2:13, ESV

13 for it is God who works in you, both to will and to work for His good pleasure.

James 4:13-15, ESV

13 Come now, you who say, "Today or tomorrow we will go into such and such a town and spend a year there and trade and make a profit" — 14 yet you do not know what tomorrow will bring. What is your life? For you are a mist that appears for a little time and then vanishes. 15 Instead you ought to say, "**If the Lord wills,** we will live and do this or that."

As humans we want to make as many of our own choices as we can, we desire to maintain control of our lives. Some people believe that God is only a supervisory force to turn to only occasionally while we all carve out our own lives for ourselves. People take pride in their own hard work, accomplishments, and successes, and tend to blame God or others when they're disappointed, or don't go their way. To think we can control anything but our reactions, our behaviors, our words and our motivations is foolish. God's plan for us began before we were conceived, according to the bible, and He knows what we're going to do before we do it (Hebrews 4:13, Psalm 139:1-6). What motivates us drives our actions, beliefs, words and behaviors comes from deep within us. Are you motivated by the respect of others, the adoration of your social media friends, or greed, lust, power? The Lord wants our motivation to be to love and serve Him, and love others as we love ourselves (Deuteronomy 28:47).

Keeping not just our hearts, but our minds and actions focused on Christ should be our goal, as His followers. We should be motivated by Christ, want to seek His guidance, and re-model our lives after His. We may be able to make our own *choices*, but we *belong* to God, our Heavenly Father. We are expected to maintain control of our motivations, to keep them wholesome as Christ's were. We are expected to follow the path God has set before each of us, and we're put through pain and tribulations to keep us on these righteous paths. Only through Jesus can we access the knowledge we'll need to progress in our faith, gain the patience, tolerance, self-control and grace we'll need, and understand our shortcomings for purpose of repentance. We mustn't become lazy in our faith, and succumb to temptations that alter our motivation from that of righteousness. After all, as Christ-followers we are seeking to model ***Christ***, and can't become tempted and distracted by the worldly sins all around us.

Psalm 24:1, ERV

1 The earth and everything on it belong to the Lord. **The world and all its people belong to him.**

May 10
Spiritual Obstacle Course?

1 John 3:6, ESV

6 **No one who abides in him keeps on sinning**; no one who keeps on sinning has either seen him or known him.

Genesis 6:5, ESV

5 The Lord saw that the wickedness of man was great in the earth, and that every intention of the thoughts of his heart was only evil **continually**.

1 John 5:19. ERV

19 We know that we belong to God, but **the Evil One controls the whole world**.

Matthew 5:48, ESV

48 **You** therefore **must be perfect**, as your heavenly Father is perfect.

Consider: Put a humanity that's prone to sin in an environment that's controlled by the devil's wickedness, and ask them to be perfect. Some people would be lying if they said they never thought to themselves, "Why would God set us up for failure like that?" When reading the bible, it's hard to ignore the impact of sin, as sin is constantly separating people from the one, true, God. We sin by the choices we make, the words we speak, the kindness we hold for ransom, and the temptations we succumb to. Many people read the bible, and come to the conclusion that they must eradicate all sin from their life in order to be holy. These people examine their sins, and the sins of others, passing silent judgement, but unable to see the bigger picture. God wants our hearts: He wants us to confess our fears, He wants us to come to Him with our questions and doubts, and He wants us to trust and confide in Him with the secrets of our hearts. God wants our loyalty, nothing less than 100% will do, and He's watching us all go through a spiritual obstacle course designed to show Him how faithful we'll be to Him (Deuteronomy 8:2, 13:3).

Our sins shouldn't be used to separate us from God, but to bring us closer to Him. It's in the act of repentance that we humble ourselves before God, and it's in God's discipline that forces our changed behavior, allowing His refining process to work in us. The sins we commit are a vehicle for this 'purification' process. We sin, we're disciplined by God through tribulation, we repent, and it's through this process our weaknesses are supplemented by the Lord. If we never knew what sins to repent for, we couldn't fill those weak places in our spirits with the Lord's grace (2 Corinthians 12:9-11). When we understand how our relationship with God is supposed to work, we can focus on being more humble, and strengthening our faith in the Lord. We must be devoted to God, to His refining process, and return to Him no matter what blessing, or tragedy, He brings upon our lives (Isaiah 45:7). Life is a test; and the sins we commit are the vehicle that proves our faith and devotion to God.

Hosea 6:6, GNV

6 "**For I desired mercy, and not sacrifice, and the knowledge of God more than burnt offerings**.

May 11
The Power Inside Us All

John 14:15-17, ICB

15 "If you love me, you will do the things I command. 16 I will ask the Father, and he will give you another Helper. He will give you this Helper to be with you forever. 17 The Helper is the Spirit of truth. The world cannot accept him because it does not see him or know him. But you know him. He lives with you, and he will be in you."

Philippians 4:13, ESV

13 I can do all things through him who strengthens me.

When we're lost, we pray. When we're hurting, we pray. We're told our prayers will be answered, but how will we know what to do, and, how does the Lord help us? For those of us following Christ, and modeling our lives after His, we are given a special 'helper.' The Holy Spirit is an invisible force that lives inside of us, sent by Jesus, to help guide and direct us. The Holy Spirit works in mysterious ways, showing us what is wrong and right in Christ through the words and actions of others (Isaiah 11:2, John 14:26). Everything in our environment is tangible, we are busy with the responsibilities we've placed on ourselves, and forget that there is an invisible war for the attention of our spirits going on unseen. (Ephesians 6:10-12) This means we're all vulnerable to unseen forces we probably don't fully understand, further highlighting our need for Jesus. Heavy, but true!

In the advice of a trusted friend, the sermon by an uplifting minister, the kindness of a stranger, perhaps a line from a song of praise or worship, or even a scene in a movie, the Holy Spirit communicates with us. Often, the Holy Spirit is that little voice in our head that tells us what we're about to do is totally wrong, but the Spirit can touch us in many ways. Some people discount this special help from the Holy Spirit, believing only what they can see and prove. It's vital that we pay attention to what the Holy Spirit is trying to communicate to us, no matter the source. We must keep open minds, trust our instincts, pray for guidance, and all we need to understand will be made known to us. Following our Lord allows the freedom from death in that we have everlasting spiritual life (John 4:24), freedom from corruption, freedom from guilt and the penalties of sin through the opportunity of repentance, and the freedom from fear. It's a pretty special power to have, and all through the love and majesty of Christ our Lord. Praise God for all He does, may we all be humbled so that we may feel His grace. AMEN!

2 Corinthians 3:17, ESV

17 Now the Lord is the Spirit, and where the Spirit of the Lord is, there is freedom.

May 12
Pray, Repeat...

Matthew 6:6-8, GW

6 **Jesus said**, "When you pray, go to your room and close the door. **Pray privately** to your Father who is with you. Your Father sees what you do in private. He will reward you. 7 When you pray, don't ramble like heathens who think they'll be heard if they talk a lot. 8 Don't be like them. Your Father knows what you need before you ask him."

Ephesians 6:18, GW

18 Pray in the Spirit in every situation. Use every kind of prayer and request there is. For the same reason be alert. Use every kind of effort and make every kind of request for all of God's people.

Many of us pray, asking for things we are sure we need, expecting that our idea of what we desire is sufficient to receive it. God knows what's best for us, even if we don't sometimes. We are told in the bible that all we need to do is ask, and we shall receive (Mark 11:24), but not all of us feel like we 'receive.' When we ask for something to help us specific to our path to righteousness, we are sure to receive it, but in the manner and timeframe the Lord sees fit. Prayers can sometimes feel unanswered, because sometimes they're not. Sometimes we ask for the wrong things, or the right things at the wrong time, and for this reason our prayers aren't answered in the way we would expect. Perhaps we're being made to wait for what we've prayed for to test our faith, patience, and reliance on God. The bible reassures us that God hears our prayers, and knowing what's best for us, we must rest on our faith that our needs will be met as **He** sees appropriate (John 9:31).

Of course, just because God hears our prayers doesn't mean He's going to grant our requests. Quiet, meaningful, simple-worded prayers that are genuine and from our hearts is what God is asking for. We aren't meant to be eloquent, or redundantly specific, or quote references from scripture when we pray, Jesus explains in the Gospel (Matthew 6:7). Churches, religions and some experts like to opine on the art of prayer, and some even require that only certain people pray. However, all humans fall short in the eyes of God, and one sinner can't tell Jesus what's in the heart of another. We are only saved through Jesus, and only heard by God through Jesus (John 14:6). Jesus' commands should take precedence over any command generated from humans, no matter how learned they may be. Jesus Christ is the only one who saves, and He teaches people how to pray. God wants us to be able to trust Him with the anxieties, the fears, the praise, the questions, and the desires that are in our hearts, and praying is how we communicate to Him. We will need God over and over, so we are expected to pray to Him over and over. So pray, brothers and sisters, then repeat. AMEN.

Luke 18:1, 7-8a, GW

1 Jesus used a parable with His disciples to show them that they need to **pray all the time** and never give up. Jesus explained, 7 "Won't God give his chosen people justice when they cry out to him for help day and night? Is he slow to help them? 8a I can guarantee that he will give them **justice quickly**."

May 13
Anything We Want?

Mark 11:24, ESV

24 "Therefore I tell you, whatever you ask in prayer, believe that you have received it, and it will be yours."

Zechariah 7:13, ERV

13 So the Lord All-Powerful said, "I called to them, and they did not answer. So now, if they call to me, I will not answer."

We must ask the Lord for what we need to obey His commandments, but just because we ask for it doesn't mean we'll receive it. If we ask for the wrong things, like money or attention, or we ask with wrong motives, with wickedness in our hearts we probably aren't going to get what we've asked for. When we judge other people, ignore someone else in need that we could help, or boast about something we're proud of we're committing sins. If we marry unwisely and then fall in love with another, an affair would still be wrong, but many humans do just that. Lust is something we may just be *thinking* to ourselves, but that is just as bad as committing the act, according to Jesus (Matthew 5:28). To think that humans can will themselves to avoid sin is ridiculous, because humans cannot be made holy without the grace of Jesus Christ. To be forgiven we need to first acknowledge our unholy behavior, feel genuine remorse for disobeying God, and seek to change our ways. What we know about unrighteousness comes from the bible: Thieves, drunkards, and angry people who shout insults are seen as unrighteous in the bible. Anyone seeking vengeance on another, someone who commits adultery, gives in to lustful feelings, practices frivolous or lude sexual acts with someone you haven't betrothed your heart to are all considered unrighteous. Our behavior stems from the desires of our hearts. We must ask ourselves, "What is it that my heart truly desires?"

Prayer is important, and what we ask Jesus for matters, after all, he knows what is truly in our hearts (Jerimiah 17:10). If we pray to be stronger, wealthier, prettier, faster, or more successful than another we may be in denial regarding our greed and arrogance. If we are seeking something in prayer because of vanity, pride, greed or vengeance, we are praying, and thinking, with unrighteous hearts, and the Lord knows it. We need to learn what God's will is, what righteousness really looks like, and work diligently to put it into practice in our daily lives. We can only reform our wicked hearts through the blood of Jesus, by reading the bible, and by pursuing the Lord's help in prayer for a more virtuous heart. When seeking true righteousness, we'll pray for patience, grace, tolerance, understanding, wisdom, forgiveness, and humility. (Psalm 51:10, Isaiah 66:2) Rest assured, that in the pursuit of *true* righteousness, the Lord sees to it that we will want for nothing.

James 4:3, ESV

3 You ask and do not receive, because you ask wrongly, to spend it on your passions.

Acts 10:34-35, ERV

34 Peter began to speak: "I really understand now that God does not consider some people to be better than others, 35 but *in every nation* the person **who fears Him and does righteousness** is acceptable to Him."

May 14
The Hardest Part

Psalm 62:8, NASB

8 Trust in Him at all times, you people; **Pour out your hearts before Him**; God is a refuge for us.

Sometimes, our shortcomings and failures seem much greater, or obvious, to us than they really are to our immediate environment. Some days we can feel like everything is going our way, and we can feel blessed beyond measure, and other days we can be left wondering where it all went wrong, and how it fell apart so quickly. God creates our circumstances, whether blessed or challenged, and watches over us as we deal with it each to our own way. We don't get to pick, or choose what happens to us, even though many of us would like to think that we do. We only get to choose *how we deal* with what God gives us, either by adapting and overcoming, or by becoming bitter and untrusting.

When we follow Jesus, we are choosing righteousness in **every** aspect of our lives, but why is being good so difficult? How we perceive our circumstances is important. From our hearts the seeds of our attitudes are sown, and we will all reap what we sow. We have all been victim to the thinking that one awful, or embarrassing moment means we *cannot do anything right*. Plenty of us are currently stuffing something down we don't want to deal with, or trying to ignore them all together. Many people are suspicious, and untrusting, because they've been hurt before. People who have been deeply hurt can be defensive, and other people blame others for something *they* have done. Still other people try reduce the sting of life by adopting all or nothing thinking, because it's easier than learning something new. When we feel wronged, we may feel we have some authority, then, to wrong someone else. Unlearning negative behavior, or coping mechanisms, that lead our thoughts to greed, suspicion and dis-trust, deceit, self-pity, or revenge is complicated.

Trusting in God is difficult because it forces us to unlearn everything we know about ourselves, our patterns of thought, our defense mechanisms, and even what drives us. These familiar thoughts, assuming, blaming, denial, jumping to conclu-sions, can be so second nature that we often don't even realize we are falling prey to them. We cannot assume we know how a certain situation will unfold, we cannot know what others are truly thinking. Everyone is incapable of perfection, and we all stum-ble over our iniquities. Each negative experience brings us challenges, and high-lights our deficits. We are all experiencing pain, mixed with blessings, we are just experiencing them in different ways, and at different times in our lives based on what God sees in us. We need to be able to trust the Lord to replace our judgmental, untrusting, arrogant, or selfish natures with His righteous, holy, humble nature. No matter what He gives us this day, how bad it may hurt, or how it may challenge us, we take everything we have to the Lord. We leave all we have at the feet of our Savior, **and let Him figure out the details**, and this, my friends, is the hard part.

Ecclesiastes 7:14, ESV

14 In the day of prosperity be joyful, and in the day of adversity consider: God has made the one as well as the other, so that man may not find out anything that will be after him.

May 15
Contrite Choices, Narrow Path

Matthew 7:13, ERV

13 Jesus said, "You can enter true life only through the narrow gate. The gate to hell is very wide, and there is plenty of room on the road that leads there. Many people go that way. 14 But the gate that opens the way to true life is narrow. And the road that leads there is hard to follow. **Only a few people** find it."

Choices, selections, and opportunities are all words that may cause us to picture houses, cars, cities & towns, extravagant dinners or parties, vacation packages, jewelry, or even a mate! These are all *tangible* things, things humans can acquire, or that the world offers. Many people would consider these things necessities to one's comfort and pleasure here on Earth, and not necessarily 'bad' things. Actually, these would be considered sinful extravagancies that *distract* from Christ, and promote further sinful choices, attitudes and behaviors (Jeremiah 9:3). This is where things get tricky, and some people shy away from pursuing a deeper faith in God through Jesus. Living modesty instead of proudly, giving what we can to those less fortunate instead of ignoring them, and not bragging or being prideful is what righteousness in Jesus Christ is all about. This is not what the world is all about, and pleasurable things like boats, lavish clothing and perfumes place evil temptation in packages we find difficult to ignore. Many people have difficulty accepting these things as unrighteous, and don't want to part with them (Matthew 6:24, John 3:19-20).

Our faith in God through Christ Jesus is meant to sustain our souls, and provide all we require throughout our life. The more we look toward Christ the more we keep our focus on what is righteous, instead of succumbing to temptation, and focusing on ourselves. Jesus knew that many people would turn away from Him (John 6:64), and said in the bible that 'few' would find everlasting life in Heaven. Yikes! The path to righteousness is tough, but those who *want* to be more like Jesus find the road rewarding and enlightening. We submit to suffering, we submit to the path laid out before us, we submit to God through Jesus Christ, and we do this because of the reciprocal love we share with our Heavenly hosts. We will always be tempted by the comforts and indulgences this world has to offer, we must realize and accept that these things pull us farther off of our path to righteousness (James 4:4, 1 Peter 2:11). We must be wise in the choices we make, pray throughout the day, and seek quiet time for reflection and fellowship. Stay strong, brothers and sisters!

Galatians 6:7-8, ESV

7 Do not be deceived: God is not mocked, for whatever one sows, that will he also reap. 8 For the one who sows to His own flesh will from the flesh reap **corruption**, but the one who sows to the *Spirit* will from the Spirit reap **eternal life**.

May 16
Forbearance in Waiting

Romans 8:25, ERV

25 But we are hoping for something we don't have yet, and we are waiting for it **patiently**.

Whatever we need, we understand that Christ will provide. When we are hurting, we pray for Him to help us to understand and work through our pain. But when we're hurting, waiting can be difficult. Not everything in life can be solved in a speedy, convenient time frame. The Lord works in His own time, and we must be patient in the waiting (2 Peter 3:8). Our faith assures us that the Lord *hears* our prayers, and offers sanctuary to *all* who seek Him. Our pain isn't as difficult to manage when we understand the lesson we are to learn from it, but we don't always understand why we are made to hurt. When we pray for understanding and wisdom from our pain, and the strength to endure the waiting we are showing God we are trusting in Him. This is when we pray to hand our burdens over to Jesus to manage. We then only need to wait, *patiently*, for Him to do His work.

Impatience can lead to bad choices. We want things in a hurry, we don't like to wait. Waiting makes us feel unimportant, passed over, unseen, and tempts us to make unwholesome choices (Ephesians 4:26). Jesus tells us that the patient person, the one who is waiting, faithfully in their suffering, will reap His extravagant rewards. If we succumb to greed, theft, gluttony, revenge, or any other deviant behavior, we will need to repent or seek the Lord's wrath (Ezekiel 18:32). What a waste of time, and you're no closer to solving your problem then you were before you acted defiantly. No one likes waiting, for *any* reason, but waiting on the Lord isn't like being in a doctor's waiting room (Isaiah 40:31). No one on Earth can offer the forgiveness, grace, rapture and salvation that comes from Jesus Christ. We should be seeking guidance and direction from Christ Jesus, the patience and grace to understand the Holy Spirit, and the wisdom and courage to change our lives as the Holy Spirit directs. We don't always get our answer in the way, or time we might expect, but this is the danger of such expectations. Waiting on the Lord may *feel* a little like being in a waiting room, but it's the Lord's waiting room and the help you'll be receiving is divine. Worth the wait! Have patience and faith, brothers and sisters, and don't let discouragement creep in! Praise God, in Jesus' name, AMEN.

Psalm 37:7-9, ERV

7 Trust in the Lord and wait quietly for His help. Don't be angry when people make evil plans and succeed. 8 Don't become so angry and upset that you, too, want to do evil. 9 The wicked will be destroyed, but *those who call to the Lord for help will get what he has promised*.

May 17
Strength, Soul, Spirit, Mind

Mark 12:30, ESV

30 Jesus said, "And you shall love the Lord your God with all your heart and with all your soul and with all your mind and with all your strength."

Our **heart** is not only an organ that pumps life-sustaining blood throughout our bodies, but it's the spiritual center for what motivates us, drives our ambitions, our intentions, goals and desires. Are we looking for tangible, or Earthly, spoils such as fame, recognition, wealth, or success? Or are we seeking, and taking in the example of Christ's love into our hearts, are we loving others like we are called to? God's understanding is able to penetrate the human **soul**; the specific, character aspects that make a person unique and individual, like a personality fingerprint, allowing Him to know us (Hebrews 4:12). We are called to 'cleanse' our unrighteous souls by seeking to live as much as we can like the only perfect human, Jesus Christ, to rest in this righteousness more naturally, and to set an example for others in the same way. Spiritual **strength** isn't physical, but the dogged persistence to know God, or endurance in resisting temptation to do or say the wrong things, and the *earnest effort* to please the Lord with our devotion and good works. Many of us find that multi-tasking is the only way to get anything accomplished, in our **minds** we should be focused on Jesus and the Holy Spirit guiding us. With all our focus we should be making a concerted effort to *understand* the scriptures, as well as apply them to our lives. We could all be using more of our brains, and because of our belief in a higher power we must remain broadminded to any direction or awareness we may receive through the Holy Spirit (John 3:12).

When we pray to the Lord, we are communicating through the Spirit, and sometimes just with our thoughts when we can't utter words aloud, so these are just as heart-felt. When we get urges, or sudden changes or inspirations of thought or conscious, we're listening to the Spirit within us communicating important messages. **Spirit and truth** is the invisible power of God through Jesus that all who accept Him into their hearts has, and the Holy Spirit guides us (John 4:24). Silent devotion of our thoughts to God, telling Him what is in our hearts in confidence, what causes us worry, and repenting for sinful or wicked thoughts doesn't require a single *physical* attribute. Going to church is fine, singing hymns of praise is excellent, but prayer, devotion, and true faith is experienced on a deeper level, unseen by human eyes. Do you feel Jesus alive in *your* heart?

John 4:23-24, ESV

23 Jesus said, "But the hour is coming, and is now here, when the true worshipers will worship the Father in spirit and truth, for the Father is seeking such people to worship him. 24 **God is spirit, and those who worship him must worship in spirit and truth.**"

May 18
Hypocrites

1 John 4:20, ESV

20 If anyone says, "I love God," and hates His brother, he is a liar; for he who does not love His brother whom he has seen cannot love God whom he has not seen.

Matthew 7:1-2, ESV

1 "Judge not, that you be not judged. 2 For with the judgment you pronounce you will be judged, and with the measure you use it will be measured to you."

To say someone is a hypocrite means they've intentionally deceived. As humans, we cannot know what's in the mind or heart of another, only God knows what is truly in our hearts (Proverbs 21:2). Therefore, we can never *really* know someone else's motive for their actions, behaviors and words. What's more, we are encouraged not to judge one another, that God has the final judgement on all of us. When we look at each other for comparison, competition, or judgement we're taking our eyes off of Christ. Forgiveness and understanding is how we should be looking at one another, after all, we're all sinners (Ecclesiastes 7:20), and we're all children of God (Galatians 3:26). We need to be mindful of *who* we are looking up to, or comparing ourselves to because all humans are imperfect and will disappoint. Only Jesus offers the perfect example we should seek to model.

As spiritual warriors on the quest to become our best selves by modeling Christ we can help one another through fellowship, guidance, support and praise. We all have different experiences in our faith journeys, and knowledge to offer another. We must beware that not all believers are *truly* following, and not everyone has a pure heart. Some people think they are more righteous than others because they have different lifestyles, because of their position or status, or because they think they're following Jesus more closely (1 Corinthians 2:11). Additionally, the devils trickery is meant to confuse us, distract us, and tempt us off our path to Jesus. We cannot trust our brothers and sisters in humankind as role models in our own lives because we are *all* imperfect, and considered sinners in the eyes of God. We can seek others for their spiritual guidance and knowledge, learning from one another's mistakes, but the only one we should be *modeling our life after is Christ*.

Luke 6:41-42, ESV

41 Why do you see the speck that is in your brother's eye, but do not notice the log that is in your own eye? 42 How can you say to your brother, 'Brother, let me take out the speck that is in your eye,' when you yourself do not see the log that is in your own eye? You hypocrite, first take the log out of your own eye, and then you will see clearly to take out the speck that is in your brother's eye.

May 19
Help: Never Too Proud

Psalm 46:1, ERV

1 God is our protection and source of strength. He is always ready to help us in times of trouble.

We all know someone stubborn, we might even *be* that stubborn person that comes to mind when we hear the word. Being stubborn, according to the free online dictionary, means to be 'dogged in their determination to **not** change their mind.' Some of us have even grown to love our shortcomings, even celebrating and bragging about being stubborn. In the bible, God chagrins stubborn people who remain inflexible, unteachable, and unaware of the truth of His word (Nehemiah 9:16). After all, how are we supposed to be humble in Christ when we're too stubborn to change, and how are we supposed to learn anything new in Christ when we're too stubborn to grow? We need to be more skeptical of what we value about ourselves, is it what the *world* celebrates, or what the **Lord** celebrates?

We make our own choices, so many that we don't always pray before we make them. When things work out we swell with pride from a plan well executed, patting ourselves on the back. Consequently, we complain to *God* when our lives don't turn out the way we've planned. No matter the issue, we try to solve our own problems, and usually bring on more challenges in the process. Stop. We didn't include God from the beginning, that's problem number one, so we shouldn't blame Him when our poor choices backfire. We may make our own choices, but who we're following is the key: are we following the Spirit, or are we following our own personal goals and desires? We cannot serve God and ourselves at the same time (1 John 2:15-17, Matthew 6:24). In the bible, we are taught to help others, but many of us are so completely self-absorbed we have difficulty focusing on anything, or anyone else. Bills, budgets, agendas and itineraries, schedules, meetings, deadlines, dates, numbers, lists, faces, and other worldly distractions win over our attention, and our priorities. Humans are social creatures, so it stands to reason that each of us will need help from another at some point in our lives. There is no room for selfish pride, vanity, ego or stubbornness when learning to be more holy. We shouldn't be too proud, or self-absorbed, to ask for help from others, or to give help without judgement or condemnation to others when we can (Galatians 6:2). Sharing our problems with our close friends or family would seem like a no-brainer, but no one on Earth can offer what Christ can. We should help one another when we can, but should be praying for *everyone*, and for help, guidance, support and direction in our own personal growth in Christ Jesus.

Psalm 34:4, ESV

4 I sought the Lord, and he answered me and delivered me from all my fears.

Hebrews 13:16, ERV

16 And don't forget to do good and to share what you have with others, because sacrifices like these are very pleasing to God.

May 20
Compassion

Psalm 78:38-39, ERV

38 But God was merciful. He forgave their sins and did not destroy them. Many times he held back His anger. He never let it get out of control. 39 He remembered that they were only people, like a wind that blows and then is gone.

Lamentations 3:22-23, ESV

22 The steadfast love of the Lord never ceases; His mercies never come to an end; 23 they are new every morning; great is your faithfulness.

Relationships come and go, family members, friends, colleagues and even enemies all change as our environment and life circumstances evolve. Sometimes people leave us because of something that went wrong, or sometimes because of new opportunities elsewhere, but change is inevitable in all of our worlds. We are all designed in God's image, and He seeks a closer relationship with each of us, and longs for us to come to Him in repentance. Being remorseful for the sins we've committed, and being earnest in not repeating them, show God our *motivation* to become more righteous. Learning from Jesus, and His disciples, about how to ready our spirits for God's divine company show's God our hearts are *truly* seeking Him.

Compassion put simply is empathy and concern for the suffering of another, or, love. God is love (1 John 4:8). God is just, though, and doesn't allow sins to be committed in His Holy kingdom. We can't get into Heaven if we don't believe that Jesus was the son of God, that He performed miracles here on Earth, and died for the sins of humanity as the perfect human sacrifice. To enter the kingdom of Heaven and into everlasting life we must prove our lives were lived as Holy as we could, repented regularly and wholeheartedly, and helped and loved our fellow man as much as we could. To some this may seem like too much to ask, and to others the path to righteousness is the toughest journey they'll ever embark on, but worth every painful step. When we think of compassion, we often think of the compassion God has for humanity, but what about humanities compassion for God?

Exodus 34:6-7, ESV

6 The Lord passed before him and proclaimed, "The Lord, the Lord, a God merciful and gracious, slow to anger, and abounding in steadfast love and faithfulness, 7 keeping steadfast love to the thousandth generation, forgiving iniquity and transgression and sin, but who will by no means clear the guilty, visiting the iniquity of the fathers on the children and the children's children, to the third and the fourth generation."

1 Timothy 2:4, ERV

4 God wants everyone to be saved and to fully understand the truth.

May 21
All Equal in the Eyes of God

Romans 3:22-23, ERV

22 God makes people right through their faith through Jesus Christ. He does this for all who believe in Christ. Everyone is the same, there is no difference, 23 for all have sinned and come short of the glory of God.

We all share an equal potential to become more righteous in the eyes of our God, from whom we *all* fall short. This is the good news, that we all have an equal opportunity to become better people. And, because it was a divine gift from God in the form of Jesus, it wasn't because of anything or anyone of this Earth. For this reason, no one should be considered in competition with anyone (Ephesians 2:8-10). It's almost impossible not to notice ourselves in relation to others, but we should be lifting one another up, helping one another, praying for others together, sharing uplifting stories together, and praising our Lord Jesus Christ together. Instead, the worst of humanity has created the world's anger, judgement, pride and conceit, which threatens our salvation. Gossip, jealously, lies and deceit, envy, financial security, and the search for respect are temptations meant to divide and classify people, and spreads hate and dissention instead of love and forgiveness. Christ calls us to love and forgive our enemies, not to compete with or gossip about them (Luke 6:27).

We are all God's creation, and Our Lord is the final judge. Since we are all sinful as a human race, not one of us will ever be fit to judge another, this is Christ's job according to the bible (John 5:22). When we pass judgement on another we are turning away from Christ, from the trust that He will judge everything fairly. Life isn't going to be fair, if it was grace and peace wouldn't be so sought after, and balance so elusive and out of our control. We shouldn't be seeking fairness, or even balance in our lives, if we are seeking Jesus, we should only be following where the Holy Spirit is leading us. This is how we show God our true devotion. Gossip might seem innocent, but it isn't, its deceit, judgement, and dissention. Vanity might seem innocent, until conceit, envy, lust and jealousy join along quietly. We can't treat one another differently, or with pre-conceived notions or stereotypes, or with contempt, or with impatience because we commit sins differently than another. Jesus calls us to treat one another with compassion, forgiveness and love. We should all check ourselves, brothers and sisters!

1 Corinthians 8:6, ERV

6 For us there is only one God, and he is our Father. All things came from him, and we live for him. And there is only one Lord, Jesus Christ. All things were made through him, and we also have life through him

May 22
Misfits

1 Corinthians 1:26-30, GW

26 Brothers and sisters, consider what you were when God called you to be Christ-followers. Not many of you were wise from a human point of view. You were not in powerful positions or in the upper social classes. 27 But God chose what the world considers nonsense to put wise people to shame. God chose what the world considers weak to put what is strong to shame. 28 God chose what the world considers ordinary and what it despises—what it considers to be nothing—in order to destroy what it considers to be something. 29 As a result, no one can brag in God's presence. 30 You are partners with Christ Jesus because of God. Jesus has become our wisdom sent from God, our approval, our holiness, and our ransom from sin.

Many of us have felt like the outcast, the 'odd one out' at a function or gathering. The bible makes it clear that no one is to be left out, and *all* are judged equally in the eyes of the Lord (Romans 2:6-10), but life doesn't always feel that way. Good people suffer, and life doesn't always seem fair, and God is directing it all (Jeremiah 49:12, Ecclesiastes 8:14, Isaiah 45:5-7). No matter what He throws at us, God wants us to turn to Him; with our problems, with our sins, with our repentance, and even with our doubt, and with our questions. We are surrounded by dark forces that want to pull us away from God's love, and this only highlights the fact that we belong to God, not the world. The bible explains that we were made in God's image (Genesis 1:27), but our souls fall short of the righteousness we need to be in God's presence (Exodus 33:20). Jesus healed the sick, and spent a great deal of time around sinners and outcasts of society, because that's where he was *needed* most.

When Moses was called by God to lead the Israelites out of slavery in Egypt, he wasn't confident in His appointment, pleaded with God to choose someone else (Exodus 4:10, 4:13), and had killed a man with His bare hands (Exodus 2:11-12). King David had an affair with His friend's wife, then had him killed to cover it up (2 Samuel 11:14-15, 2 Samuel 12:8-10). Jacob was deceitful, and lied to His father in order to get the blessing that belonged to His older brother (Genesis 27:18-19). God more than approved of each of these men (Exodus 33:17, Psalm 89:3-4, Genesis 35:10-13), and blessed them, showing that all sinners are capable of greatness, **through Him**.

It's fine if we don't feel like we fit in with the world around us, the bible tells us the world around us is controlled by the devil (1 John 5:19). Jesus calls the outcasts (Mark 2:15-17). So, rejoice, as a misfit of Christ's, fighting to maintain their righteousness among a world corrupted by sin and evil. Don't ever get too comfortable in the world, for we belong to Christ, and our eternal home is with Him in the kingdom of Heaven. It is through this hard-earned journey to righteousness in Jesus Christ that God is *able* to spend eternity with His humans who were once enslaved by the devil's deception. And, in the end good defeats evil. Sustain us, O Lord who remains steadfast forever. AMEN.

John 6:37, ESV

37 Jesus said, "All that the Father gives me will come to me, and whoever comes to me I will never cast out."

May 23
Putting Our Faith to Work

James 2:19-26, ESV

19 You believe that God is one; you do well. Even the demons believe—and shudder! 20 Do you want to be shown, you foolish person, that faith apart from works is useless? 21 Was not Abraham our father justified by works when he offered up His son Isaac on the altar? 22 You see that faith was active along with His works, and faith was completed by His works; 23 and the Scripture was fulfilled that says, "Abraham believed God, and it was counted to him as righteousness"—and he was called a friend of God. 24 You see that a person is justified by works and not by faith alone. 25 And in the same way was not also Rahab the prostitute justified by works when she received the messengers and sent them out by another way? 26 For as the body apart from the spirit is dead, so also faith apart from works is dead.

If we say we love someone, but we don't do anything to show them, do we really love them? Some people love the idea of being a child of God, but don't want to put the effort required into changing their hearts and minds. Faith isn't just the belief that the one, true God will sustain us, but actively showing Him that we love Him. The way we live our lives tells our creator how much we truly rely on Him. How often we pray, what we pray for, and the types of dreams we have tell the Lord if we're focused on serving Him, or ourselves. Pride in ourselves, our life accomplishments, and focus on ourselves keeps us from recognizing how we can help others. Some people need love, some people need clothing or food, some people need opportunities, but we all need kindness and affection. How many of us can actually say that we've done something to help the hungry, homeless, the prisoners, the widows and orphans, or the sick recently?

We all have responsibilities that keep our focus on the minutia of our daily lives, our schedules, our children, our jobs, and our friends and family. The beggar on the corner, the homeless crouched under a bridge, the employee that sits alone on their break that everyone else makes fun of, all need kindness they aren't currently getting. We all have more we can be giving. Not only should we be helping the less fortunate any way we can, we should be turning to the Lord with more of our hearts than we probably are. Are we confiding in our Savior all the desires, and anxieties, of our hearts? How often are we turning to the Lord for counsel before making a decision? Going to church occasionally, or even regularly, can't give us the amount of exposure to the Lord that is required for following Him closely in our lives. Our belief isn't worth much if we can't back it up with proof, action. We must ask ourselves, what have we really done to prove we love God, then actually make tangible changes to our lives to show Him.

John 14:21, ERV

21 Jesus said, "Those who really love me are the ones who not only know my commands but **also obey them**. My Father will love such people, and I will love them. I will make myself known to them."

May 24

Looking Inward to Move Forward

Psalm 66:17-18, ERV

17-18 I cried out to him for help, and I praised him. If I had been hiding sin in my heart, the Lord would not have listened to me.

Isaiah 59:2, NIV

2 But your iniquities have separated you from your God; your sins have hidden His face from you, so that he will not hear.

Our Lord, Jesus Christ, can see what's in our hearts even if we can't. We sinners are an imperfect and mortal group, limited in our scope of understanding and knowledge. When we sin we've turned away from God, and our repentance is required to restore our good graces with the Lord. The bible tells us that we can't hide from our sins, and we certainly can't hide our hearts from Jesus. Thinking inward, we must ask ourselves, 'How have *my* choices affected the situation?' Human beings will always be prone to sin (Genesis 6:5, Ecclesiastes 7:20), so we will always have something to repent for, as well as something to work on. The question is, are we? Many people have a difficult time accepting their imperfections, but we can't improve if we don't change, and we cannot change if we don't know where we're deficient. God sees what we cannot see, and we must trust this with the humility for which we were designed to initiate any change or improvement through Him. When we acknowledge our sins we can hand them over in prayer, and then we've learned something about ourselves that we can apply to our quest to be more righteous through Christ Jesus.

If God answered all of our prayers, He would be allowing us to guide our own lives with our limited, sinful souls in charge. We live to serve God (Luke 4:8), not because He needs us to (Acts 17:24-25), but because He wants our love and devotion, and this is how we love Him in return (John 14:15). We seek God because of His ultimate grace, righteousness, love, salvation, and all-knowing guidance, direction, and wisdom. We need God because we cannot be fairly judged by other humans, who also sin, are imperfect, and biased. We need God because we cannot be forgiven for our sins without Him. We seek the Lord our God because He is greater than us, and that's nothing to feel slighted by, because we *should* all fall short when compared to God. God knows what's best for us, especially when we don't, but accepting this fully can be difficult. We all make choices in our lives, and when they're unwholesome or not directed by God, we're expected to confess those sins and ask for forgiveness. What's more, we're supposed to try to live a more righteous life than our yesterday. When we do get gifts and mercies from God, it's His decision, and on His timeline, and it's always just. Our faith carries us through this. If we never let go of our stubborn hearts, and allow ourselves to feel guilt or shame for what we've done wrong according to God, we can't be forgiven, since we cannot repent for what we aren't sorry for. We must look inward to our hearts while keeping our eyes and faces affixed to the Lord.

1 John 3:19-20, ERV

19-20 That's how we know we belong to the way of truth. And when our hearts make us feel guilty, we can still have peace before God, because God is greater than our hearts. He knows everything.

May 25
Seeking Knowledge? Beware...

1 Corinthians 3:18-20, ERV

18 Don't fool yourselves. Whoever thinks they are wise in this world should become a fool. That's the only way they can be wise. 19 I say this because the wisdom of this world is foolishness to God. As the Scriptures say, "He catches those who think they are wise in their own clever traps." 20 The Scriptures also say, "The Lord knows the thoughts of the wise. He knows that their thoughts are worth nothing."

Proverbs 12:1, ICB/GNV

12 Anyone who loves learning accepts being corrected. But a person who hates being corrected is a fool.

Wisdom is cherished in this world, along with wealth, status, luxury comforts, power, and influence. Some people spend a lifetime accumulating wealth, status, property or other tangible luxuries, not thinking that their worldly comforts or acquisitions have anything to do with their spiritual salvation in Christ. The bible tells us that what we desire tells us how pure our hearts are (Proverbs 4:23 ESV, Matthew 5:8), and assures us that we cannot take anything with us when we die (1 Timothy 6:7). What good, then, does the achievements of this world serve us in the next? Your Pulitzer Prize, although an honor, won't secure you a seat in Heaven, nor your listing on the Fortune 500, or your SAG award, or your BRIT award, or your Grammy. Perhaps a more important question to ask ourselves is, 'How many non-believers did we bring to Jesus, how many of the hungry or underserved did we help, how many times did we actually repent and seek guidance from the Lord?

In the bible the only wisdom worth striving for is the kind that comes from our Lord and Savior (Proverbs 2:6), Jesus Christ, the kind that nourishes our souls. Wisdom the world offers may lead to greater financial success, or more influence over others, but takes us farther from God (James 4:4). Fear that the Lord knows our every thought, even the darkest ones we hide from ourselves sometimes, and that we will ultimately be judged before God is the bible's true version of wisdom. From this fear we should naturally want to *seek* Jesus to learn how to be known as righteous in the eyes of God. From this we should slowly achieve the understanding that this will be a lifetime endeavor where our faith will be tested, and we're expected to rely on God and not our *own* understanding to guide our every step in life (Proverbs 3:5-6). To say that achieving wisdom through the Lord is like the ultimate trust walk would be the ultimate understatement. Lord, we pray for deeper faith, and the strength of resolve to rely on that in all of our times of stress, oppression, pain, or anguish. In Jesus' name we pray, AMEN.

Proverbs 9:10, KJ21

10 The fear of the Lord is the beginning of wisdom, and the knowledge of the holy is understanding.

May 26
Forgiveness

Luke 6:37, ICB

37 "Don't judge other people, and you will not be judged. Don't accuse others of being guilty, and you will not be accused of being guilty. Forgive other people, and you will be forgiven."

Ephesians 4:31, ESV

31 Let all bitterness and wrath and anger and clamor and slander be put away from you, along with all malice.

Like trust, forgiveness is elusive internal process, and can be difficult to navigate. When we suffer what we think is a wrong or injustice at the hand of another, Christ calls us to forgive. As many times as we are wronged we are asked to forgive, as we would only hope for the same (Matthew 18:21-22). This can be difficult, as humans, we don't want to somehow condone a negative behavior or reduce its significance in our lives by forgiving. To forgive, we need to be in a place where we are no longer angry, and no longer bitter. We need to be able to accept that we are not the judge of another person's justice, and when we are angry we're passing judgement (James 4:11-12). When we forgive, we're acknowledging that someone else has sinned against us, but also that we ourselves are not free from sin, and shouldn't think of ourselves as somehow less of a sinner. If we are unable to forgive, we need to pray.

Buried under years of pain and regret, we can ignore the wrongs that have been done to us. Shame, guilt, remorse, pride, hate, and revenge are all extensions to wickedness, but the blood of Christ can wash us clean. We are called to forgive because Christ forgave us all with His crucifixion, and we forgive because *we* won't be forgiven if we don't forgive. We forgive because it is what is *righteous*, and *that* is what we should truly be seeking. People who are able to forgive others acknowledge that God is the final judge of a person's intensions, and understands that we all commit sins differently. Deep in our hearts, if we seek to be more righteous, we must forgive everyone who has hurt or wronged us. On our journeys to being more Christ-like, we accept our humble position, and trust in the Lord's fairness above our own. How do you feel about Christ forgiving those who have wronged you?

Matthew 6:15, ESV

15 but if you do not forgive others their trespasses, neither will your Father forgive your trespasses.

May 27
Jesus

John 3:16, ESV

16 For God so loved the world, that he gave His only Son, that whoever believes in him should not perish but have eternal life.

John 10:30, ESV

30 Jesus said, "I and the Father are one."

The power and majesty of Jesus surpasses anything we, as humans, can accomplish here on Earth, and we shouldn't be offended by that. Our job, as Christ-followers, is to try to emulate the qualities of Jesus into our lives, no matter how difficult that sounds (Luke 9:23). We are taught that Jesus died for our sins, and that because He died all of us can live forever, if we believe and repent. We follow Christ because He calls us to, and as a result we are constantly repenting, studying the Word of God, cleansing the wickedness from our hearts. We are made right with God through the blood of Jesus, and this means putting His commands into effect in our lives.

God loves mankind so much that he sent His only son to die, so that all of us could enter His kingdom despite our imperfections (John 3:16). In this act our spirits are made wholesome in the eyes of God, by the blood of Jesus, and we're allowed to enter the kingdom of Heaven for everlasting rapture (Titus 3:4-6). In the very example of love, God and Jesus did this for us, and He only asks for our love and faith in return. We love Him by our faith, by adhering to the plan God has for our lives, by repeated repentance, in our devotion to His teachings, and in our lives as we try to live by His example. Ask yourself, are you living the way Jesus would want?

John 14:15, ERV

15 "If you love me, you will do what I command."

Romans 5:19-21, ICB

19 One man disobeyed God, and many became sinners. But in the same way, one man obeyed God, and many will be made right. 20 The law came to make people have more sin. But when people had more sin, God gave them more of His grace. 21 Sin once used death to rule us. But God gave people more of His grace so that grace could rule by making people right with him. And this brings life forever through Jesus Christ our Lord.

May 28
Knowing Jesus=Following

John 8:42-47, ESV

42 Jesus said to them, "If God were really your Father, you would love me. I came from God, and now I am here. I did not come by my own authority. God sent me. 43 You don't understand the things I say, because you cannot accept my teaching. 44 Your father is the devil. You belong to him. You want to do what he wants. He was a murderer from the beginning. He was always against the truth. There is no truth in him. He is like the lies he tells. Yes, the devil is a liar. He is the father of lies. 45 I am telling you the truth, and that's why you don't believe me. 46 Can any of you prove that I am guilty of sin? If I tell the truth, why don't you believe me? 47 Whoever belongs to God accepts what he says. But you don't accept what God says, because you don't belong to God."

We believe in God, we believe in Christ, we believe that Christ died for our sins, that's terrific. Are we *following* Him, though? In the bible, Jesus says that if you "love me, you'll keep my commandments," but when was the last time we took a good look at the commandments? Some people who believe have never read the bible, but just listen to someone else tell them about it one or two verses, or a story at a time. If we don't know what the whole bible says in its entirety, we aren't getting the whole picture. Each verse, each word, each story and parable is another vital piece of a larger story, and they can be taken out of context more than we realize. We must be careful not to twist the verses to mean something other than what it was intended for (2 Peter 1:19-20). Loving each other should rid the world of hate, but hate is still all around us. Forgiving one another should rid the world of strife and deceit, but strife and deceit are still rampant.

Not everyone is following Christ, clearly. Regarding the ones that do not believe, some people will never be reached (2 Corinthians 4:4). To those that believe, we must never tire of learning more, understanding more deeply. We must guard against becoming too comfortable in our knowledge, because we could spend a lifetime trying to understand the bible's many layers and never grasp the many, multiple layers of complexity (Ecclesiastes 3:11). Some people are extremely proud of their knowledge and wisdom, but God allows us to know what we know (Proverbs 2:6), as everything comes from above (James 1:17, Psalm 24:1). We must all remember that Jesus forgave *all* people, even those of the people who cause us pain. If we accept God, we accept all He stands for, and we are working hard to incorporate the Word of God into our life. If we aren't trying to incorporate Jesus' teachings into our everyday lives, the bible tells us that we are not of God. Believing is great, but just believing isn't following, and not following is the equivalent to not believing.

John 14:15, ESV

15 "If you love me, you will keep my commandments."

May 29
Sin-Rotting from Within

Mark 7:20-23, GW

20 Jesus continued, "It's what comes out of a person that makes him unclean. 21 Evil thoughts, sexual sins, stealing, murder, 22 adultery, greed, wickedness, cheating, shameless lust, envy, cursing, arrogance, and foolishness come from within a person. 23 **All these evils come from within** and make a person unclean."

Genesis 6:5, ESV

5 The Lord saw that the wickedness of man was great in the earth, and that every intention of the thoughts of His heart was only evil **continually**.

Sins, we all commit them. Some people look down on others, classify them, categorize and label people based on the sins they commit. Jesus calls us to love, forgive, and even pray for our enemies (Matthew 5:44), so anything that separates, and divides people is wrong, not loving, and judgmental. In the above scripture from the book of Mark, Jesus explains that sin comes from *within* a person. For this reason, Jesus calls on us to change our hearts and minds (John 3:3-7, James 4:8), echoing what God had been urging people to do in the old testament (Ezekiel 11:19, 18:31, Jeremiah 24:7).

When we ignore our sins, we're ignoring our covenant with God, and passing up our opportunity to learn and grow closer to God by improving our weaknesses though Him. In the bible, greed is equivalent to worshiping wealth, and pride would be worshiping ourselves over God (Luke 12:15). Just thinking about someone else in a lustful way is the same as having committed the act, also, according to the bible (Matthew 5:28). Sin is a choice we make to give into our temptations, compulsions, and corrupts us from within. It is from our secret, wicked, unwholesome desires deep inside our hearts that establishes the foundation for the poor choices that leads us to sin. Some of us desire to fit in and be recognized as appreciated, and relevant. Other people are driven by the desire to obtain wealth, power, and influence over others. Even people who want to live as comfortable, and hassle-free a life as possible, only want to submit to their own goals and desires. Sinful from nature, humanity started off on the wrong foot by disobeying God's rules in the Garden of Eden, cursing our very natures from that point on (Gen. 3). Many people would like to think that because they aren't included in God's rules, commands, and subsequent judgement because they aren't sure if they believe entirely. Other people suppose that because they're going to be forgiven, that they don't need to worry about their sins. Humans are very good at hiding from their sins (Jeremiah 17:9 ERV), and thus highlights our **need** for our Lord and Savior in Christ Jesus. If we truly desire to follow Jesus, we'll use our sins to learn how to *follow Him closer*, not to condemn or hinder the progress of righteousness at work in our lives.

Colossians 3:5-6, GW

5 Therefore, put to death whatever is worldly in you: your sexual sin, perversion, passion, lust, and greed (which is the same thing as worshiping wealth). 6 It is because of these sins that God's anger comes on those who refuse to obey him.

May 30
Living Righteously

Romans 1:29-31, ERV

29 They are filled with every kind of sin, evil, greed, and hatred. They are full of jealousy, murder, fighting, lying, and thinking the worst things about each other. They gossip 30 and say evil things about each other. They hate God. They are rude, proud, and brag about themselves. They invent ways of doing evil. They don't obey their parents, 31 they are foolish, they don't keep their promises, and they show no kindness or mercy to others.

Has anyone out there ever been jealous of another person's home, social stature, wealth, fame or following? Perhaps we have found ourselves envious of another in the past, or told a lie, or never apologized after an argument with someone, or gossiped, but figured there was no harm. Wrong. Jealousy and envy are coveting our neighbor, and evil, according to God's commandments in the bible. Lying and gossip is corruption and deceit, and fighting doesn't beget love and forgiveness. Holiness is complicated, and is something we must work to obtain, achieve, and maintain over the course of our lives. The engine that drives our thoughts, actions, behaviors and words stems from what motivates us, our deep thoughts and desires. Jesus teaches that we are made perfect in Him (Hebrews 10:14), and that God provides all that we'll need through-out our lives (Philippians 4:19). Wanting more, wanting what we don't have, wanting something different than what we have is greedy, selfish, and disrespectful to what God has already provided, the scripture echoes.

Just as some people might be patting themselves on the back for not being a mur-derer or idolater, arrogance and pride are just as wicked (James 2:10). Our sins are our undoing, and no matter what we've done, we are all equally as guilty in the eyes of God (Romans 3:23). Jesus calls on us to love one another as he has loves us, but not all of us are trying to live by His example. Pride, bragging, wealth, lust and lack of kindness are also evil according to the Lord. Sinning is too easy for us to overlook, since we are inherently corrupt. We are surrounded by other corrupt humans who aren't repenting, or trying to make wholesome choices, their evil ways make it especially difficult to follow in Jesus' holy footsteps. Following Jesus' narrow path of holiness is the toughest thing we'll ever endeavor to do, but completely worth all the effort.

1 Timothy 4:12, ERV

12 You are young, but don't let anyone treat you as if you are not important. Be an example to show the believers how they should live. Show them by what you say, by the way you live, by your love, by your faith, and by your pure life.

May 31
Who Will I Be, if Not Myself?

Ephesians 1:4, ERV

4 In Christ, he chose us before the world was made. He chose us in love to be His holy people — people who could stand before him without any fault.

Isaiah 55:9, ERV

9 Just as the heavens are higher than the earth, so my ways are higher than your ways, and my thoughts are higher than your thoughts.

Jesus Christ knew who we would ultimately become before we were even conceived (Isaiah 44:24). As humans, we are limited in our knowledge and understanding of God's work, power and vision. It can be difficult for some to accept that God has so much control over our lives, our pride and arrogance prevents us from understanding everything clearly. That's where our faith comes in, we trust must be in the Lord, the He hears our prayers. Also, we trust His Holy Spirit at work inside us, guiding our directions, choices, and thoughts. If we're *letting* the Lord guide our lives so closely, where does free will come in? We may feel like we need to know that we have a say in who we are becoming through Christ's good work. We all have a choice, we can choose eternal life through Jesus Christ, or we can turn away from God and make our own choices (Deuteronomy 30:19-20). The good news is that we can always change our minds and repent (Zechariah 1:3, Isaiah 55:7).

Each of us have a different story to tell, a different history, and consequently, different pain. Our pain, our past experiences, shape our boundaries or what we will and will not tolerate from others. We also have different skills, talents and gifts, and all of these things make for a uniquely made warrior for Christ (1 Peter 4:10). What's more, what Jesus can do far exceeds what we can do with our limited power and knowledge. Our journeys are unique to us, our individual pains like stepping stones building us up slowly to the people we will ultimately become in Christ. We need to trust His process.

Jesus is the son of the most ultimate power in the universe. Jesus knows us by our names, knows our hearts, and knows what we're going to do before we do it. Jesus loves us, died for us, and wants to help us reach our potential as human beings through His teachings. Jesus has gifts made especially for us to use in our work to spread His word, and wants to teach us to use these gifts. As you allow Him to mold you, He will bring out the very best in you (Jeremiah 18:6). So, you'll still be you, only better. Why would you *want* to interfere with that?

Isaiah 64:8, ESV

8 But now, O Lord, you are our Father; we are the clay, and you are our potter; we are all the work of your hand.

June 1
Take Up Your Cross and Follow Jesus

James 2:19-20, ESV

19 You believe that there is only one God; you do well. Even the demons believe this—and shudder!
20 Do you want to be shown, you foolish person, that faith apart from works is useless?

John 14:21, ERV

21 Jesus said, "Those who really love me are the ones who not only know my commands **but also obey them**. My Father will love such people, and I will love them. I will make myself known to them."

Many of us grew up with the impression that as long as we believed in God, and in Jesus, and generically tried to be a 'good person' we would be assured a place in Heaven. Popular culture and tradition, different church leader's interpretations, and society at large help to form ideas that can turn into expectations. In the bible, we are given Jesus' own words, which came with specific direction, we just need to take the time to understand it. Jesus commands His disciples to make disciples of all the nations, to forgive their enemies, pray for them even, and to love one another as He loved them (Matthew 5:44, 28:19). Jesus also calls on us to take up our cross and follow Him, to keep His commandments, and to repent (John 14:15, Acts 3:19).

Jesus calls us to stop thinking about our own goals and desires in exchange for the holy example He calls us to (Mark 8:34-37). A more righteous life directed by modesty, humility, self-control, forgiveness, service and love for one another will look, and feel, completely different than one guided by false confidence, deceit, competition, greed, selfishness, wickedness and sin. We may not be forced to change careers, or home towns, by following Christ more closely, but we *may* end up with different friends, hobbies, language, attitudes and hearts. Conforming to God's idea for our lives here on Earth may not seem fair to some, as people long to be the rulers of their own lives, and hesitate to place full trust in God. How can we love God if we don't fully trust Him? Anything that clouds our view of God's grace, generosity, power, and love, or prevents us from fully understanding, or accepting Him is the work of the devil (Matthew 13:19). If we truly love our God, our Lord and creator, we are expected to obey His commands for us, including cleaning up our dirty, sinful hearts and minds, down to our language and lifestyle.

Matthew 16:24-25, ERV

24 Then Jesus said to His followers, "If any of you want to be my follower, you must stop thinking about yourself and what you want. You must be willing to carry the cross that is given to you for following me. 25 Any of you who try to save the life you have will lose it. But you who give up your life for me will find true life."

June 2
Wisdom = Fear?

Job 28:28, ESV

28 And he said to man, "Behold, the fear of the Lord, that is wisdom, and to turn away from evil is understanding.'"

Proverbs 1:7, ESV

7 The fear of the Lord is the beginning of knowledge; fools despise wisdom and instruction.

The bible says that 'fear of the Lord is the beginning of wisdom,' but what exactly does that mean? Wisdom is acquiring, and knowing how to best utilize and interpret the knowledge we obtain. Some of us were blessed with more wisdom than others, some are blessed with kinder hearts, others may be blessed with the gift of healing, teaching, or leadership. We all have different gifts, and all gifts are from God, but how we use the tools and gifts we were given is our choice. The Lord wants us to know that nothing on Earth compares to the kingdom of Heaven (Rev. 21:1-5), nor can anything escape God's final judgement and divine justice (Jerimiah 23: 23-24). God wants us to use our wisdom to protect our souls from the evil in the world, so we can remain righteous for His kingdom and eternal life with Him. Integrity means doing the right thing, even when no one is looking, and this holds its weight because we know that God see's all.

If we are *afraid* of the Lord, we are *humbled* by His divine love and power, and *submit* to Him in faith. This, in turn, leads to our virtual integrity and peace through Christ Jesus. The bible also explains that foolish people despise wisdom and correction, and choose not to abide by God's rules or direction (Proverbs 1:27-31). We always have a choice, and the Lord is hoping that we will learn to love Him enough to trust in *His love* for us. By living a more righteous lifestyle, caring for others by our good works, forgiving our enemies, and spreading the good news about Jesus we show God that we love Him, and are faithful to Him. As we are all works in progress, we must repent our sins to God through Jesus, and ask for forgiveness before we can obtain righteousness. Daily action toward attitude, and priority reform in our lives is necessary to be Holy in the eyes of God, and we should *want* these improvements. Jesus died for our eternal salvation, He should be worth the effort.

Exodus 20:20, ESV

20 Moses said to the people, "Do not fear, for God has come to test you, that the fear of him may be before you, that you may not sin."

Matthew 10:28, ERV

28 "Don't be afraid of people. They can kill the body, but they cannot kill the soul. The only one you should fear is God, **the one who can send the body and the soul to be destroyed in hell.**"

June 3
Suffering, Enduring

1 Peter 4:12-3,18-19, ICB

12 My friends, do not be surprised at the painful things you are now suffering. These things are testing your faith. So do not think that something strange is happening to you. 13 But you should be happy that you are sharing in Christ's sufferings. You will be happy and full of joy when Christ comes again in glory. 18 "It is very hard for a good person to be saved. Then the wicked person and the sinner will surely be lost!"19 So then those who suffer as God wants them to should trust their souls to him. God is the One who made them, and they can trust him. So they should continue to do what is right.

We notice all kinds of things about one another; our posture, our teeth, our laugh, our punctuality, our attitudes and demeanor. When we make assumptions, opinions, and judgements on other people we're placing ourselves above someone, or something, else, as if we didn't have any faults, or make any mistakes. We must remember that only the Lord has the authority to judge us. Forming judgements on one another has become so natural to us, we have also formed our own opinions on justice, fairness, right and wrong, and appropriate discipline. We might be the lawmakers for our society, but the law we are all called to live by is the law set by God, and that law says we serve Him (Matthew 22:37). The feeling of injustice, or outrage, stems from the feeling of discrimination, something feels *unfair* about the pain we're experiencing. In order to deem something *unfair* we must first have judged and come to a conclusion on said pain. And, here we go, judging again. Our judgements are misplaced, for only God has the power to judge. When we think of our pain as unfair or unjust, we want to blame someone, and silently expect God to swiftly rescue us out of the situation. The point is, *everyone* is suffering, and we aren't capable of judging what is just and unjust. We must ask ourselves; are we trying to understand, repent, and learn from Jesus how to make better choices in our lives, or are we complaining, judging, scheming, harboring anger and resentment? We aren't being measured by the type, degree, or amount of pain and suffering we experience, but how we **deal** with that pain and suffering. God is watching.

God knows we are going to suffer, and is waiting for us to return to Him for comfort. God wants us to love, depend on, obey, and rely on Him. We can choose to accept His love and forgiveness or not, it's our choice, but we will all experience hardships and strife in this life regardless. As followers of Christ we are called to *emulate* Christ, and He was 'the suffering servant.' Christ was beaten, whipped, and murdered for us, **He** suffered. So the point isn't really if, or even how much pain we experience, but how we deal with it that defines us, *and* our faith.

1 Peter 2:19-20, ESV

19 For this is a gracious thing, when, mindful of God, one endures sorrows while suffering unjustly. 20 For what credit is it if, when you sin and are beaten for it, you endure? But if when you do good and suffer for it you endure, this is a gracious thing in the sight of God.

June 4
Having Diligence in Our Faith

James 3:10-11, NIV

10 Out of the same mouth come praise and cursing. My brothers and sisters, this should not be. 11 Can both fresh water and salt water flow from the same spring?

1 Corinthians 15:58, ESV

58 Therefore, my beloved brothers, be steadfast, immovable, always abounding in the work of the Lord, knowing that **in the Lord your labor is not in vain**.

Life is exhausting. Schedules, meetings, deadlines, relationships, goals, family, all combine daily to produce a cornucopia of responsibilities for us to deal with. We share our lives, our world, with other humans who aren't necessarily as interested in modeling their lives and attitudes after Jesus. Temptations, irritations, obstacles, and not praying for help in time when our grace is challenged can even cause the most faithful followers to stumble on their path with Jesus (James 3:2). We need to use Jesus' love and light like a lantern, keeping us warm and lighting our path so we don't lose our way. Hey, we're not *designed* to walk this life path alone, or without any help from God (Acts 17:24-27). God loves us and wants to cleanse us of our wickedness so we can dwell among Him in the kingdom of Heaven, and the devil wants to separate God from what He loves most, and we're caught in the balance. It should be no wonder, then, to learn that our lives will be tumultuous and confusing (John 16:33, 1 John 5:19).

As followers of the one true Savior, we must work diligently to keep our small, sterile, holy pocket of the world righteous, and yet interesting and engaging. Moral decency is difficult in our current environment, but not impossible, that's our test of faith and burden to bear, and we must bear it with dignity in Christ Jesus. We must keep trying to find new ways to celebrate Jesus, to partake in fellowship with other Christ-followers trying to keep strong in their faith. Time management can be difficult, and elusive in our worlds, but the way we devote our time reflects our priorities (Ephesians 5:16). We should all be making time each day to devote directly to God, reading the bible, daily prayer, and for reflection. Fellowship, praise, and worship are all joyful ways of celebrating our amazing Lord, but solemn, somber, contrite moments of devotion and study are vital to growing in our knowledge, and faith, in Christ Jesus. Not only does this nurture our devotion to the Lord, but grounds our faith as we spread the good news to others through our words and example, and this pleases the Lord.

Galatians 6:9, ESV

9 And let us not grow weary of doing good, for in due season we will reap, if we do not give up.

Proverbs 13:4, ESV

4 The soul of the sluggard craves and gets nothing, while **the soul of the diligent is richly supplied**.

June 5
Only Ourselves to Blame

Romans 5:12, ERV

12 Sin came into the world because of what one man did. And with sin came death. So this is why all people must die—because all people have sinned.

God first created the world, and then placed humans on it in His image, and it was good, the bible recounts (Genesis 1:24-31). When humans began making choices, though, *they invited evil* into the world with their desire to seize autonomy for themselves instead of trusting God's rules (Genesis 3:1-7). So, it's us, humans, that have invited the sin into our world, from the choices we've made through History. In the bible, the wage for sin is death, and that's harsh knowing we are all inherently evil by nature. No one wants to think of themselves as evil, but there is good news, we always have a choice (Deuteronomy 30:19).

From the way we speak and treat others, to what motivates our goals and desires, we can exchange our evil natures for a more righteous one, through Jesus (1 Corinthians 1:30, 2 Corinthians 5:21). It is through following the teachings and example of Jesus Christ that we learn how to reject evil for love, and choose humility and generosity for greed and arrogance, and contempt for forgiveness. We are given this gift from God, not because of anything humans could ever do, but because of God's great love for us. We are given this choice, to believe in, and to follow Jesus, for eternal life with God. So our choices are; repent, follow and believe in Jesus and have eternal life with God, or not believe and follow our own selfish desires, not repent, and just die without eternal life with God or worse! Choose wisely, brothers and sisters.

2 John 9, ESV

9 Everyone who goes on ahead and does not abide in the teaching of Christ, does not have God. Whoever abides in the teaching has both the Father and the Son.

1 John 5:19, ESV

19 We know that we are from God, and the whole world lies in the power of the evil one.

Ephesians 2:8, ESV

8 For by grace you have been saved through faith. And this is not your own doing; it is the gift of God.

June 6
Choices

Hebrews 10:26, ERV

26 If we decide to continue sinning after we have learned the truth, then there is no other sacrifice that will take away sins.

Jeremiah 8:6, ESV

6 "I have paid attention and listened, but they have not spoken rightly; no man relents of his evil, saying, 'What have I done?' Everyone turns to his own course, like a horse plunging headlong into battle."

God wants a closer relationship with us, which indicates a commitment to certain behavior and a more righteous lifestyle than we're currently comfortable with. As humans, we have a choice to engage in a closer relationship with God or not (Revelation 3:20). Just because we believe, doesn't mean we're ready to change our lives for Him, and some people will never move past that place. If you really love someone, assimilating to their lifestyle and habits should be seamless, cohesive, and mutually beneficial. By believing in Jesus' crucifixion and resurrection, and by repentance, God gives us chance after chance at everlasting life with Him in Heaven (Matthew 3:8, James 4:8). If we choose to live our lives our own way, ignoring God's will for us, we're telling Jesus, "No thanks, man, I've got this."

All humans carry the potential to sin, and we all commit moral crimes. Most us would agree that crimes, even moral ones, should be dealt with judiciously. But, if all humans are sinful, how will we be able to render proper judgement? The answer is, we can't, and this is why we need Jesus. Following Jesus means sacrificing our worldly comforts sometimes, it means forgiving those who hurt or wrong us, it means loving our enemies instead of judging and condemning them. We will have to change some things about our lives when following Jesus, brought on by the changes in our attitudes, choices, and priorities. If we don't love God enough to try and be better people, than He will let us walk away. Forced love isn't love, and God is love (1 John 4:16). We *can* make our own choices, our own priorities, and reset our morals to suit our own convictions, but just because we can, doesn't mean we should. We can't possibly get through our lives, let alone get through the gates of Heaven by navigating our lives all by our limited selves. We don't have to follow God's rules, but we must live with the consequences of the choices we make. We cannot hide from ourselves, or God. Choose wisely.

Romans 1:21, ESV

21 For although they knew God, they did not honor him as God or give thanks to him, but they became futile in their thinking, and their foolish hearts were darkened.

June 7
Take Care of Your Body

1 Corinthians 6: 19-20, ESV

19 Or do you not know that your body is a temple of the Holy Spirit within you, whom you have from God? You are not your own, 20 for you were bought with a price. So glorify God in your body.

Ephesians 5:29, ERV

29 because no one ever hates His own body, but feeds and takes care of it. And that is what Christ does for the church.

Too tall, too short, too fat, too thin, our bodies don't always look the way we'd like them to. We aren't random beings, wandering aimlessly among one another, baffled and mystified at our surroundings, we are intentional and relevant children of a supreme God. Some people are a little more aimless than others, but all of us are important to our Heavenly Father. Actually, we're all just spiritual beings traveling in different shaped human forms, made from God's likeness (Genesis 1:27). We're only restricted by our bodies limitations, of which there are many. Life on earth is a gift, and our spiritual after-life in Heaven has been paid for by Christ's death on the cross, but our bodies are temporary. We only have our human bodies while we're here on Earth, and how we maintain them is up to us, and spare parts are hard to find.

Some people put bumper stickers on their cars, or keep a lot of knick-knacks on their dashboard or rear windows. We spend a great deal of time in our cars commuting to and from work and running errands, so much so that some of us take a lot of effort into personalizing them. Cars are as individual as the humans driving them. Whether the interiors of our cars are cluttered or kept in pristine condition, we must keep them in good running condition if we want to continue to travel in them. Our bodies are much the same in that we need to properly maintain them to keep them operating efficiently. Eating too much, or exercising too little can create health issues for our bodies, and indicates an unholy lack of self-control. We are called to love ourselves, as well as others, with respect, modesty and self-control (Proverbs 31:30, 2 Timothy 1:7, Leviticus 19:18). How we treat ourselves reflects our love, and respect, for God, and the body He's loaned us (Ecclesiastes 12:7). Food, water, rest and moderate activity are physical necessities, just as love and counsel from Jesus Christ is a necessity for our souls salvation. We should treat our bodies, and our souls, with respect, and honor for the price at which they were obtained.

1 Peter 3:3-4, GW

3 Wives must not let their beauty be something external. Beauty doesn't come from hairstyles, gold jewelry, or clothes. 4 Rather, beauty is something internal that can't be destroyed. Beauty expresses itself in a gentle and quiet attitude which God considers precious.

June 8
Soul and Body

Galatians 6:8, ESV

8 For the one who sows to His own flesh will from the flesh reap corruption, but the one who sows to the Spirit will from the Spirit reap eternal life.

Matthew 26:41, ESV

41 "Watch and pray that you may not enter into temptation. The spirit indeed is willing, but the flesh is weak."

Many of us have at least considered the possibility that who we are isn't resigned to just the physical form we look at in the mirror, that deep inside us somewhere, is a soul. Much like a fingerprint, our soul makes us individuals, and houses our spirit, our heart, what motivates and drives our intentions, goals and desires. Not giving it much more thought, many of us allow ourselves to become entrenched in our worldly lives, schedules, friends, social engagements, deadlines, and relationships. Whew! Our worlds, our lives, keep us all pretty busy one way or another, even though we all live different lives. We all seek something different, some seek recognition and respect, others seek financial or emotional security, others seek success and wealth. Many of us have goals that include retirement, modest travel, and some social pleasure activities with family or friends, perhaps. How many of us give any thought to our souls?

Our spirits need nourishment opposite of what our bodies desire (Galatians 5:17), and due to our narrow minded human thinking, our spiritual health often gets neglected. Our bodies long for elaborate petting and grooming, sensual seduction, gluttonous culinary delights, and adoration of other humans. These are all sinful, as they represent greed, lust, gluttony, envy and pride. Our spirits will thrive on the truth of Jesus Christ, which is service to others, love and forgiveness, modesty, humility, and penance. Modesty and humility is the complete opposite of pride and envy. Above most of our understanding is a larger battle being waged between good and evil, God wants us to return to Him while the devil wants to tempt us away to spite God. It might be difficult to nourish a righteous spirit in a sinful world, and the opportunity for strife is ripe, but where there is strife, there is an opportunity to help our fellow brothers and sisters. Gracious Lord, we plead with you to fill our spirits with holy nourishment that can only come from you, fill us up today with Your grace, merciful Jesus. Amen.

Jeremiah 3:15, NASB

15 (God said) "Then I will give you shepherds with hearts like Mine, who will feed you knowledge and understanding."

John 6:63, ESV

63 (Jesus said) "It is the Spirit who gives life; the flesh is no help at all. The words that I have spoken to you are spirit and life."

June 9
Scripture

2 Timothy 3:16-17, CJB

16 All Scripture is God-breathed and is valuable for teaching the truth, convicting of sin, correcting faults and training in right living; 17 thus anyone who belongs to God may be fully equipped for every good work.

More than three thousand years have passed since the bible was first composed, and many people think that the writing is either obsolete or question its authenticity. Written by an unknown group of authors by divine inspiration, the bible offers us a priceless gift of knowledge, and is widely accepted to contain the word of God, our Heavenly Father, and creator. Discounting the bible is a mistake, for there is no expiration date on God's love, or His Word (Exodus 15:18). As humans, we seek and derive knowledge from many different sources, and the bible was given to us to help us understand our ongoing relationship with God. Offering not only God's promise to provide eternal, spiritual sanctuary for His people, the bible teaches us God's law and commandments, chronicles the life and ministry of Jesus, shows us what living righteously by Him should look like, and warns of punishment for disobeying. When the world we live in creates more of a hinderance to our righteous salvation than we're prepared for, it can certainly be easier to question the bible's authenticity or relevance instead of following it's teachings.

If we're only seeking God when it's convenient for us, or not at all, we aren't really understanding how our relationships with God is supposed to work. All of humanity has entered a covenant with God, as He is our creator, and no one is immune or exempt because of their beliefs (Revelation 21:8, John 8:24). Our only hope of *true* salvation from our sinful natures is being *true* to our covenant with the one true God. As followers of Christ constantly seeking to grow in our faith, we should be conscientiously studying the Bible and comparing its teachings to today's religious organizations and fellowships, and more importantly, to our own lives. We can never hope to overcome the deceptions that are so prevalent in our world if we don't align our hearts with God's. If we never read the bible in its entirety, we don't really know the full story. What's more, if we don't know what God's word really says, we won't be able to recognize when we're being led falsely.

Deuteronomy 11:18-19, CEV

18 Memorize these laws and think about them. Write down copies and tie them to your wrists and your foreheads to help you obey them. 19 Teach them to your children. Talk about them all the time—whether you're at home or walking along the road or going to bed at night, or getting up in the morning.

June 10
God's Law, Believe It or Not?

Romans 2:11-13, ICB

11 For God judges all people in the same way. 12 People who have God's law and those who have never heard of the law are all the same when they sin. Those who do not have the law and are sinners will be lost. And, in the same way, people who have the law and are sinners will be judged by the law. 13 Hearing the law does not make people right with God. The law makes people right with God only if they obey what the law says.

The bible not only explains how we are supposed to live, but also what happens if we disobey God, and what happens after we die. After we die, your soul will either be lost forever, or be judged for passage into Heaven (Matthew 10:28, Revelation 20:15, 21:8) . When we are judged, the bible tells us that we will get what we deserve and earn based on God's verdict, which is fair and just. The bible also tells us that whether you believe the word of God or not, we will all go through the process as it is written, no human is exempt based on their beliefs. We are given a choice here on Earth, believe and repent or be lost forever.

We *can* choose to follow our own path in life, making our own choices and neglecting to follow Christ's example. But, while we're here, we will still have troubles and tribulations throughout our life like all other humans, and if we aren't abiding in Christ, we'll be without His divine help, peace, direction, salvation and gifts (2 Thessalonians 1:8-9, Psalm 28:5). Hey, we weren't meant to get through this life without Jesus' salvation (Matthew 19:26), and when we try we are usually disappointed. Cut off and lost from God sounds pretty awful, especially when we can only get forgiveness, salvation and everlasting happiness by following Christ. The person who represents Christ is always more gentle, less prone to anger, gives and forgives readily. The person who doesn't represent Christ tends to be lazy or ignorant in their faith, petty, compares themselves to others, passes judgement, and is deceitful. Think about which sounds more attractive to God? 'The grass withers, the flower fades, but the word of our God will stand forever,' (Isaiah 40:8).

Romans 11:19-22, ICB

19 You will say, "Branches were broken off so that I could be joined to their tree." 20 That is true. But those branches were broken off **because they did not believe**. And you continue to be part of the tree only because you believe. Do not be proud, but be afraid. 21 If God did not let the natural branches of that tree stay, then he will not let you stay if you don't believe.22 So you see that God is kind, but he can also be very strict. God punishes those who stop following him. But God is kind to you if you continue following in His kindness. If you do not continue following him, you will be cut off from the tree.

June 11
Actions Speak Louder Than Words

1 John 3:18, ESV

18 Little children, let us not love in word or talk but **in deed and in truth**.

1 Timothy 6: 18, ESV

18 They are to do good, to be rich in good **works**, to be generous and ready to share.

Have you ever heard someone tell you, show me don't tell me? We can promise many things with our words, but only our actions can prove our words to be true. Deep in our heart we are either motivated by God's selfless love, or our own selfish greed and pride. Are we in a rush to get somewhere, stern-faced and driven, or compassionate and welcoming? Do we shove people out of the way to get the last spot in the elevator, honk our horns impatiently in our cars, say short, curt or unkind words to others, or roll our eyes when we're behind someone with a larger load at the checkout? We are often so wrapped up in our own selves that we are oblivious to the way we are behaving, we're just trying to get somewhere, or get something accomplished. Our actions are an outward expression of our inner thoughts and attitudes (Matthew 6:21).

Whatever we do, we represent the Lord. As Christ-followers, we should be setting the example of 'Christ like behavior,' both in what we say to people, and how we treat them. We can be very hurtful to others with our words, gestures and facial expressions. We are all sinners (1 John 1:8), surrounded by temptation (Matthew 26:41), and must be strong in our conviction to be more righteous. We should stop and give thanks for all the help and guidance the Lord provides, as well as the salvation we're offered. Words are powerful, and once spoken cannot be taken back. Words penetrate into people's minds, transforming our thoughts. Actions speak louder than words. Ask yourself, what have *you* done to show the Lord your love Him lately?

James 1:22, ESV

22 But be doers of the word, and not hearers only, deceiving yourselves.

Colossians 3:17, ESV

17 And whatever you do, in word or deed, do everything in the name of the Lord Jesus, giving thanks to God the Father through him.

June 12
Just What *Is* a Parable?

Matthew 13:18-23, ERV

18 (Jesus said) "So listen to the meaning of that story about the farmer: 19 What about the seed that fell by the path? That is like the people who hear the teaching about God's kingdom but do not understand it. The Evil One comes and takes away what was planted in their hearts. 20 And what about the seed that fell on rocky ground? That is like the people who hear the teaching and quickly and gladly accept it. 21 But they do not let the teaching go deep into their lives. They keep it only a short time. As soon as trouble or persecution comes because of the teaching they accepted, they give up. 22 And what about the seed that fell among the thorny weeds? That is like the people who hear the teaching but let worries about this life and love for money stop it from growing. So it does not produce a crop in their lives. 23 But what about the seed that fell on the good ground? That is like the people who hear the teaching and understand it. They grow and produce a good crop, sometimes 100 times more, sometimes 60 times more, and sometimes 30 times more."

A parable is a story used to illustrate a moral lesson, and the bible is full of them. Morals are the clear understanding of spiritual right and wrong, or what is ethically just in the eyes of God. The ten commandments, by example, illustrates what God considers a moral code intended for us to live by (Exodus 20:1-17). Some people have a difficult time with faith in a God they cannot see, cannot feel, or simply don't agree, or submitting to any righteous lifestyle changes through Jesus. Still others who hear the teaching don't understand it because their lust to continue living their sinful way of life has blinded them to fully understanding and accepting the truth about Jesus. Still others have no problem accepting the truth of Jesus but let their worries and anxieties about this life, or love for money, stop it from growing. These people don't rely on God to provide all they need without seeking more, or fixing their problems on their own without God. As soon as trouble or persecution comes because of the teaching they accepted, people weak in their faith give up, not having a deep enough trust of the everlasting life promised by Jesus. Acceptance in Jesus requires a humble, blind trust, a deep faith, and persistence through tribulations.

Stories based on moral lessons are difficult, as people may interpret them differently. Jesus taught many parables, but all having to do with loving one another, service to one another, forgiveness, patience, acceptance, righteousness and love. (Matthew 13:34-35) Humbling ourselves to admitting we'll never know everything, being thankful to God for all we have in our lives, and submitting to lessons and tests of faith in order to build our faith and endurance is what following Jesus is all about. God's purification process isn't going to be easy, or painless, but promises to be worth our every effort. It is in this way that we honor His teachings, and show Him we love Him in return. This is what righteous devotion looks like, brothers and sisters. Praise the Lord! AMEN.

June 13
Enlightenment

Ecclesiastes 5:1b, ERV

51b Fools often do bad things, and they don't even know it.

Psalm 119:130, ERV

130 **As people understand your word, it brings light to their lives.** Your word makes even simple people wise.

Not everyone wants more of God in their lives, unfortunately, many people just don't understand their relationship with God. Our relationship with God started on page one of the book of Genesis, not on the day of our birth. We are all part of God's creation, His humans, and we all follow a pre-set course that God has planned for our lives-like it or not (Psalm 33:11, Proverbs 16:9). When we do evil, sinful things we are turned away from God, the bible explains (Isaiah 59:2). Only humility and repentance turn our faces and hearts back to God, where we can receive His comfort and forgiveness for our prayers. When we are truly focused on God, and wanting to live better lives through Him, God knows we are truly devoted. As devoted followers who read the word of God, we can gain insight into the teachings, parables and stories which are paramount to understanding how God wants us to live, and how to ward off sin and wickedness. Reading the bible is a prerequisite for understanding the current spiritual battle vying for our souls (Ephesians 6:12), or God's sincere desire for us **all** to return to Him (Joel 2:13, Malachi 3:7, Hosea 14:1, Nehemiah 1:9, Zechariah 1:3), and how this affects our daily lives today. Deep, layered, emotional, and complex, the bible is our 'instruction manual' in navigating our personal relationship with God. God's word hopes to purify our hearts evident by changed behaviors, actions, choices, and words, and into souls suitable for His Holy Kingdom.

Many people wrestle internally with the question, "Should I trust God, or just try and do the best I can on my own?" Trust is difficult for many, especially if we don't know all of the facts. If one is to make an informed decision, one must be learned in all the facts, so read the bible! Only from reading the bible will one learn the true nature of God, versus the true nature of man, and the results might be surprising to some. The closer we get to God, the more we will be able to understand the complex meaning deep within His word. All knowledge and understanding we have is given to us by God, (Proverbs 2:6) Only, **God chooses who He wishes to be close to Him, while the only choice we have is how devoted to Him we're going to be** (John 6:44). Not everyone will believe, not everyone will understand, and not everyone who believes and understands will follow. If we approach God with skepticism, or with contempt, anger, or resentment in our hearts, we aren't approaching in the right state of mind. If a person's heart is evil and focused on themselves and worldly acquisitions, they are unable to learn and understand God's word (Isaiah 26:10).

Isaiah 35:8, ERV

8 There will be a road, this highway will be called "The Holy Road." Evil people will not be allowed to walk on that road. Only good people will walk there. People who don't follow God and His wise teachings will not walk on it.

June 14

Wisdom

1 Corinthians 2:6-12, ERV

6 We teach wisdom to people who are mature, but the wisdom we teach is not from this world. It is not the wisdom of the rulers of this world, who are losing their power. 7 But we speak God's secret wisdom that has been hidden from everyone until now. God planned this wisdom for our glory. He planned it before the world began. 8 None of the rulers of this world understood this wisdom. If they had understood it, they would not have killed our great and glorious Lord on a cross. 9 But as the Scriptures say, "No one has ever seen, no one has ever heard, no one has ever imagined what God has prepared for those who love him." 10 But God has shown us these things through the Spirit.

Scholars are revered in this world as the ultimate authorities on science and technology, aerospace, meteorology, physics, theology, and medicine as examples. We all must earn livings to provide for our, and our family's needs, and education often fosters more success than people who are less educated. Often wealthier, or more prominent classes of society have access to the best education, and most often, more opportunities. In our current world, as was the same historically, the more successful the person the more power and influence they would have over their environment. This power struggle involving the different socioeconomic classes has been going on since the beginning of mankind. Over time, how society viewed, or classified, an individual was more valued and sought after than a person's spirit, or how holy they were (Romans 12:2).

The bible teaches us that the Holy Spirit lives inside of those who love God and are faithful in prayer and repentance to Jesus Christ (John 14:15-17). It is in the Holy Spirit that we gain comfort, strength, direction, and how we grow in our knowledge of Christ Jesus. The more we learn, apply to our lives, and humble ourselves in prayers of thanks to our Lord, the more we will be able to see with the Holy Spirit. When prayer replaces our natural instincts to make our own choices, or to be defensive and hide our sins, or deal with daily problems and issues on our own, we become more knowledgeable in the Holy Spirit. As our hearts become more meek under the power of Christ Jesus, holy behavior will be easily discernable where once that understanding was elusive. This is the kind of wisdom that teaches us how to live more righteously, what good works are, what loving our neighbor really means, and how to incorporate this knowledge into our lives. When we adapt our lives, purging our old, sinful behavior we begin to see the difference between righteous and unrighteous behavior more clearly.

James 3:13, ESV

13 Who is wise and understanding among you? By His good conduct let him show His works in the meekness of wisdom.

June 15
The Lord's Will

1 Timothy 2:2-4, ERV

2 You should pray for rulers and for all who have authority. Pray for these leaders so that we can live quiet and peaceful lives — lives full of devotion to God and respect for him. 3 this is good and pleases God our Savior. 4 God wants everyone to be saved and to fully understand the truth.

We may not always think our world leaders have our best interests in mind some of the times, after all, passing judgement is easy for the arrogant. We are all balancing temptation with powerful emotions and difficult decisions, and not all of us are trying to live our best lives in the process. Compassion and empathy for our friends and loved ones comes rather naturally, while positive attitudes toward our enemies or strangers can be quite elusive. If we profess to love God, but don't bother to learn what He wants from us we aren't being faithful to our love for Him. Loving God means abiding by Him, praising Him, learning, and repenting. We will do this over and over in our lives due to our propensity for committing sins (Matthew 3:8). Evil is everywhere in the form of lies, deceit, anger and wrath, vengeance, violence, envy, and lust. Wicked people don't give a hang about God or Jesus, and plow through life leaving a trail of pain in their wake. Others believe they are following God simply perfectly, and couldn't possibly have anything to repent about while they pass judgement on the sins of others. True righteous people *want* to know their sins so they can repent for them, learn from them, and show God their faith and love for Him.

God wants to rescue all of us from the evil rampant in this world, but we must choose this as it requires our cooperation. With our repentance comes our promise to avoid similar sinful choices in the future, and to follow the teachings of Jesus Christ. To follow Christ means we are willing to change our lives, to follow closely the guidance of the Holy Spirit. Every choice we make either pulls us farther from the Lord, or closer to Him. Every word, every action from us reveals our heart to a God who is watching all the time (Proverbs 15:3). As Christ's followers, we must be wise to the opportunities to make more Holy choices with our words, works, behaviors and actions toward others.

Ephesians 5:15-20, ERV

15 So be very careful how you live. Live wisely, not like fools. 16 I mean that you should use every opportunity you have for doing good, because these are evil times. 17 Therefore do not be foolish, but understand what the will of the Lord is. 18 Don't be drunk with wine, which will ruin your life, but be filled with the Spirit. 19 Encourage each other with psalms, hymns, and spiritual songs. Sing and make music in your hearts to the Lord. 20 Always give thanks to God the Father for everything in the name of our Lord Jesus Christ.

June 16
Resting in God's Good Work

John 16:33, ESV

33 "I have said these things to you, that in me you may have peace. In the world you will have tribulation. But take heart; I have overcome the world."

Romans 2:5b-7, ERV/ESV

5b On that day everyone will see how right God is to judge people. 6 He will render to each one **according to his works**: 7 Some people live for God's glory, for honor, and for life that cannot be destroyed. They live for those things by always continuing to do good. God will give eternal life to them.

We can all feel good after a hard day's work, after completing a list of errands, or finally accomplishing a long sought-after goal. A sense of achievement gives us peace of mind as humans. The world can offer many pleasant distractions with our mortal triumphs, but true peace can only come from Christ's love. If we continue to search for peace in the world we will always be broken-hearted, disappointed, and unfulfilled. Christ overcame the world and died for our sins, this He did so we wouldn't have to. He did all the work, all we have to do is follow Him. This might be a lot easier said than done, actually. We are called to live righteous lives, as God is holy, but the world we live in is the devil's playground. Sin and wickedness await us at every turn in the form of hate, fighting, obsession, losing our tempers, being competitive with one another, opposition, conflict, selfishness, group rivalry and 'cliques,' jealousy and envy, drunkenness, and partying (Galatians 5:19-21). From our pride, arrogance, greed and lust these sins form, and they challenge us all.

If being a good Christ-follower was *easy* everyone would be one, and we know that certainly isn't the case. Consider it an honor to toil over scripture in the attempt to understand God's love and wishes for us, not all of God's children do. Take pride in the act of praying more in order to communicate with Christ more deeply, not everyone cares enough to change any circumstance of their busy life for their Savior. Rest assured that you are being a good steward of your faith when you try to understand the wishes of the Holy Spirit in your life. At the end of the day you showed up and tried a little harder than yesterday, and will be rewarded with an honest effort worthy of rest and eternal sanctuary with the Lord. No matter how bad a day we have, *nothing* can take that away from us. Rest in your good works through Christ Jesus, and praise God for all you're given.

Hebrews 4: 10-11, ERV

10 God rested after he finished His work. So everyone who enters God's place of rest will also have rest from their own work just as God did. 11 So let us try as hard as we can to enter God's place of rest. We must try hard so that none of us will be lost by following the example of those who refused to obey God.

June 17
Full Court Press

1 Peter 1:15-16, ERV

15 Be holy in everything you do, just as God is holy. He is the one who chose you. 16 In the Scriptures God says, "Be holy, because I am holy."

2 Corinthians 10:5, ERV

5 We tear down every proud idea that raises itself against the knowledge of God. We also capture every thought and make it give up and obey Christ.

Many of us have relationships where we only see that person occasionally, like weekly or monthly. These people are friends, maybe even family, but our infrequency of visits indicate they aren't in our immediate family circle of people we would consider the most important to us. Some believers aren't attending church weekly, or praying daily, but still defend that they're loving God, and are an active part of His eternal family. But are they, really? God doesn't just want our praise, He wants us to live like Jesus did, to love and treat one another with love, to be more righteous. So again, are we, really? In the bible, we are called to be Holy, by God Himself, because He is holy, and in everything we do. No easy feat for a sinful humankind.

The bible calls us to make our thoughts give up and obey Christ, but a lot of people have problems with words like, 'give up,' and 'obey.' Unsure of their place in their relationship with God, some people say they love God but don't think there is anything wrong with the way they live their life. *All* humanity is sinful and disobedient to God, He tells us Himself in the book of Genesis (Gen. 6:5), explaining that humanity is sinful **by nature**. We are also told, as if we should even need to be told, that God is our creator and final judge (2 Corinthians 5:10). We were designed to worship and need Him, we were made to obey Him. People who have trouble accepting His role as supreme and Sovereign God (Isaiah 45:18), our Lord and Savior in Christ (John 10:30), and Holy Spirit (John 15:26) aren't really being honest with themselves as far as the depth of their belief. If we love God, we want to obey God, we shouldn't be opposed to changing our lifestyles, attitudes, behaviors and choices for Him. Not only that, but if we truly were faithful to God, and putting Him first in our lives like He's told us, we would be including Him more often in our life than just at church or when we're in need. All God, all day, with Jesus in our hearts and driven by the Holy Spirit, this is the way to true salvation. Praise be to God through Jesus Christ, forever. Amen.

1 John 5:3, ERV

3 Loving God means obeying His commands. And God's commands are not too hard for us.

Ephesians 5:1-2, ESV

1 Therefore be imitators of God, as beloved children. 2 And walk in love, as Christ loved us and gave himself up for us, a fragrant offering and sacrifice to God.

June 18
Persistence

Colossians 1:11-12, ICB

11 God will strengthen you with His own great power. And you will not give up when troubles come, but you will be patient. 12 Then you will joyfully give thanks to the Father. He has made you able to have all that he has prepared for His people who live in the light.

Living a righteous lifestyle reveals itself in stages as we grow in our walk with Jesus. Just when we learn one concept, another challenge presents itself, and we often find ourselves re-evaluating our hearts, and lifestyles, once again. Life ebbs and flows, as do our sinful natures, and some days will be better than others. As humans, as followers of Christ, we must not grow weary of trying to live a more holy and righteous life, for the forces of evil and darkness are just waiting for another believer to walk away from God (Ephesians 6:11). All of Christ's followers are sinners, trying to live better by Him while each facing different trials, tests of faith, spiritual endurance, and devotion.

If we want to be part of a more wholesome habitat we must look to ourselves to see how we've, not only contributed to a sinful, evil world, but how we can change it for the better through our example. Following Jesus' example in our own lives is sure to highlight the areas we need to focus, and repent on. Growing in righteousness is like carving a beautiful sculpture, some pieces will have to be cut off to reveal the final product. Trusting God's work in us through Jesus' example and the Holy Spirit's communication assistance, we can accomplish anything (Philippians 4:13). God's love for us surpasses anything we humans can offer to one another, and He's proved it through His death on the cross. Resting in Him is our sanctuary, our struggle strengthens our faith as well as our character, which is pleasing to God.

James 1:2-4, ESV

2 Count it all joy, my brothers and sisters, when you meet trials of various kinds, 3 for you know that the testing of your faith produces steadfastness. 4 And let steadfastness have its full effect, that you may be perfect and complete, lacking in nothing.

Micah 7:8, ICB

8 Enemy, don't laugh at me. I have fallen, but I will get up again. I sit in the shadow of trouble now. But the Lord will be a light for me.

June 19

Study Jesus Any Way We Can, No Church, No Problem!

1 Corinthians 3:16, ERV

16 You should know that you yourselves are God's temple. God's Spirit lives in you.

Matthew 18:20, ESV

20 "For where two or three are gathered in my name, there am I among them."

Jesus' disciples didn't always have a temple or synagogue to pray in, but never went a day without praying, several times. Prayer is our connection to Jesus, through the Holy Spirit and the silence of our intentional thoughts, or the sound of our quiet voice speaking to the unseen Heavenly hosts. Through prayer we can tell Jesus of our anxieties and concerns, repent for poor or unholy choices we've made, and ask and receive guidance for decisions in our lives. If we are following Christ, we are praying throughout the day, and not just praying in a church intermittently or on holy occasions. We are told in the bible, and by not only the disciples but Jesus Himself to pray regularly (Matthew 6:6, 1 Thessalonians 5:17-18).

When we accept Jesus into our hearts we are given the Holy Spirit to help us understand how to grow in Christ (Acts 2:38). Prayer, learning and understanding the scripture, sharing and learning with others in Christ is not only rewarding, but another way we build one another up in Christ. This is a great example of loving one another, by fellowship, devotionals, bible study groups, communing with others who are also trying to grow in the Holy Spirit. Jesus wasn't afraid to break down barriers, met in people's homes, on the road, and wherever people were gathered. After all, the spirit of the Lord lives inside of us, and we carry that with us wherever we go, keeping us company though we may be alone. Although celebrating God in the church is an awesome and uplifting way to praise Jesus with other followers of Christ, we don't *have* to be in a church to pray to Jesus. Reach out to the Lord at the height of your need, and not just as an afterthought, or when it's convenient. Pray without shame, brothers and sisters.

Matthew 6:9-13, ESV

9 "Pray then like this: Our Father in heaven, hallowed be your name. 10 Your kingdom come, your will be done, on earth as it is in heaven. 11 Give us this day our daily bread, 12 and forgive us our debts, as we also have forgiven our debtors. 13 And lead us not into temptation, but deliver us from evil."

June 20
From Death to Life, God's Grace

Ephesians 2:1-3, ERV

1 In the past you were spiritually dead because of your sins and the things you did against God. 2 Yes, in the past your lives were full of those sins. You lived the way the world lives, following the ruler of the evil powers that are above the earth. That same spirit is now working in those who refuse to obey God. 3 In the past all of us lived like that, trying to please our sinful selves. We did all the things our bodies and minds wanted. Like everyone else in the world, we deserved to suffer God's anger just because of the way we were.

Some people have a difficult time with the many rules that being righteous demands, and think that having to avoid sinful temptations and worldly pleasures is asking too much. Perhaps some people are uncomfortable with limits set on them by someone else, and in their arrogance don't think they need God on a daily basis. Sin is in our thoughts, on our lips and tongues, in our ignoring the homeless, in not caring about other brothers or sisters in need, sin is lust in any form, and it's in our gossiping and judgement of others. Not lusting after people, being kind to our enemies, and not wishing to be proud, respected or wealthy is torturous for people who are comfortable living in darkness (John 3:19). Loving and praying for our enemies is difficult, watching the innocent suffer is excruciating to our souls, knowing we'll always be sinners is humbling, and though it all we trust in the one, Almighty God. We all stumble (James 3:2). There is a battle that has been going on since the beginning of time between the forces of good and evil, humanity is the pawn, and many of us are oblivious to this occurring all around us (Ephesians 6:12). Those who turn a blind eye to God and fail to incorporate the teachings of Jesus into their own lives and turn away from sinful choices are doomed to suffer God's justice.

The bible was written over two thousand years ago, but the teachings of Jesus are moral in nature and are intended to last forever (1 Peter 1:25). Giving us the ability to repent, Jesus' divine sacrifice allows for us to turn our salvation around from the sinful evil that holds us captive to the righteous grace set by His example. We obey God because this world is only temporary digs for us, where we spend eternity is up to us. We always have a choice to follow and obey God or to go it on our own, thankfully, He always gives us the choice to come back to Him.

Ephesians 2:4-7, ESV

4 But God, being rich in mercy, because of the great love with which he loved us, 5 even when we were dead in our trespasses, made us alive together with Christ—by grace you have been saved— 6 and raised us up with him and seated us with him in the heavenly places in Christ Jesus, 7 so that in the coming ages he might show the immeasurable riches of His grace in kindness toward us in Christ Jesus.

June 21
Self-Focused

Proverbs 3:6, ESV

6 In all your ways acknowledge him, and he will make straight your paths.

Philippians 2:3-7, CEV

3 Don't be jealous or proud, but be humble and consider others more important than yourselves. 4 Care about them as much as you care about yourselves 5 and think the same way that Christ Jesus thought: 6 Christ was truly God. But he did not try to remain equal with God. 7 Instead he gave up everything and became a slave, when he became like one of us.

Humans are selfish creatures, and we don't like to admit it. Too many of our thoughts and behaviors are self-focused, and we should all be concentrating more on the Lord. For example, when we're focused on what others may be thinking about us, or what *we* may be thinking about *them*, we can't be focused on the Lord. Comparing our lives with others feels natural, but often leads to assumptions, stereotyping, and unbalanced expectations. Also, when we're focused on checking every task off of our daily itineraries, trying to squeeze one more productive minute out of our days, we are more focused on what *we* can accomplish than what the Lord can accomplish *through* us. Additionally, when we're just trying to mind our own business, we can be oblivious to the needs of others around us. Likewise, when we obsess over the sins others have committed, but aren't doing anything to change our own behaviors, we're being arrogant. If we become outraged after something has gone wrong in our lives, this too, is arrogance.

We are proud, proud of our hard work, proud of our educations, our families, our jobs, our possessions, and our social status. Pride in ourselves ignores the presence, power, and control the Lord has in our lives. Pride, therefore, chokes our ability to be humble before the Lord. God came to us in the form of a man, renounced His position as the creator to become one of us, the creation, in order to die and become the Holy Spirit to live inside of each of us. God's love and sacrifice for His humanity was done through grace, humility, and righteous holiness, and sets an example of the kind of humility that's expected of us. With Christ's help, repeated prayer and repentance, trials and testing, we too can learn to be humble. Accepting, and being truly thankful for our stations in life, helping, building up, and forgiving one another takes grace, genuine love for one another, and humility. **Let us again refocus on what the Lord wants from us, instead of what we want from the Lord.**

James 3:14-15, CEV

14 But if your heart is full of bitter jealousy and selfishness, don't brag or lie to cover up the truth. 15 This kind of wisdom doesn't come from above. It is earthly and selfish and comes from the devil himself.

June 22

A Deeper Look

Psalm 119:59, ESV

59 When I think on my ways, I turn my feet to your testimonies.

Lamentations 3:40, CEB

40 We must search and examine our ways; we must return to the Lord.

When we come back to God in repentance, we are vowing to not repeat the sins we've just confessed. Many of us repeat the same sins despite this, but why is that? We all sin, we all need to ask for forgiveness, and we all need to change our ways to prevent making the same mistakes. Some of us are committing the same mistakes because our hearts and minds haven't changed, and we are still courting the same sinful, deviant behavior. We pray for deliverance, but suffer from our own stubbornness, ignorance and unwillingness to change. In order to be more righteous we all have to stop **wanting** the wrong things. If we search our hearts we'll find what motivates us (Proverbs 4:23), whether we're seeking acceptance, balance, justice, forgiveness, or love, for instance.

Searching our hearts more often is necessary in learning what sins we're committing, need to repent for, and avoid. The bible shows us early on (Genesis 6:5) that sin lives inside of all humans, and causes us to do and say the sinful things that we succumb to. When something goes wrong in our lives, when we suffer pain or conflict, we must ask ourselves what *our* role was, and how we might have contributed to the outcome, or situation. Revisiting what are our intensions behind a decision were, or why we handled a particular situation like we did, is critical information in determining what *motivates* us. Are we really serving others, or ourselves? This knowledge can help us to know what we need to pray for, and where to seek additional knowledge, or support. In order to change our hearts, we mustn't be afraid to uncover the ugly truths deep inside of us. After all, anything is possible through Christ Jesus. Gracious Lord, please help us to truly seek purer hearts. Praise and glory be to the Lord forever. AMEN!

1 John 3:19-20, ERV

19-20 That's how we know we belong to the way of truth. And when our hearts make us feel guilty, we can still have peace before God, because God is greater than our hearts. He knows everything.

June 23
Modesty

Proverbs 31:30, GW

30 Charm is deceptive, and beauty evaporates, but a woman who has the **fear of the Lord should be praised.**

Proverbs 11:22, ESV

22 Like a gold ring in a pig's snout is a beautiful woman without **discretion.**

Many people insist on leaving the house completely dressed for the day, a coordinated outfit, hair styled and looking well-cultivated. Some people don't seem to care, neither about themselves **nor** others, and still others want *everyone* to know their thoughts and opinions. Humans are social, and many people become fixated on how they appear to others, as well as the way others appear. We form judgements on people, subconsciously, as we observe the way they walk, talk, order food, and treat other people. Many of us want to appear attractive to others, relevant, and interesting. For many people, outside appearance, style, charm and attitude are very important. Some people are attracted to loud personalities, displays of toughness and pride, designer or well-styled clothing, and fancy cars. We want other people to see us as relevant, with something to offer, we want to be accepted and loved. Although the personal clothing styles and social norms have certainly changed from bible times, the reasons why people pursue outer appearance hasn't changed.

If God wants us all to come to Him, and repent, so He can forgive us and welcome back into His kingdom, why do we need the approval of other humans? (Galatians 1:10) The worldly acceptance, and superficial successes the world can offer us is superfluous compared to the eternal salvation God offers our spirits after we've passed from this *temporary* world. We must remember that true followers of Christ are loving and forgiving to everyone, even enemies (Matthew 5:44), so acceptance shouldn't have to be sought after. God provides all we need, we only need to seek Him and trust, so needing more of anything isn't necessary. Whenever we pursue something from our own desires, and not as a result of the Holy Spirit guiding us, we're giving in to sin. *Pray for it, or repent because of it, but seek God through the life of Jesus.* Live in modesty, brother and sisters, not in 'more.'

Isaiah 3:16, GW

16 The Lord adds, "The women of Zion are arrogant. They walk with their noses in the air, making seductive glances, taking short little steps, jingling the ankle bracelets on their feet."

1 John 2:16, GW

16 Not everything that the world offers—physical gratification, greed, and extravagant lifestyles—comes from the Father. It comes from the world.

June 24
Confidence, from the Lord?

Psalm 118:8, GW

8 It is better to **depend on the Lord** than to trust mortals.

Jeremiah 17:7, GW

7 Blessed is the person who trusts the Lord. **The Lord will be His confidence.**

Most of us are confident that the sun will rise every morning and set every evening. Confidence is a slippery quality that seems to come and go in us all, and appears stronger in some than others. We can get assurances from the world around us in the way of employer reviews, comments from friends, and love from family that let us know we're important, relevant, and appreciated. Sometimes our self-confidence waxes and wanes based on the type of day we're having, or how others treat, or receive us. Coming from many different sources depending on the person, often our external environment is used in place of God for the reassurances that feed our confidence.

True confidence can come from only one source. God provides for those who call on Him, the bible assures us, and those who have a strong faith rely on this when in need (Psalm 37:39-40). Praying to God with all of our anxieties, worries, concerns, and needs is how we reassure God that we believe in His love, and have faith that He will deliver us. Turning to God instead of relying totally on our own ideas, or our friend's comfort, or a professional, to guide and comfort us is how we show God He is first in our lives. God may work on His own timeline, but He never forsakes someone who calls upon Him in faith. Friends, family, and even professionals can offer much needed support in our lives, but God is the only one we should allow to guide our lives. Sometimes what we pray for isn't in our best interest at the time, and sometimes God's way of saying no is not to say anything. We humans can have a difficult time understanding God, but we are called to place all of our faith and trust in our creator (Proverbs 3:5-6). We will have what we need, when we need it, because God's love never changes. When we let go of our worldly reassurances and have patience in God's timing, we will never be without what *God* thinks we need. Confidence in the world is vanity and wickedness, but confidence in God is faith.

2 Corinthians 3:5, ESV

5 Not that we are sufficient in ourselves to claim anything as coming from us, but our sufficiency is from God,

Hebrews 4:16, CSB

16 Therefore, let us approach the throne of grace with confidence, so that we may receive mercy and find grace to help us in time of need.

June 25
Phonies

1 So do you think that you can judge those other people? You are wrong. You too are guilty of sin. **You judge them, but you do the same things they do.** So when you judge them, you are really condemning yourself. 2 God judges all who do such things, and we know His judgment is right.

James 1:22, ERV

22 Do what God's teaching says; don't just listen and do nothing. When you only sit and listen, you are fooling yourselves.

Some people are over-zealous with their religion, silently judging and stereotyping other sinners because they corrupt their lives with sin differently than they do. Others say they believe in God but still think they can do and say anything they want because they'll be forgiven. Humanity reflects many different levels of faithfulness, and unfortunately, many different interpretations of the bible's knowledge. True love for our neighbor, as Jesus calls us to, is more about forgiveness and love than about judgement and contempt. If our brother or sister is sinning, we can help them to realize this by bringing it to their attention, but that's where the help should end. It is up to the heart of the individual to repent, and seek redemption for their sins. In the same respect, we can't go on sinning when we know it's wrong just because we know we'll be forgiven.

If we judge other people while sinning ourselves, we are hypocrites. Only God has the power to pass final judgement, as He is the only one who sees all. Our moral conscience is dynamic and ever-changing, influenced by not only our faith, but dark forces trying to keep us from a deeper faith, friends and family who are sinning all around us, and our own desires tempting us. This is why we suffer. Everyone's journey to righteousness is different, and there is a fine line between helping a fellow sinner and judging, ostracizing, and condemning them for it. Righteousness is difficult, and humans will always be fallible, but a more Holy heart is what we should **all** be striving for. Righteousness will flow more clearly when we replace our greedy, sinful, selfish hearts with more humble, forgiving, loving hearts. *We* might be able to ignore the contempt, or the jealousy, or the deceit, or the lust in our hearts but *God* knows what's in our hearts (Luke 16:15). When we seek a purer heart, our actions and behaviors will stem from that purer heart, and our actions, words and behaviors will reflect that. Keep the devotion flowing, the faith strong, and praise the Lord, brothers and sisters. AMEN.

Mark 7:6, ESV

6 And he said to them, "Well did Isaiah prophesy of you hypocrites, as it is written, "'This people honors me with their lips, but their heart is far from me"

June 26
Don't Compare Journeys

Galatians 6:4-5, GW

4 Each of you must examine your own actions. Then you can be proud of your own accomplishments without comparing yourself to others. 5 Assume your own responsibility.

Psalm 37:7, ESV

7 Be still before the Lord and wait patiently for him; fret not yourself over the one who prospers in His way, over the man who carries out evil devices!

We are all in different places on our faith journey's with Christ. Some people are avid bible readers, understanding the scriptures and making the best use of their lives by them, some people are active in their church communities, others do a great deal of community service, and still others are struggling to understand how it all fits together in their lives. Different backgrounds, hometowns, habits, skills, education levels, fears, and goals make us as unique as fingerprints to one another. As perpetual sinners with different skill sets, beliefs, and levels of faith, we humans have just enough in common to become easily tempted to compare ourselves to one another, but different enough to become miserable and confused in doing so.

Living among each other, working together, humans are observant and emotional, and absorb a great deal from one another. Jesus calls us to love one another, forgive one another, and to support our fellow brothers and sisters. Only God knows what is in an individual's heart, we cannot know one another's true heart, and cannot accurately assume anything about each other. To compare, or judge, or engage in jealous rivalry is wrong, it isn't loving toward our neighbor, it isn't humble, but selfish, greedy and vain. Christ is the one we are all striving to emulate, no human can offer that divine inspiration and spiritual leadership. Instead of classifying, ostracizing, judging and condemning each other, Christ calls for us to build one another up in support and love. Our reassurance, our relevance, our inspiration, and our hope should all be coming from our Savior in Christ Jesus, not *anything* the world has created. When we take our eyes from the Lord, we lose our focus, and are succumbing to the wickedness around us.

Philippians 2:3, ESV

3 Do nothing from selfish ambition or conceit, but in humility count others more significant than yourselves.

James 3:16, ESV

16 For where jealousy and selfish ambition exist, there will be disorder and every vile practice.

June 27
Prayer, a Deeper Look

Luke 18:7, ERV

7 God's people shout to him night and day, and he will always give them what is right. He will not be slow to answer them.

1 Thessalonians 5:17, ESV

17 Pray without ceasing.

Romans 8:27, ERV/NIV

27 God already knows our deepest thoughts. And he understands what the Spirit is saying, because the Spirit intercedes for God's people in accordance with the will of God.

Even though God knows our deepest thoughts, and knows what is in our hearts He still desires us to come to Him in prayer. From a parental point of view: Even if we know which child broke the lamp, we still want them to come to us to confess. God wants to know we are being completely honest with Him, trust Him, and are looking to Him for guidance in our lives. God wants us to know we're safe with His judgement, and protected by His love, but requires us to know and understand our place in our relationship with Him. (Revelation 4:11) As our creator, God has a plan for our lives if we'll just comply, serve Him, and stop chasing after what we want for ourselves. Many people find this too difficult, and with too many unknowns. Most people have trouble relinquishing any control they *think* they have to anyone else, while others may not be aware that we should be. We can't be sure what God's plan for us is, and what if He plans to make changes we don't like?

When we profess our belief in Jesus, and repent for our sins, we are given the Holy Spirit, which dwells inside of us. If we pray, and listen closely to our 'inner voice,' we'll hear the Holy Spirit working inside of us, guiding and comforting us. The Holy Spirit knows what's in our hearts, even if we don't. If we allow someone else to pray for us, we're denying God that intimate connection that He is seeking, for no one can accurately convey what's in another's heart. If praying through a religious official was sufficient on its own, there wouldn't have been a need to send Jesus down to earth to offer the Holy Spirit to each individual. Prayer is helpful to communicate our needs to God, but what about responses to our prayers? When we are quiet, calm, humble, and at peace we can hear the Holy Spirit through silent thoughts, the words of another, or sometimes through the changing of our life circumstances (Galatians 2:20). We can ask for knowledge and understanding, comfort, guidance, strength, patience, grace, humility, and purer hearts through prayer. We should be seeking these things daily, and listening for the Holy Spirit through quiet reflection. Pray on, Brothers and sisters!

Jeremiah 29:12, ERV

12 "Then you will call my name. You will come to me and pray to me, and I will listen to you."

June 28
The Spirit Guide

Romans 8: 5,6, ERV

5 People who live following their sinful selves think only about what they want. But those who **live following the Spirit** are thinking about what the Spirit wants them to do. 6 If your thinking is controlled by your sinful self, there is spiritual death. But if your thinking is controlled by the Spirit, there is life and peace.

The Spirit of God, given to us by Jesus through His crucifixion on the cross for our sins, is an invisible force guiding our thoughts, morals, and ethics of daily life (Isaiah 11:2). We all have access to this when we pledge our hearts and lives to Christ Jesus (Acts 2:38), but only some are paying attention, and listening, to this gift of the Holy Spirit. Helping us to remember what Jesus taught, how we should live, governing over our decisions, and constantly re-setting our moral compasses, the Holy Spirit is God working in us (1 Corinthians 2:12-14). We always have choices, but often the right ones are hidden amongst a plethora of evil, sinful, choices that are often more appealing. Drunken parties, harmless flirting, swearing in anger, lying, passing judgement, deception, pride, greed and lust for money or physical pleasure outside the sanctity of marriage are all considered sinful behaviors. Can any of us honestly say we didn't cuss, harbor an angry or ill thought, pass judgement toward another, or didn't tell a single lie all day? (1 John 1:8)

Righteousness is tough, and this is why many people give up. The bible tells us that the path to Heaven and Eternal life is narrow, and that 'few' will enter (Matthew 7:13). We must make everyday life choices that reflect who we are as devout followers of Christ, from the way we speak to others, to what governs our thoughts, to our actions and behaviors toward our brothers and sisters. What's more, we need to repent when we sin, and then actually try understand better why we commit those sins. God is asking us to give up certain aspects of our lifestyles forever that we might be uncomfortable with, at first. We should remember that this too, prevents people from understanding the true nature, and inevitability of human nature to sin and seize autonomy from God, and the true salvation that can only be found in Christ (Matthew 13:19). Trust the Spirit inside of us, brothers and sisters, and yield to the Sovereign will of the Lord. Praise be to God, forever, AMEN.

Romans 8: 12-14, ERV

12 So, my brothers and sisters, we must not be ruled by our sinful selves. **We must not live the way our sinful selves want.** 13 If you use your lives to do what your sinful selves want, you will die spiritually. But if you use the Spirit's help to stop doing the wrong things you do with your body, you will have true life. 14 **The true children of God are those who let God's Spirit lead them.**

June 29
Follow, Don't Lead

Jeremiah 10:23, CSB/**ICB**

23 I know, Lord, that a person's way of life is not His own; **No one can control His own life**.

Proverbs 19:21, ESV

21 Many are the plans in the mind of a man, but it is **the purpose of the Lord that will stand**.

Some people look at the academic degrees, diplomas, awards, trophies and certificates displayed in their office and swell with pride at their achievements. Others pull into their large home in a secure, or elite, neighborhood and smile at the life they've secured for themselves. Any achievement takes work, and the pride we develop from a job well done feels justified after the effort and diligence put into a goal. Success takes a great deal of work and discipline, it's only human nature to feel a sense of autonomy and pride at what we can accomplish when we set our minds to a specific goal. Many people have a difficult time accepting that God's plan for us has been pre-established, and we have less control than we would like to admit sometimes. However, the bible is very clear on this; God created humanity, and the Lord establishes our steps. Perhaps we aren't *supposed* to know what the Lord has planned for our lives, and only God knows why. Since we don't really control our destinies, all we can hope to control is our *response* to His will for us, or, how much we intend to obey Him.

We are designed to need God, and, hopefully, follow the example He's left for us. In the bible, God calls on us to worship Him with all of our strength, soul, might, and mind (Mark 12:30), and assures us that we will be taught the way in which to live (Micah 6:8). Our pride, our egos, our need to be relevant and important to the society we live in and those in our immediate environments take our focus off of the Lord, and place the weight of importance on our lifestyles instead of what is in our hearts. We must live in this world, but many people insist on thriving. Thriving in this world is about cars, houses, money, a healthy body, jewelry, clothes, physical attractiveness, education, power, success, and financial security. In this world made up of wickedness, backward thinking and sins, cynicism, conceit, stubbornness, ego, and deceit is rewarded with power, fame, adoration and success. As wonderful as the world's successes are, it's our *spiritual* success that God is concerned with (Ephesians 6:12). The more we keep our focus on things that make us successful *in this world*, the farther we distance ourselves from the humility, service and love to others, self-control, modesty and contrition that God calls us to, and values so. God is watching as He corrects and educates, observing not just how obedient we all are to His commands, but how we treat others *and* God as He surprises us over and over again in our lives. How obedient will God find *you*?

Proverbs 16:9, ESV

9 The heart of man plans His way, but the Lord establishes His steps.

Psalm 32:8, ESV

8 "I will instruct you and teach you in the way you should go; I will counsel you with my eye upon you."

June 30
God's Waiting for Us to Return

Zechariah 1:3, ERV

3 So you must tell the people what the Lord Almighty says, **"Come back to me, and I will come back to you."** this is what the Lord Almighty said.

2 Peter 3:9, ESV

9 **The Lord is** not slow to fulfill His promise as some count slowness, but is patient toward you, not **wishing that** any should perish, but that **all should reach repentance**.

It may be difficult to imagine that we should be repenting daily, are humans really that bad? Yes, yes we are. We're impatient, proud, arrogant, focused on ourselves, we can harbor an ill feeling toward another, hold impure thoughts, say unkind words to one another, and give in to indulgences. We should always be praying for guidance, and for kind and pure hearts that love our neighbors. The Lord our God knows our hearts, knows our life before we do. If we do everything we're called to do, but we do it merely for our own self-preservation, God knows this. God knows if we're going to eventually return to Him or not, if we truly believe in our hearts, and those that don't, He leaves (Romans 1:28). Yikes.

Repentance just means we *know* we messed up, and sinned, and we're not only sorry but we *genuinely* want to *improve* in our faith. Admitting we aren't perfect just means that we know we need Jesus to be complete and better people, not that we're worse than others. Our lives aren't between us and everyone else, God isn't going to ask us about *anyone else's sins* (Ezekiel 18:4), it's a personal relationship between us and our creator, through Jesus. For this reason, *everyone* is in need of Jesus to be complete people, there are no exceptions, there are just people who don't fully accept. God knows we need Him, and wants *us* to understand that too. When we repent and pledge to do better, promising to stay a little closer to Jesus, we are returning to God which makes Him happy. Prayer and reflection can show us what to repent for, and we must never get tired of cleaning ourselves up each day for God. No matter where we are in our faith, or what sins we've committed, God is always ready to hear us repent.

Joel 2:13, ERV/**ESV**/ICB

13 Tearing your clothes is not enough to show you are sad. Let your heart be broken. **Return to the Lord your God,** for he is gracious and merciful, slow to anger, and abounding in steadfast love; and he relents over evil.

Jeremiah 24:7, ESV

7 "I will give them a heart to know that I am the Lord, and they shall be my people and I will be their God, for they shall **return to me** with their whole heart."

July 1
Build Each Other Up

Philippians 2:3, ICB

3 When you do things, do not let selfishness or pride be your guide. **Be humble and give more honor to others than to yourselves.**

"Did you see that blouse she was wearing, yuck!" People can be so cruel to one another. "Hey, watch where you're going, idiot!" We can have so little tolerance for others who might be struggling. As humans, we're typically only focused on ourselves, and we don't want anyone else's mess to slow us down. After Covid our individual worlds shrank a little as our communities quarantined and distanced themselves, and we like to have as much control over our environments as we can. When we share our environments with others, at the park, at the bank, at the store or coffee shop, we don't want other people to get in our way, or otherwise negatively influence our personal itineraries. In fact, some of us may feel like other people are more of a hindrance than a help at times. In a hurry, focused on our own worlds, many of us have blinders on to the help we could be giving one another. A kind word, a friendly gesture, or a compliment to a stranger can mean the difference in someone's day, and takes very little effort. We can't stop fighting the good fight because a few discouraging non-believers make it more challenging. Christ asks us to be encouraging to one another, to lift one another up (Romans 14:19). Are we doing as we were told?

It takes a great deal of patience not to lose our tempers when our takeout order is incorrect, or someone takes the last parking space we were about to pull into. It takes an enormous amount of the Lord's grace working inside of us to not hold people's mistakes against them, to be non-judgmental and accepting, and to forgive. Not everyone is doing their part, and if that makes the rest of us have to work a little harder, so be it. We should all make a stronger effort to show love, and do good work. Spread the word of Jesus by setting an example of someone who didn't lose their temper, helped a neighbor pick up something they've dropped, complimented a stranger, showed a stranger directions, or let someone go in front of them in line. Jesus wants us to be the one who worked a little harder to show humanity that good deeds have not died, that His love is still right here among us. God sees *all* we do (Psalm 33:13). Every effort, large or small, is a move in the right direction with Christ. Seize opportunities to be a better human being in your daily life, in the car, at work, at the grocery store or running errands, or in a conversations with friends and family. Choose to be more tolerant, forgiving, patient, gossip less, and encourage more in your interactions with others.

Hebrews 10:24-25, ERV

24 **We should think about each other to see how we can encourage each other to show love and do good works.** 25 We must not quit meeting together, as some are doing. No, **we need to keep on encouraging each other.** this becomes more and more important as you see the day Christ will come to judge all people draw nearer.

July 2
The Commandments

Exodus 20:3-4,7a-8a, 12a-17, ESV

3 "You shall have no other gods before me. 4 "You shall not make for yourself a carved image, or any likeness of anything that is in heaven above, or that is in the earth beneath, or that is in the water under the earth.. 7 "You shall not take the name of the Lord your God in vain 8 "Remember the Sabbath day, to keep it holy. 12 "Honor your father and your mother, 13 "You shall not murder. 14 "You shall not commit adultery. 15 "You shall not steal. 16 "You shall not bear false witness against your neighbor. 17 "You shall not covet anything that is your neighbor's."

Some of us read the commandment about adultery and think we're safe because we've never acted on impulse, but what about our commitment to God? Even if we don't act upon our sinful, or lustful desires, we may still have them, and *that's* the issue. In the bible, Jesus explains that just thinking something sinful is as bad as actually committing the act itself (Matthew 5:28), and that it's from within our own mind that evil desires originate (Mark 7:20-23). Jesus is telling us that we are our own problem, and that it's our sinful, human, desires, ambitions, cravings, needs, and demands that is our undoing. Just like our own personal relationships, we show honor to our commitment by our love, loyalty, and support. Likewise, if we're not putting the Lord first in our lives, we may be guilty of adultery to our covenant with God (Matthew 22:37). If we just read the commandments, and not the rest of the bible in its entirety, how can we truly know the complete context of our covenant with the Lord we say we love? To know God is to understand His word, His story and our place in it, and the one He sent to save us all, Jesus. God wants our love in the form of devotion. We can strengthen our devotion to God by fortifying our trust in Him, in combination with our sincerity, and repeated repentance. **To love God is to know Him, to understand what He asks of us, and to put that into regular, faithful, and diligent practice.**

Reading the commandments once, then plunging into our lives, making our own choices, and just checking in with God once in while is a half-hearted effort, at best. Just believing isn't really showing devotion (James 2:18-26), but only with routine prayer, repentance, listening, obeying do we show our love for Jesus (John 14:15). As we follow the Lord more steadfastly, the more understanding we will glean on why we commit the sins we do. When we know what our shortcomings are will we strengthen our self-control in those weak areas, and avoid committing the same sins again? Or, will we neglect the lesson, give *in* to sin again, once again turning away from God? Some of us don't want to look at our own sin, unable to come to terms with our own imperfections. Others are too busy looking at the sins of others, hoping theirs will seem less severe in the eyes of God. When we truly love others as ourselves, we should *want* to treat them with kindness instead of contempt. After all, we *all* sin, so pointing fingers, forming bias, and opinion about each other's sins is waste of time. Not only that, but dissention is wickedness trying to rob us of the righteousness we're all working toward. As followers of Christ, our quest for righteousness will require our sacrifice, hard work, and a **genuine heart** that longs to become a closer, more *faithful* servant to our Lord and Savior.

July 3
A Deeper Understanding: Jesus; Seed Parable

Matthew 13:18-23, GW

18 "Listen to what the story about the farmer means. 19 Someone hears the word about the kingdom but doesn't understand it. The evil one comes at once and snatches away what was planted in him. This is what the seed planted along the road illustrates. 20 The seed planted on rocky ground is the person who hears the word and accepts it at once with joy. 21 Since he doesn't have any root, he lasts only a little while. When suffering or persecution comes along because of the word, he immediately falls from faith. 22 The seed planted among thornbushes is another person who hears the word. But the worries of life and the deceitful pleasures of riches choke the word so that it can't produce anything. 23 But the seed planted on good ground is the person who hears and understands the word. This type produces crops. They produce one hundred, sixty, or thirty times as much as was planted."

There are many lessons one can derive from this story told by Jesus in the book of Matthew. Jesus tells us that not everyone will *understand* His teaching, and that the devil is the reason for this. When we're too focused on ourselves, our own goals, desires, our own code of justice, our personal boundaries, we aren't focused on the Lord's will for us. Our Lord and Savior also explains that some people hear and understand Jesus' teaching, accepting it with great enthusiasm, but when they go through suffering or persecution they turn away from their faith. Being outraged at the pain or tribulation we're given doesn't indicate a humble heart that fears God. God gave us ten commandments to live our lives by, and Jesus reiterated their importance when He tells us, "If you love me, you'll follow my commandments," (John 14:15). When we truly understand God's message to us through Jesus' teaching we understand that God will see to all of our needs, and He will never abandon us. When we trust in this, even though we suffer sometimes, we show God that we truly understand His love for us. God sent Jesus to die for our sins, *in the midst of humanities sin and wickedness*, showing His love for us by His divine, compassionate heart. When we wait patiently on the Lord's comfort, *through our time of affliction, knowing* He'll show up for us, we're showing Him our love and devotion. When we trust that the Lord will comfort and guide us through our pain and tribulation, we show our devotion to Him. Jesus explains that we must remain open-minded and humble to understand His teaching, and expects us to trust Him fully through **all** of our dark moments, no matter how long it may take to get through them. Many of us can admit doubting the Lord on a particularly painful, or difficult emotional time. Again, Jesus expresses the importance of coming to Him to repent for our sins, including our doubt, our anger, our ignorance, and our petulance. Pray on, repent, and understand the good news! AMEN.

July 4
The Waiting Room

Psalm 27:14, ESV

14 **Wait for the Lord**; be strong, and let your heart take courage; **wait for the Lord!**

Proverbs 8:34, ESV

34 "Blessed is the one who listens to me, watching daily at my gates, **waiting beside my doors.**"

When things go wrong, when we've been badly hurt, we all react differently. Under pressure, some of us will lose our tempers, some of us lash out verbally at others, some complain about injustice to anyone who'll listen, others will break down and cry. Anytime we lose our mental and spiritual composure, we should be praying to get through it, praying for strength, grace, patience, guidance and comfort. Praying is always the best solution, but what happens when we pray, and it seems like nothing has happened? Patience is part of faith, God is going to repeatedly test our faith (Isaiah 48:10). If we didn't suffer, we wouldn't have a reason to call upon God for help, and God desires this from us. Getting impatient, and deciding on a man-conceived solution instead of patiently waiting on the Lord is inviting more uncertainty and problems, and not putting our trust in Him (Lamentations 3:25).

We need to remember that the Lord is looking for our humility, our repentance, the concerns deep in our hearts, and our confidence that He'll provide all we need to sustain us. The patience we need in waiting for the Lord should feel like we're alone, waiting without worry or concern, in a non-descript, yet tranquil waiting room. In this 'hypothetical' waiting room nothing exists that would distract our attention from the Lord, and His work in us. If we're thinking of solutions to the problems we've just prayed about, if we continue to worry and stew over the concerns we've just prayed for, we're not really *waiting* for the Lord to sustain us. We need to let go of the rules of justice we've created ourselves, and trust in the Lord's view of what should be done in a given situation. We need to practice patience, all good and bad in our lives comes from the Lord (Isaiah 45:7), and He always has a reason why we go through what we do. Trusting this is part of our faith; having a deep, and unmovable trust in God's love for us, especially when we don't completely understand the Lord's will for us.

Doubting that our prayers are being heard, unsure if we'll be taken care of, or that the Lord will be able to meet all of our needs is the devil trying to separate us from God's wisdom and enlightenment. God's answer will always be the correct one, but we need to show Him faith, and patience, in the midst of our pain to be rewarded by His comfort and enlightenment. God is in charge of every life, and even though He's going to test our faith over and over, and in different ways, He will never abandon any of us (Deut. 31:8). Loving and forgiving Christ, bless us with a more robust faith, a stronger understanding of your word, a deeper trust in you, and hearts that seek you. Praise be to God forever! AMEN.

Isaiah 40:31, ESV

31 But they who wait for the Lord shall renew their strength; they shall mount up with wings like eagles; they shall run and not be weary; they shall walk and not faint.

July 5
God's Sovereign Discipline

2 Kings 19:28, ERV

28 (God said) "'Yes, you were upset at me. I heard your proud insults. So I will put my hook in your nose and my bit in your mouth. Then I will turn you around and lead you back the way you came.'"

Psalm 32:8-9, GW

8 The Lord says, "I will instruct you. I will teach you the way that you should go. I will advise you as my eyes watch over you. 9 Don't be stubborn like a horse or mule. They need a bit and bridle in their mouth to restrain them, or they will not come near you."

We can all be discouraged when we didn't get that job we were hoping for, or that promotion we thought we deserved. Financial setbacks test our patience and honesty, and we all feel the pressures of trying to measure up to our own expectations, as well as that of others. Stressful social situations, competition with others around us, or comparing our lives to others can test the self-control of even the most righteous person. Many people suffer traumas in their lives, or injustices, and shake their fists at God, thinking they are being treated unfairly. Some people may disagree with the way God is directing their lives, and they voice their disdain instead of asking for guidance, patience, forgiveness and grace.

Stubborn people aren't teachable, and proud people don't think they need correction. God finds fault in people who are like this, the bible displays (Proverbs 1:7, 12:1, Jeremiah 8:6). God tells us personally that He will teach, instruct, advise us in the way we should live our lives, and that He will turn us around and lead us back to where He wants us when we stray. People that continue to keep their obedience from God will continue to be bridled like a mule, according the bible. Even though God's discipline is firm, it is fair, and He only intends to make us more holy, more devoted people. There is no excuse for misunderstanding God's intensions, or our role as His servants, as the bible has been around our entire lives for us to learn this. Our devotion is what God wants, and rightly deserves as our creator. Even though we all offer different levels of devotion, God made the non-believers as well as the believers, and He is Sovereign over all. We must remember that the same mighty hands that correct also welcome, forgive and love.

Job 5:17-18, ERV

17 You are fortunate when God corrects you. So don't complain when God All-Powerful punishes you. 18 God might injure you, but he will bandage those wounds. He might hurt you, but His hands also heal.

Job 2:10a, ERV

10a Job answered, "You sound like one of those fools on the street corner! How can we accept all the good things that God gives us and not accept the problems?"

July 6
Be Strong

Deuteronomy 31:6, ESV

6 "Be strong and courageous; don't be terrified or afraid of them. For it is the LORD your God who goes with you; He will not leave you or forsake you."

Joshua 1:9, ESV

9 "Have I not commanded you? Be strong and courageous. Do not be frightened, and do not be dismayed, for the Lord your God is with you wherever you go."

Being strong, having strength, can mean a lot of different things. Some people are proud of their physical prowess, business or financial power. In Jesus Christ, strength is faith. It's important to remember in our walk with Christ that not everyone we run into along our path with be an asset to our journey to be more Christ-like. Not everyone believes that Jesus Christ actually walked the earth the human form of the living God, and died for our sins. What's more, even some who do believe in our Lord and Savior don't believe in repentance to Him, or that they have to change any aspect of their life for that belief. Jesus encourages us to be strong in our faith, and not to hide it, or become corrupted because we're surrounded by people who aren't following Christ. Loving Jesus means following Him by example, by love and forgiveness, no matter what is surrounding us. Temptation, peer-pressure and social expectations can affect the way we represent ourselves.

In our journey to become better versions of ourselves through Christ we must remain strong in who the Holy Spirit is forming us to be. Be authentic, and not afraid of what others around us may think about our choice of words, or activities, or what we might now abstain from. Pray in front of others, use alternative words to swear words, gossip less, and encourage more instead of going along with the crowds negativity. As followers of Christ, we need to remember that our attitudes, actions, and words must set the example, not the exception. Don't cave when temptation teases you with envy, jealousy, greed or other unholy dirty deeds. Stand strong in your faith, and in the better you you're becoming. Carry yourself strong and with humble confidence, because you don't walk alone!

Ephesians 6:10, ESV

10 Finally, be strong in the Lord and in the strength of His might.

Romans 1:16-17, ESV

16 For I am not ashamed of the gospel, for it is the power of God for salvation to everyone who believes, to the Jew first and also to the Greek. 17 For in it the righteousness of God is revealed from faith to faith; as it is written, "But the righteous man shall live by faith."

July 7
Fear Is a Trap

Philippians 4:6-7, NIV

6 Do not be anxious about anything, but in every situation, by prayer and petition, with thanksgiving, present your requests to God. 7 And the peace of God, which transcends all understanding, will guard your hearts and your minds in Christ Jesus.

Proverbs 29:25, ICB

25 Being afraid of people can get you into trouble. But if you trust the Lord, you will be safe.

Rejection, uncertainty, failure, loneliness, change, loss of control, being judged, are all common fears humans have. We all want to feel significant, relevant, loved, and accepted. Our anxieties and fears can negatively affect our actions, thoughts, and behaviors toward others, resorting to deception and gossip to quell our doubts and suspicions. We can all be threatened, and feel unsettled at times. When we allow ourselves to become afraid from an outside threat we need to remember that God will never forsake us (Deut. 31:8, Matthew 28:20), and to put our complete trust in Him to get us through. The only fear we should respect and acknowledge is the fear of God, everything is in His power. Fear is another form of deception, and places our focus on the strife, and away from God's grace. God assures us He will provide all we need (Matthew 6:31-33). Fear is a trap, God is in control, not the world.

We are told to vent our concerns in prayer, and wait patiently for God to address us. Just because we think we need something, doesn't mean it's the right solution (James 4:3). Justice is served in God's way, and in His timeframe, not ours. Fear of God is acknowledging the power *He* has in our lives, and this is healthy and righteous. However, when we focus too much on our fears they can take our focus off of the Lord. We love God, and we know all that happens does so according to His will (Isaiah 14:24), so we must turn that love into trust. Our father in Heaven knows what century we live in, and what we need. God doesn't have an expiration date. When we become fearful, of anything, we need to pray and ask God to guide us through it. No matter what is unsettling us, or how big our problems or needs appear to be, the right answer is **always** going to be to rely solely on God. Merciful and most gracious Lord, guide and comfort us through our weaknesses, for in you we find strength. Thanks be to the Lord, for in Him we rest. AMEN.

2 Timothy 1:7, ICB

7 God did not give us a spirit that makes us afraid. He gave us a spirit of power and love and self-control.

Isaiah 41:10, ESV

10 "fear not, for I am with you; be not dismayed, for I am your God; I will strengthen you, I will help you, I will uphold you with my righteous right hand."

July 8
Give More, Want Less

Ecclesiastes 7:18-20, ICB

18 Those who honor God will avoid doing too much of anything. Even God's followers will do some good things and some bad things. 19 Wisdom gives a person strength. One wise man is stronger than ten leaders in a city. 20 Surely there is no one on earth who always does good and never sins.

Psalm 37:16, GW

16 The little that the righteous person has is better than the wealth of many wicked people.

A well-paying job, a comfortable home in a safe neighborhood, recognition from peers and colleagues all sound like reasonable goals, right? Of course, there is a difference in wanting what is necessary for a healthy life in this world, and wanting bigger, better, or more because of vanity or pride. We should be satisfied with what we have been given (Hebrews 13:5, 2 Corinthians 9:8), and not want for anything in order to live the humble lives we are called to as Christ-followers (Matthew 23:12). Even less talking, according to the bible, and more listening (James 1:19), is required and not just to others around us in fellowship but also in response to our prayers. In appreciating what we *currently have* we put ourselves in a thankful, and humble, position before our Lord. Consequently, when we long for more we've set our priority to worldly acquisitions over our spiritual assets, we are straying farther from God. Anytime we turn our faces *away* from Jesus, the trickery of the devil has won one more battle in the war for our souls (Ephesians 6:11-12, 2 Corinthians 11:14).

We must be mindful of what drives us; money, wealth, the attention of others, revenge are all sinful, extravagant selfish indulgent attitudes. We should only want to attain more love for one another, more forgiveness for ourselves and one another, and kinder hearts through Christ. Nothing else that the world is offering should matter to us anymore, for the world we live in is temporary (Mark 13:31). That may sound extreme, but so are the consequences of our sins without repentance, or faith without changed behavior according to the bible. Persistent prayer and reflection can change our hearts and minds to be more righteous, but only through the power of the Holy Spirit through Christ our Lord. In the eyes of God, the only advantage of having more of anything is the ability to **give more** to the less fortunate. Righteousness is characterized by a quiet, peaceful, unassuming demeanor, with a modest, loving disposition. Less anger, less pride, less greed, less deception, less envy, less dissention and division, less immorality, less stubbornness is what the bible teaches us to strive for (Philippians 2:3-4, James 3:16, James 1:19-20). Less is more, brothers and sisters.

1 John 2:5-6, ERV

5 But when we obey God's teaching, His love is truly working in us. this is how we know that we are living in him. 6 If we say we live in God, we must live the way Jesus lived.

July 9
We Are Not in Control: Fact

Isaiah 45:6-7, GNV

6 "That they may know from the rising of the sun, and from the West, that there is none besides me. I am the Lord, and there is none other.7 I form the light, and create darkness: I make peace, and create evil: I the Lord do all these things."

Job 12:10, ERV

10 Every animal that lives and everyone who breathes—they are all under God's power.

Some people believe in God staunchly, others go most of their lives 'unsure,' still others say no to God all together. It may be easy to assume that if someone doesn't believe in God then they're immune to God's laws and commandments. Wrong. The bible reminds us repeatedly of God's omnipresence and overall management of everything. God's plan to refine and purify humanity in preparation for eternal life is the status quo for every individual (Isaiah 48:10), and His plan takes precedence over anything we plan for ourselves. (Proverbs 16:9). The need for God to purify humanity comes into play almost immediately in the bible, and our creator's first discipline is handed down to Adam, Eve, and the devil (Genesis 3:14-19). What some may not realize is that since Adam and Eve both sinned, and defied God, *all* of their offspring will sin (Genesis 3:15, Romans 5:12). We may like to think we know right and wrong, but God doesn't think so (Malachi 3:18). Although some people have a difficult time accepting God's truths, we *all* need His holy guidance, His supreme wisdom, His divine mercy, and His divine judgement.

God knows where our hearts lie, even if we don't sometimes. There will always be people who don't think they need God, and plenty of believers who, sadly, never actually change their lives and lifestyles for Him. Too comfortable in the sin they've gotten used to, and the truths they've created for themselves, some people will never come out of the darkness of their wicked ways (John 3:19-20). God has a master plan that encompasses all of humanity, and we are unable to truly fathom it completely. When we *trust* in God without knowing our own futures, we are displaying our faith in Him. God is the creator of the universe, creator of **us**, and he has final word over all creation. No one is immune to God, and it's our arrogance that can prevent us from accepting this, because of the humility that understanding requires. God is fair and just, and this faith tells us that we must grow to trust His plan for us. Nonbelief isn't immunity (Luke 6:46), and even non-compliance isn't excused to those who believe, for noncompliance is *infidelity*.

Ecclesiastes 7:14, ERV

14 When life is good, enjoy it. But when life is hard, remember that God gives us good times and hard times. And no one knows what will happen in the future.

Proverbs 19:21, ERV

21 People might make many plans, but what the Lord says is what will happen.

July 10
Patience, Again?

Lamentations 3:25, NIV

25 **The Lord is good to those who wait for Him**, To the person who seeks Him.

Proverbs 8:34, GW

34 Blessed is the person who listens to me, **watches at my door day after day, and waits by my doorposts.**

We can become impatient because we're worried about the outcome of a certain situation, when we're interrupted, when we're in a hurry, when we feel our needs are overlooked, or when our expectations have been thoroughly dissatisfied. What makes us feel like our time is more valuable than someone else's, or that our needs are somehow more important than another person's, that makes us subconsciously put ourselves first? When we are wronged, we feel outraged, and we feel justified in our indignation. In order to surmise that we've been wronged we have to first pass judgement on the situation, and this is where we make our first mistake. We will never be able to see the whole picture (Ecclesiastes 3:11), our lives belong to God (Ezekiel 18:4), we cannot hide from Him (Hebrews 4:13). God is the only one who can render fair judgement, as He is the only one who knows, and has control over everything. When we consider our relationship with our Lord, and place all of our trust in Him, we realize we don't have any authority to feel outraged, indignant, or impatient about anything. We are called to forgive, to *not* judge others, and be humble in all we do. Impatience comes from our arrogance and pride, our expectations, and for this reason is unrighteous.

We will all suffer throughout our lives, no one is exempt from God's master plan. God's purification process through affliction not only test's our faith in Him, but our patience, grace, and self-control. We must realize that God works on His timeline, and in His way (Isaiah 55:8-9), so the results of our prayers will always surprise us. It is important, then, not to have expectations when waiting on the Lord to comfort, or heal, or answer, or guide, or refill, or direct us. When we wait for the Lord, with the hope and open mind of a child (Matthew 18:3) we will get all the Lord see's fair to give us. Although we do sometimes, we shouldn't want or need more than this. The bible explains that we shouldn't worry about anything, but to pray (Philippians 4:6-7), and trust that He knows what we need better than we do (Job 28:24). Trust takes time to develop, but we can pray about this too! Even the Lord exhibited frustration (Matthew 17:17), emotions are powerful, and we all have a great deal at stake. It's important to remember our place, not to feel like we're in a position to demand anything, and to always be grateful for what we *do* have. Thanks be to God for all His graciousness, and grace be to all brothers and sisters in the Lord Christ, AMEN.

2 Peter 3:9, ICB

9 The Lord is not slow in doing what he promised—the way some people understand slowness. But **God is being patient with you. He does not want anyone to be lost.** He wants everyone to change His heart and life.

July 11
Laughter

Job 8:20-21, ESV

20 Behold, God will not reject a blameless man, nor take the hand of evildoers. 21 **He will yet fill your mouth with laughter**, and your lips with shouting.

Psalm 126:2, ESV

2 Then **our mouth was filled with laughter**, and our tongue with shouts of joy; then they said among the nations, "The Lord has done great things for them."

Humans laugh at the expense of others, and, sometimes, at the expense of themselves. It is common to justify any laughter as good for the soul, but is it? Everyone's sense of humor is a little different, and most people can agree that a good, hearty laugh is a positive and enjoyable experience (Ecclesiastes 3:4). In the bible, good, healthy laughter is associated with praise and rejoicing in Jesus' name for the mercy and compassion He's shown us. It is important to remember that crude, indelicate, or insensitive humor is unholy in the eyes of God, and something we would need to repent for if we partook in (Ephesians 5:4, Colossians 3:8). We can't help what makes us laugh, but that's just the point. Someone who is *truly* righteous would be *offended* by crude or indelicate humor, not tempted to laugh at it. Our hearts hold our righteousness, however big or small, reveal our true selves, and our sense of humor is another extension of this.

The Lord's new covenant says we are made new in Christ, through His crucifixion and resurrection, allowing us to become new people. (Ephesians 4:22-24) That means just what it says it does, God wants to replace our sinful, corrupt hearts with righteous, holy hearts. When we give our love and lives to Jesus we become new, and through His guidance and the Holy Spirit we are slowly changed into the righteous versions of ourselves God intended. Through different choices, changed attitudes, more love and forgiveness for others, and increased love for humanity God cleanses our spirits. In our lives, we remain steadfast and disciplined in our faith by eliminating sinful distractions and habits, by daily prayer and reflection, and surrounding ourselves with people who are also following Christ. Just because righteous piety isn't synonymous with wild, raucous party's and reveling, it doesn't have to be boring and somber all of the time. Being righteous is its own reward, and delight in our heart is the result. When laughter is the result of happiness, and within the boundaries of God's righteousness it's another wonderful gift from our Heavenly Father to enjoy.

Proverbs 17:22, CSB

22 A joyful heart is good medicine, but a crushed spirit dries up the bones.

July 12
Gifts

1 Peter 4:10-11, ERV

10 God has shown you His grace in many different ways. So be good servants and use whatever gift he has given you in a way that will best serve each other. 11 If your gift is speaking, your words should be like words from God. If your gift is serving, you should serve with the strength that God gives. Then it is God who will be praised in everything through Jesus Christ. Power and glory belong to him forever and ever. Amen.

We are all broken. Flawed, with a past full of mistakes, and pain, we are all a work in progress under God. We are all human, we all make mistakes every day, and we all need to be forgiven. We all have different skills, talents and gifts that make us unique and individual. Together, we, as God's creation fit together like broken pieces that make up a beautiful yet exclusive mosaic. We aren't talented on our own, or because we're more exceptional that the next person God created, but because the Holy Spirit decides who gets what gifts. Humans like to think they have more power and control over their lives, and their futures, than they *actually* do.

God has a plan for each human, He knows their heart, and knows their life plan as their Creator. As His creation, we either accept His will or we fight it and struggle in pain and strife, a victim of our own unfaithfulness. Jesus taught to love and serve others, to consider others more important than ourselves. Our gifts are meant to be used for the service of others, as an important, functioning part of a larger mechanism, an honor to God. We are all children of God, with gifts and talents to offer one another in our quest to be righteous like Christ. How we use them is up to us, but God see's all. Contempt, criticism, competition are evil in the eyes of God. **Forgiveness of our enemies is a requirement for the kingdom of God, and humility replaces pride and ego on the path to holiness.** If we don't know what our gift is, or how we're to use it in our lives we should be praying. We must be driven by the love we have for our Creator God, steadfast in our pursuit of Jesus, and want to be better people who truly, and deeply love others. Strength of spirit and faith is far more attractive to God than wealth, success, or anything the world can offer.

1 Corinthians 12:7,11, ERV

7 Something from the Spirit can be seen in each person. The Spirit gives this to each one to help others.
11 One Spirit, the same Spirit, does all these things. The Spirit decides what to give each one.

July 13
Helping One Another Is Helping God

Matthew 25:40-46, GW

40 "The king will answer them, 'I can guarantee this truth: Whatever you did for one of my brothers or sisters, no matter how unimportant they seemed, you did for me.' 41 "Then the king will say to those on His left, 'Get away from me! God has cursed you! Go into everlasting fire that was prepared for the devil and His angels! 42 I was hungry, and you gave me nothing to eat. I was thirsty, and you gave me nothing to drink. 43 I was a stranger, and you didn't take me into your homes. I needed clothes, and you didn't give me anything to wear. I was sick and in prison, and you didn't take care of me.' 44 "They, too, will ask, 'Lord, when did we see you hungry or thirsty or as a stranger or in need of clothes or sick or in prison and didn't help you?' 45 "He will answer them, **'I can guarantee this truth: Whatever you failed to do for one of my brothers or sisters, no matter how unimportant they seemed, you failed to do for me.'** 46 "These people will go away into eternal punishment, but those with God's approval will go into eternal life."

It's easy to pass up haggard individuals holding a sign pleading for assistance on busy street corners, while making every excuse for why we can't help the person. We can easily turn our face away from a fellow brother or sister begging for help, telling ourselves someone else will probably take care of them. Some people avoid going to church, so they won't be approached to volunteer their time for a function they don't have time for. People are in need all around us, and some of us are more empathetic than others. Most of us want to have everlasting life in Heaven with our creator, but not everyone will earn God's approval. Jesus tells us directly, in the above passage, that if we ignore a fellow brother or sister we're ignoring Him. Many of us don't want to admit we've ignored our fellow man in the past, but there is always time to turn our attitudes toward one another around. It is important to realize that we are all brothers and sisters in Christ, and we shouldn't ignore, or turn our hearts away from someone we could help. Even if someone treats us badly, Christ tells us we're to forgive them, pray for them, and give them our best (Matthew 5:44). Some people have a difficult time seeing themselves as equal, equal to the man who is begging on the street, or equal to the man in prison, but we all have an imperfect soul the Lord wants to rescue. When we help one another in any way we can we're loving each other as Christ asks us. Not everyone has time to devote to the wonderful missionary work local churches can accomplish, but food, clothing, or monetary donations are always helpful in any community. Put a package of food and some basic supplies in a disposable shopping bag, keep it in your car, and the next time you see someone in need you'll be ready to help! Using our talents and gifts, we can all do a little more to help one another. Our very salvation depends on it.

July 14
God of Comfort

Psalm 94:16-19, ERV

16 No one helped me fight against the wicked. No one stood with me against those who do evil. 17 And if the Lord had not helped me, I would have been silenced by death. 18 I know I was ready to fall, but, Lord, your faithful love supported me. 19 I was very worried and upset, but you comforted me and made me happy!

John 3:16-18, ESV

16 (Jesus said) "For God so loved the world, that he gave His only Son, that whoever believes in him should not perish but have eternal life. 17 For God did not send His Son into the world to condemn the world, but **in order that the world might be saved through him**. 18 Whoever believes in him is not condemned, but whoever does not believe is condemned already, because he has not believed in the name of the only Son of God."

Trying to get comfort in a sinful, corrupt world like ours is like trying to draw milk from a stone. Some people spend their entire lives trying to find true happiness from the world we live in, in the way of physical comforts, respect, wealth, and consider God a once-in-a-while distraction. With so much pain and strife in the world, and considering God's strict rules, what comfort does life offer us outside of God? Teaching us how to live like Jesus offers us salvation, peace, a thriving spirit, and a softer heart. Having our sins forgiven shows us compassion and love on a scale only God can provide. Being able to communicate with God through prayer via Jesus and the Holy spirit can bring wisdom and grace the world cannot offer. Knowing we're loved enough to be given another chance at spending eternity with our creator, despite our sinful nature, is also love beyond human measure. By dying for us, offering forgiveness for our sins, showing us how to be more Holy and to rebuke sin, Jesus literally gave our souls an opportunity to be saved from evil forever.

God didn't bring sin into the world, humans did that by rebuking God (Romans 5:12). Out of love for us, God sent Jesus to die to save us from the sin *we* had brought into the world. The world we live in can never offer us the comfort of salvation that is offered through Jesus Christ, but many spend their entire lives trying to do just that. Still others set out to prove they don't need God or Jesus, never *admitting* their vulnerability, or submitting to the humble state God requires of us. Only Jesus can offer the peace, grace, and love that comes from God, we must *seek* Christ earnestly to receive the comfort that comes from studying Him (Revelation 3:20).

2 Corinthians 1:5, ERV

5 We **share** in the many **sufferings** of Christ. In the same way, much **comfort** comes to us through Christ.

Deuteronomy 32:39, ESV

39 "See now that I, even I, am he, and there is no god beside me; I kill and I make alive; I wound and I heal; and there is none that can deliver out of my hand."

July 15
Mercy

Proverbs 28:13, ESV

13 Whoever conceals His transgressions will not prosper, but he who confesses and forsakes them will obtain mercy.

Isaiah 1:18-20, ICB

18 The Lord says, "Come, we will talk these things over. Your sins are red like deep red cloth. But they can be as white as snow. Your sins are bright red. But you can be white like wool. 19 If you obey me, you will eat good crops from the land. 20 But if you refuse to obey and if you turn against me, you will be destroyed by your enemies' swords." The Lord himself said these things.

Many of us would have to admit that talking about the things we do wrong isn't our most favorite subject. In fact, many people go to great lengths to ignore their sins and transgressions. Some people have a difficult time accepting anything they do as wrong, and still others tend to blame other people for their mistakes. We **all** fall short in the eyes of God (Romans 3:23), so it shouldn't be a shock to learn we're **all** sinners. If we all make mistakes, why do some people still try to hide from them? Perhaps they don't want anyone else to discover they aren't perfect. Surprise! Instead of mourning our status as imperfect, we should repent our prideful attitudes and seek a more realistic viewpoint through a healthy dose of humility. Jesus sustains us, offers us a way to repentance, offers fair judgement, remains divinely holy forever, and offers us grace. Hallelujah!

Hey, we all stray from our righteous path sometimes. After all, nobody's perfect (Romans 3:10-12). Because we all commit sins, what matters is that we're being honest with ourselves when it comes to repenting for them. Taking time at the end of our day to consider our words and behaviors with humble reflection, learning what we could have done better is important. We must ask ourselves, could we have chosen better words, or how could we have been more forgiving, inspirational, or loving to another? If we present our sins before God and ask for forgiveness that's a great first step toward righteousness. We want to be sure to not only avoid committing these sins again, but we need to understand *why* we're committing them in the first place if we're going to avoid them in the future. If we're truly seeking repentance, we will want to ask God to help us to change so that we can actually step away from our old, sinful behaviors of the past. Only God's power can replace in us the tendency to judge others, or our deceitful behavior, or the lustful temptations we desire, or the stubborn heart that doesn't want to change or forgive with humility, self-control, modesty, and love. Only God can truly change the motivations within our hearts (Jeremiah 24:7). Brothers and sisters, seek the Lord's mercy a little more each day for optimal results.

Luke 15:10, GW

10 So I can guarantee that God's angels are happy about one person who turns to God and changes the way he thinks and acts."

July 16
The Sheild of God

Ephesians 6:11-12, ERV

11 Wear the full armor of God. Wear God's armor so that you can fight against the devil's clever tricks. 12 Our fight is not against people on earth. We are fighting against the rulers and authorities and the powers of this world's darkness. We are fighting against the spiritual powers of evil in the heavenly places.

Silent forces of good and evil afoot among us almost sounds like the theme of a scary movie, more than the current state of humanity. The devil, or Satan, was an angel in Heaven before he was kicked out for exalting himself above God in His heart (Isaiah 14:12-15), and has power here on earth (Job 1:7, Matthew 4:8-9). The spirits of those who have passed away, are sleeping, according to the bible (Luke 8:52-53, Psalm 13:3). Ghosts, apparitions, and unembodied spirits aren't from those who have passed, then, they are far more sinister. The devil employs the use of demon spirits to aid him, and the bible warns of these dark and evil spirits on Earth, trying to separate man from His true relationship with God (1 Samuel 16:14, 1 Timothy 4:1). Masquerading as an angel of light, Satan deceives us into thinking unholy thoughts, wanting sinful things, and spreading hate and suspicion among us (2 Corinthians 11:14). Playing on our insecurities and vulnerabilities, evil preys on our desire to be exalted by making us desire to be more, and have more than our neighbors.

Spiritual powers of darkness have corrupted many people on Earth through war, murder, violence, hatred, prejudice, fear, contempt, conceit and lust. Any of these can be found in the music people listen to, the movies and shows people watch, the language they use toward one another, and on the lips of the leaders of Nations. Some people who actually believe in God are under the power of dark spirits and may not even know about it. Search your heart, do you still have suspicions, doubts and fears? If we fully trust in the Lord our God, we don't fear anything but Him, and our salvation in Him, and we rest in that faith instead of worldly anxieties. Praying to Jesus in prayer is a much better solution than anything sinful or corrupt we could come up with on our own. Following Jesus more closely, studying the bible more thoroughly in the true context the stories were written, and praying devoutly and regularly is always going to be the best 'armor' to guard against being corrupted by the devil's sin and temptations.

1 John 4:1-4, ESV

4 Beloved, do not believe every spirit, but test the spirits to see whether they are from God, for many false prophets have gone out into the world. 2 By this you know the Spirit of God: every spirit that confesses that Jesus Christ has come in the flesh is from God, 3 and every spirit that does not confess Jesus is not from God. this is the spirit of **the antichrist**, which you heard was coming and now **is in the world already**. 4 Little children, you are from God and have overcome them, for he who is in you is greater than he who is in the world

July 17
Only the Holy?

Revelation 21:27, CJB

27 **Nothing impure may enter** it, nor anyone who does shameful things or lies; the only ones who may enter are those whose names are written in the Lamb's Book of Life.

Hebrews 12:14, ESV

14 Strive for peace with everyone, and for the **holiness without which no one will see the Lord**.

Sinners can't get into Heaven, but if we're all sinners (Ecclesiastes 7:20), where does that leave us? Consider this scenario, brothers and sisters: Two people sit in the same pew in church, awaiting the offering plate, both with donations at the ready. The first man, well dressed, smiles proudly as he places two $20 bills in the church offering plate. The second man, dressed in shabby clothes, places only $2 in the offering plate, and quickly looks away in shame. Can you tell the difference between a person with a pure heart, and one who is only focused on their own gain? On the outside, it appears as if one man takes his faith more seriously, taking the time to dress in nice clothes respectable for church services, and placing a large donation to the offering. What no one can see is that the first man donated quite a bit less than he could've, is proud of his status, and concerned only with his wealth. What no one could know, just from their offering or attire, is that the second man lost his job the week prior, and has only a couple of hundred dollars to his name, and has given considerably more, respectively. Hypocrisy, self-preservation, and false humility cannot always be seen.

If we pray with someone to help them through a pain they are experiencing, but later become outraged when we experience a perceived injustice ourselves, we're being hypocrites. Similarly, when we pray before dinner at home, but not in a restaurant we're hypocrites to our faith. Looking around a busy restaurant dining room, we cannot tell the difference between someone who doesn't typically pray before a meal, and who does, but isn't. Our purity of heart, devotion to the Lord, or depth of faith is not always visible to others.

The bible tells us we need to believe in Jesus (John 14:6), and have the heart of a child to enter the Kingdom of Heaven (Matthew 18:3), but what does that mean exactly? We need to be humble, accept correction and tests of faith from God without disdain or hostility, and follow the righteous life of Jesus to a purer heart by understanding the word of God, and repeated repentance for the sins we commit. That may sound like a tall order for a sinful humanity, but that's just the point. The blood of Jesus covers our sins, but we must repent with pure hearts in order to be forgiven for them. Not everyone will make the effort to know Jesus, not everyone will humble themselves for God, and not everyone wants to endure what one must in order to have a purer heart for God. When reading the word with understanding, it's clear that God wants us to have the right balance of fear and humility, like that of a 'small *child*.' Lord, help fortify our faith and devotion to you through a purer heart. Humble us, O Lord, and make our hearts into that of a child's with your grace, love and forgiveness. AMEN.

Hosea 6:6, ERV

6 "This is because **I want faithful love, not sacrifice**. **I want people to know God**, not to bring burnt offerings."

July 18
The Prodigal Son

Luke 15:11-14, 17-23, 30-32, ICB

11 Then Jesus said, "A man had two sons. 12 The younger son said to His father, 'Give me my share of the property.' So the father divided the property between His two sons. 13 Then the younger son gathered up all that was His and left. He traveled far away to another country. There he wasted His money in foolish living. 14 He spent everything that he had. Soon after that, the land became very dry, and there was no rain. There was not enough food to eat anywhere in the country. The son was hungry and needed money. 17 The son realized that he had been very foolish. He thought, 'All of my father's servants have plenty of food. But I am here, almost dying with hunger. 18 I will leave and return to my father. I'll say to him: Father, I have sinned against God and against you. 19 I am not good enough to be called your son. But let me be like one of your servants.' 20 So the son left and went to His father. "While the son was still a long way off, His father saw him coming. He felt sorry for His son. So the father ran to him, and hugged and kissed him. 21 The son said, 'Father, I have sinned against God and against you. I am not good enough to be called your son.' 22 But the father said to His servants, 'Hurry! Bring the best clothes and put them on him. Also, put a ring on His finger and sandals on His feet. 23 And get our fat calf and kill it. Then we can have a feast and celebrate! 29 The older son said to His father, 'I have served you like a slave for many years! I have always obeyed your commands. But you never even killed a young goat for me to have a feast with my friends. 30 But your other son has wasted all your money on prostitutes. Then he comes home, and you kill the fat calf for him!' 31 The father said to him, 'Son, you are always with me. All that I have is yours. 32 We had to celebrate and be happy because your brother was dead, but now he is alive. He was lost, but now he is found.'"

Some of us know, or heard of, family members who haven't spoken to each other in years because of some epic, Historical family quarrel. Some people look differently upon others because they sin differently, assuming they know what's in another's heart based solely on their own perceptions. We cannot exclude, or withhold forgiveness from others because we don't know all of the facts, only God can judge truly us. Tolerance, acceptance, and forgiveness are allusive, and can be equally hard to ask for as it can be to grant. Once we've distanced ourselves because of our sins, poor choices, vengeance or anger, our pride makes a peaceful solution impossible (Hebrews 12:14). Some people remain in their pride or stubbornness, unwilling to admit they were wrong, presumptuous, or acted out of ignorance or pain (Ephesians 4:18). Humbling ourselves starts with holding ourselves accountable for our actions, behaviors, thoughts, and words. Acknowledging that we make mistakes isn't comfortable, but correction isn't usually comfortable, and is vital in understanding what actions, behaviors, thoughts, and words we need to change. Peace and resolve can be incredibly difficult to attain through the hardships we suffer, but God is the one, constant source of comfort and direction. We are all going to sin, we are all going to stray from God (James 3:2), and what was true when the bible was written is still true today. Although the sins we commit are noteworthy and important, only *one* sin is unforgiveable (Matthew 12:32). Our sins show us why we need God, and from the parable of the prodigal son we can derive the meaning God sends to us all: *I don't care what **you think** you've done, just come home, and return to me.*

July 19
God's Judgement Doesn't Neglect

Jeremiah 17:10, ESV

10 "I the Lord search the heart and test the mind, to give every man according to his ways, according to the fruit of his deeds."

We can all feel frustrated in a rush, or even agitated, when our schedules are unexpectedly hindered by a passing train. We can feel, anxious, exasperated, or even angered when no one holds the elevator door for us while we're clearly rushing to catch it. We can feel like a strange injustice has been done when we're passed up for a promotion we counted on securing. What we can't know is that a drunk driver ran the stop sign beyond the railroad tracks we were waiting at, and if we hadn't been stopped by the train they would've hit us. We also cannot possibly know that the elevator we missed was going to be stuck between two floors for ninety minutes, and we would've missed an important meeting. And again, we can't see the file on the applicant who *did* receive the promotion, or that their experience eclipses ours. Only God can see all, only He can render proper judgement on who is supposed to receive what, when, and why. Working from wisdom and knowledge we cannot comprehend, we place our faith in the one, true, God for so many reasons. Not only is God our creator, but our judge, and our redeemer.

What we think is fair is based on a limited, restricted, viewpoint. Our own justice will always be incomplete, because none of us will ever be able to see the complete plan God has for humanity (Ecclesiastes 3:11). As tempting as it is to render a verdict from the sense of justice we've created from our own judgement, we shouldn't, because we can't possibly be fair every time. No one human is better than another, and God wants ALL humanity to return to Him in repentant humility. Because no one of us is better, only God should be intervening when one thinks another is wrong. Forgiveness cannot occur where judgement is taking place, and love for one another should be stronger than the differences between us. Let us treat one another with forgiveness, tolerance, acceptance, love, and grace, because we would want others to treat us with the same. Trust in God, brothers and sisters. If **your** final judgement day was tomorrow would *you* be ready?

Romans 2:6-11, ESV

6 He will render to each one according to His works: 7 to those who by patience in well-doing seek for glory and honor and immortality, he will give eternal life; 8 but for those who are self-seeking and do not obey the truth, but obey unrighteousness, there will be wrath and fury. 9 There will be tribulation and distress for every human being who does evil, the Jew first and also the Greek, 10 but glory and honor and peace for everyone who does good, the Jew first and also the Greek. 11 For **God shows no partiality.**

July 20
Listen and Focus on God

Deuteronomy 8:2-3, ERV

2 And you must remember the entire trip that the Lord your God has led you through these 40 years in the desert. **He was testing you. He wanted to make you humble. He wanted to know what is in your heart. He wanted to know if you would obey His commands.** 3 He humbled you and let you be hungry. Then he fed you with manna—something you did not know about before. It was something your ancestors had never seen. Why did the Lord do this? Because he wanted you to know that it is not just bread that keeps people alive. People's lives depend on what the Lord says.

Isaiah 59:1-2, ERV

1 Look, the Lord's power is enough to save you. He can hear you when you ask him for help. 2 It is your sins that separate you from your God. He turns away from you when he sees them.

Many popular stories involve a strong, sturdy hero saving the innocent victim from a dangerous, evil oppressor with good triumphing in the end. Humanity has a collective sense of fairness and order, and when the unrighteous aren't completely decimated immediately, and to our total recompense, we can feel a sense of outrage. Evil should be squashed without hesitation upon offense, and the righteous blessed beyond measure uniformly, this is the code of justice **humanity has largely conceived.** The Lord's divine justice and balance is so complicated, He Himself explains that we cannot understand it (Isaiah 55:8). Instead of learning what God wants, we've decided for ourselves, and we can look down on God when His ways don't conform to our preconceived notions of justice.

Many successful people have proved through their words and actions that they aren't very righteous, or just people, and yet they seem to thrive. Too many times we see rotten, wicked or evil people enjoying unabated power, good fortune and success while decent, law abiding citizens who try to do what's right seem to struggle unreasonably. God wants only faithful servants in His Heavenly kingdom, and is testing us to see who will keep coming back to Him in true faith (Psalm 14:2). Perhaps we suffer financially, or medically, or with poor relationships and disappointments, but we are all tested, and we are all tested differently. Testing the righteousness of an individual who is dwelling among other righteous people isn't a very accurate test, but testing the righteous person among sinners and strife will yield a more accurate measure of that individual's faith. How we react to life's constant flux and unbalance, its injustice, and its unfairness is just as revealing as how much we help others, spread God's word, or how often we pray. Life isn't about fairness or even balance, as humankind views it. Like it or not, life is a test of faith. How much are *you* currently relying on God in your life?

Psalm 37:7-8, ERV

7 Trust in the Lord and wait quietly for His help. Don't be angry when people make evil plans and succeed. 8 Don't become so angry and upset that you, too, want to do evil.

July 21
What Service Means

Job 41:11, GW

11 God said, "Who can confront me that I should repay him? **Everything under heaven belongs to me!**"

Colossians 3:23-24, ESV

23 Whatever you do, work heartily, as for the Lord and not for men, 24 knowing that from the Lord you will receive the inheritance as your reward. **You are serving the Lord Christ.**

Galatians 5:13, ESV

13 For you were called to freedom, brothers. Only do not use your freedom as an opportunity for the flesh, but **through love serve one another.**

When things go wrong, it is helpful to know why in order to prevent a reoccurrence. When we, or someone we care about, suffers what we perceive as an injustice we can be outraged if it's not resolved to our satisfaction. We cannot see everything leading up to a disaster, nor can we prevent them, as all things are under God's control. We were meant to use the Holy Spirit as a moral compass for all we do, allowing God to lead us (John 14:26, Romans 8:14). In the same way, God may give us a shovel, but *we're* intended to dig the hole. None of us chose to be born, or what color the ocean was going to be, or how bright the sun needed to be. Admitting we are powerless to control our destinies, or of those we love, is humbling, and it's meant to be. God has been refining humans from their sinful heritage through affliction for thousands of years (Isaiah 48:10), and does so in His own mysterious ways (Isaiah 55:8). We are not entitled to an explanation of why things are the way they are, or faith wouldn't be faith. If we read our bibles, we would have a far greater understanding of our Lord and Savior's ways. God doesn't owe us anything, as He does not serve us, He governs over us with Sovereign power. We weren't meant to just check in with God every once in a while, we are meant to *serve* God, with daily repentance and praise.

Sometimes we have to learn what our sins were from a process of elimination to understand what we've done wrong by God, but this is all part of the learning process. Prayer is helpful when asking for understanding, and to convey our humility before our one, true, Heavenly Father. On earth, humans are the dominant species, and we like to think we rule over all creation. We don't, we *are* the creation. Being burdened with hard work until destruction sounds pretty unpleasant, but we can easily forget our place. God created the world and everything on it, He sent prophets to help people understand what He would, and wouldn't tolerate, He ensured the drafting of the bible and oversaw the work of the authors (2 Timothy 3:16) so future generations could also benefit from His word. God sent Jesus not only to die for the sins of all humans, but to lead us in spiritual cleansing through faith in Him (1 John 1:7). All God is demanding is respect, love and true devotion in our hearts, and He's more than earned it.

Mark 10:45, ESV

45 "For even the Son of Man came not to be served but to serve, and to give His life as a ransom for many."

July 22
Who Are We Trying to Please?

Galatians 1:10, ESV

10 For am I now seeking the approval of man, or of God? Or am I trying to please man? If I were still trying to please man, I would not be a servant of Christ.

What do you think of my new haircut? Do these pants make my butt look big? Did you see his shoes? Many people walk around, preoccupied with how other people perceive them, while wondering how they are perceived by others. Our confidence can wax and wane, depending on how we feel the world receives us. We all want to be loved, appreciated, and recognized as relevant with something to offer the world. All the while we're looking, and thinking, and forming preconceived perceptions of one another, we're looking for reassurances we *should* be getting from God. Despite the intellectual capabilities of the human brain, we don't really know what's best for our lives, so other *people* certainly don't know what's best for our lives. God is the all-powerful creator who sees and know what's in the hearts of us **all** (Jeremiah 17:10), and has the power to create and to destroy. It shouldn't be too much of a revelation to realize that we are supposed to be looking to God *more* in our lives.

Confidence comes from the faith, the belief that all we need in our lives God will provide for us (Hebrews 11:6). He creates all triumph and strife for His reason, His plan. It's when we aren't listening, or paying attention to God that we can become outraged and angry with Him when life gets too painful, difficult, or complicated. He's trying to get us to refocus on what pleases Him; repentance and devotion to Him, forgiveness, grace, self-control, humility, service to the underserved, and righteousness. Only God knows what's in our futures, *we* certainly don't, any more than the next mortal. Instead of looking at one another, the bible urges us to look at God, since He's in control of everything (Psalm 146:3-6). 'His will be done,' means just that; God's will, not our own. When we live our lives with the aim to please our family, friends, society, or ourselves instead of God we will always carry the potential to be disappointed, and short-changed. We must ask ourselves who, or what, is our priority? We should be giving the salvation of our souls more than just a passing glance. Thankfully, it's never too late to begin praying to our Lord and Savior, and putting Him first in our lives. Lord, help us to focus on you more, give us hearts that seek you and your holiness. Great is your faithfulness, O Christ, our merciful Savior. AMEN.

James 4:13-15, ESV

13 Come now, you who say, "Today or tomorrow we will go into such and such a town and spend a year there and trade and make a profit" — 14 yet you do not know what tomorrow will bring. What is your life? For you are a mist that appears for a little time and then vanishes. 15 Instead you ought to say, "If the **Lord wills**, we will live and do this or that."

July 23
Staying Righteous

Ephesians 4:26, ERV

26 When you are angry, don't let that anger make you sin, and don't stay angry all day.

Faith during painful experiences, devotion during correction, and grace under pressure is elusive. It's hard to be righteous when you don't get what you paid for, or feel you got the short end of someone else's half-hearted effort. It's hard to forgive when we feel we've been wronged, because we want retribution, we want our own view of justice to proceed expeditiously. We can be so focused on ourselves, on the pressures in our lives, instead of on what God is trying to teach us. When we get away from true righteousness, we tend to judge for *ourselves* how we think our life circumstances should proceed, and can even get outraged when those expectations aren't met. We can slip into old patterns of thought, old behaviors all too easily when we feel pressured, or stressed. Righteousness by example is love for others, praying for our enemies, accepting the Lord's correction, remaining steadfast during tests of faith, and never considering ourselves better, or more worthy than another.

Being inconsiderate, fear, laziness, fatigue, lack of conviction, and vengeance are all reasons why people put in half-hearted efforts. When we seem to be less concerned with someone else's injustice we have become de-sensitized to the plight of others, our love for others should generate a natural compassion. Being 'in control' of our own lives, focused on our own goals and desires, we are more self-focused than many of us realize, and we can all succumb to sinful behaviors and attitudes. Humility is more elusive than we realize, and we must work hard to remain unassuming in the knowledge that we are all naked and exposed in the eyes of our God (Hebrews 4:13). All good, and bad, in our lives comes from God (Isaiah 45:7), and we should be relying on Him more than most us of us currently are. We are all saved, but not because of anything we did or could do, but because of the love, grace, death, and resurrection of Christ Jesus (Titus 3:5)(Ephesians 2:8-9). If we come across as unwelcoming because we make other people feel inferior, we need to remember that we all have different gifts, and one person's isn't worth more than another's. When we become incensed at another's sins, not able to understand why they commit them, or when we indulge in self-pity after correction from God, we're allowing our arrogance to overshadow our righteousness. Being righteous is a constant struggle, and it's balance difficult to maintain.

Matthew 6:1, NIV

1 "Beware of practicing your righteousness before men to be noticed by them; otherwise you have no reward with your Father who is in heaven."

Psalm 34:15, GNV

15 The eyes of the Lord are upon the righteous, and his ears are open unto their cry.

July 24
A Test of Faith

Genesis 22: 1-2, 9-12, ESV

1 God tested Abraham and said to him, "Abraham!" And he said, "Here I am." 2 He said, "Take your son, your only son Isaac, whom you love, and go to the land of Moriah, and offer him there as a burnt offering on one of the mountains of which I shall tell you." 9 When they came to the place of which God had told him, Abraham built the altar there and laid the wood in order and bound Isaac His son and laid him on the altar, on top of the wood. 10 Then Abraham reached out His hand and took the knife to slaughter His son. 11 But the angel of the Lord called to him from heaven and said, "Abraham, Abraham!" And he said, "Here I am." 12 He said, "Do not lay your hand on the boy or do anything to him, for now I know that you fear God, seeing you have not withheld your son, your only son, from me."

Some people only see their pain as pain. Trauma, tribulation, disappointment, suffering, death, hardship, and loss are all saddening, and difficult to process emotionally. As humans, we made life difficult when we disobeyed God in the garden of Eden (Gen. 3). Since the first humans chose to disobey God, and seek autonomy for themselves, humanity has been born into the same, a pre-destined tribulation. As a result, God has been abandoned by humanity for false Gods (Judges 3:7), and their own desires since our creation (Jeremiah 8:6). Giving us both blessings, and hardships, God's looking into our hearts while watching how we deal with both. Hoping we'll praise, acknowledge, and seek Him for all we receive, or confront in our lives, God tests our faith in Him. Similarly, God studies how we deal with pain, if we'll turn *to* Him, or turn *away* from Him. (James 5:13) In this way, God tests our hearts, and only those with pure hearts will be called His people (Proverbs 17:3, Psalm 24:3-4, Deuteronomy 8:2). If we think life's unfair, it is. We must be mindful not to judge God, how and when He brings forth growth and change in our lives.

Not processing our pain creates bitterness, cynicism and resentment. Many of us can relate to these emotions, we've all had to work through difficult situations. Not understanding our pain prevents us from accepting our role in our own tribulations, and prevents us from growing, and moving forward. Looking at our situations with humility instead of expectations can show us where we've made our mistakes, and our mistakes tell us where we need to work harder, or change. When we're treated unjustly do we let it make us chose sinful anger and resentment, or do we swallow it with grace, patience, and forgiveness? When we suffer, and we *will* suffer, are we turning to God for comfort and direction? Or, are we trying to navigate the life God created for us by ourselves, untrusting, and unable to humble ourselves before our creator? Our pain may look different to other people, but no one is immune, we all deal with it differently. Accepting our role in our own suffering is important, we should be using it to repent and learn from it. If we have trouble accepting our sins, or don't know why we're made to suffer, we need to be careful not to invoke our *own* ideas of justice. Trusting God, whether we're lost, hurt, angry, suffering and in need of comfort or direction, is what faith is all about. Knowing that God will give each their due justice for their actions is resting in that faith. No matter how we're tested, how many times we fail, or how many times we succeed, who we turn to and how we handle what we're given is what tells God what's in our hearts.

July 25
Purification

Jeremiah 9:5-7, ESV

5 "Everyone deceives His neighbor, and no one speaks the truth; they have taught their tongue to speak lies; they weary themselves committing iniquity. 6 Heaping oppression upon oppression, and deceit upon deceit, they refuse to know me," declares the Lord. 7 Therefore thus says the Lord of hosts: "**Behold, I will refine them and test them, for what else can I do, because of my people?**"

Since Adam and Eve made the first choice representing humanity's need for independence from God's law's and restrictions, and sinned by disobeying God, all of humanity became prone to sin (Romans 5:12). The bible chronicles humanities propensity for sin by the example of God's ongoing, and often tumultuous, relationship with Israel. We need purifying, according to our creator, and Father in Heaven. Those of us that scoff at this, thinking we're not included in this purification process because we don't really believe, or because the bible was written so long ago, are sorely mis- informed (Psalm 103:19) If people think a loving God wouldn't make them suffer, these people are also misinformed (Proverbs 16:4, Isaiah 48:10). God loves us, and wants to purify as many of us that'll let Him, so He can bring us into His eternal kingdom with Him. God purifies us with good discipline when we stray from Him, and tests us to strengthen our faith in Him. This is how God brings us closer to righteousness, by molding us into who He needs us to be (Isaiah 64:8).

Life seems to be one booby-trap after another, pain and trouble seem to find us wherever we go. Many people ask, 'Why me?' or, 'why this?' instead of **what** is God trying to show me? How we deal with our problems tells God a great deal about our faith, our self-control, and our reliance on Him. Sometimes, it can feel like we've been given more troubles than we can deal with appropriately (1 Corinthians 10:13). Under pressure and feeling stressed, we can easily allow our troubles to make us bitter, angry, or resentful toward God. Being comfortable all the time, finding suc- cess in everything we do, and never losing someone we love isn't our reality. Things will be taken from us sometimes, other things will be kept from us other times, and through it all we're called to never stop relying on God to help us put the pieces back together. Praying for strength, praying for healing, praying for our spirits to be renewed are all things the Lord can, and does, provide to His faithful servants (Psalm 51:10). If we never had trouble, how would God *really have proof* that we would rely on Him?

1 Peter 1:7, ICB

7 These troubles come to prove that your faith is pure. This *purity of faith* is worth more than gold. Gold can be proved to be pure by fire, but gold can be destroyed. But the purity of your faith will bring you praise and glory and honor when Jesus Christ comes again.

2 Corinthians 7:1, NIV

Therefore, since we have these promises, dear friends, let us purify ourselves from everything that contaminates body and spirit, perfecting holiness out of reverence for God.

July 26
God Let's People Choose

Revelation 3:20, ESV

20 "Behold, I stand at the door and knock. If anyone hears my voice and opens the door, I will come in to him and eat with him, and he with me."

Deuteronomy 30:19, ESV

19 "I call heaven and earth to witness against you today, that I have set before you life and death, blessing and curse. Therefore **choose** life, that you and your offspring may live."

Jesus let people walk away if they didn't believe in Him, He expected it (John 6:64), and focused His ministry on those who *would* accept His teaching. In the same way, God lets us reap what we sow. When we make poor, sinful, or unholy decisions with our lives we pay the consequences. Sometimes, we aren't aware of the sin, or sins, we committed and are left wondering why God allows us to suffer. Sometimes good people suffer, and their faith is sorely tested, and the world doesn't offer much in the way of comfort for suffering (2 Timothy 3:12). God's comfort is eternal spiritual salvation, not a comfortable and easy life while on earth, even so, the Lord can offer us comfort, grace, forgiveness, hope, and direction. Our faith can't make the suffering on Earth any the less painful when we experience it, but it can assure us a well-deserved Heavenly rest at the end of a well-fought journey. People lose their faith, sometimes for days, weeks, or even years. People often neglect their faith because they are lost, confused, and hurt. The answers we seek can only be found through a closer relationship with Jesus Christ, and by understanding His ministry.

Impure thoughts only lead to impure actions and choices, and impure thoughts come from a heart that is focused on sin instead of righteousness (James 1:14-15, Mark 7:20-23). This cycle of wickedness must be stopped by willpower and self-control, and we can derive this strength from the Spirit through prayer and grace. (Romans 6:17-18) Humans don't possess this strength or grace naturally, nor the humility that's required to approach the Lord. Our attitude during prayer is a vital, as prayer is such a crucial tool, a conduit, connecting us to Christ. It's the Almighty power of Jesus through the Holy Spirit that allows us to endure temptations and tribulations, gives us the grace we need to bypass and remain sustained through them. If we choose to rely on our own wit and guile to sustain us, we've chosen not to include the Lord, and whoever isn't with the Lord is against Him (Matthew 12:30). Forced love isn't love, and God let's people walk away (Isaiah 53:6). By relying on Jesus and the Holy Spirit to get through, we have the power we need to deny sinful acts, as well as grow more holy, whereas on our own we are insufficient. We cannot re-interpret the scriptures, if we're even reading them, to suit our own interpretation of God's word. We have a choice, follow the rules of righteousness or don't, but if you're relying on your staunch belief instead of your heart and good works you're not doing enough. Don't be one of those whom God 'let's go' of, read scripture, and go forth humbly my brothers and sisters.

July 27
Where Arrogance Hides

1 Samuel 15:23, CEV

23 Rebelling against God or **disobeying him because you are proud is just as bad as worshiping idols** or asking them for advice. You refused to do what God told you, so God has decided that you can no longer be king."

Someone who can't acknowledge their own faults, or who thinks they're the most attractive person in the room, or most talented, or who never needs the advice or counsel of another would easily be considered vain. Vanity, a form of pride, is wicked in the eyes of God. Although some forms of arrogance, like vanity, can seem obvious to us, others hide in some all too common places. Arrogance cannot coexist with the humility that God calls us to, many of us are guilty, and some of us many not be aware of it.

When something goes wrong in our lives, we can be outraged if we don't receive quick, and expeditious restitution. We can have a very different opinion on what proper, and situationally balanced, restitution should look like, and can be indignant if we don't get what we expect from a situation. When we rest on our own, self-appointed justice, we remove God as the ultimate judge. When we work diligently to follow the golden rule (Matthew 7:12) but see that others don't, we can take offense. Some people assume they deserve respect, thinking they have the right to things other people seem to have: a better car, a bigger house, better family or friends, more opportunities, or more success. Expectations are ignorant when we assume we know more than we actually do.

Arrogance tricks us into thinking we are superior in some way, causes us to be entitled, forms presumptuous, or assuming attitudes. When we think this way we aren't putting other people first. We may be attending church, praying regularly, and even donating to charities, but unless we're operating from a humble perspective in every mindset we're likely to fall prey to the wickedness of arrogance. Only God can see into our hearts and minds, and give us what we are truly due, while humans will always be biased and fallible. When we receive blessings from the Lord we should be thankful, and should never assume we know what we deserve. Likewise, when we are challenged, scorned, or afflicted by the Lord we should trust Him to teach us, redirect us, correct us properly, and comfort us at just the right time, and in just the right way. Lord, help our faith and trust in you to grow, and bless us with humble hearts in all we do. Blessed is the Lord's faithfulness, and in His name we pray, AMEN.

Romans 12:16, NIV

16 Live in harmony with one another. **Do not be proud**, but be willing to associate with people of low position. **Do not be conceited.**

Hebrews 4:13, ESV

13 And no creature is hidden from his sight, but all are naked and exposed to the eyes of him to whom we must give account.

July 28
What It Means to Follow Christ

Ephesians 2:15, 18, ICB

15 The Jewish law had many commands and rules. But Christ ended that law. Christ's purpose was to make the two groups of people become one new people in him. By doing this Christ would make peace. 18 Yes, through Christ we all have the right to come to the Father in one Spirit.

Matthew 5:17-18, ESV

17 "Do not think that I have come to abolish the Law or the Prophets; I have not come to abolish them but to fulfill them. 18 For truly, I say to you, until heaven and earth pass away, not an iota, not a dot, will pass from the Law until all is *accomplished*."

When reading these two scriptures, they can seem to contradict one another. One says Christ abolished the laws, in a sense, and in the other Jesus tells them He's not here to abolish, but to *fulfill* the law. Often using parables, or analogies to tell stories, illustrate messages, commands and lessons, but also to sing songs of praise, the bible is full of apparent contradictions. One advantage of the use of parables is that it is centered around a moral lesson, and moral lessons are meant to be passed on from generation to generation. The old testament is full of Jewish law, how to be clean and pure in the eyes of God, and includes hundreds of laws they are expected to obey. When Jesus died, He instructed His disciples to preach His good news to all the nations, which included non-Jews. (Mark 13:10) The idea of bringing people of different faith backgrounds, customs, and beliefs together was to unite all of His followers together in one body, under Christ.

Jesus and His disciples teach over and over that the body perishes, for all of us, and that it's in **our spirits** that we have eternal life. God wants our souls, He wants them abiding in Him, obeying His laws and commandments with all our heart, soul, spirit, and strength. Anything having to do with the body passes away, so **what** we do with them is secondary to **why** we do what we do. So, although following God to His letter is what He's asking of us, it's our hearts, our spirit that needs the most preparation for eternal salvation in Him. Here, the message and moral code of living Christ was trying to teach, and convert in the hearts of all humanity, was to be passed on for future generations so that *all* of humanity could be included in Christ's message. Even though these stories are thousands of years old, we can still derive meaning from them and apply them to *our* lives. The bible didn't come with an expiration date (Matthew 24:35). We should re-familiarize ourselves with the Holy Bible, the commandments, *and* the laws, so we can truly **understand** the message God is sending to us about cleanliness, purity, and contriteness in our hearts, minds and lives.

Matthew 22:36-40, NKJV

36 "Teacher, which is the great commandment in the law?" 37 Jesus said to him, "'You shall love the Lord your God with all your heart, with all your soul, and with all your mind.' 38 This is the first and great commandment. 39 And the second is like it: 'You shall love your neighbor as yourself.' 40 On these two commandments hang **all the Law and the Prophets.**"

July 29
Abide in Him

John 15:4-5, ESV

4 "Abide in me, and I in you. As the branch cannot bear fruit by itself, unless it abides in the vine, neither can you, unless you abide in me. 5 I am the vine; you are the branches. Whoever abides in me and I in him, he it is that bears much fruit, for apart from me you can do nothing."

1 John 3:24, ESV

24 Whoever keeps His commandments **abides** in God, and God in him. And by this we know that he abides in us, by the Spirit whom he has given us.

When Christ calls us to 'abide' in Him, he's asking us to *accept* Him into our hearts and minds. We do this when we chose to live by His righteous example instead of choosing to walk by our old, sinful ways. For example, being kind and forgiving instead of blaming or judging of others, and by choosing humility and love instead of pride and hate are ways we can abide in Christ. Avoiding gossip, flirting, cussing, and obscene conversations, and do a little more for those in our communities who are less fortunate or need special help, this is also how we can abide in Christ. Devoting more of our personal time to prayer, confiding and trusting more to God, is also how we can abide in Christ. We know we'll make many mistakes on our righteous quest to be more like Jesus (James 3:2), but it's in the sincerity of our attempt that shows God our devotion to Him (Psalm 14:2, Proverbs 8:17).

We are sinful, we, as in the human race. Temptation, frustrations, expectations, obnoxious pride, selfishness, ignorance, quick and easy solutions, and deception to get what we want are real, every day booby traps for those of us who have chosen to follow Jesus. In the book of Job, God allows a man to be tested by the devil (Job 1:6-12), in Genesis (22), Abraham is called to sacrifice His son, and in the desert Jesus was tempted by the devil three times (Matthew 4:1-11). We are all temped, in different ways, and we can all make mistakes and poor choices at times. Some of us do everything we can to hide from our mistakes, others are content to judge others while ignoring their own sins, and some people like to hang themselves on their sins without giving themselves the benefit of forgiveness. If we truly love Jesus, it isn't too much to ask to evaluate ourselves, repent our sins for goodness sake, and seek direction from Christ. Remember brothers and sisters, Jesus died for all, but not all will die for Him.

2 Chronicles 7:14, NKJV

14 "If My people who are called by My name will humble themselves, and pray and seek My face, and turn from their wicked ways, then I will hear from heaven, and will forgive their sin and heal their land."

1 John 2:6, ESV

6 whoever says he abides in him ought to walk in the same way in which he walked.

July 30
Think Spiritual, Not Physical

Romans 7:6, GW

6 But now we have died to those laws that bound us. God has broken their effect on us so that **we are serving in a new spiritual way**, not in an old way dictated by written words.

Sins are wicked choices according to God, and come from our physical needs and desires (James 1:14-15). Some people have a desire to have what someone else owns so they covet, deceive, or steal to get it, all of which are sins. If we lust for another, whether or not we act upon that the bible tells us that simply the lustful thought is as bad as actually acting upon it (Matthew 5:28). Some people want to be seen as important, so they ignore our fellow man to accomplish their goals for power, wealth, or success. These wants and desires are entwined with our individual pursuits of happiness, and the physical, social, and economic world we live in. We need our houses as shelter, but they don't need to be mansions. We need cars to drive to work, but they don't have to be fancy. If we are blessed with more than we need, we should give it to someone who needs it instead of padding our lives with 'more.'

No matter what we try to tell ourselves, we can't be righteous, holy and humble if we're greedy, selfish, and in pursuit of worldly comforts while ignoring the plight of our fellow man. We can't love and forgive our enemies while we covet them, or harbor deceit in our hearts toward them. We can't judge another on the sins they've committed while committing sins ourselves, that's self-exaltation. What may seem impossible to us really isn't, with God's help (Matthew 19:26). God can transform our greedy, selfish, arrogant hearts into more loving, forgiving and humble hearts if we would only pray and ask Him for that. When we pray for things in the pursuit of righteousness we're assured to get what we ask for (Mat.7:7). How we feel about other people, what we secretly wish for, what we're afraid of, what touches our soul is what comprises our spirit, and this is what God is asking us to purify. The things about us that make us who we are, what makes us different than the next human, is what God wants to save. We all need saving and purifying, no matter what we try to tell ourselves, and reading the scriptures will start us on the path to righteousness.

Romans 8:2, ICB

2 I am not judged guilty because in Christ Jesus the law of the Spirit that brings life made me free. It made me free from the law that brings sin and death.

Mark 12:24-27a, ICB

24 Jesus answered, "Why did you make this mistake? **Is it because you don't know what the Scriptures say? Or is it because you don't know about the power of God?** 25 When people rise from death, there will be no marriage. People will not be married to each other but will be like angels in heaven. 26 Surely you have read what God said about people rising from death. In the book in which Moses wrote about the burning bush, it says that God told Moses this: 'I am the God of Abraham, the God of Isaac, and the God of Jacob.' 27a God is the God of *living* people, not dead people."

July 31
A Spiritual Battle

Ephesians 6:11-13, ESV

11 Put on the whole armor of God, that you may be able to stand against the schemes of the devil. 12 For we do not wrestle against flesh and blood, but against the rulers, against the authorities, against the cosmic powers over this present darkness, against the spiritual forces of evil in the heavenly places. 13 Therefore take up the whole armor of God, that you may be able to withstand in the evil day, and having done all, to stand firm.

We don't really think of life as a spiritual battle when we're twelfth in line, waiting at a stoplight, or in a crowded elevator stopping at every floor. Our lives keep us busy, sometimes to the point of being oblivious to the larger battle waging inside and all around us. Even if this battle started a million years ago, we are all involved since we all belong to the human race, which God created for His purpose. The bible makes it clear that the devil wants to spite God for kicking him out of Heaven and sending him to Earth (Isaiah 14:12-15). We are told that he is the 'deceiver,' and 'murderer,' (John 8:44) and he is all lies and wickedness, spreading sin and trying to corrupt the souls of man to turn away from their faith in the one Almighty God (2 Corinthians 11:14).

Some of us want to stay out of it and just mind our own business, but turning a blind eye to the importance of the 'unseen battle' we've inherited doesn't make us less a part of it. We will be tempted by the devil, given tests of strife, endure pain, and be subjected to sin no matter what we think is justified by our own standards. God's will is more powerful than our own, like it or not. Many are distracted by their work, families, or our social lives, but nothing should never take us away from our first priority, which should be our devotion to God. The bible clarifies God as Spirit (John 4:24), and that we should pray and meditate in a quiet place to receive Him (Matthew 6:6). Devoting our time, our hearts in prayer, and our lives to the changes He's planning to direct, with or without our consent, is the key to peace, and salvation for our spirits. The salvation of our spirits is important to God, and should be important to us as well.

Psalm 1:1-2, GW

1 Blessed is the person who does not follow the advice of wicked people, take the path of sinners, or join the company of mockers. 2 Rather, he delights in the teachings of the Lord and reflects on His teachings day and night.

August 1
3000 Year Old Love Affair

1 John 4:16, ESV

16 So we have come to know and to believe the love that God has for us. God is love, and whoever abides in love abides in God, and God abides in him.

God has been wrestling and negotiating and applying His special kind of holy justice on the sins of a corrupt humanity since the beginning of time. The bible is full of betrayals of God by humans, only to be given forgiveness and continued grace and opportunities for His everlasting salvation (Proverbs 1:28-31, Proverbs 19:3, Jeremiah 12:8, Jeremiah 32:33, Ezekiel 21:13, Amos 4:6-12). Despite what some people may think, this pattern continues to this day between a faithful, forgiving God and His self-seeking humanity that continues to stray from Him by sin. Worldly desires, temptations surrounding us, and other humans distracting us exacerbate our natural propensity to make unrighteous choices. God only wants our love, and for us to lead as righteous a life as we can, loving one another. That doesn't seem like much to ask, so why do we keep letting God down?

We cannot love what the world has to offer and love God at the same time (James 4:4). Anytime our focus is on anything that pertains to the world, our jobs and careers, our finances, or our possessions we aren't focused on God. God loves humans, all of us. There is no greater love than someone who lays down their life for another. God literally did that, came down to Earth as a human in the form of Jesus and died for ALL of our sins. That's love. Jesus calls us to love Him by following His commands (1 John 2:3-6). How can we, as humans, *not* love the Lord for His sacrificial love? We are part of the same human family as the characters in the bible (Genesis 9:19), and God's documented love for them equally applies to us as a result. We are in a relationship with God, He is waiting for us to seek Him with His divine forgiveness and grace. Let us pray to Him now, and renew our vows to put Him first in our lives. We have everything to gain and only our sins to lose! Merciful and loving Lord, restore our hearts to those that seek you first, forgive us our iniquities, and draw us nearer to your grace and truth. Praise be to the Lord, King of the Universe, always and forever, AMEN.

John 15:13, ESV

13 Greater love has no one than this, that someone lay down His life for His friends.

Jeremiah 31:3, ERV

3 From far away, the Lord will appear to His people. The Lord says, "I love you people with a love that continues forever. That is why I have continued showing you kindness."

August 2
Our Teacher In Jesus

Jeremiah 30:21-22, ERV

21 The Lord says, "One of their own people will lead them. That ruler will come from my people. People can come close to me only if I ask them to. So I will ask that leader to come to me, and he will be close to me. 22 You will be my people, and I will be your God."

John 14:6, ERV

6 Jesus answered, "I am the way, the truth, and the life. The only way to the Father is through me."

Many churches have beautiful alters, a lovely or ornate cross, and maybe a sculpture or two. Pastors, preachers, ministers, rabbis, and priests lead their congregations in worship and praise, following years of tradition. These Godly men and women take very seriously their commitment to teaching the word of God as their religion directs. Whether we're in the congregation or leading the worship, we all have a responsibility to serve God as He's asked us to. As individual people, we are to follow and serve our one, Almighty God, and He has very specific ideas about how we should be worshiping. Tradition can serve a lot of people to grow in righteousness, but they must be led by the truth of the word of God. The bible has sixty six books, written at different times in History, and from different people in the service of the one, true God. Just like one cannot understand the story properly if it isn't read in its entirety, the bible cannot truly be understood and respected unless it's been read completely.

If we're simply learning God's word one or two bible verses at a time, we're not really following the word of God, but another human beings interpretation of God's word. Churches can provide a place to worship God with other believers, but unless we're actually reading the bible for ourselves, we're not going to understand how to follow God, or what the truth is. Jesus was sent to take the sins for all humanity, giving birth to the Holy Spirit, and eternal salvation for all of those who would follow Him. Jesus was sent as a form of God (John 1:18), witnessed firsthand the disbelief of His creation, and died for them so that they could be made Holy. Jesus is a filter for God (John 5:22). Jesus decides our fate. We can't add to the scriptures to make it easier, or more fun to follow. We aren't supposed to be praying to Mary, or the Saints, or our late Grandma who always knew what to do (1 Corinthians 3:23). Just because the most notable people according to the world say it's the right thing to do, doesn't mean it is. All truth in God is written in the bible, if we don't know what it says, how can we say really love God, a God we can't possibly understand? Read on, pray, repeat, brothers and sisters!

Revelation 22:18-19, ERV

18 I warn everyone who hears the words of prophecy in this book: If anyone adds anything to these, God will give that person the plagues written about in this book. 19 And if anyone takes away from the words of this book of prophecy, God will take away that person's share of the tree of life and of the holy city, which are written about in this book.

August 3
Adultery

James 4:4, ESV

4 You adulterous people! Do you not know that friendship with the world is enmity with God? Therefore whoever wishes to be a friend of the world makes himself an enemy of God.

Isaiah 24:5, ESV

5 The earth lies defiled under its inhabitants; for they have transgressed the laws, violated the statutes, broken the everlasting covenant.

Although many people may think of an unfaithful mate when they read the word, 'adultery,' unfaithfulness to God is what the bible is referring to. God knows we have to live in this world, He knows we'll need things to survive here. God calls us to live modestly, giving what we can to those in need or less fortunate, to show kindness to our neighbor, and attribute all we have to the Lord instead of our own brilliance, tenacity and free will. Wealth, fame, properties, possessions, cars, yachts, jewelry, extra-marital affairs and liaisons, gambling and fighting are all sinful acquisitions that put hostility between us and God. Gossip, obnoxious or stubborn attitudes, flirtatiousness, and ignoring the plight of our fellow man are also sinful acquisitions that put hostility between us and God. The bible is clear that God is looking for calm, generous, humble, modest-living, faithful, disciplined souls who love and treat others as well as they do themselves (Micah 6:8). It's only the world we live in, our changing, fickle, wicked society that puts focus on the unrighteous behavior- this separates us from God's grace.

Some people seek worldly pleasures, thinking some are less sinful than others, not wanting to believe or accept that God frowns upon *any* behavior that leads to sin. Still others commit one sin after another without regard to God at all, ignoring and suppressing any part of themselves that may be curious about a closer relationship with God. In the bible, the agreement between God and all of humanity is referred to as a 'covenant,' where He agrees to bless us with eternal life in return for our faithfulness and obedience (Romans 3:26, 29-30). A 'covenant' is equivalent to a marriage, a bond, a pledge, a contract, an agreement, and measures our love and faithfulness. Still taking this as serious as the day it was made over three thousand years ago, (Hebrews 13:8) God is still evaluating us while humanity continues to march up and down on the Earth, demanding its own will, and gradually forgetting God all together. Who will repent, and re-pledge their love to a forgiving God who waits patiently for them to return?

Ezekiel 16:59-60, ERV

59 this is what the Lord God said: "I will treat you like you treated me! You broke your marriage promise, since you have despised the oath by breaking the covenant. You did not respect our agreement. 60 But I will remember the agreement we made, and I will establish a permanent covenant with you, an agreement with you that will continue forever!"

August 4
Irreparable Damage?

Isaiah 46:9-10, 12, CEV

9 "I alone am God! There are no other gods; no one is like me. Think about what happened many years ago. 10 From the very beginning, I told what would happen long before it took place. I kept my word 12 You people are stubborn and far from being safe, so listen to me."

Ezekiel 21:13, CEV

13 "I am testing my people, and they can do nothing to stop me. I, the Lord, have spoken."

Not everyone likes surprises, especially when they're traffic related, or pose a threat to our safety, happiness, or salvation. We are all hurting, we all suffer, and many of us don't deal with this in healthy, righteous ways. Turning the other cheek when we feel wronged is tough, especially when the pain is choreographed by God. Trust is difficult, and human emotion, expectations, and secret anxieties make focusing on the Lord challenging. Make no mistake, we are all being challenged, and we are all failing the Lord in some way. We are made imperfect, to need the Lord, yet many of us try to make ourselves righteous on our own in our ignorance. No matter what our emotions may be telling us, no hurt is too much for the Lord. We are assured that **all of our sins**, except contempt against the Holy Spirit, **will be forgiven** (Matthew 12:31-32). No damage is *Irreparable* (Jeremiah 32:27).

God tests us sometimes, to see if we're worthy of the blessings we're about to receive. God reproves us when we make poor decisions, don't repent for our wrongdoings, or have the wrong attitudes toward one another (Jeremiah 2:19). Sometimes, God hurts us to see if we'll seek Him, or if our love and obedience toward Him diminishes (Deuteronomy 8:2). God can tell if we're indignant and outraged in our hearts at the pain we're experiencing, or if we're patient and humbly waiting for Him to repair our broken hearts. Make no mistake, God Himself, is responsible for all we feel, think, and experience in our lives. When we fail to acknowledge the Lord's power, and presence in our lives, we only put ourselves in a position to make more mistakes. We must have faith that the Lord will restore us, even when it doesn't feel like that will ever happen. Pain and anxiety causes our perspective to narrow, and we must understand this, especially when we are under pressure, feeling afflicted, scorned, or spiritually wounded. Lord, strengthen us, restore us, and help us to understand how to please you better, blessed is the name of the Lord in Christ Jesus. AMEN.

Psalm 6:1-4, CEV

1 Don't punish me, Lord, or even correct me when you are angry! 2 Have pity on me and heal my feeble body. My bones tremble with fear, 3 and I am in deep distress. How long will it be? 4 Turn and come to my rescue. Show your wonderful love and save me, Lord.

August 5
Our Souls on a Wanted Poster

Ephesians 6; 14-18a, GW

14 So then, take your stand! Fasten truth around your waist like a belt. Put on God's approval as your breastplate. 15 Put on your shoes so that you are ready to spread the Good News that gives peace. 16 In addition to all these, take with you the shield of faith. With it you can put out all the flaming arrows of the evil one. 17 Also take salvation as your helmet and God's word as the sword that the Spirit supplies. 18 Pray in the Spirit in every situation.

Some of us might think stories of the good guy fighting the evil bad guy is an over-used cliché, but that's what our tightrope walk of faith is all about. God wants to bring us into His eternal kingdom, but we must achieve a certain level of righteousness to get there. The devil and His evil spirits are busy at work to separate God from what He loves the most, us. Caught in the middle of an unseen, holy war, between good and evil is the salvation of the human spirit. Wow, that's really heavy. Maybe we weren't expecting to be involved in a three thousand year old chess match of life and death when we endeavored to develop a closer relationship with Jesus, but, we are.

Evil hides in common places, like gossip, lust for money, physical lust for another, anger and arguing, judging other people, assuming we know more than we do, self-aggrandizing appearances and pride, and ignoring the plight of those less fortunate. Over and over, righteousness is described as being humble, modest in our lifestyles and appearances, forgiving others, treating others with kindness, patience, love, and always maintaining self-control. Our world isn't designed to foster a holy relationship with God through Christ Jesus, through their repeated poor choices and need for autonomy, humans have made it a breeding ground for sin and wickedness. The good news is that our sins are forgiven through Christ Jesus, if we believe in Him, repent, and turn away from our sinful behavior and follow His example for our lives. Consider that for a moment, because it's easy to make promises without truly thinking about, or fully understanding the consequences. If we don't repent for all of our sins, give up our sinful behaviors, and follow Jesus' righteous lifestyle we risk being exiled from His eternal kingdom forever (Romans 11:22). Many people can accept believing in Jesus, even repenting their wrongs isn't too tough, but changing their lifestyles, or giving up comforts they've grown accustomed to having is too much for them. God's love may be strict, but His rewards are plentiful, and His love is never-ending. Nothing on Earth can compare to the glory, the love, the depth of understanding God has for us. All we need to do is come to Him in prayer, over and over, and seek Him first in our lives. Choose wisely, brothers and sisters.

Acts 26:18, ERV

18 Jesus said to His disciples, "You will make them able to understand the truth. They will turn away from darkness to the light. They will turn away from the power of Satan, and they will turn to God. Then their sins can be forgiven, and they can be given a place among God's people—those who have been made holy by believing in me.'"

August 6
Heaven or Hell, Got Reservations?

Matthew 25:41, ESV

41 Jesus said, "Then he will say to those on His left, 'Depart from me, you cursed, into the eternal fire prepared for the devil and His angels."

Matthew 13:40-43, ESV

40 Jesus said, "Just as the weeds are gathered and burned with fire, so will it be at the end of the age. 41 The Son of Man will send His angels, and they will gather out of His kingdom all causes of sin and all law-breakers, 42 and throw them into the fiery furnace. In that place there will be weeping and gnashing of teeth. 43 Then the righteous will shine like the sun in the kingdom of their Father. He who has ears, let him hear."

For many, the question of Heaven and Hell can be literal or metaphorical, and on this there will always be debate. The bible describes Hell as a 'fiery inferno,' a place of eternal suffering and damnation away from God's love and light (Matthew 18:9, Revelation 20:10, 2 Thessalonians 1:8-9). Heaven is described as a 'new Eden,' a place where there is no suffering, and we can enjoy God's love and light forever (Isaiah 65:17-19, 2 Peter 3:13, Revelation 21:1). God always gives humanity a choice, but we don't always make good ones. Choosing the narrow path to Heaven is daunting, and requires staunch belief in God's love for us through Jesus and His sacrifice, plus a lifetime of repentance, and a devotion to actually living more holy lives.

Choosing the way of Christ is a difficult road, and following His narrow path of righteousness amongst our sinful, greedy, evil world can be nearly impossible (Matthew 7:13-14). After all, our world is a place where evil holds sovereignty. Our life's choices here on Earth reflect our motivation, the desires in our heart, and this we cannot hide from God (Jeremiah 17:10). Do you want more money, more recognition, or more respect? If so, you are driven by selfish, sinful desires. Jesus calls His followers to limit their desires to wanting to live a more 'Christ-like' lifestyle, a spiritual cleansing and growth, holiness and righteousness by example. Keeping our focus on Jesus, and not ourselves or other humans, will help us avoid a reservation in hell.

Matthew 10:28, ERV

28 Jesus said to His disciples, "Don't be afraid of people. They can kill the body, but they cannot kill the soul. The only one you should fear is God, the one who can send the body and the soul to be destroyed in hell."

August 7
Going Our Own Way

Ecclesiastes 7:29, ERV

29 "There is one other thing I have learned. God made people good, but they have found many ways to be bad."

Isaiah 29:15-16, ERV

15 Look at them! They try to hide things from the Lord. They think he will not understand. They do their evil things in darkness. They tell themselves: "No one can see us. No one will know who we are." 16 You turn things upside down. You think the clay is equal to the potter. You think that something that is made can tell the one who made it, "You did not make me!" this is like a pot telling its maker, "You know nothing."

From what we'll wear to what we'll do with our time, to who we'll spend it with, what we'll have for lunch to what we spend our money on, we make a lot of decisions in our day. Over the course of history man has waged war, made laws, enforced punishments, and learned new discoveries. It would seem as though one can accomplish anything one sets their mind to, but this is only a half truth. Because the first humans disobeyed God, we will all have to work hard for what we have (Genesis 3:19), but all that we have has been provided by our Father in Heaven (Deuteronomy 10:14). At the end of a long day we can be satisfied with our hard work and all we've accomplished, but when do we acknowledge God? All we've gone through in the day was due to the course God set out before us, perhaps to teach someone something about God, or to learn something about God from someone else.

When we say we love God, but only pray when we're in trouble, we're hypocrites. God isn't a supervisory force merely watching and only intervening when something huge or miraculous happens, He is the power that fuels our world, and the force that binds us all together as His creation. God wants us to model our lives by Jesus, to rid our lives of all sin forever, and live according to His commandments and direction. Many of us say they believe in God, but that's where it ends. Praying for guidance and direction means to seek Him for all of our choices and decisions. When was the last time you consulted God in prayer before making a decision?

Isaiah 48:8-10, ERV

8 "But even in the past you didn't listen. You didn't learn anything. You never listen to what I say. I have always known that you would turn against me. You have rebelled against me from the time you were born. 9 But I will be patient. I will do this for myself. People will praise me for not becoming angry and destroying you. You will praise me for waiting. 10 Look, I will make you pure, but not in the way you make silver pure. I will make you pure by giving you troubles."

August 8
Choices & Behaviors

Romans 2:4-9a, GW

4 Do you have contempt for God, who is very kind to you, puts up with you, and deals patiently with you? Don't you realize that it is God's kindness that is trying to lead you to him and change the way you think and act? 5 Since you are stubborn and don't want to change the way you think and act, you are adding to the anger that God will have against you on that day when God vents His anger. At that time God will reveal that His decisions are fair. 6 He will pay all people back for what they have done. 7 He will give everlasting life to those who search for glory, honor, and immortality by persisting in doing what is good. But he will bring 8 anger and fury on those who, in selfish pride, refuse to believe the truth and who follow what is wrong. 9a There will be suffering and distress for every person who does evil.

Luring us away from the soul-saving grace of God's forgiveness, the devil confuses and tempts us away from the path of true righteousness (1 John 5:19). Our world provides a plethora of unwholesome distractions where people can satisfy their immoral sexual desires, give in to the lust for money and wealth, or succumb to bitterness and revenge. The devil likes to spark our passions, spawn arguments and create suspicion among family members, the bible warns us (1 Peter 5:8). Those who don't believe that our behaviors reflect what's in our hearts, or don't think any of it really matters, are being deceived. Perhaps some of us have forgotten, or simply don't believe, that God is responsible for all we have, and not us (Romans 11:36). Some of us have difficulty bringing ourselves down to a humble state before God, which is required to witness His forgiveness and grace.

A little gratitude for all God has done to help us gain access to His eternal kingdom is required from all of us, for we are all God's creation. We have been given His commandments and laws in the bible, we have been given Jesus and the Holy Spirit for the forgiveness of our sins, and guidance to the path of righteousness. When we humble ourselves and ask for forgiveness, we are promising God we'll change our actions and behaviors, otherwise we aren't really sorry. There is a big difference between being sorry we've been caught doing something we shouldn't and feeling genuine remorse, God knows when we're faking it. Genuine remorse generates the desire to improve oneself, using the guilt as a lesson of behavior to avoid a second time. If we don't really think about our actions as a representation of our true heart's desire, we're being deliberately distracted or confused. We are not only called to change the way we think and act, but be *persistent* about staying in the righteous light of God's word and commandments. Pray on, repent, and remain steadfast in faith, brothers and sisters!

John 3:17, GW

17 God sent His Son into the world, not to condemn the world, but to save the world.

August 9
Honesty

Proverbs 12:22, GW

22 Lips that lie are disgusting to the Lord, but **honest people are His delight**.

We have all received a gift we didn't like, but pretended we did. We have all told someone, "It'll be fine," when we really didn't think all would be fine. When we try to spare someone unpleasant, or hurtful, news, we may think a lie is justified. No matter how noble the intension, choosing sin is never the wise choice. A righteous solution is only a prayer a way, and the word of God is in our hearts for us to draw upon. Asking ourselves, "What would Jesus do?" is always going to be better than any solutions we could come up with on our own. Whether drumming up excuses on why we were late, or why we weren't where we were supposed to be, or what we said to someone else, a lie is deceit. When we're focused on how we look to others we're not focused on Jesus, and when we assume we know what is best for another, we are arrogant, and both are sins. God decides what our ultimate fate is going to be, not humanity or the world we live in, so our focus should always be on Him. Once the world tempts us to lie, one lie leads to another, and other sin to cover the lie, and before we know it we're not just chasing after sin and wickedness, we're running after it! (Jeremiah 8:6)

Doing the righteous thing isn't going to be easy, especially when it seems like the entire world is caught up in sin's wicked conquest, pride and competition. Persistence under pressure is a sign of true faith, and when we pray to God for strength and resolve when we're under strain, He hears us. We don't always have the best answers, we don't always make the right choices, and we've all disappointed someone at one time in our lives. Confessing our imperfections to the Lord should be private (Matthew 6:5), and not anything we need to profess loudly to the world. We know our sins, the Lord knows our sins, and that's all that matters. We can't hide from ourselves, our sins follow us wherever we go, spawning more sins until we've handed them over to Christ. Truly brothers and sisters, the world doesn't care about our honesty or integrity, but it'll sell us theirs for the right fee. Our salvation is worth more than what the world has to offer, not because of how special we are, but because of how special Christ is. Denial is a trap, we are all meant to repent and humble ourselves before the Lord, honesty is the only way to true salvation. Peace to all brothers and sisters! Amen.

2 Timothy 2:15, ICB

15 Do the best you can to be the kind of person that God will approve, and give yourself to him. Be a worker who is not ashamed of His work — a worker who uses the true teaching in the right way.

Mark 8:36, KJV

36 For what shall it profit a man, if he shall gain the whole world, and lose His own soul?

August 10
Discouragement and Doubt Don't Belong

Psalm 112:4-9, GW

4 Light will shine in the dark for a decent person. He is merciful, compassionate, and fair. 5 All goes well for the person who is generous and lends willingly. He earns an honest living. 6 He will never fail. A righteous person will always be remembered. 7 He is not afraid of bad news. His heart remains secure, full of confidence in the Lord. 8 His heart is steady, and he is not afraid. In the end he will look triumphantly at His enemies. 9 He gives freely to poor people. His righteousness continues forever. His head is raised in honor.

Psalm 33:18, GW

18 The Lord's eyes are on those who fear him, on those who wait with hope for His mercy.

Many of us are mature enough to realize we're not always going to get what we want in life. Disappointment and unmet expectations threaten even the most successful, and even the most righteous person. Praying our anxieties to Jesus is the first step, and then we are called to be patient and trust in Him. We can become impatient in waiting for the Lord to answer our prayers and concerns, and this can lead to frustration and doubt. Our troubles don't always go away, and others seem to work themselves out or vanish. Many people attribute the answer to their problems was their own ingenuity, hard word, determination, or luck. God controls the good and bad in our lives (Isaiah 45:7), and works on His own mysterious timeline. Even though we are told we will never be forsaken by God (Hebrews 13:5), His timeline can test what little patience we do have. When we pray for patience and guidance along with our request for healing and comfort, we are showing the Lord we have faith in Him.

Patience is tough, especially when we, or someone we love, is hurting or having trouble in their life. It can be easy to allow impatience to turn into frustration, and neither of these are the right mindset to hear the Holy Spirit. When we are calm, humble, and trusting in the Lord we are seen and heard by Jesus. We may not get the answer we expect, but what's right according to God is what will happen, not what we think is the right solution. Trusting that God hears our prayers, but also that what will be done is justified by the Lord. If we are truly listening, and remain strong in our faith, we will be pleasing to the Lord. In the end, a strong faith and works that are pleasing to the Lord should be our true goal, not our idea of justice or balance. Faith is having patience when we're feeling disappointed, let down, discouraged, or even doubtful, patience and confidence that God will heal us. We can, and should, pray for a faith that can withstand what God gives us. After all, discouragement leads to doubt, and doubt takes us away from the very grace of God we seek.

2 Corinthians 4:16-17, ESV

16 So we do not lose heart. Though our outer self is wasting away, our inner self is being renewed day by day. 17 For this light momentary affliction is preparing for us an eternal weight of glory beyond all comparison.

August 11
Seeking Praise

Matthew 6:1-4, ERV

1 "Be careful! When you do something good, don't do it in front of others so that they will see you. If you do that, you will have no reward from your Father in heaven. 2 When you give to those who are poor, don't announce that you are giving. Don't be like the hypocrites. When they are in the synagogues and on the streets, they blow trumpets before they give so that people will see them. They want everyone to praise them. The truth is that's all the reward they will get. 3 So when you give to the poor, don't let anyone know what you are doing. 4 Your giving should be done in private. Your Father can see what is done in private, and he will reward you."

We all like to be complimented, after all, it feels good to be recognized pleasantly by others. We want our employers to see us as reliable and efficient, our subordinates to see us as capable leaders, and our loved ones to see as important and loving. As nice as it feels to be loved and accepted by other people, seeking the acceptance of people above God is not being faithful to Him, according to scripture (Romans 2:11, Colossians 1:17). Seeking praise from our Heavenly Father should be driving more of us. Daunted and confused by the complexities of the bible, Gods relationship goals for us fall by the wayside for many of us. Which rules do we follow, how will we know if we're doing it right, and how to decipher the Spirit at work inside of us can all be too perplexing for some people to stay the course with God. Many people become discouraged, disillusioned and disappointed with the narrow path, and restricted course, that the Lord's righteousness offers. We must be diligent to unlearn our expectations of God, and re-familiarize ourselves with what He is truly asking of us.

Humans are good at overthinking and overcomplicating things, after all, God simply wants our faith and devotion. Blessings from God doesn't give us the kind of instant gratification that comes from diving headlong into sinful indulgences, or cash prizes, or awards, or notoriety we can brag about to our friends and colleagues. Righteousness brings about peace of mind, wisdom that fuels our spirit growth that only comes from God, and opportunities to spread His word to others through good works of faith. We should *want* to seek God because He is our creator, and offers us eternal salvation and rest for our souls through His sacrifice in Jesus. We can find God in the written word, the teachings of Jesus, and through prayer, not through conquests of things the world offers. Capable, loving, efficient, and prosperous are the qualities we should want God to see in us. If we aren't seeking God actively and daily, how are we showing Him we love Him?

John 5:44, ERV

44 You like to have praise from each other. But you never try to get the praise that comes from the only God. So how can you believe?

August 12
Tough Love

Jeremiah 7:23-24, CEB

23 "Rather, this is what I required of them: Obey me so that I may become your God and you may become my people. Follow the path I mark out for you so that it may go well with you. 24 But they didn't listen or pay attention. They followed their willful and evil hearts and went backward rather than forward."

Learning to be holy in our lives the way God requires us is going to take a life-time of overcoming insurmountable odds, trusting through unanswered questions, and working through devastating pain. Our world has been corrupted by human sin and wickedness, and offers us competition, conquest, dissention, and deceit instead of forgiveness, service, grace, and love. If we question where God is when we experience strife, or become despondent or impatient when we don't feel comforted for each and every affliction we are being arrogant. Sometimes, the biggest blessings come first from challenges that seem to devastate us. These challenges can make us question ourselves, our gifts, our faith, and are meant to bring us to our knees before God. If we were never challenged, we could never actually 'prove' that we're relying on the one, true God for everything in our lives.

Challenging us in ways we don't expect, God can appear to hide His face from us when we feel we need Him the most (Psalm 27:9). Overwhelming us with difficulties accompanied by little to no respite, the Lord can sometimes give us more than we can handle to see if we'll come to Him in true faith when we break. The pain the Lord can inflict upon us is often deep, personal, and shakes the foundations of our trust in Him. Knowing our hearts, our mistakes and why we make them, The Lord knows what it's going to take to redirect us properly on our path of righteousness. We are asked to trust in the Lord, to trust His ways over our own (Psalm 118:8, Proverbs 3:5-6), and taking an "It's not fair" attitude doesn't represent a full trust in the Lord.

Our walk of faith, our relationship with the Lord, is like walking on a path through the woods (Proverbs 3:6). As we walk we learn what righteousness looks like, and adapt our behaviors and attitudes to suit the Lord instead of ourselves. As we get closer to becoming who God wants us to be the challenges He gives us to forward us along that path become increasingly more difficult as the path becomes more nar-row to reflect the strict righteousness we must adhere to. He is refining us (Jeremiah 9:7), making us holy, making our faith stronger, our grace more abundant, and our endurance greater so we'll be prepared for the next challenge we get from Him. The holy walk of faith we undertake with the Lord will become more narrow as we progress along it, through affliction, and the tough love of the Almighty God. Eventually, the path will become so narrow and fine that it'll disappear completely, leaving just our faith to sustain us. Is your faith currently strong enough?

Isaiah 37:29, NIV

29 "Because you rage against me and because your insolence has reached my ears, I will put my hook in your nose and my bit in your mouth, and I will make you return by the way you came."

August 13
Looking for Blame in All the Wrong Places

Genesis 3:12-13, CEB

12 The man said, "The woman you gave me, she gave me some fruit from the tree, and I ate." 13 The Lord God said to the woman, "What have you done?!" And the woman said, "The snake tricked me, and I ate."

Romans 2:3, ESV

3 Do you suppose, O man—you who judge those who practice such things and yet do them yourself—that you will escape the judgment of God?

The clothes we wear, the way we spend our money, the way we stand, the way we walk, to the cars we drive, to the way we order our coffee, humans judge one another. Some people who judge others are looking for any weakness to exploit themselves as more significant than another. Others judge because they are trying to see where they fit in with the rest of society, trying to classify themselves and others from predetermined conceptions. It's noteworthy to mention that 'all humanity falls short,' and is considered, 'wicked,' and 'sinful,' according to God in our beloved bibles (Romans 3:23, Genesis 6:5). As unpleasant as the disparity of mankind is, it makes us all equal in the eyes of God, and equally gives us the potential to disappoint one another. In fact, the disparity of mankind means that no one really has the *right* to accuse, judge, condemn, make ill-conceived or unfair opinions on one another, for any reason. If we're all rotten, all guilty, then pointing fingers isn't going to change, lessen, take away your sins, or make them less offensive in the eyes of God.

Behind the sins we commit are motives, *why* do we do the things we do? Why we make the choices in our lives comes from our heart, the deep need or desire that we are trying to fill. Some of us desire to fit in, some of us desire success, some of us desire a deeper spiritual relationship with our creator. We all make our own mistakes, all God's asking us to do is bring them before Him, not parade them for the whole world to see. Likewise, He's asking us to not advertise our fellow brother's and sister's sins, if we know them, because we'd be hypocrites. Anything that assigns blame, apportions guilt, criticizes, condemns, rebukes or attacks is against God, the bible tells us (Ephesians 4:31-32, Colossians 3:12-17). Not only that, but we're asked to forgive, and even pray for, our enemies (Matthew 5:44). *In the dictionary, the opposite of blame is forgive*. If we would all take a closer look at what **God** expects, and compare them to our **own** actions, we'd be spending more useful time, than comparing rotten apples to rotten oranges.

Galatians 6:4-5, ERV

4 Don't compare yourself with others. Just look at your own work to see if you have done anything to be proud of. 5 You must each accept the responsibilities that are yours.

August 14
Something to Talk About

James 4:16, ESV

16 As it is, you boast in your arrogance. All such boasting is evil.

Matthew 6: 1, 4, ERV

1 "Be careful! When you do something good, don't do it in front of others so that they will see you. If you do that, you will have no reward from your Father in heaven. 4 Your giving should be done in private. Your Father can see what is done in private, and he will reward you."

1 Samuel 2:3, GW

3 Do not boast or let arrogance come out of your mouth because the Lord is a God of knowledge, and he weighs our actions.

We all know someone who patronizes people when they speak, or someone who doesn't like to consider the opinions of others, or someone who has a distorted opinion of their abilities, or someone who doesn't like to accept their limitations, or someone who thinks their knowledge is superior to another's. These are just a few examples of arrogance. Having an inflated view of your importance, gifts and abilities, or being focused on the lack of your gifts and abilities is focused on self. Self-absorption is pride due to our 'self' wanting to be elevated, and the cause is really secondary, because in our arrogance we're focused on ourselves and not God. Pride and arrogance is at the root of turning away from God (Psalm 10:4). When we suffer, and have been arrogant or prideful, we can be outraged when our prayers aren't answered. It shouldn't be too difficult to see that human sin is tricky, also that its everywhere, and should leading us to repentance.

As in the case of pride or arrogance, once we understand that we have been sinful, we should be less concerned with how we got there, and more with substituting that pride and arrogance for humility and modesty. Of course, to know *why* we sinned is important in reforming the heart, but only to once again refocus on Jesus. When we keep our thoughts to our Lord and Savior, what *He* did, what *He* said, how *He* handled Himself, we gain clarity in how righteousness looks, sounds, and behaves. Getting close to the Lord, our God and Savior, should be the only motivation in our lives, and all we need to brag about.

Ephesians 2:8-9, ESV

8 For by grace you have been saved through faith. And this is not your own doing; it is the gift of God, 9 not a result of works, so that no one may boast.

Jeremiah 9:23-24, GW

23 this is what the Lord says: "Don't let wise people brag about their wisdom. Don't let strong people brag about their strength. Don't let rich people brag about their riches. 24 If they want to brag, they should brag that they understand and know me. They should brag that I, the Lord, act out of love, righteousness, and justice on the earth. This kind of bragging pleases me," declares the Lord.

August 15
Remain Strong in Faith

1 John 4:2-3, ERV/ESV

2 This is how you can recognize God's Spirit. One spirit says, "I believe that Jesus is the Messiah who came to earth and became a man." That Spirit is from God. 3 Another spirit refuses to say this about Jesus. That spirit is not from God. This is the spirit of the antichrist, which you heard was coming and now is in the world already.

James 1:12, ESV

12 Blessed is the man who remains steadfast under trial, for when he has stood the test he will receive the crown of life, which God has promised to those who love him.

The older we get, the longer the days seem to be, and yet our struggles continue. Financial, health and relationship crises strike us all, and all on top of the many different responsibilities we already carry. Anytime we take our focus off of what the Lord has done for us, what He has provided, how He's directed us, and focus on our own world for too long we can lose sight of true righteousness. Faith, sincerity, forgiveness, modesty, righteousness, and penitence are all examples of attitudes full of contrite morality, characteristics of someone holy. But beware brothers and sisters, boredom, confusion, betrayal, lust, envy, suspicion, frustration, and hope-lessness are deceitful emotions that the devil likes to exploit in order to separate people from God's grace.

We are assured that all of our lives will be a struggles (Genesis 3:19), and this is due to many reasons. Sometimes to refine us (Zechariah 13:9), other times to humble us (Isaiah 23:9), other times to see what's truly in our hearts (Jeremiah 17:10), and other times to discipline us (Job 5:17-18). Not everyone understands the nature of their struggles, and unholy desires plague us all. We all have different weaknesses, but we are all made strong in our weaknesses by the grace of Jesus Christ (2 Corinthians 12:9). We must not allow our emotions to deceive us into thinking the Lord has forgotten us, isn't being fair with us, or doesn't care what is happening to us, because He always has a reason for what He does. We have been assured we'll never be forsaken, and that God's love for us is eternal (Deut. 31:6, Jeremiah 31:3), and we can't let anything in our world try and tell us otherwise. As God's love for us is eternal, so too should our faith in Him be. Through all He puts us through, we should be patient, accepting of His will, repentant, and thankful to Him for all He is providing for us in our lives.

Ephesians 4:2-3, GW

2 Be humble and gentle in every way. Be patient with each other and lovingly accept each other. 3 Through the peace that ties you together, do your best to maintain the unity that the Spirit gives.

August 16
Avoid Backsliding in Your Faith

Jeremiah 8:4-7, GW

4 "Say to them, 'This is what the Lord says: When someone falls, he gets back up. When someone turns away from me, he returns. 5 The people of Jerusalem turned away from me without ever returning. They still cling to deceit. They refuse to return. 6 I have paid attention and listened, but they weren't honest. They don't turn away from their wickedness and ask, "What have we done?" They go their own ways like horses charging into battle. 7 Even storks know when it's time to return. Mourning doves, swallows, and cranes know when it's time to migrate. But my people don't know that I, the Lord, am urging them to return."

If we look on our cell phones, our emails, our chats and messages with family and friends we'll see who we devote the most time to, people that we consider priority. Our jobs, our loved ones, our families all tend to get the most of our attention. We must ask ourselves, how much time are we devoting to God each day? We all slip in our faith, we all get lazy. Our Lord knows we will stray from Him from time to time, but He also knows our hearts. We have to remember our lives create a great deal of distraction in the way of cell phones, computers, games, texting and a multitude of other applications. To be in tune with the Holy Spirit we must be calm, relaxed, free from distraction and focused on Christ Jesus. Our attention shouldn't be divided, and this is a challenge.

We are told to submit our needs and sins in prayer, but how will we do this if we're not devoting the proper time? What's more, we want to understand God's will responding to us through the Holy Spirit, but we can't really be listening if we're not paying attention. We may be busy people, but we can all make a little more time for Jesus in our lives. Whether in prayer, in devotionals, meditation during alone time, journaling, or simply reading the scripture, carve out time in your day to devote to the Lord. It doesn't matter how many times we stray from our virtuous path, we must always return and ask for forgiveness for our absence and sins (Matthew 18:21). In search of righteous salvation, we will find it in Christ, every time.

Isaiah 48:8, ERV

8 "But even in the past you didn't listen. You didn't learn anything. You never listen to what I say. I have always known that you would turn against me. You have rebelled against me from the time you were born."

Hebrews 2:1-3, ICB

1 So we must be more careful to follow what we were taught. Then we will not be pulled away from the truth. 2 The teaching that God spoke through angels was shown to be true. And anyone who did not follow it or obey it received the punishment he earned. 3 The salvation that was given to us is very great. So surely we also will be punished if we live as if this salvation were not important. It was the Lord himself who first told about this salvation. And those who heard him proved to us that this salvation is true.

August 17
A Father's Discipline

Hebrews 12:4-11, ERV

4 You are struggling against sin, but you have not had to give up your life for the cause. 5 You are children of God, and he speaks words of comfort to you. You have forgotten these words: "My child, don't think the Lord's discipline is worth nothing, and don't stop trying when he corrects you. 6 The Lord **disciplines** everyone he loves; he **punishes** everyone he *accepts* as a child." 7 So accept sufferings like a father's discipline. God does these things to you like a father correcting His children. You know that all children are disciplined by their fathers. 10 Our fathers on earth disciplined us for a short time in the way they thought was best. But God disciplines us to help us so that we can be holy like him. 11 We don't enjoy discipline when we get it. It is painful. But later, after we have learned our lesson from it, we will enjoy the peace that comes from doing what is right.

We are all grown adults, and, as such we should know to carry ourselves with grace and self-control instead of pride, power, and false charms. Motivated by a deeper, spiritual code of conduct and contrite morality, followers of Christ know that modesty and humility are favored by God, and pride is the complete opposite of humility. To know how to please God, one must understand what God wants, and that's where the bible comes in. Deriving all necessary information from the bible, followers of Christ can begin to understand what brings on God's divine correction. A deeper look into this passage reveals that God doesn't accept everyone, and this shouldn't surprise us really, since Jesus explains that not all will get to Heaven (Matthew 7:14). When we're accepted as God's child, we receive the Holy Spirit, who gets immediately to work trimming the wickedness from us. Excising the natural propensity to commit sin is similar to carving a beautiful sculpture: pieces have to be cut off, trimmed, shaved, or compressed before the final, beautiful masterpiece is revealed (Isaiah 64:8). Not all humans will be accepted by God, and not all will be saved (1 John 2:22-23, Luke 10:16, John 3:36, Proverbs 1:24-26, Jeremiah 15:6). God even rejects people (Jeremiah 6:30), those who refuse His word, refuse His correction, and deny the fact that Jesus is the Messiah.

What a wonderful and, yet, frightening thought to know that our one true God has His Almighty hands on us. When we accept Jesus into our hearts, souls, minds *and* lives, our choices and behaviors begin to change, reflecting the divine sculpting process at work inside of us. Those who seek a closer relationship with God will find it, we are assured (Proverbs 8:17), which is a blessing and a curse. We are called to be loving, forgiving, and service-oriented in a world cloaked in sin and wickedness, all the while never stepping out of the righteous light of our Lord in Christ. Staying holy in an evil world, full of evil people who don't give a hang about being a better person in Christ isn't *supposed* to be easy. We should **want** to please our creator, and only those who are truly wicked will resent God's will to change them. God doesn't want to have to destroy us, and pleads with His creation to change their ways, but He can, does, and will (Genesis 19:24-26, Genesis 7:4, Exodus 14:17-18). Fear God, and pray on, brothers and sisters.

August 18
Jesus Is Always the Answer

Acts 4:12, ESV

12 And there is salvation in no one else, for there is no other name under heaven given among men by which we must be saved.

1 Timothy 2:5, ICB

5 There is only one God. And there is only one way that people can reach God. That way is through Jesus Christ, who is also a man.

Our lives are an opportunity to build a close relationship with our Savior in Christ. When we accept His sacrifice and resurrection as our truth, we're given the Holy Spirit as a guide on our journey with Him (Acts 2:38). We're building our relationship up to *utilize* it, not just when our lives are in danger, but in our everyday lives. Jesus is the model for our moral behavior, our comfort and guidance when we're weak, and is our forgiveness when we stray. Working through the secret, silent thoughts from deep within our hearts, the Holy Spirit grooms and reshapes us into the forgiven, righteous, holy people God calls us to be. We cannot do this on our own, as we ourselves are not holy, but wicked and sinful (Mat. 19:25-26). Even as we grow in Christ we make mistakes, this is how we grow and learn to be better people, people God views as righteous and deserving. Those people who remain stubborn to the Lord's correction only bring on more correction, and discipline if repentance isn't forthcoming. Unfortunately, it can be difficult to see God's correction as beneficial to us, and bitterness, frustration, confusion, and anger can develop.

We are ultimately responsible for the words we speak, and for the choices we make. What we are truly seeking, whether it be attention, recognition, respect, wealth, love or acceptance, is what lies in our hearts. From here, all of our choices, behaviors, attitudes, and words will come. God's plan is to determine which souls can be devoted to Him, and which souls won't ever accept His word (Jeremiah 9:7). Jesus is always the answer. As a human, He was sin-free, and set an example for all humans to live by. Dying for us all, Jesus is the Savior, the Messiah, and Lord we happily serve. Generous and forgiving, we are taught how to be our very best by the only one who **can** show us: Christ Jesus, our Lord (Colossians 3:23-24). Helping us to make choices that reflect obedience to God's word, the Holy Spirit guides us though the big problems, as well as the small everyday decisions. When we rely on the Lord, trusting in Him, and praising His goodness and grace, we strengthen our relationships with Him.

1 John 1:7, GW

7 But if we live in the light in the same way that God is in the light, we have a relationship with each other. And the blood of His Son Jesus cleanses us from every sin.

2 Corinthians 9:8, NIV

8 And God is able to bless you abundantly, so that in all things at all times, having all that you need, you will abound in every good work.

August 19

Inward Focused?

Ezekiel 14:20, ERV

20 "If Noah, Daniel, and Job lived there, those three men could save their own lives because they are good men. But I promise by my own life that they could not save the lives of other people — not even their own sons and daughters!" This is what the Lord God said.

It's pretty clear, we can only save ourselves, and even then only by the grace of the Lord. Instead of focusing on what the other person has, or doesn't have, or how much we have, we should be focusing on our own salvation. When we analyze ourselves in comparison to other people, we are deceiving ourselves (2 Corinthians 10:12). Other people have nothing to do with our own, individual relationship with our Lord. We cannot change the heart of another, only God can do that. We shouldn't focus or dwell on other people, their obvious sins, or their outward success, we cannot save anyone but ourselves. Being saved from our sins, of which the penalty is death, Jesus' death on the cross opened the door to Heaven for all humanity (Matthew 28:19). By believing in Jesus' sacrifice, and by following His example in our lives, we too can be saved from our sins.

Forgiveness is the way to true repentance, and the 'apology' to God for the sins we've committed. The bible tells us that when we sin, we're actually turned away from God, and He doesn't hear us (Isaiah 59:2). Repentance is the process of turning back to God, *humbly* asking Him to forgive us, and to show us the righteous way (Acts 3:19). Because we will always be prone to sin, it is important to realize this cycle of sin, repentance, and forgiveness will constantly repeat throughout our lives (1 John 1:8, James 3:2). We need to repent and ask for forgiveness, not just *once*, but *each* time we find ourselves sinning. We learn, we make new mistakes, we repent all over again, and we grow in Christ this way. Our correction comes from our **inward focus**, and the remodeling of our hearts (Matthew 3:8). When we compare ourselves to the teachings of our Lord Jesus Christ, we clearly see our iniquities, and purifying these darkened parts of ourselves leads to the salvation of our souls through His grace. We cannot get discouraged, we cannot allow our faith to weaken, and we must always give thanks to God through Jesus. We can offer guidance to another when we know we can offer them something that they do not have, but this doesn't mean we are better than another. We all walk our own journey in Christ, we all grow differently, and should *want* to help one another through difficult times. Some of us are more stubborn, or bitter, or misguided than others, but no one is less worthy or important (Titus 2:11). We cannot change another human being's heart, they must seek and accept the truth of Jesus themselves, and believe in their *own* heart. God is spirit, and God is superior, and the more we are able to humble ourselves and accept this the more righteous we become. How comforting it is, and such a blessing, to have such a wise, loving and gracious God! AMEN.

2 Corinthians 7:10, ERV

10 The kind of sorrow God wants makes people decide to change their lives. This leads them to salvation, and we cannot be sorry for that. But the kind of sorrow the world has will bring death.

August 20
Faith by Example

Hebrews 11: 1, ESV

1 Now faith is the assurance of things hoped for, the conviction of things not seen.

Matthew 5:14-16, ERV

14 You are the light that shines for the world to see. You are like a city built on a hill that cannot be hidden. 15 People don't hide a lamp under a bowl. They put it on a lampstand. Then the light shines for everyone in the house. 16 In the same way, you should be a light for other people. Live so that they will see the good things you do and praise your Father in heaven.

The sun disappears over the horizon every night, but returns each morning. As humans, we hold a lot of faith in what we can see and touch, what is tangible, and what we can prove. Most of us have worked hard for what they have, and are fearful of things in their life being changed or taken away without our consent. As Christ-followers, we are supposed to want to seek Christ's judgement. As good stewards of our faith we seek to better ourselves through Christ. How are we to do that if we don't give Christ consent to change us, and consequently, our lives? If we truly want to live as good Christ-followers, than we should expect the Holy Spirit to initiate changes in our lives.

We cannot see Jesus, but when we pray we can feel His presence. When we pray, and are at peace, we can feel the Holy Spirit whispering to our thoughts, guiding our convictions and morals (Ezekiel 2:2, John 16:13). We all have choices, but the choice to put into practice that which we are being guided to do by the Holy Spirit should be the most important. We pray for the understanding it takes to follow our guided paths, and it's the Lord's courage that helps us to follow it closely. If we want to put our 'money where our mouths are,' we will chose to change our actions and behaviors for Christ. Let's put our faith to use in our daily lives more by the good works that we do, and by the good examples we set.

James 2:17-18, ERV

17 It is the same with faith. If it is just faith and nothing more — if it doesn't do anything — it is dead. 18 But someone might argue, "Some people have faith, and others have good works." My answer would be that you can't show me your faith if you don't do anything. But I will show you my faith by the good I do.

August 21
Actions

Romans 12:2, ERV

2 Don't change yourselves to be like the people of this world, but let God change you inside with a new way of thinking. Then you will be able to understand and accept what God wants for you. You will be able to know what is good and pleasing to him and what is perfect.

The bible describes the relationship between God and humanity as back and forth in nature, a corrupt humanity being called out for their sins, they repent and are remorseful for a time and come back to God, only to commit another sin, repeating the cycle over again. God wants us to be more like Him, as the bible describes us being called to repentance and accept His truth over and over (Psalm 14:2, Isaiah 30:15). After telling us and sending messengers in the way of prophets like Isaiah and Daniel didn't help to change humanities propensity for sin, God sent Jesus to actually show us what He's looking for from us. 'A new way of thinking,' referenced above in the book of Romans eludes to an error in the way humanity *naturally* thinks, and challenges us to understand *and* accept this. The Bible attempts to educate us on the fact that God wants something different from us than what we find comes naturally to us (Ezekiel 11:19). God calls us to live a morally upright, contrite, righteous life fueled by a heart with a greater love for others than ourselves, and guided by the Holy Spirit. Many people would argue that they are already living a morally upright life, and that this message *must* be for someone other than them. **Surely no one but God can accurately determine what is righteous,** and, as the bible explains, no human is completely without sin.

Evil is more a part of our lives than we would like to admit, hiding in every-day conversations, situations, comforts and choices. Some people have lost sight of what evil and sin looks like, while some people have never learned. Silent lust not acted upon, innocent flirting, and *any* physical pleasure, or lustful act outside of a marriage is considered adultery in the bible. What's more, thinking of *anything* as greater than God, including yourself, or anyone else, is also considered adultery by the bible's standards. Not completely adhering to the commandments set forth by God in The Bible, or not believing in God or Jesus fully, is also considered adultery in the eyes of God according to collective works of the Bible. Bragging, pride, envy, and lying are all recorded plainly as sins in the Bible, but most of us see and hear it in some form every day. Additionally, anger, vengeance, theft, violence and ignoring the plight of the less fortunate are sins reported in the bible. Humans are *prone* to sin, and are dwelling in, among and around other sinful humans who aren't necessarily aware, or interested, in avoiding their comfortable wickedness. The Bible tells us that God is looking for people who seek God by *obeying* Him. How faithful would God consider *you* to be?

Colossians 3: 5, 8-10, ESV/ERV

5 So put everything evil out of your life: sexual sin, doing anything immoral, letting sinful thoughts control you, and wanting things that are wrong. And don't keep wanting more and more for yourself, which is the same as worshiping a false god.8 But now you must put them all away: anger, wrath, malice, slander, and obscene talk from your mouth. 9 Do not lie to one another, seeing that you have put off the old self with its practices 10 Now you are wearing a new life, a life that is new every day. You are growing in your understanding of the one who made you. You are becoming more and more like him.

August 22
Never Too Righteous

Mark 16:15-16, ERV

15 Jesus said to them, "Go everywhere in the world. Tell the Good News to everyone. 16 Whoever believes and is baptized will be saved. But those who do not believe will be judged guilty."

Proverbs 24:1-2, ESV

1 Be not envious of evil men, nor desire to be with them, 2 for their hearts devise violence, and their lips talk of trouble.

We are all in different places on our faith journey. Some people are just believers, not willing to give up, or change their sinful ways, or live any differently. Other people are busy studying, learning the scripture, and reassessing every infinitesimal aspect of their lives in their own righteous 'quest.' Wherever we lie in our faith journey, we must remember that righteousness will always be a journey, dynamic and flowing, with good days and not so good days. As humans, we are all prone to, and tempted by sin (Genesis 6:5). Perhaps sin tempts us in the form of innocent flirtation, or a little white lie, or a judgmental or patronizing attitude. Others allow themselves to become tempted by conceit, believing they are superior to others in talent, skill, charm, ability, power or intelligence. Still others might be tempted to fall back into old patterns of thought, turning our hearts and minds away from the steadfastness and salvation that can only be found in Christ Jesus (Matthew 13: 22). Temptation is sin, sin is wicked, and wickedness is from the devil, and we're all guilty of falling prey to some sort of impulse, desire, or compulsion.

With a more righteous, Christ-like heart and mind comes a lifetime of diligence, repentance, correction and learning. In order to bring other people to Christ, we must go out into the world, for Christ calls for everyone to hear the good news. Some people who have become proud of their righteousness might scoff at associating with people whom they classify as less holy. No matter how righteous, or unrighteous a brother or sister may be, no one is more or less worthy to God as a result (Deuteronomy 10:17). We are all children of God, and we cannot know the truth in the heart of another the way our Heavenly Father does. Besides, if we only associate with other righteous people, people who have *already* accepted the good news, we'll never reach the people who need to hear the 'good news' about Jesus the most. It is important to take care to not lose oneself when being among less righteous people, and to maintain our self-control, but we are all one creation under God (Psalm 1:1). We shouldn't allow ourselves to get sucked into other people's sin by association, but we must remember that not one of us should ever be too righteous to associate with another. We all deserve love, and we all deserve forgiveness. Many people need to find Christ in their own way, but we can never underestimate the power of planting the seeds of righteousness in another!

Acts 5:29, ESV

29 But Peter and the apostles answered, "We must obey God rather than men."

August 23
What We Need & What We *Think* We Need

Matthew 6:31-33, ESV

31 "Therefore do not be anxious, saying, 'What shall we eat?' or 'What shall we drink?' or 'What shall we wear?' 32 For the Gentiles seek after all these things, and your heavenly Father knows that you need them all. 33 But seek first the kingdom of God and His righteousness, and all these things will be added to you."

Think before we act is prudent advice, but some of us give more pause than others before we act or speak. Some people are *proud* to blurt out the first thing that comes to mind, proud of their bluntness, their boldness, their obnoxiousness really. Others like to draw a certain kind of attention to themselves, secretly longing to tempt or fascinate other people with their wiles, charm or cleverness. This is pleasure-seeking behavior, wanting to please the world (others) instead of the Lord, sinful, wicked, and selfish. Wondering how we're going to pay the bills, what extra-curricular activities we can afford, and making sure our families have all they need can seem like chores unrelated to our faith, or God somehow. Nothing could be further from the truth, as the bible illustrates we should cast ALL of our anxieties to the Lord, and He will provide (1 Peter 5:6-7, Psalm 145:15-16). When we run every aspect of our life through God in prayer, asking for guidance, direction, comfort, and strength, we are acknowledging God as a priority. If we aren't connecting, communicating with the Lord, our focus isn't *on* the Lord, but on ourselves, or the minutia of our lives. After all, if we want the grace, patience, and self-control we'll need to prevent the world's wickedness from shattering our spiritual countenance, we'll have to continually pray for it. It doesn't matter what century we live in, God is still God, and has power over everything. Just because the bible didn't come out last month, or isn't on the 'best-seller' list this week, doesn't mean it doesn't have vital information in it that we can all use in our lives today, about love and self-control, forgiveness and salvation.

Have faith, God's will is going to be done no matter what we do, as He is capable of anything He desires (Ezekiel 12:25). We are limited in our understanding of just how much power God has in our lives, and many of us don't *want* to know. We are called to believe in a God we cannot see, we are called to believe that our God loves us, even though we will suffer in our lives sometimes; this is faith. We are called to believe that opportunities can always arise, opportunities lead to hope, and hope is faith. The more we pray for strength in our faith to help us believe in opportunities and change, the better our odds are of getting it. If God created the stars, the Heavens, the mountain ranges, the rivers, and controls the thunder and lightning we shouldn't place limits on what He can do in our own lives.

Matthew 19:26, ESV

26 But Jesus looked at them and said, "With man this is impossible, but with God **all things** are possible."

August 24
Clean

Zechariah 7:9-10, ESV

9 "Thus says the Lord of hosts, Render true judgments, show kindness and mercy to one another, 10 do not oppress the widow, the fatherless, the sojourner, or the poor, and let none of you devise evil against another in your heart."

Proverbs 6:16-19, ESV

16 There are six things that the Lord hates, seven that are an abomination to him: 17 haughty eyes, a lying tongue, and hands that shed innocent blood, 18 a heart that devises wicked plans, feet that make haste to run to evil, 19 a false witness who breathes out lies, and one who sows discord among brothers.

God punishes the wicked, some of us know this firsthand, but the bible assures this in several ways. Wickedness isn't a gray area left open to our interpretation, but is clearly defined in the bible as specific to avoid (Mark 7:20-23, Proverbs 4:14-19). When we speak to others are we giving direction, building up, or condemning? Are we treating others with kindness, forgiveness and love, or are we trying to avoid any unnecessary interactions with our fellow man? Some of us don't give much thought to questions like these, questions about what lies in our hearts. Comparably, certain other people aren't paying close enough attention to what motivates them, whether good, *or* evil. It is important to take a closer look at ourselves, our hearts, to see what is truly inspiring them. Do our hearts seek the reassurances of man, the wealth, power, security, or influence the world offers? Or do our hearts long to be more like Christ? The more our hearts desire righteousness, the easier it will be to not only discern wickedness, but avoid it more readily.

Bringing people together in Christ becomes more and more difficult, with war, dissention, and divergence in social classes intensifying the struggles we all face in our world. Some people will never consider caring for those less fortunate, forgiving and being kind to those who oppose them, or relinquishing what they've spent a lifetime building, in order to be more humble. Stubborn tenacity and humility cannot coexist, and the Lord asks us to *submit* to Him (Psalm 81:11-12). We are able to wash ourselves clean of the mistakes of our past, but are called to walk away from them completely in the process. Our Lord calls us to learn, to change, to become better people *through* Him (Luke 9:23). Submitting to this is our faith, the faith that assures us we will have all we need, that assures us a place in Heaven if we follow Christ Jesus, and that forgives us of our sins.

Isaiah 1:16-17, ICB

16 "Wash yourselves and make yourselves clean. Stop doing the evil things I see you do. Stop doing wrong! 17 Learn to do good. Be fair to other people. Punish those who hurt others. Help the orphans. Stand up for the rights of widows."

August 25
Repeating Sins

James 4:17, GW

17 Whoever knows what is right but doesn't do it is sinning.

1 John 3:9, AKJV

9 Whosoever is born of God **doth not commit sin**; for His seed remaineth in him: and **he cannot sin**, because he is born of God.

Ecclesiastes 7:20a, ESV

20a Surely there is not a righteous man on earth who does good and never sins.

1 John 1:8-10, ESV

8 If we say we have no sin, we deceive ourselves, and the truth is not in us.

There is no such thing as someone who never sins? The bible certainly can send what seems to be mixed messages, at times. Some people assume from the scriptures that Christ-followers who accept Jesus in their hearts, magically, no longer sin. Lost in translation and human interpretation, the scriptures in the bible weren't meant to stand alone. We must love the Lord enough to read the bible in its entirety, and when we do we find that even the most righteous and holy leaders in the bible were people that had sinned (James 3:2). Our sins are important, vital even, to understanding our insufficiencies and how to correct them through a closer relationship with Christ Jesus. We should all be seeking a closer relationship with Jesus, and this will highlight our moral inadequacies. Assuming we'll never sin again because we have Jesus in our hearts is arrogance, and desensitizes the reminder of our daily need for God's guidance in our lives. We should never come to a point where we think we're safe, because it's too easy for us to become lazy and complacent in our faith. Reading the scriptures is a surefire way of keeping God's word fresh in our minds, and in our hearts. What's more, we can't assume we know where another stands in their righteousness just because they may practice a different faith, or lifestyle, than we're accustomed to. We are *all* broken and in need of the Lord's mending, and we will all stumble at times. We shouldn't be comfortable with committing sins, we should feel bad enough to *want* to repent and seek improvement. What the scriptures tell us is to never stop *coming back* to the Lord for forgiveness, for spiritual refueling, for guidance, for enlightenment, and for moral cleansing. The purifying and holy sanitizing of our souls is a dynamic process, and the human variable brings us to our individual judgements before God, not one another.

Psalm 143:2, ESV

2 Enter not into judgment with your servant, for no one living is righteous before you.

1 John 1:9, KJ21

9 If we confess our sins, He is faithful and just to forgive us our sins, and to cleanse us from all unrighteousness.

August 26
Not So Smart

Proverbs 26:12, ESV

12 Do you see a man who is wise in His own eyes? There is more hope for a fool than for him.

Proverbs 28:26, ERV/ESV

26 Whoever trusts in His own mind is a fool, but he who walks in wisdom will be delivered.

Some people explore the knowledge of the world, putting great effort in their studies, and come away with intelligence, wisdom, and success. Along with this success, however, frequently comes an upgrade in social status, financial earnings, sometimes even power or influence, and, eventually, pride. Many people would argue that there is nothing wrong with being proud of one's accomplishments, but pride is a sin according to the bible (James 4:6, 1 John 2:16). Pride is pride, whether it's pride in your collection of prostitutes, riches, knowledge, family successes, or awards, and all pride is a reflection of wickedness, sin and temptation. When we allow one sin to take hold, thinking we can handle it, we're already blinded by temptation and risk accumulating more sins. When we discount some sins as worse than others we are rewriting the scripture to suit our needs and desires (James 2:10). Are we really only thinking about how we can help one another by our skills and talents, or do we secretly see ourselves as superior to others by them? Our confidence is from the Lord, by the blessings we received from Him, and we shouldn't hold ourselves in a higher regard than anyone else.

A superior intellect is a blessing and a curse, like wealth or recognition and many other things that are sought after, and don't lead one to less problems or stress. Quite to the contrary, the more successful a human becomes according to the world, the harder it will be to remain in a righteous light (Matthew 19:24). For what the world values is wealth, boisterous personalities with sharp opinions, success, manipulation and power while Christ Jesus values service to one another, love and forgiveness, modesty, grace, integrity, humility and gentleness. These are two very different worlds, *opposing* worlds in fact. Sin and righteousness cannot coexist, the bible explains (2 Corinthians 6:14). Humans are subject to sin, and we all sin differently, but we all need daily forgiveness from our Heavenly Father. Pride, greed, anger and contempt, impatience, manipulation, theft, cussing, lust and flirtation surround us all day long, tempting us to join everyone who is partaking of sinful behavior. What *truly* matters isn't how big, or wonderful, our gifts are, but how we use them to help one another.

Ephesians 5:15-16, ERV

15 So be very careful how you live. Live wisely, not like fools. 16 I mean that you should use every opportunity you have for doing good, because these are evil times.

August 27
Longing...

James 1:13, ESV

13 Let no one say when he is tempted, "I am being tempted by God," for God cannot be tempted with evil, and he himself tempts no one.

Matthew 15:18-19, ESV

18 But what comes out of the mouth proceeds from the heart, and this defiles a person. 19 For out of the heart come evil thoughts, murder, adultery, sexual immorality, theft, false witness, slander.

Everything on the Earth eventually ruins, all things die; plants die, animals die, minerals eventually decay, the ozone layer depletes, and each human body has an expiration date. Paradise with our creator in a place where there is no suffering, only love eternally, sounds pretty nice, and this available to all of us. This is the *only truth* that lasts forever, and it's only found in Jesus Christ (Acts 4:12). Temptation is a part of living on an Earth controlled by the devil, and is meant to distract us from God's truth. We are all tempted, tempted to steal when no one is looking, to run the stop sign when no one else is there, to gossip when it seems benign, or to pass quiet judgement without expressing our growing prejudices to anyone, or lying to ourselves saying it's anything less than deceitful. Many of us fall victim to temptation without knowing it, still others fall prey to the devil's trickery, spreading fear and suspicion among us.

Whether we have to suffer a hardship first hand, watch someone we love suffer unjustly, or suffer the consequences of our own poor decisions, we must rely on our faith to sustain us. How we respond to hardship is more important than the misguided justice we seek to validate it (Hosea 6:6). We rely on our faith to show us our wrongs for the purpose of repentance and correction. We rely on our faith to communicate our anxieties, concerns and needs to our Savior who hears and comforts us. We rely on the Holy spirit to guide and administer to our spiritual growth in Christ Jesus, as we seek a more righteous life. A deeper faith will sustain us through tribulation, and is what we should always be seeking. Trusting and abiding in Christ is how He asks us to show Him our love for Him. Temptation is another opportunity to show God our love by faith, by praying through the temptation, and believing He'll sustain us through it. Crave Jesus, brothers and sisters!

1 Peter 1:7, ERV

7 These troubles test your faith and prove that it is pure. And such faith is worth more than gold. Gold can be proved to be pure by fire, but gold will ruin. When your faith is proven to be pure, the result will be praise and glory and honor when Jesus Christ comes.

August 28
Ok with God Hurting You?

Jeremiah 2:19, CEB/CJB/ICB

19 **"Your wrongdoing will punish you. your own backslidings will convict you;** know therefore and see that it is evil and bitter for you to abandon the Lord your God. It is wrong not to fear and respect me." This message is from Lord God All-Powerful.

John 9:1-3 ESV

1 As he passed by, he saw a man blind from birth. And his disciples asked him, "Rabbi, who sinned, this man or his parents, that he was born blind?" Jesus answered, "It was not that this man sinned, or his parents, **but that the works of God might be displayed in him."**

'I haven't done anything wrong, how can anyone who truly loves me allow me to suffer like this?' We have all asked God this question, or, at least, thought about asking God this question at some point in our lives. Pain comes from many different forms, from minor irritations to devastating life changes, emotional, physical, and spiritual pain can drain the righteousness right out of us. When we're hurting we often *can't* see God's light shining in our lives, we can only see the pain, the disappointment, the unmet expectations, the heartache. Some people abandon their faith in God when He inflicts pain or discipline they don't understand (Matthew 13:20-21). When we feel like something important has been taken from us, or kept from us, or we feel an injustice has been done to someone we love the hurt we feel can overshadow things we cannot see. What we think we understand clearly we may not, and what we think we understand may be incorrect. What makes pain so devastating is its ability to mask the hope, joy, courage, patience, and even the faith we need to rise above our painful experience (Psalm 78:21-22).

As humans, we've inherited a love affair between the one, true God and His fledgling humanity. Over and over again, our Heavenly Father has been betrayed by humanity (Psalm 78:8, Psalm 106:43), and as a result is having to assay us (Jeremiah 9:7). We don't see what God sees, we can't know what He has planned for our futures, or what it's going to take to prepare us for it. Even if we don't think we've done anything wrong to produce God's wrath, correction, or discipline, we shouldn't assume. God is refining us, building up our endurance, character, hope, righteousness, and fortifying our fear in the one true, Almighty God. (Proverbs 10:17, Romans 5:3-4, James 1:2-4).

When we feel dismayed, disillusioned, and devoid of all hope we must pray, for this is when we are most vulnerable. Our devotion to God needs to be stronger than the pain He's putting us through. Even though we hurt, we must reach out to our Heavenly Father with the faith that He hears us calling to Him and will offer us comfort. God's timing is perfect, ours isn't. God's love is steadfast and pure, ours isn't always. God is wisdom, and upholds righteousness, where humans will always fall short. **God is love.** We must **trust** in God's love, brothers and sisters, even when we hurt.

Job 5:18, ICB

18 God hurts, but he also bandages up. He injures, but his hands also heal.

August 29
Only God

Genesis 20:2, KJ21

2 And Abraham said of Sarah His wife, "She is my sister." And Abimelech king of Gerar sent and took Sarah.

Numbers 20:12, ICB

12 But the Lord said to Moses and Aaron, "You did not believe me. You did not honor me as holy before the people. So you will not lead them into the land I will give them."

2 Samuel 12:8-10, ICB

8 I gave you His kingdom and His wives. And I made you king of Israel and Judah. And if that had not been enough, I would have given you even more. 9 So why did you ignore the Lord's command? Why did you do what he says is wrong? You killed Uriah the Hittite with the sword of the Ammonites! And you took His wife to become your wife! 10 So there will always be people in your family who will be killed by a sword. This is because you showed that you did not respect me! And you took the wife of Uriah the Hittite!'

Abraham, David, and Moses were three of the most notable characters in the Old Testament. God chose Abraham to father the Nation of Israel, God's chosen people (Genesis 17:5). God found favor in Abraham, and blessed Him (Genesis 12:2). Moses led the Israelites out of slavery from Egypt (Exodus 13:3), received the commandments and laws from God directly (Exodus 20), parted the Red Sea (Exodus 14), and led the Israelites through the desert for 40 years to the land promised to them by God. Moses also found favor in the eyes of God, (Numbers 12:7-8). David was Israel's second king, he restored Jerusalem, and brought the arc of the covenant, which housed the tablets with the ten commandments, back to God's temple there. David also fathered the long line of Israel's kings, which including Jesus Christ (Matthew 1:1). As amazing as these biblical figures were, blessed by God to do wonderful things for Him, they weren't perfect. David had an affair with His friends wife, fathered a child with her (2 Samuel 11: 27), and then had His friend killed to cover it up. Moses used harsh words and arrogance when doing something the Lord instructed, and was unable to enter the promised land as a result. Abraham was deceitful when he lied to king Abimelech, the king of Israel at the time, about Sarah being his sister, when she was actually His wife.

Clearly, the sins of these great servants of God didn't prevent them from being forgiven, and even blessed by God. On their own, they were just flawed human beings with an abundance of faith in God, doing what God instructed them to do the best they could. All of them repented by humbling themselves before God, and praised God for all they had in their lives. That's all any of us can do. Our faith in God is what earns us blessings, not the greatness of the acts themselves. Everyone has done something wrong, something human, something sinful. We can't ignore our sin, nor can we use one another's sins to condemn one another. Even though we all come from different walks of life, we are all descendants of Noah (Genesis 9:19), and we should love one another (John 13:34). God has made His point: **we need Him.**

August 30
He Walked Among Us

Colossians 2:9-10, ERV

9 I say this because all of God lives in Christ fully, even in His life on earth. 10 And because you belong to Christ you are complete, having everything you need. Christ is ruler over every other power and authority.

John 1:18, ERV

18 No one has ever seen God. The only Son is the one who has shown us what God is like. **He is himself God** and is very close to the Father.

The bible uses real life accounts mixed with symbolism and hyperbole, it can be difficult to determine where to derive the proper meaning from the stories contained in it. In several different verses we are told that Jesus was God in human form (John 10:30, Philippians 2:5-8, John 8:58). Jesus was ridiculed by His own people, brutally bound, stripped, and mercilessly whipped, then His hands and feet were nailed into the cross. He endured this to save our souls from evil. We can all have eternal life through Jesus Christ, and this could only have been made possible by God's love for us. God knew that only He could cleanse His sinful humanity from their own wickedness, and gave His human life for all of ours.

Jesus came to do what no other human could do, offer a perfect sacrifice for humanity. No human born on the Earth could ever live a sin-free life of perfect righteousness, even the most revered biblical leaders fell short in God's eyes according to the bible (Romans 3:23, Ecclesiastes 7:20). In order to save humanity from its evil self, God came to Earth in the form of Jesus, literally tearing a piece of Himself off and sending it down to earth. Down here on Earth, Jesus was able to spread His teachings about God's love and the way he wants us to live our lives. This was more than some people could wrap their heads around, and those people feared Jesus. Others hated Jesus for the lifestyles He was asking them to give up, and they didn't want to walk away from their greedy lives for anyone, including God. We inherited this divine relationship and are just as much a part of it as the characters in the bible were, our choice is to submit to God's love and choices for our lives, or to our own desires and eternal damnation. Choose wisely, brothers and sisters.

John 17:20-21, ESV

20 Jesus said, "I do not pray for these only, but also for those who will believe in me through their word, 21 that they may all be one, just as you, Father, are in me, and I in you, that they also may be in us, so that the world may believe that you have sent me."

John 14:6, ESV

6 Jesus said to him, "I am the way, and the truth, and the life. No one comes to the Father except through me."

August 31
Make a Spiritual U-Turn!

Luke 24:46-48, ICB

46 He said to them, "It is written that the Christ would be killed and rise from death on the third day. 47-48 You saw these things happen—you are witnesses. You must tell people to **change their hearts and lives**. If they do this, their sins will be forgiven. You must start at Jerusalem and preach these things in my name to **all nations**.

Change is difficult, we rely on so many habits and rituals for daily comfort, we can really be shaken when our environment changes. When change occurs in our lives many of us feel our *control* has been threatened, and we can become defensive and unmovable. Many of us are reluctant to change any aspect of our daily lives, even for Christ Jesus. Nothing happens outside of the watchful eye of the ever-present, Almighty God (Proverbs 15:3, Matthew 6:4), many people have a hard time accepting God's power, and ultimate, influence in our lives. This only further highlights the needs we humans have for the Lords forgiveness, guidance, and love.

The Lord invites us, *pleads* with us even, to return to Him and repent our sins (Ezekiel 33:11, Matthew 4:17). If we do this, after examining our sins, and expressing our remorse, we are offered forgiveness. Jesus is giving all of us a fresh start if we just confess our sins to Him in prayer. Some people aren't interested in looking at their faults, or look at them and never move on. Our faults are shown to us in our life lessons, sent by God, to offer us knowledge in what to repent for.

Some people continue to bring undue strife into their lives by committing the same sins over and over again, thinking Christ's repentance gives them reason to live any way they wish. The bible assures us that we reap what we sow (Galatians 6:7). If we don't really want to live righteously, the way Jesus calls us to, then we've chosen *not* to follow Him. Just believing in Christ's salvation doesn't magically bestow holiness upon us, we must learn, apply, repent, and pray. Righteousness takes work for a perpetually sinful humanity. If we truly love Christ, we'll love Him enough to change our lives to be more righteous like Him. Make a personal vow to clean up one aspect of your life each day, for the sake of your salvation in Christ. Do this not just for one day, one week, or one month but from now on.

Isaiah 55:7, ERV

7 Evil people should stop living evil lives. They should stop thinking bad thoughts. They should come to the Lord again, and he will comfort them. They should come to our God because he will freely forgive them.

2 Corinthians 7:10, GW

10 In fact, to be distressed in a godly way causes people to change the way they think and act and leads them to be saved. No one can regret that. But the distress that the world causes brings only death.

September 1
Watchful

1 John 5:19, CSB

19 We know that we are of God, and the whole world is under the sway of the evil one.

1 Peter 5:8, KJ21

8 Be sober, be vigilant, because your adversary the devil walketh about as a roaring lion, seeking whom he may devour.

Ephesians 4:27, CEB

27 Don't provide an opportunity for the devil.

Sometimes we wake up feeling stressed, unrested, irritated, or distracted by a bad dream. Many of us shrug this off as we begin the rituals of our day, thinking about what is going to be expected of us and how we'll deliver that expectation. It doesn't take long for something else to go wrong, the car won't start, or too many questions from the family on the way out, and we can totally lose our tempers. Some people lose their tempers more often than others, some people yell, throw things, some people blame those around them, and some people cry. Although we may all react differently to anger, our wrath usually propagates some sort of provocation. Many of us aren't thinking the devil is afoot in all our mishaps, or the sole reason we make poor, sinful choices, but his wickedness is all around us. Sin and wickedness can hide in some surprisingly common, everyday places.

As followers of Jesus Christ, we are given the Holy spirit to follow, that little voice in our heads warning us of poor choices, and calling us to do the right things (Ezekiel 36:27). The bible warns humanity of the devil's trickery, his deceit, and of his goal to turn people away from God. We are a part of this, like it or not, because we are all considered part of God's humanity (Genesis 9:19). God is supreme, more powerful than any one of us, and His will is going to take precedence over anything we think or believe ourselves. Angry at God for kicking His conceited angel out of heaven, the devil uses God's creation against Him, turning his wrath against God by spreading wickedness, dissention, hatred, and disbelief among us. If the devil can't ruin you with sin and temptation, he will confuse you with deception, and no one is immune. Be watchful, pray to Jesus for constant guidance, and the wisdom to detect the devil's schemes. Read the word, learn what is, and isn't, considered wicked so that the devil's deceit is more transparent. Pray when we're at the height of our anger, or in the midst of a heated argument, or when we're feeling persecuted, singled out or put on the spot. The *very moment* our emotions are at a climax, and we're on the verge of losing control and making a poor decision, **this** is when we need to pray. This is when God hears our hearts calling out to Him. In the battle of good versus evil, how well are *you* prepared?

1 Corinthians 10:13, ESV

13 No temptation has overtaken you that is not common to man. God is faithful, and he will not let you be tempted beyond your ability, but with the temptation he will also provide the way of escape, that you may be **able to endure** it.*

September 2
Got Humility?

Luke 18:9-14, CEV

9 Jesus told a story to some people who thought they were better than others and who looked down on everyone else: 10 "Two men went into the temple to pray. One was a Pharisee and the other a tax collector. 11 The Pharisee stood over by himself and prayed, 'God, I thank you that I am not greedy, dishonest, and unfaithful in marriage like other people. And I am really glad that I am not like that tax collector over there. 12 I go without eating for two days a week, and I give you one tenth of all I earn.' 13 The tax collector stood off at a distance and did not think he was good enough even to look up toward heaven. He was so sorry for what he had done that he pounded his chest and prayed, 'God, have pity on me! I am such a sinner.' 14 Then Jesus said, When the two men went home, it was the tax collector and not the Pharisee who was pleasing to God. If you put yourself above others, you will be put down. But if you humble yourself, you will be honored."

Society seems to operate by an invisible hierarchy; those with the wealth and power, have all the influence, while those with less continue to be oppressed by the imbalance. We can easily consider ourselves more righteous than someone we see coming out of a bar late at night, drunk, and acting raucous and unholy. Prisoners, drug addicts, and people who don't go to church may appear to be less spiritually adept to those of us who pray and repent daily. What other people see of us is only a small portion of a notably larger life, much of which occurs in private, through prayer and personal reflections, remaining largely unseen by others. Many of us have deceived ourselves into thinking we have more control or influence than we actually do. Because humans are arrogant, and assume they know more than they usually do, God humbles us each in different ways according to our inner-most thoughts and desires. Just reading about King Nebuchadnezzar in the book of Daniel, chapter four, illustrates God's power to humble even the powerful and influential. Altering our life circumstances, and allowing us to suffer the consequences of our own poor decisions (Galatians 6:7), are just a couple of the ways our Lord humbles us. Minor irritations wear us down, and remind us that we aren't going to always get our way, or feel comfortable in every aspect of our lives. Tragedies remind us just how frail and helpless we are under the mighty power of God. It's tempting to stamp our feet indignantly, and declare something in our lives as 'unfair,' but this requires judgement that we don't have the authority for. Our afflictions reveal the way we deal with adversity, and how much trust we have in the Lord through them. Stay strong under pressure, brothers and sisters, and never lose faith in the Lord.

September 3
Alterations by God

Ezekiel 36:26-28, ESV

26 "And I will give you a new heart, and a new spirit I will put within you. And I will remove the heart of stone from your flesh and give you a heart of flesh. 27 And I will put my Spirit within you, and cause you to walk in my statutes and be careful to obey my rules. 28 You shall dwell in the land that I gave to your fathers, and you shall be my people, and I will be your God."

When we decide we want something, it is human nature to subconsciously make a plan to acquire it. Our different choices stem from motivations deep within each of us. By ourselves, humans aren't pure enough for God's kingdom, and He's been forced to test us to see what's truly in our hearts (Jeremiah 17:9 -10). Humans naturally want to make their own choices, and often find the Lord's commandments and laws burdensome, and impossible to completely adhere to. When we commit to the Lord, we're submitting to the righteous changes needed to make us purer in the eyes of God. Like an uncultivated piece of hardened clay, the Lord is shaping us into our greatest potential. In this process, like a sculptor's clay, pieces will need to be carved off, removed, molded, and smoothed out to produce the final masterpiece we'll ultimately be in Christ. It is through repeated mistakes, repentance, humility, and patience that we learn the way the Lord wants us to live.

When we read the bible, we learn what Jesus' righteousness looks like. What's more, we can look around and clearly see that the world is not set up to follow, or even celebrate Christ Jesus. Everywhere we turn we can see greed, dissention between groups of people, poverty, oppression, conquest, and lust for wealth, power, and control. Jesus taught to love one another, promote peace, forgive one another, and to help the poor and underserved. Certainly, if all of us were doing our part, as Jesus asked, then we wouldn't see the amount of wickedness that we do. Just because righteousness is harder to achieve and maintain, doesn't mean it's not possible (Matthew 19:25-26). Every time we choose to walk away from gossip, dissention, or judgement toward another, we're choosing righteous behavior instead of the sinful behavior we may have been used to.

Isaiah 64:8, ESV

8 But now, O Lord, you are our Father; we are the clay, and you are our potter; we are all the work of your hand.

2 Corinthians 3:18, ERV

18 And our faces are not covered. We all show the Lord's glory, and we are being changed to be like him. This change in us brings more and more glory, which comes from the Lord, who is the Spirit.

September 4
What God Really Wants

Isaiah 58:6-10, ERV

6 (God said) "I will tell you the kind of day I want—a day to set people free. I want a day that you take the burdens off others. I want a day when you set troubled people free, and you take the burdens from their shoulders. 7 I want you to share your food with the hungry. I want you to find the poor who don't have homes and bring them into your own homes. When you see people who have no clothes, give them your clothes! Don't hide from your relatives when they need help. 8 If you do these things, your light will begin to shine like the light of dawn. Then your wounds will heal. Your "Goodness" will walk in front of you, and the Glory of the Lord will come following behind you. 9 Then you will call to the Lord, and he will answer you. You will cry out to him, and he will say, "Here I am. Stop causing trouble and putting burdens on people. Stop saying things to hurt people or accusing them of things they didn't do. 10 Feel sorry for hungry people and give them food. Help those who are troubled and satisfy their needs. Then your light will shine in the darkness. You will be like the bright sunshine at noon."

Many of us only donate to the needy during the Holidays, pretending we don't see the brother or sister on the corner begging every day for assistance of any kind. Society today reflects the fear of the wicked, and people don't welcome strangers into their homes as a result. Since we don't feel like it's safe to let a stranger into our homes today, some of us think that helping another person in need is the job of the government as well. As we pass the homeless by in our cars we turn away with the thought that they aren't our responsibility, but God says they are. There is no argument that we could all be doing a little more to help our brothers and sisters in need. Many of us have more than we need; too many clothes, too many possessions, full pantries, toys, and the burning desire for still more. Some people believe that because *they* work hard for what *they* have, naturally the person without must deserve to be. The bible tells us not to judge others, or compare ourselves to others, because we all fall short in the eyes of God, and we are all sinners (Romans 3:10). We cannot really judge the person who has less, or the person who lost everything as being deserved of their fate, only God has the power to do that. When we judge that person and drive right by them without shame we are driving right past the Lord in need (Mat. 25:45). We are called to love one another, and especially those who are in need. Donate that bicycle in the garage no one rides, or the extra clothes choking our closets, these may mean the world to someone without. Giving money to churches, or donating to local clothes closets, community gardens, or food pantries are all ways of helping others. Instead of passing someone else's plight off as not our responsibility, we should be using our clever minds to figure out ways we can help them. We should *want* to help others, and why not? For we all come from the same God, we have all committed sins, and we all need to be forgiven. Pleasing God should be our priority, following His commands our desire, so helping others should be the result. Our hearts should be forgiving and accepting of our fellow brothers and sisters, after all, life isn't a competition. Life is about our relationship with God, learning to be holy, and following our Savior in Christ Jesus. Pleasing God requires giving up our stubborn pride, and selfish individuality for a more humble, righteous, loving, community service oriented, God-fearing person. What's not to like?

September 5
Humility, Again?

Matthew 23:12, GW

12 Whoever honors himself will be humbled, and whoever humbles himself will be honored.

James 4:10, ERV

10 Be humble before the Lord, and he will make you great.

It's normal to be proud of academic achievements, philanthropic work, or a large well-earned paycheck. But, what is the reason for the goals we set? If we are seeking success, fame, recognition, respect of our peers or the admiration of others we are choosing in vain. Don't do good work just to outdo another or look favorably in someone's eyes, doing the right thing for the wrong reason is still wrong. (Matthew 6:3-4) We should strive to accomplish things in our life because it feels good to be a good person, to help others, and do the right thing. It's not enough to just *do* good things for others, but the reason *why* we do these things is even more important that the act itself. True greatness isn't measured in the amount of awards one can acquire, the amount of friends one can accumulate, or the amount of academic accolades one can be awarded. All we have, all we are, all we can become is due to the grace and will of the Lord. Therefore, since we're all sinners, we're only proud out of our own arrogance.

True greatness is how the Lord Jesus Christ, and the example He set, not how our world views greatness. Our perspective must change to match that of Jesus' before we can truly change, but we need to get over our egos before we approach the Lord. Our desire to impress should only extend to the *Lord*, no one else's opinion really matters. We often lose sight of that as we are surrounded by other humans, some of whom will never stop the foolish race to be better than another. Once we can view greatness from the *Lord's* perspective, we will know what behaviors are truly congruent with greatness, and seek them. Humility means we don't see ourselves any better, or worse, than all the other sinners walking around in human bodies. The motives for our behavior must be authentic, we must truly *want* the Lord to view us more favorably. Ask yourself if the Lord saw your behavior today, would *He* be proud?

Ephesians 4:2, ERV

2 Always be humble and gentle. Be patient and accept each other with love.

Isaiah 13:11, GW

11 "I will punish the world for its evil and the wicked for their wrongdoing. **I will put an end to arrogant people** and humble the pride of tyrants."

September 6
Worship

John 4:24, KJV

24 God is a Spirit: and they that worship him must worship him in spirit and in truth.

John 14:6, KJV

6 Jesus saith unto him, "I am the way, the truth, and the life: no man cometh unto the Father, but by me."

Every prayer is a form of worship. The Free online dictionary confirms this, stating: "A reverent petition made to God, a God, or other object of *worship*," and many wouldn't argue thar prayer is a form of worship. In the bible, God makes it pretty clear that we should worship no other Gods. Jesus says, "Serve God, and Him only," so it's pretty clear we should be praying to Jesus, and Him only (Deuteronomy 6:13). Many people inspire us, show us the true nature of God through mentoring, moving personal stories, and their heroic acts of service, charity and love. Being inspired, moved, motivated and encouraged by people propagates love and hope, and these things please God. However, the only one we should be looking to for all of our comfort, needs, and direction is God, and through His Word.

The bible outlines rules, commands, and laws of behavior and lifestyle that many people find difficult to understand, or hard to live with. Jesus came to show humanity what is expected of them, how to live, talk, love, and treat others. Jesus also came to die for our sins, so that those who believed and followed Him would have everlasting life. This is why we pray to Him through the Holy spirit, which He gives to those who believe in Him, because in no one else can we be saved (Acts 4:12, 1 Timothy 2:5, John 14:6). When we worship, we celebrate God, *through Jesus,* with others who want to love and praise Him. Worship is such a broad word, and there are many ways to celebrate our Sovereign Lord. People worship with prayer, we worship with songs of praise, reading His word, sharing uplifting stories of faith and courage, and a growing love for one another that we display through righteous acts of service. From the verses on this page we get this information: God is spirit, Jesus is the only way to God, we shall worship only God, pray in private, and don't change or re interpret any of His rules. this sounds like a roadmap for a personalized invitation to seek God individually through prayer to Jesus Christ, and **only** Jesus Christ.

Matthew 6:6, KJV

6 "But thou, when thou prayest, enter into thy closet, and when thou hast shut thy door, pray to thy Father which is in secret; and thy Father which seeth in secret shall reward thee openly."

Deuteronomy 4:2, DRA

2 You shall not add to the word that I speak to you, neither shall you take away from it: keep the commandments of the Lord your God which I command you.

September 7
God-Sanctioned Purity

Psalm 119:9, ESV

9 How can a young man keep his way **pure**? **By guarding it according to your word.**

Isaiah 1:16-17, ESV

16 "Wash yourselves; **make yourselves clean**; remove the evil of your deeds from before my eyes; cease to do evil, 17 learn to do good; seek justice, correct oppression; bring justice to the fatherless, plead the widow's cause."

Just taking someone at their word would be considered naïve, as people will always carry the potential with them to disappoint. People change their minds, they hesitate, loyalties and priorities can shift like the wind. God provides the only constant in our lives; constant in love, generosity, wisdom, justice, power, and grace. God is purifying those who profess belief in Him, because only those with pure hearts will pass into everlasting life in the Kingdom of Heaven (Matthew 5:8). Through pain, affliction, trials, and tests of faith, God's purification program is the gold standard. Not always will we understand the pain in our lives, or the tribulations God chooses for us to endure. Watching over us all as we make decisions and choices, the Lord decides what each of us will receive based on what's in our hearts (Jeremiah 17:9-10). Sometimes we don't know what's in our hearts, and our emotions can cloud our judgement. Only God can deliver what is fair for each person, and trusting this without becoming bitter at the trials we receive from Him can be a challenge for any believer!

If we were going to prove someone faithful, we'd want them to prove it by an action of some sort. Taking someone's word, especially a sinful person's word, just isn't going to provide enough proof of their loyalty. In this way, God's purification plan is rationalized. (Zechariah 13:9) **We can tell God we love Him, that we're completely devoted to Him, but we still sin despite our faith.** We sin because the first humans sinned, condemning us all until Jesus came to save us by His crucifixion and resurrection. We follow Jesus' example, we incorporate His teaching into our daily lives, and we repent when we learn of our sins because we want to be cleaned. We continue to repent because we all stumble (James 3:2), and we take our sins seriously to heart. We do this because we want to please the Lord more than we want to please ourselves, and this is what it means to have a pure heart. A pure heart desires to serve the Lord, not themselves. Clean and purify your spirit in the name of the Lord, brothers and sisters. Praise be to God through Christ Jesus, AMEN.

Psalm 24:3-4, ESV

3 Who shall ascend the hill of the Lord? And who shall stand in his holy place? 4 He who has clean hands and a pure heart, who does not lift up his soul to what is false and does not swear deceitfully.

September 8
Pain and Lessons Learned

2 Corinthians 7:10, ERV

10 The kind of sorrow God wants makes people decide to change their lives. This leads them to salvation, and we cannot be sorry for that. But the kind of sorrow the world has will bring death.

Life just plain hurts sometimes. People can say hurtful things to one another when they are in pain, they can be vindictive and persecutory when they feel wronged or insulted, and can even impart physical harm when anger is left to violence. It is difficult to comprehend how any suffering can be a good thing, but our relationship with our Heavenly Father is complicated, spiritual, and dynamic. Christ suffered on the cross, He suffered through the crown of thorns cutting into His flesh, He was beaten and whipped, and all while He was being mocked (Mark 14:65, John 19:1). We suffer because Jesus suffered for us, sometimes we suffer because of the choices we make, sometimes we are disciplined or humbled, but all suffering is a test of our devotion.

We have all made mistakes, and will all continue to make them. This is a fact, as the bible points out that humans are sinful, and some people have a difficult time accepting this. What we should be focused on is learning our indiscretions for the purpose of enlightenment and repentance, for we cannot move forward on our journey to righteousness without spiritual growth and improvement. When we are tested, or endure suffering *whatever* the reason, we need to rely on Christ for the comfort and solutions we need to endure. After we've prayed all of this away to our Savior, we wait, and we trust that God will present the solution to us in His timeframe. This is the tough part, because of the temptation to come up with solutions to our problems and anxieties when we should be trusting in the Lord. Patience and trust in the Lord is how we learn from our pain and suffering while strengthening our faith and spiritual endurance.

1 John 1:9, ESV

9 If we confess our sins, he is faithful and just to forgive us our sins and to cleanse us from all unrighteousness.

Job 6:10, ERV

10 I am comforted by this one thing: Even through all this pain, I never refused to obey the commands of the Holy One.

September 9
God's Purpose

Isaiah 48:9-10, ERV

9 "But I will be patient. I will do this for myself. People will praise me for not becoming angry and destroying you. You will praise me for waiting. 10 **Look, I will make you pure**, but not in the way you make silver pure. I will make you pure by giving you troubles."

The bible is full of stories of God offering humanity a choice, and allowing people to live with the consequences (Romans 1:28). Wickedness descended to the Earth and tempted humans to follow their own path, and we've been second-guessing God's judgement ever since (Genesis 3:1-5). Deep down, humans wonder if we could do it better, and some people just don't want to remain faithful to God's strict rules. Living righteous and holy is difficult, near impossible in the environment we have created for ourselves. When we deviate from our righteous quest, and give in to sin, we are corrected and repurified by God through our repentance. Even the righteous aren't above having their faith tested by God, hoping we'll turn to Him for all of our needs and comforts. Evil tempts us to question whether we really need God's authoritarian love, and convinces us we don't really need God. God created us, died for us through Jesus' crucifixion, and continues to give us multiple opportunities for repentance throughout our lives. God's love may be conditional on us following His commandments, but His love is divinely perfect and never-ending.

God has been warning and urging humanity to submit to Him for over three thousand years; those that follow God through Christ Jesus are promised everlasting life in Heaven while non-believers suffer the fate of death and permanent exile from God's love (Revelation 21:8). Believers aren't able to rest in the comfort of their belief, we are called to live more holy, like Jesus (1 John 2:6, Ephesians 5:1-2). The penalty for our sins is spiritual death (Ezekiel 18:4), God came down to Earth as a man in the form of Jesus Christ (Hebrews 2:17), so that we may have spiritual 'life' through Him. We may receive trials and affliction at times, but the same hand that corrects and disciplines also restores, comforts, and heals (Job 5:17-18). Reach out to Jesus in prayer, it's never too late to return to God's light.

Zechariah 13:9, ERV

9 "Then I will test those survivors by giving them many troubles. The troubles will be like the fire a person uses to prove silver is pure. I will test them the way a person tests gold. Then they will call to me for help, and I will answer them. I will say, 'You are my people.' And they will say, 'The Lord is my God.'"

Romans 6:23, ESV

23 For the wages of sin is death, but the free gift of God is eternal life in Christ Jesus our Lord.

September 10
It's Not Really About Our Sin

Acts 13:38-39, ERV

38-39 Brothers, understand what we are telling you. You can have forgiveness of your sins through this Jesus. The Law of Moses could not free you from your sins. But you can be made right with God if you believe in Jesus.

Isaiah 66:2, ESV

2 "All these things my hand has made, and so all these things came to be," declares the Lord. "But This is the one to whom I will look: he who is humble and contrite in spirit and trembles at my word."

Taking the Lord's name in vain when we're under more pressure than we can handle gracefully, coveting something someone else has, and participating in idle gossip or passing judgement are common sins many of us commit. Telling 'innocent lies,' being lazy in our devotion to God, swearing, and making decisions without regard to the Holy Spirit working hard inside of us, trying to guide us, are some other, not so obvious sins that are easy to succumb to. In the bible, sin is described as disrespecting what God says is right, either in action, or simply in thought (James 4:17, Matthew 5:27-28). We know from the bible that all humans sin (Romans 3:23), are looked upon as equal in the eyes of God (Romans 10:12), and are all being refined by God (Jeremiah 9:7). We also know from the bible that *when* we repent, all sins but one will be forgiven (Matthew 12:31-32). Given all of these factors, the key to a closer relationship with God isn't about the sins we're committing, but how devoted to God we are through His refining process. Our sins are merely the vehicle that proves to God either our humility and repentance, or our arrogance and rebellion.

Over and over in the bible, God expresses His disdain when His people don't turn to Him, rely on Him, and appropriately praise Him for all they are going through (Proverbs 1: 28-32). Sins occur when we give into the secret, wicked, desires of our hearts, and Jesus explains that this comes from inside of us (Mark 7:21). God sent a piece of Himself down in the form of Jesus, as a gift for our salvation (John 3:16). Our sins show us how we've strayed from God, and are meant to be used as a tool to refine us into more holy people. If we're trying to eradicate all the sin from our lives, we may be focused on the wrong things. After all, If we could be doing something to EARN Christ's grace, then it wouldn't really be a gift (Romans 11:6). We are meant to seek God, to learn what pleases Him, and through Jesus, develop purer desires from within. God wants our desire to be to seek Him, not ourselves. God wants our devotion, so leave the purifying to Him (Psalm 14:2). Praying more, admitting our sinful thoughts and desires more transparently, and seeking repentance for all of our known, as well as unknown wrongs is more important than sorting, judging, and classifying our never-ending sins. Our faith walk with Christ is more about our devotion to God, and not totally eradicating sin-we will always be imperfect.

John 16:8, ERV

8 (Jesus said) "When the Spirit comes, he will show the people of the world how wrong they are about sin, about being right with God, and about judgment."

September 11

Why We're mistaken about Sin

Proverbs 1:28-33, ERV

28 "Fools will call for me, but I will not answer. They will look for me, but they will not find me. 29 That is because they hated knowledge. **They refused to fear and respect the Lord. 30 They ignored my advice and refused to be corrected. 31 They filled their lives with what they wanted. They went their own way,** so they will get what they deserve. 32 "Fools die because they refuse to follow wisdom. They are content to follow their foolish ways, and that will destroy them. 33 **But those who listen to me will live in safety and comfort. They will have nothing to fear."**

When a newborn baby wraps it's tiny hand around an adults finger, or when the early morning fog brilliantly settles on a meadow under a breathtaking sunrise, we can easily see and feel God's majesty. Some of the signs God leaves are obvious, but many times He works in more mysterious ways (Isaiah 55:8-9). Outside of His commandments, loving one another, and praising Him in regular worship, some people think of God as the Sunday dinner guest; important, but anything more than an occasional experience is unnecessarily excessive. If we aren't making changes to ourselves, to the way we live our lives, the way we think and organize our priorities, we're putting God on a shelf. God is spirit (John 4:24), so listening and following Him is a learning process that begins with looking inward at ourselves. When we repent, and accept Jesus into our hearts, we receive the Holy Spirit (Acts 2:38). The Holy Spirit is Jesus' Spirit inside of us, guiding us and refining us into holier people worthy to dwell in the Kingdom of Heaven. We listen, and follow according to the will of the Holy Spirit, and we do this knowing that it is pleasing to God, and because we're going to receive blessings in our lives from the Lord when we do (James 1:12).

Our faith alone, nor our own diligent hard work, will ever be enough to cleanse our hearts and minds the way God needs them to be to dwell among Him (Ephesians 2:8-9). In the bible, God explains that people refused to fear Him, respect Him, refused His wisdom and advice, and refused to be corrected by Him. We are meant to follow God's commandments, but we were designed to need Jesus Christ to do that (Hebrews 9:22 ,1 John 1:7). Giving up gossip, gambling, conquests and competition, and the pursuit of wealth or worldly comforts is more change than some people are willing to accept. A more loving, forgiving, accepting heart can only come from God. When people chase after what they want without regard to God's direction for them, this is a form of betrayal. God wants us to love Him with all of our hearts, souls, and strength (Deuteronomy 6:5). When we submit to the Lord's wishes for us instead of chasing after goals we've set for ourselves, we're doing that.

Romans 8:2-4, ESV/ERV

2 For the law of the Spirit of life has set you free in Christ Jesus from the law of sin and death. 3 **For God has done what the law, weakened by the flesh, could not do** : He sent his own Son to earth with the same human life that everyone else uses for sin. God sent him to be an offering to pay for sin. So God used a human life to destroy sin. 4 He did this so that we could be right just as the law said we must be. Now we don't live following our sinful selves. We live following the Spirit.

September 12
What Our Sins Reveal

Matthew 15:18, ESV

18 But what comes out of the mouth **proceeds from the heart**, and this defiles a person.

Luke 12:34, ESV

34 For where your treasure is, there will your heart be also.

The bible tells us that humans are sinful (Gen. 6:5)(Romans 3:23, Ecclesiastes 7:20), and the world around us certainly highlights our greedy, selfish, deceitful, uncaring nature. Scattered among what seems like the few acts of human kindness, forgiveness, generosity and love are ten times the acts of revenge, hate, discord, conquest, vanity, indifference, intolerance, apostacy, wealth, and avarice. Reading the scriptures tells us where human sin originated, but how do we recognize our own sins from that of the world around us? First, we must understand, and accept, that sins are violations of our covenant with God (Matthew 22:37-40). God's laws were intended to show us our sins, why we need God, and what to repent for (Romans 3:20).

Choices, decisions, actions, and words come from what we are all motivated by. Some people are motivated by work, a paycheck, and supplying all their family's needs, while others are searching for peace of mind, reassurances, and emotional contentment. We sin when we stray from the righteous path the Lord sets before us, when we go after what **we** want instead of what He desires for us. God knows what's in our hearts, and produces all the bumps, curves, and obstacles in our path to keep us moving in the correct direction. If we pay close attention to the lessons God is teaching us in our lives, we'll learn what truly motivates our hearts, and the results might surprise us. If God is regularly humbling us, we might have a problem with arrogance. Likewise, if God is testing our courage we might need more self confidence in the person He's creating in us. Even if we find ourselves to be 'fairly decent' people, but we're always focused on ourselves more than we are Christ, we might need our attention re-focused (Psalm 26:2). How God corrects us reveals what kind of heart we have, and how He's purifying it.

We set individual goals for the things we want, and what we want says a lot about us. Nothing the world offers, physical comforts, wealth, power, influence, awards, or even our terrific family can be taken with us when we die. Only what's in our hearts, our spirit, will endure, and only if it's pure enough by God's standards. We are all sinful, have sinful desires and thoughts (Romans 7:18), and the only way to correct them is through Christ Jesus. No one else can change our hearts, not our minister, not our best friend, cousin, partner, spouse, auntie, or very determined boss. Do you know what motivates *your* heart?

Acts 8:22, ESV

22 Repent, therefore, of this wickedness of yours, and pray to the Lord that, if possible, **the intent of your heart may be forgiven you.**

1 Timothy 1:5, ESV

5 The aim of our charge is love that issues **from a pure heart** and a good conscience and a sincere faith.

September 13
Churches

Revelation 22:18-19, ESV

18 I warn everyone who hears the words of the prophecy of this book: if anyone adds to them, God will add to him the plagues described in this book, 19 and if anyone takes away from the words of the book of this prophecy, God will take away His share in the tree of life and in the holy city, which are described in this book.

There was a time when families would get dressed up and go to church, or place of worship, every Sunday, or specific weekday, following the religious traditions of their families for generations. Often including regimented praise hymns interspersed with scripture readings, sermons, the occasional communion, and other traditions, organized religion allows large groups of different kinds of people exposure to God on a fellowship level. Relying on organized religion can serve a specific purpose, but bible verses can easily be misinterpreted, and mistakenly misused. Our relationship with God is just that, a relationship, and we must treat it accordingly. Scripture reading, actually *understanding* the bible in its entirety from Genesis to Revelation, so we *actually* understand what happened, what was said, and how *we* fit into every-thing also makes sense if we truly want to understand God and our relationship with Him. If we're only going to church occasionally, and praying infrequently but still consider ourselves devoted to God, where's the exchange of spirits in communication that fosters a relationship? One scripture, read by someone else, and explained by yet another, three or four times per month sounds like a half-hearted effort at a relationship, at *best*.

Church and other forms of worship can be great ways of participating in fellow-ship, *community* worship, but are we also worshiping God **individually**? Devoting time to silent meditation or reflection, quiet moments through prayer, reading the scrip-tures on our own, and listening to praise music, are all great ways of reconnecting with God individually. If we aren't actually reading, and understanding, the bible ourselves we won't know the difference between someone's educated interpretation of the scripture and the true meaning of it. What's more, what will we have to *offer* if we only listen to others and not learn for ourselves, what are we really offering our fellow brothers and sisters in faith then? Learning from the bible should be firsthand knowledge, not secondary, this is what Christ calls upon us to do as His followers (Matthew 22:29, 4:4). We should consider it an honor to pass the stories of the bible down to the next generation of people in search of a deeper understanding of their Lord and Savior. We are to look to God for guidance through prayer to Jesus Christ, and to others as an example of righteousness at work in fellow sinners. Churches and organized religions can help to *educate us* and *lead us in worship*, but should not be the *sole source* of our connection to God. May the Lord bless us all with a deeper faith and devotion to Him, AMEN!

Matthew 15:6-9, ICB

6 Jesus said to the pharisees, "You teach that it is not important to do what God said. You think that it is more important to follow the rules you have. 7 You are hypocrites! Isaiah was right when he spoke about you: 8 'These people show honor to me with words. But their hearts are far from me. 9 Their worship of me is worthless. The things they teach are nothing but human rules they have memorized.'" (*Isaiah 29:13*)

September 14
Death of a Loved One

1 Thessalonians 4:13-18, ESV

13 But we do not want you to be uninformed, brothers and sisters, about those who are asleep, that you may not grieve as others do who have no hope. 14 For since we believe that Jesus died and rose again, even so, through Jesus, God will bring with him those who have fallen asleep. 15 For this we declare to you by a word from the Lord, that we who are alive, who are left until the coming of the Lord, will not precede those who have fallen asleep. 16 For the Lord himself will descend from heaven with a cry of command, with the voice of an archangel, and with the sound of the trumpet of God. And the dead in Christ will rise first. 17 Then we who are alive, who are left, will be caught up together with them in the clouds to meet the Lord in the air, and so we will always be with the Lord. 18 Therefore encourage one another with these words.

We all experience tragedy. Each life is so precious, and so fragile, and intricately intertwined with other lives. Whether it is expected or not, death of someone we love can bring clouds of intense grief into our lives. No one likes to see someone they care about suffer, and we can offer one another some pretty empty words in clumsy efforts to console. "It'll be ok," and "You're so strong to deal with this," although well-intentioned can make someone feel more isolated and alone. "Time heals all wounds," isn't true, as if simply waiting it out for an undetermined amount of time can make the sadness magically disappear. Intense grief cannot be cured, as if it were a sickness, it isn't a problem that can be fixed. Everyone responds differently to grief and sadness, and it can change over time.

Perhaps a bit of genuineness, despite the awkwardness is the best remedy when trying to communicate with someone who's going through a tragedy. "It really hurts to see you hurting," or, "I wish I could say something to make the pain go away," will go a lot farther than false platitudes. Honestly, God is the one responsible for our triumphs, as well as tragedies (Isaiah 45:7), and only He can change our hearts. Listening, having compassion, patience, and empathy for our fellow man who is struggling is the best way to show we care. Resist the urge to compare experiences, comfort should be about them, not us. Love hurts, and we won't always get to know why. We hold fast to the Lord, and we pray and give thanks for all we have in our lives. We should be supporting one another with love and compassion, not approaching life like it's a series of problems we must solve, but a journey to a stronger faith in God. When we comfort one another we should be listening, and preparing our heart to feel some pain, and asking for ways to help. Loving Christ, we lift up all those who are grieving right now. Comfort and sustain us all, Lord, help us to seek solace in your loving, healing grace. Strengthen our faith in you, merciful Jesus, whose love overcomes all. Praise be to God, through our Messiah in Christ Jesus. AMEN.

Revelation 21:4, ESV

4 'He will wipe every tear from their eyes. There will be no more death' or mourning or crying or pain, for the old order of things has passed away.'

September 15
Creating Divisions

Romans 16:17-18, ESV

17 I appeal to you, brothers, to watch out for those who cause divisions and create obstacles contrary to the doctrine that you have been taught; avoid them. 18 For such persons do not serve our Lord Christ, but their own appetites, and by smooth talk and flattery they deceive the hearts of the naive.

If we're truly followers of Christ we want to celebrate and commune with fellow followers, or help bring a lost soul to faith. Inevitably, we will discuss our different thoughts about faith among one another, and not everyone is gracious to those with differing opinions. Forming opinions and judgments about one another can be dangerous, but we must all remember a few things before we let our imaginations run away. First, the bible reminds us that we are all sinful in the eyes of God, and therefore all of us sin (Romans 3:10). Next, Jesus died for all humanity, for those who believed in Him, so everyone is eligible (Romans 10:13). Further, Jesus calls us all to repent for the sins we've committed (Mark 1:14-15). Finally, God is the final judge, and He will have final say on final sentencing as well.

Of the many commandments and laws discussed in the bible, Jesus repeated the importance of loving one another more than many of the other commandments (Mark 12:28-31). Jesus displayed love only the Messiah could offer, by dying on the cross for the sins of all humanity. Since Jesus paid for the sins of all, *all* are worthy of righteousness and forgiveness. Jesus calls us to follow Him, emulating and living a lifestyle like the one He led. Helping the sick and underserved, feeding the hungry and sheltering the homeless, aiding the widows and less fortunate was the example Jesus left for all of us to follow. Criticizing, separating into unapproachable 'cliques,' leaving others out, condemning, or judging others is completely opposite to Christ's teachings, and spreads hate, suspicion, envy, and dissention. Including others, forgiving people, being understanding of one another is a step closer to Jesus. One small action, one smile, one invitation to lunch, one awkward conversation can mean the first in a wave of righteous changes we can not only spread in our own world, but to our brothers and sisters in Christ. After all, spreading love is what we're all called to do more of!

Titus 3:10-11, ESV

10 As for a person who stirs up division, after warning him once and then twice, have nothing more to do with him, 11 knowing that such a person is warped and sinful; he is self-condemned.

Jude 17-19, ESV

17 But you must remember, beloved, the predictions of the apostles of our Lord Jesus Christ. 18 Christ said to you, "In the last time there will be scoffers, following their own ungodly passions." 19 It is these who cause divisions, worldly people, devoid of the Spirit.

September 16
Speaking from the Heart

Proverbs 12:18, ERV

18 Speak without thinking, and your words can cut like a knife. Be wise, and your words can heal.

James 1:26, ESV/ERV

26 If anyone thinks he is religious and does not bridle His tongue but deceives His heart, this person's religion is worthless, as your careless talk makes your offerings to God worthless.

Words are powerful, they describe, penetrate, and are grossly underestimated. Some people like to share every aspect of their lives on social media, or to their family, friends and co-workers. Other people like to charm everyone with an outward smile, ingenuine yet pleasant word for everyone, witty conversation, and come away with the adoration and acceptance of others. Our words reflect our righteousness, or unrighteousness. An agreement or vow between two people can most often be broken, or not always taken as serious as maintaining a healthy relationship requires. Some people talk and talk, to fill the silence, afraid of being alone for too long with their own thoughts. Other people say what they think others want to hear, trying to please everyone. What we say reflects our attitude, what's in our hearts (Luke 6:45). Words are powerful, igniting emotions in others, and can build up or tear down. Once spoken, words cannot be taken back.

What we say, and how we say it, represents who we are. If we call ourselves Christ-follower, but we give the driver that cut us off the middle finger as they go by, then we're not accurately representing a dutiful Christ-follower at all. If we publicly support a friend or family member, but silently we condemn them we are hypocrites in our faith. If we say we believe in Christ, but don't change our hearts and minds to focus on His righteousness instead of our own thinking, then we aren't true followers of Christ the bible explains (James 2:14-26). The word of God was transcribed by sinful, fallible humans under divine direction, and it's all we have to guide us in the life of Jesus, as well as humanities ongoing position in the relationship between God and His creation. God's words, the ten commandments along with the commandments Jesus spoke of (John 13:34-35, Matthew 22:36-40), is the way, the truth, and everlasting life-but we need to abide by them. Reading the words, even understanding them isn't enough, we are expected to apply them to our lives. We should challenge ourselves to examine our own, individual lives to see where we could make tangible changes toward righteousness through better choices, improved attitude, and kinder, more relevant words backed with love and self-control.

Matthew 24:35, ESV

35 Heaven and earth will pass away, but my words will not pass away.

Hebrews 4:12, ESV

12 For the word of God is living and active, sharper than any two-edged sword, piercing to the division of soul and of spirit, of joints and of marrow, and discerning the thoughts and intentions of the heart.

September 17
God Changes Us

Ephesians 4:22-24, GW

22 You were taught to change the way you were living. The person you used to be will ruin you through desires that deceive you. 23 However, you were taught to have a new attitude. 24 You were also taught to become a new person created to be like God, with a life that truly has God's approval and is holy.

Isaiah 64:8, ESV

8 But now, O Lord, you are our Father; we are the clay, and you are our potter; we are all the work of your hand.

Before a sculptor finishes an exquisite piece of art, they must start with an over-sized block of blank material, or clay. Pieces of the clay must be carved, or cut off in order to reveal the final, beautiful and meticulously thought out, masterpiece. In the same way, we are the clay, and the Lord is our sculptor. We must all endure pieces of ourselves being cut off, changed, removed or remodeled in order to reveal who we are truly called by God to be, our true righteous selves. Many of us offer God a tough, stubborn material that finds every cut impossible to endure, and they struggle with their faith as they are molded. Some people have difficulty accepting God's Sovereign power over us as His creation (Deuteronomy 30:8-20), these people don't want anyone but themselves to sculpt them. It is important to remember that forced love isn't love, and God gives us a choice (Revelation 3:20). After all, God is love (1 John 4:8). It isn't uncommon to be fearful of what God's final product in us will look like, or if we'll like the changes He's making. Change is scary, and trust is difficult to grow and maintain. Many people are skeptical of God.

If we truly love God and want to be pleasing to Him so that we can be assured eternal life with Him, then we should want to learn how to become more righteous for Him. When we exchange bad, sinful, or indulgent choices for more modest, humble or righteous choices we are living out God's vision for us. The more righteous we become, one better decision at a time, the more righteous we'll *want* to become. We should readily accept training in how to be more humble, less judgmental, less argumentative, less proud, and be more accepting of lifestyle changes incurred by the Lord's 'righteous makeover,' as the *sculptor* of our souls. God's plan includes each and every one of us, no matter what we've done (2 Chronicles 7:14, Matthew 12:31). Our quest for righteousness begins and ends with Jesus Christ (Revelation 22:13), and we should be modeling our hearts after **His** gracious, loving heart. God's will is going to be done, we are who **He** says we're going to be, but the journey doesn't have to be miserable. The more we trust in God, repent our sinful ways, and obey His word, the more pleasing we will be in His eyes. Righteousness is its own reward, brothers and sisters, and the Lord gives us much to sing about in praise! God's ways will *always* be superior to our own (Isaiah 55:8-9), no matter what we want to believe, or tell ourselves. Trust on, brothers and sisters!

Romans 12:2, GW

2 Don't become like the people of this world. Instead, change the way you think. Then you will always be able to determine what God really wants — what is good, pleasing, and perfect.

September 18
Correction, Not Oppression

Proverbs 15:32, ESV

32 Whoever ignores instruction despises himself, but he who listens to reproof gains intelligence.

Proverbs 9:7-9, ESV

7 Whoever corrects a scoffer gets himself abuse, and he who reproves a wicked man incurs injury. 8 Do not reprove a scoffer, or he will hate you; reprove a wise man, and he will love you. 9 Give instruction to a wise man, and he will be still wiser; teach a righteous man, and he will increase in learning.

We should be always *wanting* to learn and grow, and never assume we will be superior to anyone. In the world, there will always be someone better, quicker, smarter, faster, wealthier, or more powerful, but in the kingdom of Heaven we are all one in Christ. Christ directs our paths, and sustains all of our needs as we are all inferior in the eyes of God. This is good news, and comforting to those who seek righteousness, but not to those who seek autonomy through their pride and arrogance. We aren't meant to know our shortcomings to condemn ourselves, but to understand what to avoid and how to improve. Likewise, we aren't meant to understand our shortcomings to judge one another by them, as God is the final judge of us all. When we are wronged we are called to forgive, and we pray for comfort and healing as we trust in our faith. We aren't judged by how we're treated, but how we treat God when we're suffering or lost (Deuteronomy 4:30-31, Isaiah 45:22).

When we are corrected for the use of building us up, learning from our past sins so we don't repeat them again, or to encourage growth, we can rest assured it is positive. Any correction for the use of deceit, discord, or passing judgement isn't really correction, it's slander, dissension, deceit, and sinful wickedness at work. None of us are immune to wickedness, but we don't have to submit to it. The more we study what is righteous and what isn't, the easier it will be to discern gentle correction from wickedness and deceit. A wise person is always in the position of accepting knowledge, learning no matter the source. All wisdom can be used to build one's faith and trust in God, to discern the truth from deception. Our faith allows us to trust that God's love gently corrects for our growth. If we're being corrected by God, He considers us one of His children, and not everyone who is called will be chosen (John 3:3). We must be humble in order to be pure in the eyes of God, and human arrogance hides in unlikely places. Lord, humble us and correct us with your gentle hand. Retrain our hearts, merciful Jesus, to seek your will and not our own. Teach us, gracious Christ, in the wisdom of your ways. All praise, and glory, be to the Lord. AMEN.

Hebrews 12:7-8, ERV

7 So accept sufferings like a father's discipline. God does these things to you like a father correcting His children. You know that all children are disciplined by their fathers. 8 So, if you never receive the discipline that every child must have, you are not true children and don't really belong to God.

September 19
Body Language

Jeremiah 17:9, ERV

9 Nothing can hide its evil as well as the human mind. It can be very sick, and no one really understands it.

1 Peter 3:10, ESV

10 For "Whoever desires to love life and see good days, let him keep His tongue from evil and His lips from speaking deceit."

Many people greet one another by asking them, "How are you?" or, "How's your day going?" but their body language is saying, "I really don't give a hang about you or your day, I'm just trying to sound polite." Of course, some people manage to look more convincing than others, how did such blatant inauthenticity become an everyday, accepted mannerism? Nodding, shrugging, blushing, sweating, arms crossed, bowing, feet shuffling, eyes rolling are all ways of sending a distinct message *without* words. Many of us don't realize that our body language accompanies everything we're saying, we all do it. Sometimes a person's body language doesn't match what they're saying, and this indicates some sort of deception. It stands to reason that if we feel we need to hide something inside of us from others, we would have to be sharply focused on the way other people perceive us. Even though it is human nature's instinct to form opinions about one another, the Lord is the final judge of us all. Shouldn't God's opinion of us matter more than opinions of other people? (Galatians 1:10)

Perhaps to defend ourselves from being seen as vulnerable, some of us are purposely misrepresenting what's in our hearts. Coming across as confident and self-assured, successful, intelligent and capable, or attractive to others is important to many people. Some of us are trying to hide the fact that we're scared, or that we feel inadequate, or unsure, or wrong. Many of us don't want to admit these all too human emotions to ourselves, and certainly not to other people. Perhaps these people are afraid that they'll be seen as less in the eyes of others, or that other people will see their uncertainty. It might help those people to know that *all* humanity is sinful and fall short in the eyes of their creator, according to the bible (Rom. 3:23). What God thinks of us matters more than what the world, or other people think of us. Offering us a way to His eternal salvation, God sent Jesus to atone for the sins of all humanity, and this good news is for everyone. No matter what we're afraid of or hiding from, God knows our hearts and offers forgiveness. We might have to appear more than we are to impress the world, but not to our Heavenly Father, who loves us *despite* our sins. Keeping sending the right messages, brothers and sisters. AMEN!

Psalm 12:2, NIV

2 Everyone utters lies to His neighbor; they flatter with their lips but harbor deception in their hearts.

September 20
Not a Life Sentence

Job 5:17, ESV

17 Behold, blessed is the one whom God reproves; therefore despise not the discipline of the Almighty.

Matthew 3:8, ESV

8 Bear fruit in **keeping with repentance**.

Many people can float through life feeling very little guilt for the strife they cause, but other people have trouble with forgiveness and trust. After being hurt and disappointed over and over again through life, many people find it easier to stop trusting all together. The bible assures us that with repeat repenting our spirits will bear fruit through Christ Jesus, which gives us all hope. In order to follow Jesus, we must leave our sins behind, and make different choices. In order to do this we must know what sins we've committed, we cannot guess, or we'll repeat our mistakes. The bible calls us to be holy, not perfect (1 Peter 1:16). If we continue to be focused on our mistakes after they've been forgiven, we aren't acknowledging that Christ paid for that sin on the cross. We sin, we repent, we learn, **we move on**.

When we let the Lord correct us, and allow ourselves to be humbled before Him, we are acknowledging Him as our Heavenly Father. Learning from our sins, trying not to repeat them, and trusting in the forgiveness Jesus Christ provided for us is how we can atone for our transgressions. When we keep our eyes fixed to the Lord guiding us through the Holy spirit, we will be able to see, and choose righteousness more easily. When we make mistakes, we'll be corrected by the Lord in His own way. To try and eradicate all the sin from our lives is futile because we will always be making mistakes, or we wouldn't be asked to *keep repenting*. When we're called to learn another lesson we'll get another lesson from the Lord, and no two are alike. Likewise, if we're called for a brief respite in our tribulations we praise Jesus and celebrate His grace in our lives. If we are called to help another, we look for every opportunity to do so, and give all we can responsibly. Bottom line, we follow the path Christ sets before us, expecting to learn and grow along the way. Our past mistakes are helpful in learning what to watch out for in the future, but not to wear as a token reminder of our mistakes.

Isaiah 43:18, ICB

18 The Lord says, "Forget what happened before. Do not think about the past."

Proverbs 28:13, ERV

13 Whoever conceals His transgressions will not prosper, but whoever confesses their sins and stops doing wrong will receive mercy.

September 21
Eternal Life

John 14:6, ESV

6 Jesus said to him, "I am the way, and the truth, and the life. No one comes to the Father except through me."

Hebrews 9:28, ESV

28 So Christ, having been offered once to bear the sins of many, will appear a second time, not to deal with sin but to save those who are eagerly waiting for him.

When we celebrate communion, or the *Eucharist*, we are honoring the life, ministry, and death of Jesus on the cross, as well as His ultimate offering of sacrifice for the forgiveness of sins (1 Corinthians 11:26). Symbolized by fresh bread and wine or grape juice, we are offered 'the body and the blood' of Christ during times of worship. Placing the morsal of bread into the wine or juice then into our mouths we are putting Christ 'in' us, literally and figuratively. This is an act of symbolism, a re-affirmation to Christ Jesus that we will maintain righteousness as He did. On the last day, the bible tells us that Jesus will return for us (John 6:54). We must remain steadfast in our faith to God through Jesus, by following Him as best we can. When we sin, and we *will* sin, we are to learn and repent, then try harder. We have been given the Holy scriptures to aid in learning the ways of Jesus, His humility, service and love. We should be studying these, and trying to model our lives after them.

We all have but one life to give, then we face death, and after that Christ comes to take us to final judgement (2 Corinthians 5:10). Until that time comes, which no one but God knows (Matthew 24:36-38), we will all sleep in the waiting (Job 14:10-12, Daniel 12:2). God's plan has a beginning, and an ending (Isaiah 46:10, Revelation 22:13), and what happens in between is largely determined by us (Revelation 22:14). We need to strengthen our faith, increase our knowledge of God's word, and clean out the unrighteousness from our hearts in repentance to the Lord in order to receive the gift of eternal life. We have been told that just believing isn't enough to save us (James 2:14-26, Hebrews 12:14), and that we must practice righteousness to make our souls holy. If just our faith was enough to secure our everlasting lives in Heaven, God wouldn't be asking us to change our lives for Him (Acts 3:19, 2 Timothy 3:16, Matthew 18:3, Ephesians 4:23, Romans 12:2). We may not have to follow the hundreds of Jewish laws that are in the old testament, but we do have to cleanse our unrighteous souls of the wickedness we readily cozy up to. Emulating Jesus is impossible, true, but it's in the *effort*, the *repentance*, and the acts of good works that bring us back into righteousness. After all, it's an effort worth eternal life! Praise be to the Lord, AMEN.

John 14:3, ESV

3 "And if I go and prepare a place for you, I will come again and will take you to myself, that where I am you may be also."

September 22
Holiness

Leviticus 20:7, ERV

7 "Be special. Make yourselves holy, because I am the Lord your God."

Hebrews 12:14, ERV

14 Try to live in peace with everyone. And try to keep your lives free from sin. Anyone whose life is not holy will never see the Lord.

Holiness isn't something that's promoted on billboards or advertisements, it's not something you can learn in five easy steps, and it isn't something you can purchase on Amazon, or steal from someone else. Holiness also doesn't appear to be something on the minds of some people. Holiness isn't just what God is all about, it's a pre-requisite for entering the kingdom of Heaven. Usually in a hurry, or trying to get too many tasks done, vainly yet ignorantly focused on their own needs and goals, most working human beings are dedicated to their own individual worlds. People can often find themselves too busy for God; they don't include Him in their daily lives, but still expect to enter the kingdom of Heaven. This type of thinking is incongruent, unbalanced, unreasonable and is refuted in the bible (Deuteronomy 13:4, Mat.22:14,Mat.7:21). What the world thinks is important is opposite of holy: vulgar humor and language, large egos and attitudes, greed, power, boisterous personalities and opinions, wealth and influence. What God thinks is important is obedience and faith, for only the holy will enter the kingdom of Heaven. Many of us aren't remotely close to holy.

Obeying God's rules *makes* us pure, for His laws are *designed* to do this by the grace given to us by the death of Jesus on the cross (Romans 3:28-31). Humans don't naturally gravitate toward holy and righteous behavior, and holiness takes a lifetime of diligence, sacrifice and work to achieve. **Jesus was the example to us, a part of God Himself, given as a mercy sacrifice, and real-life guide to holiness by example.** We were meant to follow Jesus' example, inheriting everlasting life in the kingdom of Heaven by way of righteousness in our *own* lives. As we show God we're seeking Him, we're praying daily to communicate with Him, and we're genuinely looking for ways to change our lives, He will bless us with righteousness (Mat. 5:6). As God reveals what righteousness in our own individual worlds looks like, we are expected to emulate this and actually walk, talk, think and feel differently. Love, humility, peace and forgiveness is to be our guide, not survival, conquest or competition. Only with prayer, questions, trial and error, and diligence in seeking holiness will we get closer to the righteousness God desires, and expects from us. Work hard and carry on, brothers and sisters!

2 Timothy 2:21, ESV

21 Therefore, if anyone cleanses himself from what is dishonorable, he will be a vessel for honorable use, set apart as holy, useful to the master of the house, ready for every good work.

2 Corinthians 7:1, ERV

7 Dear friends, we have these promises from God. So we should make ourselves pure—free from anything that makes our body or our soul unclean. Our respect for God should make us try to be completely holy in the way we live.

September 23
Divine Assurances

Isaiah 32:17, ESV

17 And the effect of righteousness will be peace, and the result of righteousness, quietness and confidence forever.

Proverbs 3:25-26, CSB/ICB

25 Don't fear sudden danger or the ruin of the wicked when it comes 26 for the Lord will be your confidence He will keep you from being trapped.

Humans like to receive compliments from others, but we all react differently to them. Some people become shy and bashful by compliments, not liking to have too much attention drawn to themselves. Other people truly enjoy hearing positive things about themselves, while others seem to *expect* compliments. Human self-esteem can range from feeling completely inferior to others, to feeling arrogant and superior to others. When we feel proud we may innately consider this a good thing, something we can use to bolster our self-esteem. After all, we all want to feel good about ourselves, and many even want others to feel good about us too. Whoah. Pride is considered a sin in the bible (James 4:6), so how are we to feel good about ourselves if we're not *supposed* to be proud? Our focus should be on the Lord, on His forgiveness, guidance, and love, not on ourselves. When we have trouble, we pray for comfort, and when we have blessings and joy, we praise Him in thanks. We celebrate God's light shining through one another's stories, through the scriptures, and through our beautiful differences. Shining the light God gave us isn't wrong, and being happy and thankful is appropriate, but exalting ourselves because of those gifts is pride. Everything given to us can be taken from us (Job 1:21).

True confidence comes from our faith. Our faith in God tells us that our Father in Heaven knows our hearts, is aware of our needs (Psalms 7:9, Matthew 6:31-33). The bible is our closest written link to God's word, and the life and teachings of Jesus Christ. Scripture also tells us to put all of our worry and concern to God in prayer, and He will hear us. All that happens to us, whether triumph or struggle, comes from God (Isaiah 45:7). The bible tells us that we are all God's creation, that God knows us by name, and has a plan for each of us according to His will (Psalm 33:11, John,10:14-15). When we rest in our faith we can be confident because of that faith. God's got our backs.

God is spirit, the bible explains (John 4:24). We cannot see, hear, touch, smell or taste God, we must *feel* Him. God is interested in our spirits, how righteous our hearts and souls are. Nothing anyone can do to our bodies can take away our belief and devotion to God. Likewise, nothing that temporarily tricks or deceives our minds can change in any way the strength of our faith, or our ability to *connect* with our God. When we derive our confidence from comparing ourselves to the world around us, and other people, we're taking our eyes away from God. Our relationship is with God, and its spiritual, it's not between us and the rest of the world. We can't take the rest of the world with us at our final judgement, that will only between us and God, so God should get more of our focus now. **All** that happens to us in our lives God is allowing for some reason, and we won't always know why. When we're following and listening closely to God, our confidence will come from the knowledge that He is watching over us. Any confidence not born of our one true faith in God is considered vanity, and false confidence (Jeremiah 17:5). Trust on, brothers and sisters!

September 24
Don't Look Back

Luke 9:62, AMPC

62 Jesus said to him, "No one who puts his hand to the plow and looks back [to the things behind] is fit for the kingdom of God."

There are many obstacles on our path to righteousness through Christ Jesus. Sins can be tricky to spot through God's correction, and we all handle this refining process differently. No matter where we lie on the 'sin' spectrum, we all commit them, and this is valuable information. When we know what our sins are, we can understand what truly motivates us; whether it's acceptance, reassurance, comfort, security, or wealth. What's more, when we know what we've done wrong by the eyes of God, we can bring that iniquity to Him in repentance, and receive forgiveness. Believe it or not, some people never get past the 'investigation stage," constantly reviewing, identifying, classifying themselves and others merely by the sins they commit, but taking this information no farther. *What we do with the* **knowledge** of our sins reveals more about our true natures than the actual sins themselves. Once our sins are forgiven, they are forgotten, blotted out (Isaiah 43:25). If our Heavenly Father can forgive our sins, we should be able to as well. We can't remain fixed on our sins, or our past mistakes, we're meant to learn from them, repent, and move on.

As distracting as our sins can be, some people stumble over the complexity of understanding, comprehending, and communicating with God. Understanding God's love and our covenant with Him can be complicated, let alone learning to communicate with His invisible, Holy Spirit. Guiding us, directing us, comforting us, and sustaining us, the Holy Spirit is God's love through Jesus working inside of us (1 Corinthians 3:16). Our Sovereign Lord communicates to us through many conduits, we only need to **seek Him** (Jeremiah 29:13). Seeking and understanding are two very different aspects of our relationship with God, and close-mindedness is another obstacle for many people (Ephesians 4:18). Silent thoughts that aren't are own, familiar song lyrics that *suddenly* feel like a personal message, an inspirational story, meme, or encouragement from a friend, an unexpected, yet dramatic shift in life circumstances, the Holy Spirit can touch us in many mysterious ways. If we're **only** tuned into the **tangible world** around us, our cellular devices, tablets, TVs, or other people, how can we expect to hear, let alone understand the Lord? Many of us get tripped up by looking for assurances in our own world; assurances that we're a good person, that we're doing things correctly, that we're loved and appreciated. If we're looking anywhere other than to Christ Jesus for our assurances, we'll always come up with an empty sack. God needs to be important to us, a regular fixture in our daily lives. No matter what our personal obstacles are, God waits for us all to seek Him. If we truly love the Lord our God, and want to serve Him, we won't let any obstacles, including our sins, or our past, come between that love. Keep moving forward in faith, brothers and sisters.

Isaiah 43:18, GW

18 Forget what happened in the past, and do not dwell on events from long ago.

Job 17:9, NLT

9 **The righteous keep moving forward,** and those with clean hands become stronger and stronger.

September 25
Body and vs. Soul

Romans 8:7, ESV/ERV

7 For the mind that is set on the flesh is hostile to God, for anyone whose thinking is controlled by their sinful self is against God. They refuse to obey God's law. And really they are not able to obey it.

Galatians 5:19-23, ESV

19 Now the works of the flesh are evident: sexual immorality, impurity, sensuality, 20 idolatry, sorcery, enmity, strife, jealousy, fits of anger, rivalries, dissensions, divisions, 21 envy, drunkenness, orgies, and things like these. I warn you, as I warned you before, that those who do such things will not inherit the kingdom of God. 22 But the fruit of the Spirit is love, joy, peace, patience, kindness, goodness, faithfulness, 23 gentleness, self-control; against such things there is no law.

We're all traveling around in different bodies, and our differences can be equally beautiful and mysterious as they can be intrusive and threatening. We are all different people, following different moral compasses, having different sets of boundaries, and different sets of priorities for our lives. Our spirits are one with our bodies now, but they won't always be, and this is the struggle the bible talks about (Matthew 26:41). Many of us don't think about what we do with our bodies, and how it affects our spiritual growth in Christ in our daily lives. By example, the passage in Galatians 5 (above) could describe what many would consider a good party, unfortunately. Anything impure physically highlights a heart given to indulging in sinful pleasures, lack's righteous willpower and restraint, and hides secret unholy longings. True repentance is a change in behavior, a change in the way we think, a change in what motivates our heart. Instead of longing for success, worldly comforts and financial security we should be longing for a purer heart, and a more righteous life in service to God. Some people don't like to give up things that give them pleasure, they don't like following rules set by another to govern over their moral choices. These people, whether they believe it or not, are not following God (1 John 2:15). Just thinking about these activities fondly is as bad as committing them in the eyes of God, because He sees your heart's true desire.

If we ask for a more disciplined heart, more righteous, contrite, and holy, the bible assures us that anything we ask for in regards to the improvement of our Spirits, we will receive (John 14:13-14). However, we must understand that we will receive what **God** thinks we have earned, and *He* will direct our improvement, and on *His* timeline. How accepting we are is up to us, but all that we will need to say 'no' to sin God will provide. Being a better person through Christ Jesus may not be as exciting as a rousing drunken brawl or orgie with people whom you cannot trust, but the peaceful grace and moral decency that comes from being more righteous is its own reward. Holy people and true stewards of their faith in Jesus don't really want or desire impure things that satisfy the flesh, they pray through temptation and rely on their self-control and discipline learned through a stronger faith. Gracious Lord, please recycle our sinful, fleshy desires into spiritual cravings for your righteousness and holiness. Create in us, merciful Christ, hearts that are pure and worthy of your grace. Praise be to the Lord, forever. AMEN.

September 26
God Is Greater

Job 38:4, ERV

4 God said to Job, "Where were you when I made the earth? If you are so smart, answer me."

Most of us blast through our day, one coffee, tea, or latte at a time, checking the time and hoping to get as much done in a day as we can. We put off less important tasks or events for another day when our schedules become over-stuffed. Inwardly focused, we are usually happily oblivious to the plight of our fellow man, motivated by our own goals and desires. Humans are a morally corrupt species, time has proven, and as Christ-followers we know we'll be sinning again tomorrow. We, sometimes, make unwholesome choices and just add it to our mental list of indiscretions we'll repent for, expecting to be forgiven. Some people go for weeks, months, or even years without praying and then when faced with death frantically call out to God.

We take much for granted. We don't control time, we certainly don't control our own deaths, and we certainly don't control the physical environment in which we dwell. We are God's children, on God's planet, and should be including thanks to Him in our daily lives. Many of us aren't giving God proper praise in our lives, or offering Him regular repentance for our sins (Matthew 3:8). God is all knowing, and is all powerful, we are not (1 John 3:20). God is able to see the master plan for all humanity over a timeline we, as humans, couldn't possibly fathom (Ecclesiastes 3:11). It's ok, even expected, to need God in our lives. God loves us and wants us to seek Him, he wants to partake in a loving relationship with humanity. Turning to God for forgiveness, guidance in our daily lives, and in our growing relationship with Him is a prayer away. Take a few minutes out of your day to thank God for the good in your life, as well as your daily opportunities for love and growth in Him.

Psalm 94:9-11, ERV

9 God made our ears, so surely he can hear what is happening! He made our eyes, so surely he can see you! 10 The one who disciplines nations will surely correct you. He is the one who teaches us everything. 11 The Lord knows what people are thinking. He knows that their thoughts are like a puff of wind.

Isaiah 45:5-7, GNV

5 "I am the Lord, and there is none other; there is no God besides me: I have given thee strength, power and authority, though thou hast not known me. 6 That they may know from the rising of the sun, and from the West, that there is none besides me. I am the Lord, and there is none other. 7 I form the light, and create darkness: I make peace, and create evil: I the Lord do all these things."

September 27
Perfect Parent

Malachi 2:10, ERV

10 We all have the same father. The same God made every one of us. So why do people cheat one another? They show that they don't respect the agreement. They don't respect the agreement that our ancestors made with God.

Romans 5:8, ERV

8 But Christ died for us while we were still sinners, and by this God showed how much he loves us.

Being a parent is painful, difficult and challenging. As parents, we don't get to decide who our children will ultimately become, what they'll do with their lives, or even how much of us they'll want in their lives when they're grown. As we watch our children grow, make choices, and make mistakes we can't help but see priceless pieces of ourselves in them. Most parents would easily claim we only want our children to have every opportunity in life for success, and that we want them to be happy. Many of us profess love for our children that is so deep and strong, that we would even give our lives for our children if we had to, and if we could. As sinners, we parents will ultimately make some mistakes with our children, but we must not stop trying to do the best we can with what we are given.

God is our Father in Heaven, and we can derive all that we need to not only survive, but spiritually thrive through Jesus and the gift of the Holy Spirit (2 Corinthians 9:8). this is the message we must pass on to our children. Anytime our hearts are separated from our children, we have a small taste of the pain God must be feeling from the many disbelievers that are still spreading sin and hate. We cannot forget the sacrifice on the cross, of Jesus being mocked and beaten by the very people he was saving. We will worry, cry, be afraid for our children, and wish we could choose *for* them sometimes, but that is the sacrifice of being a parent. God knows this all too well, as the first, and original parent of us all. Along with these challenges we will, at times, be moved to tears because of them, rejoice in their growth, and enjoy celebrating in their love through the years as a gift from our Heavenly Father. God is the ultimate parent, and understands all too well the pain we parents suffer, along with that special kind of love that we all have for our children.

It can be easy to forget that these children will eventually grow into adults with their own opinions, views and convictions. As much as we'd like to directly guide their lives in certain aspects, our children will have to find Jesus on their own, and in their own way. As parents, it is our responsibility to plant the mustard seed about Jesus Christ and the good news He brings (Deuteronomy 6:6-7). Exposing them to a church community, or prayer, or readings and stories from the bible, are all good ways of teaching our children about Jesus. These send messages that guide our moral knowledge of right and wrong, as well as how to live our lives. As followers of Christ, we know of the power of the Lord in our lives, but we cannot produce a conviction in someone else. As we are all praying for our children today, we should also pray for them to want to seek Christ.

3 John 4, ESV

4 I have no greater joy than to hear that my children are walking in the truth.

September 28

"I Am"

Exodus 3:14, KJ21

14 And God said unto Moses, "I Am That I Am." And He said, "Thus shalt thou say unto the children of Israel, 'I Am hath sent me unto you.'"

Isaiah 43:11-12, ESV

11 "I, I am the Lord, and besides me there is no savior. 12 I declared and saved and proclaimed, when there was no strange god among you; and you are my witnesses," declares the Lord, "and I am God."

God is real. Scientists like to study physical, tangible, provable origins and cross reference these findings with divine theories and derive at a conclusion to explain the unexplained. Seeking ultimate knowledge, or ultimate notoriety and recognition for their discoveries, intelligent people like to debate and question the origins of the Earth, and of humanity, seeking alternative explanations. Faith is believing in what we cannot see, but something we feel in our hearts (Hebrews 11:1). Nothing but God can explain the complexities of the human soul and spirit, what delights us, motivates us, and drives us from within (Ecclesiastes 12:7). In getting closer to God we will inevitably come face to face with our own shortcomings and sins, and this is the whole point. None of us can improve, spiritually, without learning, and growing in Christ through God's purification process (1 John 3:3). It is difficult to look at ourselves in an unpleasant or unfavorable light, and some people go to great lengths to hide themselves from themselves.

Reigning from the unseen Heavens, God also dwells inside of us because, the bible tells us, God is spirit (Genesis 1:2). An invisible force of unimaginable love divinely combined with stern discipline, God is the beginning and end of time as the bible additionally explains (Revelation 1:8). Many people have difficulty with things they cannot prove, and turn away from God for fear of too many unknowns in their life. We can always pray for a deeper faith, and a wider spiritual understanding without rejecting God in our lives hastily. Believing in God, trusting in Him, will only bring out the best in us. Putting God first in our lives *will* bring change. Change we don't have control over in our lives brings about fear that wants to resist God's will, and not accept God's truth as better for us. We can pray about our fear, we can pray for reassurance, but all relationships are going to take effort. We are always a part of God's world, even when we don't allow Him in ours.

John 8:57-58, ESV

57 So the Jews said to him, "You are not yet fifty years old, and have you seen Abraham?" 58 Jesus said to them, "Truly, truly, I say to you, before Abraham was, I am."

Jeremiah 23:23-24, ESV

23 "I am a God who is near," says the Lord. "I am also a God who is far away. 24 No one can hide where I cannot see him," says the Lord. "I fill all of heaven and earth," says the Lord.

September 29
Understanding

Proverbs 2:6-9, ERV/ESV

6 The Lord is the source of wisdom; knowledge and understanding come from his mouth. 7 He gives good advice to honest people and shields those who do what is right, 8 guarding the paths of justice and watching over the way of his saints. 9 Then you will understand righteousness and justice and equity, every good path.

Deuteronomy 29:4

4 Yet to this day the Lord has not given you a heart to know, nor eyes to see, nor ears to hear.

Learning to become a more righteous person through the life and teachings of Jesus can certainly be easier to read about than interpret through the Holy Spirit. Our life circumstances are directed by God, who knows our hearts, as well as what we each deserve. This is a complicated fact to live by given our autonomous nature, and propensity to give in to sinful desires. God's purifying process can be a bewildering, and sometimes painful, experience. As quick as we are to feel outraged when we are deceived, afflicted, or betrayed, many of us don't realize how selfish this is. We experience everything for God's reason, no matter what we may, or may not, understand about our circumstances. We don't get to see, or know, what our Father in Heaven does, and therefore we can never accurately judge if our life circumstances are fair or not. Just because we *feel* hurt, treated unfairly, or unjustly persecuted doesn't mean **we are**, and, so what if we are? If we love God, we will turn to Him for **all** that is going on in our lives, no matter how bad it hurts. When we decide and assign blame, we are judging, and the Lord tells us this is wrong (Matthew 7:1-2).

We are wrong sometimes. We can misinterpret, and we read into things at times when we shouldn't. Also, we can let our emotions trick us into thinking falsehoods, and can misunderstand the communication we share with the Holy Spirit. God is trying to purify His chosen children (John 1:12-13), and only He knows what each of us need to reach true righteousness, or what is needed to prove our devotion. Only God can allow us to know, and understand, and only God can mend our hearts once they've broken. When we are hurt, confused, and feeling forgotten we need to remember God's love and mercy for us extends beyond what we can comprehend. Reaching deep into our faith, we will begin to see that all we go through is meant to show the Almighty power, and grace, that can only come from God. Working through our pain by praying through Christ Jesus, repenting, trusting in the Lord, and listening more closely to the Holy Spirit, we can learn and grow from our trials. If we don't understand something we are going through we should pray, and then wait, not jump to wrongful, impulsive conclusions. Our trust in the Lord is the foundation of our faith, that, no matter what He puts us through: God knows best, and the Lord will never forsake the one's that love Him. May the Lord fortify, and strengthen, each and every one of us in Jesus' name, AMEN.

Proverbs 9:10, GNV

10 The beginning of wisdom is the fear of the Lord. He showeth what true understanding is, to know the will of God in his word.

September 30
Choosing Wisely

2 Corinthians 6:14, ERV

14 You are not the same as those who don't believe. So don't join yourselves to them. Good and evil don't belong together. Light and darkness cannot share the same room.

Romans 16:17, NIV

17 I urge you, brothers and sisters, to watch out for those who cause divisions and put obstacles in your way that are contrary to the teaching you have learned. **Keep away from them.**

If one apple has rotted, it'll spread the spoilage to the apples nearest to it, and it must be removed or spoil the whole bushel. Negativity spreads like cancer, with attitudes and behavior usually to follow, and it can be difficult to break the cycle. Criticism, competition, prejudice, hate, jealousy and envy are on the lips and minds of those foundering in the darkness. Some people are happy to remain there, uninterested in the salvation Jesus' teachings offer. If we can bring people to Jesus, we should, but we must remember that we can't reach everyone. Not everyone *wants* to take an active role in learning the scripture, in getting closer to Jesus. Some people just want to live in peaceful anonymity, and don't want to change for anyone, even God. While some people are fighting desperately to find their way out of the dark, still others are content to live in the darkness. (John 3:19-20) As sinners searching for salvation through righteousness, we cannot afford to be led astray from what we know to be true about Jesus. If someone in our lives is determined to remain in the darkness, **and not know and accept Jesus' commandments**, then God asks us to disassociate with them. Harsh, but clear.

Got friends? Got *good* friends? It's imperative that we take a good look at the people we associate ourselves with. Not everyone around us has our best interest at heart, and we must be vigilant to our surroundings. All people are sinners, but some are trying harder than others to be, and stay, wholesome through Christ. We must be careful when speaking with people that we don't pass judgement on them, because only God knows what is truly in a person's heart (Jeremiah 17:9-10). We can only listen to their words, and observe their behaviors and attitudes toward others, to determine a person's righteousness. People who aren't interested in improving themselves through the teachings of Jesus Christ are living in the darkness, and their negativity, and taciturn attitude toward Christ's salvation, will only spread more of the same negativity. This is why God has said to be selective in who you allow to penetrate your inner social circle, and be clear on the intensions in their hearts. We are who we associate with, so look around, are we among a pack of lost souls foundering in the shadows, or a spiritual gangster fighting in the army for Christ?

Proverbs 12:26, NIV

26 The righteous choose their friends carefully, but the way of the wicked leads them astray.

Luke 17:3, ESV

3 Pay attention to yourselves! If your brother sins, rebuke him, and if he repents, forgive him.

October 1
The Bible's Importance

John 6:63, ESV

63 "It is the Spirit who gives life; the flesh is no help at all. The words that I have spoken to you are spirit and life."

Matthew 4:4, ESV

4 But he answered, "It is written, 'Man shall not live by bread alone, but by every word that comes from the mouth of God.'"

Education is respected in our society, and if the price is right, any amount of knowledge can be learned. Scholars and scientists struggle daily to find the answers to life's greatest mysteries, find cures for diseases, and solutions to world and global problems. Intelligence gives people choices, opportunities and a false sense of security. World knowledge is only necessary to the extent one needs to understand the laws, and expectations of one's immediate environment. World knowledge is useless in Heaven, however. What's more, the smarter we think we are, the more foolish we are in the eyes of God. Humility doesn't favor pride in one's intelligence, however well it may serve us here on Earth.

The bible is God's word for us, and we're called to live by that word. People who dismiss the bible are dismissing God, for in no other place will His knowledge be found in written word. Some people misinterpret the bible, or just read certain portions of it, missing the whole picture. Understanding our relationship with the characters from the bible is vital, showing us how to change our hearts, our minds, and our very lives to follow in the footsteps of the divine. We cannot know what God's truth is if we don't understand it from the source. If we're going to be able to decipher what is trickery, man's interpretation, or derive any knowledge from the bible we're going to have to read it for ourselves. Offered in many forms, with many study guides available, there is no excuse for not endeavoring to read the holy bible from cover to cover. If we say we love God, then we should want to get to know Him firsthand. Churches, fellowship with other bible scholars, and even bible study classes are helpful in getting closer to God, but nothing should replace the personal relationship that develops from reading and understanding God's word independently. Jesus tells us that we are to 'live by every word that comes from the mouth of God,' so we should know it!

2 Peter 1:20-21, ERV

20 Most important of all, you must understand this: No prophecy in the Scriptures comes from the prophet's own understanding. 21 No prophecy ever came from what some person wanted to say. But people were led by the Holy Spirit and spoke words from God.

Hebrews 4:12, ESV

12 For the word of God is living and active, sharper than any two-edged sword, piercing to the division of soul and of spirit, of joints and of marrow, and discerning the thoughts and intentions of the heart.

October 2

God's Way, Not Our Way

Isaiah 53:6, ERV

6 We had all wandered away like sheep. We had gone our own way. And yet the Lord put all our guilt on him.

Proverbs 18: 1-2, ERV

18 Some people like to do things their own way, and they get upset when people give them advice. 2 Fools don't want to learn from others. They only want to tell their own ideas.

Many of us grow up and go to college, get married, have children, land a job we can tolerate doing for the rest of our lives, and all without giving much thought to the war between good and evil raging on inside of us that the Lord God is focused on. Written so long ago, some people use the vast difference in societal and ethical norms between today and biblical times to argue that the bible is basically obsolete. God is permanent, and so is His command over the entire universe (Luke 16:17). God's laws and commandments are all about loving one another, helping and respecting one another, and not making ourselves out to be more than one another, or God (Matthew 22:36-40). Many people find these rules to be too difficult to follow because humility is required, submission to God is mandatory, we will all be challenged, pressed, tempted and tested throughout our lives, and our reward doesn't happen till after we've been dead a while. These facts discourage many people from a deeper devotion to God.

God's will is going to happen, the bible tells us, and *has been* happening since the beginning of time (Isaiah 14:24). God see's people's spirits as good or evil based on the desires and intensions of their hearts in comparison with their devotion and good works displayed by their lives. How many people did we help, or how many did we ignore? Repenting for our sins is only the first step back to God, we must also change our lifestyles to be more righteous, contrite, and obey God's commandments. When we go our own way instead of submitting to God, He will correct and discipline us when we stray from Him. How we deal with God's correction helps Him determine how 'good' or 'evil' our hearts are. Many people are living wickedly without knowing this because they continue to partake in gossip, pride, judging one another, jealousy, deceit, foul language, hate and adultery. When we pray, we repent for our sins, and ask God for blessings, but we also need to listen when He communicates with us. Reading God's word, along with routine prayer, will help us to understand what God wants from us. We must listen and obey God, this shows Him our faith, and that our spirits are pursuing His righteous 'goodness.'

Proverbs 1:28-33, ERV

28 "Fools will call for me, but I will not answer. They will look for me, but they will not find me. 29 That is because they hated knowledge. They refused to fear and respect the Lord. 30 **They ignored my advice and refused to be corrected. 31 They filled their lives with what they wanted. They went their own way,** so they will get what they deserve. 32 Fools die because they refuse to follow wisdom. They are content to follow their foolish ways, and that will destroy them. 33 But those who listen to me will live in safety and comfort. They will have nothing to fear."

October 3
Committed?

Luke 14:26, 33 ERV

26 "If you come to me but will not leave your family, you cannot be my follower. You must love me more than your father, mother, wife, children, brothers, and sisters — even more than your own life!" 33 "It is the same for each of you. You must leave everything you have to follow me. If not, you cannot be my follower."

What if God was only as committed to us as we were to Him? If that question leaves you unsettled, good, as it should. To love God with all of our heart, soul, and mind, and to love one another as we love ourselves *seems* like fairly easy commandments to follow. Certainly, however, if we were all following these two commands to the letter we wouldn't see all the crime, hate, conquest, greed, and indifference to suffering that we do in our world. We each play a part in the world around us, how often are we asking ourselves, "what have I done to contribute, or what can I do to help?" People are in need all around us, hungry, homeless, oppressed, sick, and suffering. God wants us to do more to help them. (Isaiah 58:6-10). Pushy, greedy, selfish people keep their noses arrogantly to their own affairs, reassuring themselves they are good and righteous, while they ignore, step over, and shove aside everyone else around them. Not only should we be helping more where we can, but we should be showing more kindness to one another in the way of tolerance, understanding, acceptance, forgiveness, patience, and love.

Each decision, each choice we make stems from what motivates us, and at the root of them all should be God (Isaiah 30:1). When we don't include the Lord in our daily thoughts, goals for the day, concerns and needs, we are showing that we don't think we need Him. Devotion to the Lord isn't supposed to be on occasion, once in a while, or only for emergencies, or in a quick, robotic, insincere prayer. "All of our heart, soul, mind, and strength" (Luke 10:27), sounds more like "all God, all day." We all experience trouble, affliction, and pain, or blessings, peace, and grace depending on what the Lord needs to do to keep us focused on Him (Jeremiah 8:4-6). No matter what God throws at us, we need to remember that He only corrects those that belong to Him, and this is an honor not bestowed on everyone (Hebrews 12:6) (Matthew 22:14). When we hurt we should ask our Heavenly Father for comfort, even if He is the source of our hurt, because our love for Him should be stronger than our constantly changing emotions. The bottom line is, our faith tells us that we can trust that God has our best interest at heart, and will never forsake us. If we don't trust, we should be praying for that, as well as repenting for our lack of faith. A serious commitment in any relationship takes work, dedication, love, and a responsibility toward sincere devotion. How committed will God find *you*? Lord, we ask you to search our hearts, cleanse and purify them as only you can, and help us to focus on you more contritely. All praise be to God through Jesus Christ, our Lord and Savior, and reigning King. AMEN.

Deuteronomy 13:4, ESV

4 You shall follow the Lord your God and fear Him; and you shall keep His commandments, listen to His voice, serve Him, and hold fast to Him.

1 Kings 8:61, ESV

61 Let your heart therefore be wholly true to the Lord our God, walking in his statutes and keeping his commandments, as at this day.

October 4
The Devil's Trickery, Self-Doubt

Hebrews 3:12, ERV

12 So, brothers and sisters, be careful that none of you has the **evil thoughts** that **cause** so much **doubt** that you stop following the living God.

James 1:6-8, ERV

6 But when you ask God, you must believe. **Don't doubt** him. Whoever doubts is like a wave in the sea that is blown up and down by the wind. 7-8 People like that are thinking two different things at the same time. They can never decide what to do. So they should not think they will receive anything from the Lord.

Many of us have trouble placing our full trust in things we cannot see, touch or prove. God is spirit, truth and love, intangible and mysterious, but not elusive (Jeremiah 29:13). No one enjoys suffering, but we all suffer, as we all process our suffering differently. Some people rely on God, some people don't, but we all *need* God for our eternal salvation. When we're pressed, or under pressure, we are more vulnerable to the devil's trickery. When we doubt God hears us, or is working in our lives and hastily form our own plans and solutions we are allowing ourselves to be deceived. The truth tells us that the Lord is with us all the time, in the form of the Holy Spirit, which dwells within us (1 Corinthians 3:16). Forming our own plans, making our own decisions because we didn't want to wait on God, or because we didn't like His answer is a lack of faith in Him. We aren't expected to enjoy our painful tribulations, trials and tests issued by God, but we are asked to seek Him while we endure them.

Our trials, tribulations, and tests feel like pain and suffering, and the devil often tempts us by telling us we've been forgotten, that our needs aren't important to God. Bringing our past mistakes, or old pains into clear view, the devil intends to cloud our communications with God. When we ask for forgiveness, we are forgiven according to the bible, and we're told not to sin again (Hebrews 8:12). Once we've been forgiven, the past is left to the past, and we rest in the confident knowledge that the future is in God's hands. We need only wait, have patience that the Lord will address us in His timely manner, and **not** rely on our own understanding. The pain God imparts on us in our lives helps to show us where we've make mistakes, so we can retrain our thinking to a more righteous way. If we don't fully *believe* the Lord will provide for us, and in every way possible, than we don't have enough faith. After all, how can you ask God for rescue when you aren't really sure of His abilities? If we don't see or feel God in our lives, it's because we're not looking in the right places. God *is* with us, and desires us to come to Him for *all* of our needs with the faith that He **can, and will** provide for them. Self-doubt is a negative, all too human emotion, spurred by low self-esteem and the devils trickery. A stronger faith can overcome anything, as all things are possible with God to those who believe.

Mark 5:36, ESV

36 But overhearing what they said, Jesus said to the ruler of the synagogue, "Do not fear, only believe."

October 5
The Devil's Trickery, Clouded Judgement

Luke 8:12, ICB

12 What is the seed that fell beside the road? It is like the people who hear God's teaching, but then **the devil comes and takes it away from their hearts. So they cannot believe the teaching and be saved.**

Proverbs 25:26, ESV

26 Like a **muddied spring** or a **polluted fountain** is a righteous man who gives way before the wicked.

When our lives are turned upside down, or things go wrong, or we suffer from misfortunes and hardships it is natural for us to want justice and retribution. If we're not turning to God in our time of need, we really should be. Everything occurs according to the will of God, and He is the only true direction in our lives. When we pray, we might be praying for a quick solution, or fair and efficient justice served immediately based on what we determine is appropriate. If we aren't appeased the way we think we should be, and in the timeframe we think appropriate, we can become disappointed, angry, and even outraged at God. When we're down, and wondering where God is in our lives, the devil is quick to seize the opportunity to cloud our understanding, and pollutes the knowledge that our Lord sends to us through the Holy Spirit.

God will never forsake us, but He will test us. It can be easy to form our own opinions on how God *should* be working in our lives, but He is the only one that truly see's the whole picture. We can't possibly see all that is happening in the lives of others, even those closest to us. With our passions, emotions, judgements and prejudices, humans can't always provide fair and balanced conclusions, and this is just one reason why we need to rely on God. When something bad happens in our lives that we don't understand, it can be extremely painful, churns up our emotions, and it can be easy to wonder if He even *see's* our pain at all, sometimes. We need to be careful when thoughts creep into our heads like, "if God loves me so much, why am I hurting so?" or, "maybe my problems aren't important to God, maybe He's got more important things to deal with." God works in ways we don't always understand, and that's why we need to have a strong faith. When we truly and deeply trust God with all of our strength, we understand that, although we don't understand how it all works together, we know that God is fair, just and loving. We also trust with all of our hearts that God will *not* forsake us, and loves us more than we can possibly comprehend. When we trust in God through our darkest moments we show Him that we love Him too. How deep is *your* faith?

Proverbs 28:5, ESV

5 Evil men do not understand justice, but those who seek the Lord understand it completely.

1 Corinthians 14:33a, ESV

33a For God is not a God of confusion but of peace.

October 6
The Devil's Trickery, Deception

Genesis 3:13, ESV

13 Then the Lord God said to the woman, "What is this that you have done?" The woman said, "**The serpent deceived** me, and I ate."

2 Corinthians 11:3, ESV

3 But I am afraid that as the serpent **deceived** Eve **by His cunning**, your thoughts will be led astray from a sincere and pure devotion to Christ.

No one likes to admit they've been deceived, no one wants to be thought of as foolish or unaware. The bible tells us that the devil fools everyone on earth, so none of us are immune (2 Corinthians 11:14). How can we know the difference between the devil's trickery, and God's justice? The closer we get to God through prayer, repentance, devotion to understanding His written word, we learn what true righteousness looks like. Once we begin substituting evil, impure thoughts and choices with more contrite ones, we begin to understand what a sincere and pure devotion looks like.

We can't live more righteous lives if we're holding on to our old ways of thinking. Clearing out the greed, pride, arrogance, and developing a sharper focus on Jesus's life, ministry and teaching, provides a stable foundation for a deeper faith and understanding. Our thoughts are vulnerable, and fueled by the desires in our hearts. In order to share our spiritual eternity with God in Heaven, we must become holy so we can be in His presence. God is trying to change our hearts to that of a more forgiving, reserved, humble, patient, loving heart, desiring all of humanity to be with Him in Heaven (2 Peter 3:9). The more righteous we become, the easier it will be to decipher the devil's trickery from God's grace and truth. Like the pull of two attracted magnets, humans naturally gravitate to sin and wickedness. When God teaches us a lesson, its painful, and we can often feel unjustly prosecuted. The devil wants to deceive us from *understanding* God, and can deceive us into feeling like nobody knows our burdens, or even cares. This can cause us to feel lost, forgotten, and become angry or embittered against God when we're suffering. The bible reminds us to pray without ceasing, indicating we need to be patient, and lean into our faith that God will not abandon us. We cannot trust our emotions, which can deceive us, but must place all of our trust in Jesus. We must trust that God is shaping us, reforming us, bringing out our best selves, and the more we try to fight it the more tribulation, pain, and confusion we will experience.

Revelation 12:9, CEV

9 and were thrown down to the earth. Yes, that old snake and His angels were thrown out of heaven! That snake, **who fools everyone on earth, is known as the devil and Satan.**

James 4:7, ESV

7 Submit yourselves therefore to God. Resist the devil, and he will flee from you.

October 7
Losing Spiritual Composure

Proverbs 12:16, ERV

16 Fools are easily upset, but wise people avoid insulting others.

Titus 2:11-12, ESV

11 For the grace of God has appeared, bringing salvation for all people, 12 training us to renounce ungodliness and worldly passions, and to live self-controlled, upright, and godly lives in the present age.

Indulging in one too many culinary treats, letting our anxieties carry our thoughts away, and reacting impulsively out of emotion are all examples of how we, as humans, can lose our self-control. Getting angry, giving into gossip, giving into our own self-doubt, or our own self-exaltation are also examples of a loss of self-control. Many of us spend way too much time on social media responding to drama, judging other people's reactions, forming, and sharing opinions. Many people desire to impress others with their wit, humor, and clever responses. How we react and respond to others says a great deal about ourselves. Self-control is the ability to control our reactions. When we feel we're disrespected, insulted, or we feel like an injustice has been committed against us the bible calls us to turn the other cheek and forgive (Matthew 5:38-39). Many times people want to confront disrespect immediately, angry and outraged, demanding someone back off or back down or capitulate to their own demand for justice. Some people overthink everything in their lives, worried about every possible outcome, and overreact when something is out of place. Others ignore their own needs, too uncomfortable in their own skin to advocate for themselves. No matter how much self-esteem we may have, the bible educates that righteousness is all about self-control (1 Corinthians 6:12).

Many of us could stand to self-edit before we speak, respond, or react to someone in emotion. Our words and behaviors represent who we are, and we are called to be contrite, virtuous and upright. Thinking before we speak, we should ask ourselves if what we're about to communicate is necessary, truthful, and kind? Everyone carries a different idea of what self-control should look like, but there is only one example of righteousness and holiness. Jesus Christ, our Lord and Savior, walked the Earth the only truly perfect, sinless man. God calls us to live by Christ's example of true righteousness, through self-editing, self-control, willpower and restraint. We derive all we need from the Lord, including patience, wisdom, and grace. We should be building others up with our words, and holding our tongues accordingly when angered or emotional so we don't condemn or judge a brother or sister in Christ. We should be forgiving people who make us angry or cause us emotional pain, because Jesus asks us to. We should take a step back, pray, and restrain our urge to yell, cuss, gossip, or give in to a sinful temptation. Each time we lose our composure we turn away from Christ and must repent, and learn to filter our responses better. Self-control leads to wisdom and enlightenment, where lack of emotional control leads to volatility and impulsivity (Proverbs 16:32, 25:28).

2 Peter 1:5-7, ESV

5 For this very reason, make every effort to supplement your faith with virtue, and virtue with knowledge, 6 and knowledge with self-control, and self-control with steadfastness, and steadfastness with godliness, 7 and godliness with brotherly affection, and brotherly affection with love.

October 8
Righteousness

Galatians 5:19-23, GW

19 Now, the effects of the corrupt nature are obvious: illicit sex, perversion, promiscuity, 20 idolatry, drug use, hatred, rivalry, jealousy, angry outbursts, selfish ambition, conflict, factions, 21 envy, drunkenness, wild partying, and similar things. I've told you in the past and I'm telling you again that people who do these kinds of things will not inherit God's kingdom. 22 But the spiritual nature produces love, joy, peace, patience, kindness, goodness, faithfulness, 23 gentleness, and self-control. There are no laws against things like that.

Although adultery is an obvious sin, there are many sins that hide in everyday actions and words, sins that we can all fall prey to. Righteousness doesn't allow angry outbursts, room for selfish ambition, or conflicts among one another, the scriptures outline. Also, if we want to be righteous, we can't have any social cliques or divisions, we can't envy anyone, or engage in wild parties. This may sound harsh, but good people chase righteousness and self-control, and wicked people give in to their own thoughts and desires. We can't wantonly partake of sin and wickedness, then profess to be following Jesus. When we're in conflict with one another, or stand in judgement of another, or envy another, or use another's sins to exclude them we are giving into the hate and wickedness in our hearts. Knowing we're sinful shouldn't make us bitter, it shouldn't make us judgmental either, it should make us want to *improve* for our Lord. When we give into temptation we are focusing on ourselves, and not Christ. If we believe in Jesus but still partaking of wickedness *readily*, we're not really a true follower of our Lord (Hebrews 10:26, 1 John 3:9). Giving up **all** of the sinful things we take for granted every day, like swearing, passing judgement, crude humor, lust, conflict with co-workers, and cliques can seem unreasonable, and, unrealistic to some.

Just because our sins are forgiven, doesn't mean we can behave any way we like. Anger, hate, and loss of self-control only leads to more poor choices and sinful behaviors. Committing some sins and not others isn't really changing the desires in our hearts that causes us to want things we shouldn't. If we loved one another like Christ asked us to, perhaps we would all work harder to not commit sins against one another, maybe we would forgive one another more readily. In order to be more righteous, we need to change what drives our hearts desires. We should humble ourselves, and be forthright enough to address the selfishness, the prejudice, the lack of love and forgiveness in our hearts, and ask the Lord to purify them through Him. The bible assures us that God knows what's truly in our hearts (Proverbs 21:2), even if we hide from ourselves, we cannot hide our true intensions from God. A half-hearted effort is worthless, just because we 'cut down' on our bad choices, doesn't mean we're truly seeking God and not just the benefits of believing in Him. If our faith in God is true, we seek to *be like Jesus*, and to be like Jesus is to be as righteous and loving to others as we can, and genuinely, from our hearts, and not for selfish ambition, or self-preservation. We must all take a deeper look at what is motivating us, and ask ourselves if its righteous, or just our own sinful desire.

1 John 1:9, ESV

9 If we confess our sins, he is faithful and just to forgive us our sins and to cleanse us from all unrighteousness.

October 9
Simple to Understand, Hard to Follow

Matthew 7:12, NASB

12 "In everything, therefore, treat people the same way you want them to treat you, for this is the Law and the Prophets."

James 2:8-9, NIV

8 If you really keep the royal law found in Scripture, "Love your neighbor as yourself," you are doing right. 9 **But if you show favoritism, you sin** and are convicted by the law as lawbreakers.

The bible tells us we can't swear, lie, cheat, steal, covet something someone else has, to keep the Sabbath holy in honor of God, pray often, repent, praise God through good works, be holy, avoid all sin all the time, whew!-it all seems like too much. Many people come to realize they cannot possibly follow all of God's rules, and give up in discouragement. For others, they stop worrying about their own sins, because they're free in Christ, but continue to notice everyone else's sins. For some, it seems as if God has set us all up to fail by requiring us to live holy, knowing we are sinful creatures. Besides, many people think, since Christ died for the forgiveness of our sins, we can basically live any way they want. After all, we'll just be forgiven anyway. What **is** clear, is that all humans need guidance, direction and forgiveness that only our Lord and Savior can provide.

Within the pages of the Holy word are many rules defining how God's people are to live, work, and behave according to a clean and pure way, in a very meticulous outline of do's and don'ts. The ten commandments are common enough to everyone, and fairly reasonable to follow (Exodus 20:1-17). These very specific laws turn a lot of people away from God, or tempt them to change, omit, or ignore some of God's word. Jesus urges us 'not too relax' in trying to abide in these laws and commandments, knowing we'll make mistakes (Matthew 5:18-19). Jesus said the two most important commandments were love God and love others, that from these all other laws and commandments stem (Matthew 22:36-37). The Lord didn't say they were the only certain rules we needed to abide by, and others we could overlook. We are called to repent for our mistakes, because God knows we'll commit them as we try to learn to be more Holy. Righteousness is a lifestyle, a way of thinking, of behaving, a specific code of service and love from which all of the laws and commandments are derived. We might all be set up for failure in our quest for righteousness, but God knows some of us are trying harder than others.

Psalm 19:7-11, ESV

7 The law of the Lord is perfect, reviving the soul; the testimony of the Lord is sure, making wise the simple; 8 the precepts of the Lord are right, rejoicing the heart; the commandment of the Lord is pure, enlightening the eyes; 9 the fear of the Lord is clean, enduring forever; the rules of the Lord are true, and righteous altogether. 10 More to be desired are they than gold, even much fine gold, sweeter also than honey and drippings of the honeycomb. 11 Moreover, by them is your servant warned; in keeping them there is great reward.

October 10
Equality in Suffering?

Isaiah 45:7, ESV

7 "I form light and create darkness; I make well-being and create calamity; I am the Lord, who does all these things."

God is responsible for ALL that happens to us in our lives, both good and bad. God wants all of His people to seek Him for all of their needs. Many of us aren't doing this enough, or at all. Instead of being outraged at God for our pain, we should be asking Him for guidance, understanding, and comfort.

Ecclesiastes 9: 2-3a, ICB

2 Both good and bad things happen to everyone. They happen to those who are fair and to those who are wicked. They happen to those who are good and to those who are evil. They happen to those who sacrifice and to those who do not. The same things happen to a good person as happen to a sinner. The same things happen to a person who makes promises to God as to one who does not. 3 This is something unfair that happens here on earth. The same things happen to everyone.

Life isn't designed to be fair. Life is unfair to everyone, equally, and without bias, no matter what it may appear to be. This is how God's grace brings salvation, and we rest in His final judgement.

James 1:13, ESV

13 Let no one say when he is tempted, "I am being tempted by God," for God cannot be tempted with evil, and he himself tempts no one.

Temptation is wickedness luring someone into doing what God says is wrong. God isn't going to tempt us, but He is going to test us, and there is a big difference. Tests from God produces growth, a deeper faith, and enlightenment, while giving into impulses leads to sin.

Ecclesiastes 7:20, CJB

20 For there isn't a righteous person on earth who does [only] good and never sins.

All humanity is sinful, all humans will disappoint. No one is any better or worse than another in the eyes of God, because we're ALL sinful. It's in how hard we're trying NOT to be that is important.

Isaiah 59:1-2, ERV

59 Look, the Lord's power is enough to save you. He can hear you when you ask him for help. 2 It is your sins that separate you from your God. He turns away from you when he sees them.

When we're committing sins, God turns away from us. It's only after we've repented for our sins that we can be forgiven, and accepted, once again into God's good graces. If we don't know what our sins are, we should pray to God for that knowledge. God's power is available, we only need to seek it.

October 11

"Not a True Follower"

Proverbs 30:12, ERV

12 Some people think they are pure, but they have done nothing to remove the filth of their sin.

Romans 2:1, ERV

2 So do you think that you can judge those other people? You are wrong. You too are guilty of sin. You judge them, but you do the same things they do. So **when you judge** them, **you are really condemning yourself.**

"If one type of person thinks a certain way, then all of those people must think that way," is a disparaging thought some of us have fallen victim to. Humans are naturally judgmental, often assuming more knowledge and authority than we have. While some people have trouble admitting to *partaking* in such judgmental thoughts, others have trouble admitting that we're usually wrong when we think this way. All judgmental thinking is wrong, and certainly, categorizing people who may, or may not be qualified for the kingdom of Heaven is presumptuous, at best! We cannot know what is in the heart of another person, sometimes we don't even know what's in our *own* hearts. Preferences, boundaries, previous negative experiences, ignorance, and prejudice affects us all, as a result, humanity will always disappoint (Jeremiah 17:5). All people have sinned, will sin, and need God's Sovereign power, grace, judgment, and wisdom to complete the journey to righteousness. No one is above anyone else, and no one has the power to pass judgement on another. Over and over in the bible, we are told not to pass judgement on one another (Luke 6:37, Romans 14:10-12, Matthew 7:1). We are to treat everyone the way we would want to be treated. If someone professes to love God, unashamed, and wants to discuss scripture, wants to learn more about God, then we know we've found a fellow follower in Christ. We shouldn't be selective toward which groups, types, or cultures of people partake in our worship, fellowship, and love because they happen to sin *differently* than we do. Jesus called all sinners (Luke 5:32). Besides, other people's sins aren't something we should be looking at, judging, or using against them in any way (Romans 14:13). Unless someone tells us what they believe, and don't believe, we cannot assume to know.

We don't want to make a practice of associating closely and regularly with people who are non-believers, or people who make a habit of sinning without regard to their salvation in Christ Jesus. However, we don't know the internal battle people may be waging with their spirits, or how strongly they're effort to know Jesus is. Jesus wants *tryers*, people who *pursue* Him, who exalt and praise Him, and people who pray to the Lord to help them become a better person. If we deny a believer because they sin differently we are placing ourselves in the judges seat, which rightfully belongs to God (James 4:12). When we assume we know more than we do about someone, or a situation, we are being arrogant. Let God Be the Judge, and pray for a humble heart, brothers and sisters.

Matthew 12:36, ERV

36 (Jesus said) "I tell you that everyone will have to answer for all the careless things they have said. This will happen on the day of judgment."

October 12
Pride Is Bad, Accept It

Philippians 2:3, ESV

3 Do nothing from selfish ambition or conceit, but in humility count others more significant than yourselves.

Proverbs 16:5, ERV

5 The Lord hates those who are proud. You can be sure he will punish them all.

To those who are proud of their intelligence, there will always be someone smarter. To those who are proud of their appearance, there will always be someone younger and more attractive. To those who are proud of their possessions, there will always be someone else with more. Our degrees, our cars, our large client list, our prestigious position or career, though wonderful accomplishments, cannot save our souls or get us into Heaven. We may want, or even *believe*, that our accomplishments and achievements inspire others to work hard and set lofty goals for themselves, that they are good and wonderful things to be proud *of*. Pride is bad, **always.** If we're proud because of the things we've accomplished on our own, we're seeking in vain, and only giving in to self-worship. If we're proud of what we have because we know that it all comes from God's will for us, then we're not really proud, we're *grateful*, and there is a big difference.

Some people brag about making their own choices, being the masters of their own destiny, self-made, are usually intelligent people who make their own path in life, and are, unapologetically, very proud of themselves. Although many people admire this type of person, any pursuit of anything outside our path in Christ, is vanity. No matter how powerful, or strong, we want to appear to ourselves, we are all derived from a sinful, disobedient humanity, and are all in need of God's guidance in our lives. Submitting to humility instead of pride as something to strive for is a foreign notion to most people, and enough for them to turn away from God. Some people operate on the thinking that their pride in their appearance, or cars, or jewelry, or their loud, 'out-spoken' personality, is because they're a strong person with clear boundaries and a strong self-worth. Truly, pride is a sin in the bible, because it takes the glory off of God, who is the true giver and taker of all things. Those who truly know and understand God's love, and will, for them understand He is in control of every aspect of life. Humans are deceitful, prone to sin, and naturally disobedient to God, all are created equal and will be judged equally by God. To believe we have more control over our lives through our own will than God does is to believe a lie.

Psalm 10:4, KJ21

4 The wicked, in the pride of His countenance, will not seek after God; God is not in all His thoughts.

Isaiah 13:11, GW

11 "I will punish the world for its evil and the wicked for their wrongdoing. I will put an end to arrogant people and humble the pride of tyrants."

October 13
Hide and Seek?

Deuteronomy 4:29, ERV

29 But from there you will seek the LORD your God and you will find him, if you search after him with all your heart and with all your soul.

Psalm 118:8, ERV

8 It is better to take refuge in the Lord than to trust in man.

One of the downfalls of being a responsible adult is simply *having* responsibilities, the only consolation being that we can accomplish them any way we like, within the law, of course. When we think of the laws we abide by, paying taxes, not committing acts of theft or violence, civic duties, we are talking about the laws of our civilization. What about God's laws? Freedom to meet our many responsibilities isn't free, our bodies and spirits belong to God (Ecclesiastes 12:7). Many people, despite believing in God, don't want to accept the humble perspective of belonging to anyone, including God. Sinful arrogance and human pride can deceive people into believing more in their own free will and autonomy, instead of the strict guidelines of God's commands and laws. As children of the one, true, Almighty God, we have a covenant to adhere to. Being kind, forgiving, and tolerant of other people is less difficult, perhaps, than running everything we do and say before God. Although some people may be reluctant to accept it, God desires us to seek Him first, above ourselves, and those we love, and to do His will and not our own (Psalm 14:2).

Strict adherence to our covenant with God not only grooms better self-control and righteous behavior, it is also meant to correct and reproof our mistakes. Anytime we stray too far from the path of righteousness God corrects us with trials, pain, and tribulations. Sometimes, God puts pressure on us just to test our faith in Him. Some people don't welcome God's correction with a pure heart, and can become angry or embittered with God as a result (Proverbs 1:28-31). When we have troubles but don't seek God for comfort, solutions, and direction we aren't seeking God. (Zephaniah 1:6) When we trust too much in our own abilities and knowledge, we aren't seeking the Lord. Brothers and sisters, we should be beginning each day with the Lord's prayer (Matthew 6:7-13), and seeking Jesus throughout the day in prayer, for the guidance, direction, comfort and support our spirits need to stay righteous through our difficulties, and to remain steadfast in a wicked world. God is never hidden, and always desires us to seek Him for all our needs (Acts 17:27). Gracious Lord, forgive us for turning away and focusing on ourselves, help us to adhere to your covenant more closely, and bless our hearts with the desire to serve you better. All praise and glory be to God forever through the Son, who gives mercifully, AMEN.

Isaiah 65:16, ERV

16 The Lord says, "People now ask blessings from the earth. But in the future they will ask blessings from the faithful God. People now trust in the power of the earth when they make a promise. But in the future they will trust in the God who is faithful. That's because the troubles in the past will all be forgotten. They will be hidden from my sight."

October 14
'Carte Blanche'

1 John 3:8, ESV

8 Whoever **makes a practice of sinning** is of the devil, for the devil has been sinning from the beginning. The reason the Son of God appeared was to destroy the works of the devil.

1 John 5:18, NLT

18 We know that God's children do not **make a practice of sinning**, for God's Son holds them securely, and the evil one cannot touch them..

Sin is behavior contradictory to what God has commanded for humanity. Sins are bad, and we all commit them. The bible calls people who sin repeatedly children of the devil, but that seems harsh considering all humanity sins. Our world is in control of the devil (1 John 5:19), human thoughts are evil by nature (Genesis 6:5), and when the two are combined, only the power of God can break the cycle of wickedness. Many people, after reading 1John 5:18, believe that simply because of their belief in Jesus, they automatically become sin-free. It is important to remember Matthew 3:8, and what Jesus says about 'keeping with repentance.' If humans didn't sin continuously, as God alludes to in the book of Genesis (Gen 6:5), then Jesus wouldn't have said that we needed to **keep** repenting. We don't just stop sinning because we believe in Jesus, we will sin all our lives, never truly reaching spiritual perfection. We are only purified through the blood of Christ, through His crucifixion, death, and resurrection. Christ was offered as the sacrifice for the sins of humanity, so all of our wrongs have already been paid for before we even commit them. If we know we're forgiven, then what's the point in even paying notice to the sins we commit? Hey! Just because we're forgiven, doesn't give us carte blanche to do whatever we want without regard to God's commandments.

God's commandments may read easy on paper, but put those same guidelines in a sinful, wicked environment, and to a humanity prone to committing sin: it's a setup for failure; no one human can achieve righteousness simply by their own efforts. It was only through the seed of God Himself, traveling in a human body as Christ Jesus, that He was able to set the example fo the rest of us. Our God came down to Earth as a man, and died badly for the creation He loves. Anyone who doesn't automatically love God for that sacrifice, and want to do something for Him in return, belongs to the devil. This is what the scripture is intended to illustrate, and we prove our love through acts of service and devotion. We are supposed to feel badly when we commit sins against God, and want to work harder at improving our sinful selves as a result of that remorse. We'll never be able to be completely sin-free, as it is not in our nature, but it is in the effort, humility, and sincerity, with which we approach those inadequacies that prove our devotion to God. It is in our efforts to get to know what God truly wants from us (Psalm 119:11), in our genuine remorse for committing wrongs against Him, and the sincerity in our efforts to improve ourselves through Christ that will ultimately show God how devoted we are to Him.

James 3:2, NASB

2 For we all stumble in many ways. If anyone does not stumble in what he says, he is a perfect man, able to rein in the whole body as well.

October 15
The Lord's Discipline

Proverbs 15:32, ERV

32 If you refuse to be corrected, you are only hurting yourself. Listen to criticism, and you will gain understanding.

Hebrews 12:11, ESV

11 For the moment all discipline seems painful rather than pleasant, but later it **yields the peaceful fruit of righteousness** to those who have been trained by it.

We all need correction, at times, to prevent errors, to improve, and grow in our understanding. Many people proclaim to be perfectionists, which is impossible, according to the bible there doesn't exist a person who does everything perfectly all the time (Ecclesiastes 7:20). Humans are prone to sin and corruption, and will always need guidance from God. Through the commandments the Lord has taught us to follow, we are shown our sins and shortcomings (Romans 7:7-8). Not only does this show us where we need to repent and improve, but it reminds us how much we depend on the Lord for forgiveness and guidance. We are called to be perfect, because God is perfect, even though it's impossible to do so (Matthew 5:48). It might seem like the Lord our God has set us up for failure, because He has. We all handle failure differently. In testing our faith through repeated trials; those who *keep trying* to improve and perfect, despite themselves, by repentance, humility and patience show their devotion to the Lord that guides them. Conversely, those who are indignant, bitter, angry or offended are courting their autonomy *from* God, and reveal their infidelity and stubbornness *toward* God (Isaiah 48:3-4)

Some people can't ignore the urge to accumulate as much wealth, power, or status as they can, and these people, the bible tells us, are not serving the Lord (1 John 2:15-17). When we stray from the Lord's path for us, He will correct us in the manner of His choosing, none of us are immune to God's discipline. No one likes to be corrected, but we must accept the good along with the bad that God gives us in our lives if we want to prove we are devoted to Him. When we become angry, stubborn, or indignant to the Lord's correction we only push ourselves farther away, which brings on more trouble. When we comply with the Lord, and His commandments and laws, we are being faithful to Him, but this doesn't ensure a pain-free existence. God is refining us, purifying us for His eternal kingdom, and He isn't going to give up! (Hebrews 13:5) We can expect trial after trial in our lives, as God watches our actions, behaviors, and looks into our hearts while we endure His discipline. Who will remain faithful to God up to the very end?

Proverbs 29:1, ERV

1 Some people refuse to bend when someone corrects them. Eventually they will break, and there will be no one to repair the damage.

Isaiah 28:22, ERV

22 Now don't complain about these things. If you fight against them, you will only tighten the ropes around you. The words I heard will not change. They came from the Lord God All-Powerful, the ruler of all the earth, and these things will be done.

October 16

Turn the Other Cheek

Matthew 5:42-45, GW

42 "Give to everyone who asks you for something. Don't turn anyone away who wants to borrow something from you. 43 You have heard that it was said, 'Love your neighbor, and hate your enemy.' 44 But I tell you this: Love your enemies, and pray for those who persecute you. 45 In this way you show that you are children of your Father in heaven. He makes His sun rise on people whether they are good or evil. He lets rain fall on them whether they are just or unjust."

Proverbs 3:11, ERV

11 My son, don't reject the Lord's discipline, and don't be angry when he corrects you.

Hebrews 12:15, GW

15 Make sure that everyone has kindness from God so that bitterness doesn't take root and grow up to cause trouble that corrupts many of you.

When we are wronged we desire retribution, justice, and sometimes, revenge. Humans have an innate intolerance to injustice, and expect justice for every act of unfairness. Jesus teaches to turn the other cheek, not to respond with revenge or our own sense of justice. Many people would admit to being unable, or unwilling, to turn the other cheek when they're wronged. We cannot obtain forgiveness if we don't first forgive (Matthew 6:15). To forgive, we need to let our indignance go and leave deciding blame to God. Society places a great deal of emphasis on pride and respect, which leads to dissention, competition, deceit, envy, and hatred. We are called to love one another, placing others more valuable than ourselves (Philippians 2:3). We cannot forgive one another when we're focused on blame, or our own ideas about how justice should be served. God has final vengeance on wickedness, oppression and injustice, according to the bible (Romans 12:19). When God places strife and tribulation in our path, our lives can become tenuous and stressful, even leaving us with remorse and great sadness. We must remember to always respect God's place as our Lord and creator, and not become bitter and angry with Him, but always pray for a kinder heart. Nothing is impossible for God, but humans will always be limited. We will never be perfect, but we can be more righteous with God's help. How we handle ourselves in a stressful situation tells us how much faith we have in God. Sinners who have turned away from God to focus on themselves will become bitter and outraged at the strife God places upon them, but the righteous know that they will never be forsaken, and that all they need God will provide if they remain patient and humble. So we should turn the other cheek, always, for one another, but also for God.

October 17
The Parable of the Unforgiving Servant

Matthew 18:21-35, ESV

21 Then Peter came up and said to him, "Lord, how often will my brother sin against me, and I forgive him? As many as seven times?" 22 Jesus said to him, "I do not say to you seven times, but seventy-seven times." 23 "Therefore the kingdom of heaven may be compared to a king who wished to settle accounts with His servants. 24 When he began to settle, one was brought to him who owed him ten thousand talents. 25 And since he could not pay, His master ordered him to be sold, with His wife and children and all that he had, and payment to be made. 26 So the servant fell on His knees, imploring him, 'Have patience with me, and I will pay you everything.' 27 And out of pity for him, the master of that servant released him and forgave him the debt. 28 But when that same servant went out, he found one of His fellow servants who owed him a hundred denarii, and seizing him, he began to choke him, saying, 'Pay what you owe.' 29 So His fellow servant fell down and pleaded with him, 'Have patience with me, and I will pay you.' 30 He refused and went and put him in prison until he should pay the debt. 31 When His fellow servants saw what had taken place, they were greatly distressed, and they went and reported to their master all that had taken place. 32 Then His master summoned him and said to him, 'You wicked servant! I forgave you all that debt because you pleaded with me. 33 And should not you have had mercy on your fellow servant, as I had mercy on you?' 34 And in anger His master delivered him to the jailers, until he should pay all His debt. 35 So also my heavenly Father will do to every one of you, if you do not forgive your brother from your heart."

We all need to be forgiven for our sins, sins we commit every day. When we repent with humble hearts, we are forgiven. God forgives all who repent in good faith. We must be able to forgive people if we want to be forgiven, this is a simple truth explained in the bible (Matthew 6:15). Everyone should have the chance to get closer to God if they've remained faithful to His commandments, and repent with an honest heart. As followers of Christ, we should want everyone to come to repentance, ridding the world of evil one apology at a time. We shouldn't become incensed, then, when God forgives our enemies. If we are true to God's teaching, no one is an enemy, but a brother or sister in faith. Jesus tells us that the two most important commandments are to love God, and love others as yourself (Matthew 22:36-40). We cannot forgive if we don't love others, and genuinely want them to experience the glory of God's grace. We are all one humanity, under one creator, going through God's refining and purification process. Building one another up, helping those in need, forgiving one another, holding one another accountable to the faith, is what God wants from us. Denying a brother or sister in faith is the same as denying God.

October 18
Knowing Our Place

Job 38:4-6, ERV

4 "Where were you when I made the earth? If you are so smart, answer me. 5 And who decided how big the earth should be? Who measured it with a measuring line? 6 What is the earth resting on? Who put the first stone in its place?"

John 15:5, ESV

5 "I am the vine; you are the branches. Whoever abides in me and I in him, he it is that bears much fruit, for apart from me you can do nothing."

We all know someone who proudly declares that they're 'free-spirited' and independent saying, "I'll be who I want to be, and do whatever I want." Some people don't like the idea of being submissive to anything or anyone, including God. Perhaps people forget that God created the world, the universe, and all of us. Perhaps people forget that God sent Jesus to die for all of our sins, so that we could have eternal life with Him in Heaven (John 3:16). God will bring good days and bad days to our lives, He is testing our faith in Him (Isaiah 48:10). Just because we cannot see God face to face doesn't mean He isn't the driving force behind all that happens to each of us, and the power we have in comparison to His is laughable. Just because we follow God doesn't mean we're going to live a life of stringent, sterile celibacy on an isolated mountain top somewhere. *Following* God means that we understand our place in His creation, and submit to the changes that following Him will bring to our personalities and attitudes. 'Cleansing and purifying' us may be *God's* words, but being a kinder, more honest, more forgiving, more loving person is the result just the same. God's going to bring both good and bad to everyone's lives, we can't possibly compare our pain with another because we can't see all that happens in the lives of others. A shift in our perspective, a change in our priorities, a more forgiving and generous heart is what God calls us to. If someone doesn't believe in God's Sovereign power in their lives, or doesn't welcome it, they belong to wickedness, and wickedness is of the devil. Jesus says that the path to righteousness is narrow, and that 'few' will find it (Matthew 7:14), this indicates how difficult it is to live a holier life in an unholy world corrupt with sin. Loving God more than our own worlds is what it's going to take to **stay on** that narrow path to eternal life in Heaven. God should be worth it to all of us to want to walk that narrow road to righteousness. All praise and glory to our Almighty Father, AMEN.

Deuteronomy 10:17, GW

17 The Lord your God is God of gods and Lord of lords, the great, powerful, and awe-inspiring God. He never plays favorites and never takes a bribe.

John 12:46, GW

46 "I am the light that has come into the world so that everyone who believes in me will not live in the dark."

October 19
God Is the Judge, Not Other People

Matthew 7:5, ESV

5 You hypocrite, first take the log out of your own eye, and then you will see clearly to take the speck out of your brother's eye.

Matthew 23:1-4, GW

1 Then Jesus said to the crowds and to His disciples, 2 "The experts in Moses' Teachings and the Pharisees teach with Moses' authority. 3 So be careful to do everything they tell you. But don't follow their example, because they don't practice what they preach. 4 They make loads that are hard to carry and lay them on the shoulders of the people. However, they are not willing to lift a finger to move them."

Sometimes, when walking into church, people who don't recognize you stare, and you wonder if you're underdressed or in the wrong place. When the offering is passed, and we don't have much to give we can feel like we're not as worthy as someone who gives more. We hear sermons and speeches from ministers, theologians and religious leaders, and wonder if we're farther away from God than they are because of their knowledge. People are flawed, all of them (Romans 3:23), consequently all have the opportunity to disappoint. We can set ourselves up for disappointment when we have expectations that someone or something will be as we think it should. As followers of Christ, we want to bring other people into the light of the Lord, but we cannot judge them for their sins. We all commit sins, every one of us.

Other Christ-followers, and even top theologians may scoff at our choices, but we are all held accountable by God alone, not another human being. Even though some people have a great deal more understanding and knowledge about the bible, they aren't superior in any way, and make mistakes just like everyone else (James 3:2). When pride begins to rear its ugly head, knowledge and experience can lead people to sin, sounding like they know so much more and yet living in as much sin as everyone else. No one should sound, claim, or feel superior to another, this is self-idolatry according to the bible. Likewise, we should all be more willing to let go of our own pride and accept help and advice, in any form, that is helpful to our growing faith. Life's lessons don't always come from expected places, as God works in ways that are mysterious to us.

Psalm 75:6-7, GW

6 The authority to reward someone does not come from the east, from the west, or even from the wilderness. 7 God alone is the judge. He punishes one person and rewards another.

October 20
Submitting to God's Will

Isaiah 45:11-12, 21b, 22 GW

11 This is what the Lord says: "Ask me about what is going to happen to my children! Are you going to give me orders concerning my handiwork? 12 I made the earth and created humans on it. I stretched out the heavens with my own hands. I commanded all the stars to shine. 21b There is no other God except me. There is no other righteous God and Savior besides me. 22 Turn to me and be saved, all who live at the ends of the earth, because I am God, and there is no other."

We choose the college we want to attend, or if we want to attend college at all. We also choose what kind of pet we're going have, if we're going to have a pet, what kind of diet we're going to follow, where we'll work, where we'll live, and even who we'll live *with*. Our lives are full of choices and decisions, some we make with others and some on our own. The more choices we make the more confident we are that we're in control of our own lives, for better or worse. If we're following our own path, not having prayed and consulted first with God, then we're not *following* God. Just because we believe in God, just because we love God, doesn't mean we're actually following God. Maybe we didn't know we were supposed to follow God? We have all had plenty of opportunities to understand God's will for us, the bible has been available to us to read and understand, but many choose not to read or understand for themselves.

God is our creator, and is in control of everything, including our individual lives. Refining us into more righteous people who praise and obey Him, God controls both negative and positive aspects of our lives in the hope we'll come to Him with repentance. Many people stumble over the mistake of not understanding, therefore not following God most of their lives, or stumble over relinquishing everything they thought they understood. Submitting to God's will isn't easy, if it were, the world would be a much different place.

Jeremiah 10:23, ICB

23 Lord, I know that a person's life doesn't really belong to him. No one can control His own life.

Psalm 9:10, ESV

10 And those who know your name put their trust in you, for you, O Lord, have not forsaken those who seek you.

Philippians 4:6, ESV

6 do not be anxious about anything, but in everything by prayer and supplication with thanksgiving let your requests be made known to God.

October 21
God's Will

Proverbs 16:3, ESV

3 Commit your work to the Lord, and your plans will be established.

Isaiah 46:8-10, GW

8 "Remember this, and take courage. Recall your rebellious acts.9 Remember the first events, because I am God, and there is no other. I am God, and there's no one like me. 10 From the beginning I revealed the end. From long ago I told you things that had not yet happened, saying, 'My plan will stand, and I'll do everything I intended to do.'"

We get up each day and go to work because our bills won't pay themselves. For many, if they get up on time, may *occasionally* attend church on Sundays. And, of course, we love God, but maybe we don't pray every day. Many think they have all they do because they worked for it, they **earned** it. When we release our thoughts from the stubborn independence of our inherited human flaws we can submit to the plans the Lord has for us, instead of selfishly courting our own. The bible makes it clear, all things happen according to God's will (Daniel 4:35). Thinking our own free will shows the Lord what we're made of is ignorance, the bible calls us to commit to the work of the Lord. This means that what happens to us is the will of the Lord, not our own.

We want to feel like more than just God's talking dirt (Gen. 2:7), we want to be proud of our accomplishments. This is wickedness deceiving us, for we are all made incomplete without the Lord's direct intervention. We have the earth, the sky, the plants, the waters and oceans, and all the animals at our disposal, and not because of our own brilliance but because of God's will (Genesis 1:26). God's plan for humanity will play out the way He intends, for the reasons only He knows, and we are meant to follow and obey. Many people don't want to submit to God, or anyone, and don't truly understand how God's will works. On the other side of God's will is His discipline, and no one is exempt the punishment of not complying with God. When we listen and obey we're not eliminating our chance for strife, but showing God we will be faithful to Him no matter what His will declares for us. How faithful will He consider you to be?

Hebrews 12:4-6, GW

4 You struggle against sin, but your struggles haven't killed you. 5 You have forgotten the encouraging words that God speaks to you as His children: "My child, pay attention when the Lord disciplines you. Don't give up when he corrects you. 6 The **Lord disciplines everyone he loves. He severely disciplines everyone he accepts as His child.**"

October 22
Compliance

Hebrews 12:25, GW

25 Be careful that you do not refuse to listen when God speaks. Your ancestors didn't escape when they refused to listen to God, who warned them on earth. We certainly won't escape if we turn away from God, who warns us from heaven.

Hebrews 10:38-39, GW

38 The person who has God's approval will live by faith. "But if he turns back, I will not be pleased with him." 39 We don't belong with those who turn back and are destroyed. Instead, we belong with those who have faith and are saved.

Matthew 7:26-27, GW

26 (Jesus said) "**Everyone who hears what I say but doesn't obey** it will be like a foolish person who built a house on sand. 27 Rain poured, and floods came. Winds blew and struck that house. It collapsed, and **the result was a total disaster.**"

Some of us would rather admit to causing our own life calamities than confess to being under God's wrath for noncompliance. We all stray from our path, but forgiveness is a humble prayer away. When we continue to plow through life by our own choices and desires, we're refusing to acknowledge the fact that God is directing our lives. Maybe we believe that God's out there, but only to rescue us when we're really in trouble. According to God we humans are **constantly in trouble**, because we're a sinful humanity that tends to worship themselves above God (Jeremiah 17:5). Those that turn away from God face calamity and are destroyed, the bible tells us, so why *wouldn't* we want to obey God?

God is that little voice in our heads telling us what we're about to do isn't right. Through the death of Jesus, who was sent as a human form of God, we inherited the Holy Spirit to guide us. All of these gifts were from a Heavenly Father who loves us, and wants to welcome us into His Heavenly Kingdom. In order to be close to God, we need to be holy, difficult for a sinful humanity. This is our challenge, and God is watching our actions as He looks into our hearts to see what is truly motivating us (Jeremiah 17:10). Loving Him first, obeying His commandments to love and respect one another, praying, repenting and praising God isn't too much to ask for all He's done for us. Avoid total disaster, and give obedience and praise to Almighty God, because gracious and loving is He. AMEN.

October 23
Using Our Weaknesses Against Us

James 1:13, ESV

13 Let no one say when he is tempted, "I am being tempted by God," for God cannot be tempted with evil, **and he himself tempts no one.**

People can sometimes feel disillusioned by the pain and tribulation they experience, they want to believe that God only comforts and heals. Anyway, God doesn't do bad things to people, that's the devil's job, right? The devil has a job, he is the 'tempter,' and the 'deceiver,' and his job is to try and separate people from their faith in God. If we never experienced adversity or tribulations, if we never suffered, how could we prove to God we'll turn to Him? God is purifying us, testing our faith in, and devotion to Him, and that process is going to be painful, and difficult at times. Although the devil's wickedness creates the environment for adversity, tribulation, and strife, the bible tells us that God controls every aspect of this (Isaiah 45:7).

The devil uses our weaknesses against us: arrogant people are angered when things don't go their way, or outraged when they are treated badly. Similarly, self-conscious people lose their self-control when they are made to feel inferior, and greedy people can lose their self-control when what they hold dear is threatened, or taken away. We can all lose control, we all have different triggers, and those triggers can reveal what's truly in our hearts. It can be tricky to learn something from the sins we regularly commit when we're too busy being outraged by them.

Knowing our sins is our defense against falling prey to them. When we know what sins we're committing, we're essentially learning what our specific weaknesses are, and if we know how we're vulnerable, we can pray to the Lord for strengthening in that area. The devil also confuses and deceives, using our sins to distract us from repenting for them. We can spend a great deal of time thinking about recognizing sin in ourselves, in others, using them to categorize people, and going out of our way to eradicate it from our lives. Knowing our sins does so many wonderful things: we're reminded of our need for the Lords forgiveness and direction, we're reminded we're not as great as we think we are and are humbled, and we're made aware of our weaknesses. We can only be heard, and helped by the Lord if we're humble. Similarly, when we know where our vulnerabilities are we can fortify them, with the Lord's help. For instance, if we know we're vulnerable to getting impatient we pray for patience. Likewise, if we know we lose our tempers easily, we can pray for more self-control. If we are greedy, we can pray for a more generous heart. Learning, and accepting, our sins is the first step in fortifying ourselves against further sins. We do this through prayer, and repentance through Christ Jesus, our Lord and Savior.

Job 1:12, ERV

12 The Lord said to Satan, "All right, do whatever you want with anything that he has, but don't hurt Job himself." Then Satan left the meeting.

Isaiah 45:7, GNV

7 "I form the light, and create darkness: I make peace, **and create evil: *I the Lord do all these things*.**"

October 24
Changing Our Ways

Romans 1:20-24, GW/**GNV**

20 From the creation of the world, God's invisible qualities, His eternal power and divine nature, have been clearly observed in what he made. As a result, people have no excuse. 21 They knew God but did not praise and thank him for being God. Instead, their thoughts were pointless, and their misguided minds were plunged into darkness. 22 While claiming to be wise, they became fools. **23** For they turned the glory of the incorruptible God to the similitude of the image of a corruptible man, and of birds, and four footed beasts, and of creeping things. **24** Wherefore also God gave them up to their hearts lusts, unto uncleanness, to defile their own bodies between themselves:

Believing in God is terrific, but it won't get us into Heaven if we don't exchange our sinful lives with the righteous quest to follow in Christ's holy footsteps. Standing firm on their own interpretation of the bible, the commandments, the parable stories Jesus told, or certain verses that make more sense to them than others, false wisdom is a danger we should all be aware of. Only studious devotion to learning, and understanding, the scripture will provide the knowledge we all require to be successful in the eyes of God (Hebrews 4:12-16). Our choices stem from the desire of our hearts, the motivation inside of us that drives our goals, attitudes, words, and actions. These choices are what lead us to the salvation or damnation of our souls.

God wants us to turn to Him, not just for guidance in making more holy and righteous choices with our lives, but to also seek Him for comfort, repentance, and praise. If we're not praying to God multiple times per day, chances are we're not putting Him at the center of our world. (Acts 17:24-30) Whatever takes up the most space in our minds and hearts is what we're focused on, so, how often are we really thinking of God? If we say we're sorry, but we don't stop the bad behavior, are we really sorry? Actions speak louder than words, and God is going to test us to make sure our hearts and minds are focused on Him: If they aren't, they need to be. Repent, refocus and praise God, brothers and sisters. AMEN!

Revelation 9:20-21, GW

20 The people who survived these plagues still did not turn to me and change the way they were thinking and acting. If they had, they would have stopped worshiping demons and idols made of gold, silver, bronze, stone, and wood, which cannot see, hear, or walk. 21 They did not turn away from committing murder, practicing witchcraft, sinning sexually, or stealing.

October 25
God Is Good

James 3:17, ICB

17 But the wisdom that comes from God is like this: First, it is pure. Then it is also peaceful, gentle, and easy to please. This wisdom is always ready to help those who are troubled and to do good for others. This wisdom is always fair and honest.

Psalm 32:10, ESV

10 Many are the sorrows of the wicked, but steadfast love surrounds the one who trusts in the Lord.

Because we can suffer through pain and trial at God's hand, we can't forget His unfailing love and generosity to those who serve Him in good faith. Fair treatment without lies or deceit, support for widows and orphans, and steadfast love are the hallmarks of God's love for us. Through His word we grow strong in our faith, turning to Him for all of our needs. When we make mistakes, and we will make them (James 3:2), He corrects us and forgives us by **His** perfect grace. Constant and eternal, God provides the very life force we humans thrive on. When we put our complete trust in the Lord, we are setting our burdens at His feet, and we don't strategize solutions for ourselves. When we trust in God, solutions present themselves before us, and we pray for guidance in making the right choices before we act or decide anything. When we pray for comfort it might come in a form we're not expecting, so we must be open-minded, and in tune with the Holy Spirit. In a world where it can seem like everything fun, comfortable, or indulgent is a sin, God provides a peace and grace not found anywhere in our tangible world. Through the power of the Holy Spirit, given to us upon Jesus' death, we have access to our Lord and Savior to guide us through those trials and temptations. Using the bible and the Holy Spirit as a guide, we can learn and understand God's word, and intension for us to be clean and purified of sin. We are all sons and daughters of the one true God. We all sin, we just sin differently. We are all corrected, and we will all suffer at times in our lives. We are all on an *individual* journey with God, some of us are just more stubborn and lost than others. We all fall short of the glory of God (Romans 3:23), and are all called to repent. Not one of us is better than another, God wants *all* of our souls to return to Him at the end of their lives on Earth. God is the beginning and the end (Mark 13:32), here the bible assures us that there will be an 'end.' Placing our lives in the hands of the Almighty creator versus the imperfect, often deceitful plans of mankind seems like a no-brainer, especially with a finite conclusion like the one outlined in the scriptures. God is stern, but fair, loving, and forgiving. When we humble ourselves before Him, admitting we're lost without Him, He is faithful to comfort us. If we remain stubborn, bitter, independent, or indignant, we turn our backs on the divine forgiveness, eternal love and grace that only God can provide.

Psalm 25:8-10, GW

8 The Lord is good and decent. That is why he teaches sinners the way they should live. 9 He leads humble people to do what is right, and he teaches them His way. 10 Every path of the Lord is one of mercy and truth for those who cling to His promise and written instructions.

October 26
All Things

Ephesians 1:10-11, GW

10 God planned to bring all of History to its goal in Christ. Then Christ would be the head of everything in heaven and on earth. 11 God also decided ahead of time to choose us through Christ according to His plan, which makes everything work the way he intends.

Colossians 1:16, GW

16 He created all things in heaven and on earth, visible and invisible. Whether they are kings or lords, rulers or powers — everything has been created through him and for him.

We like to think that everything that we have, we've worked for to achieve, and that's true, but there is a larger force at work in all of our lives. When we feel proud of accomplishing a goal, we feel justified in that pride. However, when we have too much on our plate, or our worlds come crashing down around us faster than we can put it back together, some of us wonder why *God* is punishing us. Humans can be quick to accept the glory that rightfully belongs to God, and even quicker to blame Him for their own bad choices. Whether our pain is a lesson, a punishment from God, or if it's the consequences of our own sins and behaviors, our pain and strife are unique to us. We all suffer, but in different ways, and for different reasons. Our pain shapes who we are, by constantly reshaping how we set our boundaries, limits, goals, and attitudes.

Anything that turns us away from God is sinful, and usually stems from our own selfish, sinful desires. God is why we have good in our lives as well as bad, and He wants us to realize how much we need Him. In the passage below, we understand that even though man builds the house, God built the man. God is superior to us, as He is our creator, but some people have a difficult time putting Him first in their lives even though they believe it in their hearts. Pride, any pride, for any reason, should be subjugated for the humility of knowing that all we have is because of God, and not ourselves. Our work in a manmade society means nothing compared to the condition of our spirits in God's eyes. A successful jerk with a large bank account and position of power isn't worth more than the homeless follower who prays to God every day with a righteous heart. Society has reversed God's priorities so that what God thinks is good, like modesty, humility and forgiveness, our world sees as weak. Likewise, society places great adoration on qualities God sees as wicked such as pride, wealth, and power. God is the reason we are in the circumstance we are, and directly reflects how well we've listened and obeyed Him in our lives. We *should* be turning to God in thanks for the blessings we have, the love and health of our family, the work we are able to do, and the opportunity each day for a fresh start in our faith. Additionally, we should be turning to God with *all* of our needs and concerns. This is what we are called to do by His word, AMEN.

Hebrews 3:4, GW

4 After all, every house has a builder, but the builder of everything is God.

October 27
Fear God

Isaiah 8:12-15, ERV/ICB

12 "Don't think there is a plan against you just because the *people* say there is. Don't be afraid of what they fear. Don't let them frighten you!" 13 The Lord All-Powerful is the one you should fear. He is the one you should respect. He is the one who should frighten you. 14a If you people would respect him, he would be a safe place for you. But you don't respect him, so he is like a stone that you stumble over. 15 Many will stumble and fall, never to rise again. They will be snared and captured.

Many of us look at our homes, our cars, our lives, and congratulate ourselves on a lifetime of achievements. We work hard at our jobs and careers, working our way up to a more prestigious position for the recognition of a lifetime of diligent work, and the money we feel we deserve. Looking around, we silently compare ourselves to the other guy, building our personal empires for the health, success and comfort of our families. Many of us would say that most of this is true of ourselves, but where is God in all this life we're living? We have what we have, because it's God's plan for us, not because we're capable of creating our own destinies.

After all, God may bring us to a large hole and give us a shovel, but we have to do the work to dig a hole. We derive our strength from God, our direction, and all of our needs. The bible explains that we are all part of a larger plan God has for humanity, and we each play a role even if we're unaware of it (1 Corinthians 12:12-27). We are to praise God for all we have, pray for the things we need from Him, and repent for our sins when we stray away from His word. Many people try to cover up their sins, but God sees all. We humans can be pretty distracting to one another, but we're supposed to be working together to become more holy, not to think of new ways to defile ourselves with one another. Man created computers, technology, and wealth, but God created the world. Humans created modern medicine, and learned to save lives, admirable, but God created the human soul. God alone is in control of time, the fate of the Earth, as well as all of humanity. God alone has the final judgment over us all. All honor and glory to God, King of the universe. AMEN.

Isaiah 14:27, 26:7, ERV

27 When the Lord All-Powerful makes a plan, no one can change it. When he raises His arm to punish, no one can stop him. 7 Honesty is the path good people follow. They follow the path that is straight and true. And God, you make that way smooth and easy to follow.

Matthew 10:28, ESV

28 And do not fear those who kill the body but cannot kill the soul. Rather fear him who can destroy both soul and body in hell.

October 28
Assumptions & Judgement

Proverbs 18:13, ICB

13 A person who answers without listening is foolish and disgraceful.

Deuteronomy 17:13, ESV

13 (God said) "And all the people shall hear and fear and not act presumptuously again."

Suppose this scenario: we're out walking our dog and we wave to our neighbors, who usually wave back but don't this time. Suddenly, in our minds we're automatically coming up with reasons why they didn't respond back to us. Or; In the corridor at work, we smile at a colleague who completely ignores us. Again, our minds come up with assumptions as to why we were slighted by someone who is normally friendly with us. Standing in line at the store we notice someone with dirty clothes, and we automatically assume they are poor or underserved. We can even observe a strangers behavior and assume they *always* behave in that manner we observe them at the time, whether impolite, stuck-up, rude, or inconsiderate. Perhaps the co-worker was listening to their earbuds, and was distracted. Maybe the neighbor was focused on another task, and simply didn't see us waving. In the line at the grocery store, maybe someone just finished helping someone move and didn't have time to change their clothes before going to the store. We just can't possibly know all that goes into the actions, words and behaviors of other people. God is the only one who knows the intensions of the heart (Jeremiah 17:10).

When we make assumptions about people, or pass judgement, we aren't thinking with an open, loving, forgiving heart, we're leaning on our own, flawed understanding. We want to understand our world, our environment, and our place in it, but our assumptions give us a false sense of what is affecting our environment. When we speak or behave based on our guesses and preconceived ideas about people, we can create more problems. We shouldn't need to know more than God allows us to, and only try to control our own reactions, words and behaviors when interacting with others. We are provided all we need, according the bible, and faithful people believe this. A deeper trust in God, knowing His final judgement will be fair, should be enough to leave judging people to Him. We shouldn't be trying to classify, label or exclude anyone anyway, because we're all sinners, all children of the one, Almighty God.

Ephesians 4:2-3, GW

2 Be humble and gentle in every way. Be patient with each other and lovingly accept each other. 3 Through the peace that ties you together, do your best to maintain the unity that the Spirit gives.

1 Samuel 16:7, GW

7 But the Lord told Samuel, "Don't look at His appearance or how tall he is, because I have rejected him. God does not see as humans see. Humans look at outward appearances, but the Lord looks into the heart."

October 29
Walking in the Light

1 John 1:5-9, ESV

5 This is the message we have heard from him and proclaim to you, that God is light, and in him is no darkness at all. 6 If we say we have fellowship with him while we walk in darkness, we lie and do not practice the truth. 7 But if we walk in the light, as he is in the light, we have fellowship with one another, and the blood of Jesus His Son cleanses us from all sin. 8 If we say we have no sin, we deceive ourselves, and the truth is not in us. 9 If we confess our sins, he is faithful and just to forgive us our sins and to cleanse us from all unrighteousness.

It's pretty easy to say we believe in Jesus, but how closely we're living our lives to the way He calls us to? Confessing our sins to God in prayer is a lot easier that it sounds! The bible tells us over and over again that lying, stealing, adultery to one another, and to God's commandments, pride, selfish worship of earthly things, the love of money, and other impure acts are wicked and sinful. Allowing something to corrupt their desires, *both man and woman* defied God in the garden of Eden, so all humanity forevermore was prone to sin (Romans 5:12). If we confess our sins, we are assured that we'll be forgiven, the bible states, but first we need to know what they are. We are expected to learn what it means to be righteous, *practice* the truth, and stop committing sins. Sins are difficult to see sometimes, especially if we've been committing them so long we no longer think of them as sins. We're being called to unlearn these old habits, old patterns of thinking that have led to poor choices, weakened by, and conditioned to, sinful behaviors and attitudes like pride, bragging, gossip, judging others, competition, anger, or adultery. We can't fake this 'spiritual remodeling,' either, the bible tells us that God knows the heart of every person (1 Kings 8:39).

Not only do we need to examine ourselves, but in doing so, our lives, our choices, our words, our attitudes, our desires, our motives, **all** more closely. This isn't going to happen overnight, and there's no 'easy button,' and *many* give up (Matthew 7:13-14). Righteous change is a lifetime effort of love and dedication to our faith in Christ Jesus. Repentance requires our **humility, honesty** to our Lord, and forgiveness only comes *after* we've submitted ourselves before Him. Whatever we need and can't obtain, or need to get rid of and can't, we need to put into a prayer of supplication. When we can trust, and utilize, the assistance and guidance of the Holy Spirit trying to work inside of us, we'll see our sins more clearly. This *gradual* process will help us understand what our Heavenly Father wants from us. Pray on, brothers and sisters!

Mark 8:34-37, ERV/ICB

34 Then Jesus called the crowd and his followers to him. He said, "Any of you who want to be my follower must stop thinking about yourself and what you want. You must be willing to carry the cross that is given to you for following me. 35 Any of you who try to save the life you have will lose it. But you who give up your life for me and for the Good News will save it. 36 It is worth nothing for a person to have the whole world, if he loses His soul. 37 A person could never pay enough to buy back His soul."

October 30
We Can't Fix People

Isaiah 43:13, ERV/GW

13 "I have always been God. When I do something, no one can change what I have done. And no one can save people from my power. When I do something, who can undo it?"

Ezekiel 14:14, ERV

14 "I would punish that country even if Noah, Daniel, and Job lived there. **They could save their own lives by their goodness, but they could not save the whole country.**" This is what the Lord God said.

Our journey with our Lord and Savior is personal, a love affair between God and His creation in preparation for salvation in eternal life. Along our journey, God is purifying each soul, and we each need different types of correction and praise to accomplish this. It can be difficult to see another person struggling, or hear a doubter deny God or Jesus, or hear someone misinterpreting the scriptures as we understand them. We need to remember that we are always learning, always being tested, and we're wrong more often than we'd like to admit. God is in control of each life journey, and we have little power over what happens to us, or to those around us. No matter what we go through, or see other people go through, our devotion to God is the most important thing in our lives. Above all else, we need to protect, and nurture, our faith in the Lord.

We are all in different places in our faith, and we cannot presume to know what is in the heart of another, despite what we may see, or hear. We have far less influence over our lives than people may be comfortable with, but there is no avoiding our need for a Sovereign Spiritual Lord. God provides all we need, and choreographs our journey to righteousness through Christ Jesus. When we profess our faith in Christ, we receive the Holy Spirit as a guide, and a gift to use in service to God. Our gifts, our trials, our levels of faith and devotion, are as different as our fingerprints, and only God can tell our spirits apart. All of our fear, trust, hope, and love should be placed at the feet of God, through the blood sacrifice of Jesus Christ, because He's the one who died for our salvation.

As humans, we cannot fix one another. The best answer will always be to direct people back to God by prayer, through Jesus. If we are meant to help, the Holy Spirit will guide us to do so, and is a gift through Christ, not ourselves. Using our talents to bring another person to the same level of awareness or faith as we have isn't the right way to help one another. After all, we should be following the Lord, not one another. Spiritual mentors, close friends or family may know us better than most, but they can't know our hearts like our Heavenly Father does (1 Samuel 16:7). As we each go through different trials in our lives, we should help one another to stay righteous, and **focused on God.** Jesus is always the answer. Helping those in need, no matter who they are, forgiving those who treat us badly, avoiding sinful choices, and encouraging others to do the same, is a fantastic way of spreading God's love. (Matthew 5:16) The best thing we can do for someone in need is to let them know they are loved, and bring them back to the Lord. No matter how sincere our drive to help others ourselves, only the Lord can repair broken hearts, redirect someone back on the path to righteousness, restore faith, and mend damaged spirits.

Acts 4:12, ESV

12 And there is salvation in no one else; for there is no other name under heaven that has been given among men by which we must be saved.

October 31
Evil Is out there, Beware!

Job 1:12, GW

12 The Lord told Satan, "Everything he has is in your power, but you must not lay a hand on him!" Then Satan left the Lord's presence.

1 Peter 5:8, ESV

8 Be sober-minded; be watchful. Your adversary the devil prowls around like a roaring lion, seeking someone to devour.

"In the beginning, God created the Heavens and the Earth," (Genesis 1:1) tells us that everything has been created by God, and for His purpose, which we cannot fully understand. Evil has lived among us from the beginning (Genesis 3), luring us naturally-sinning, unsuspecting humans into lustful, vengeful, prideful, covetous, adulterous or gluttonous behavior. The devil is at work, doing what he was designed to do, having power over the earth to subject people to trial, exploit evil desires into temptations, and deceive those with weak or little faith (Job 1:7). In fact, humans have wallowed in sin for so long some don't recognize that they've lost the ability to decern good from evil. Not everybody is willing to admit they make mistakes, or commit sins, believing that if *they* think they're a good person then God will to. God's thoughts and ways are not like ours (Isaiah 55:8-9), and this is only *one* reason why we should be listening to what God wants from us, instead of us telling Him what we're comfortable giving Him. God wanted to give humans a way of escaping evil, and did so by Christ's sacrifice on the cross, while the devil wants to turn humans away from God and His light (Ephesians 2:1-2).

Caught in the ultimate battle between good and evil, humans are the pawns in a spiritual war that has been raging since the beginning of man. Those who choose to follow Jesus must tread down a strict and narrow path, full of surprise gifts along with continuous trials of suffering, but will have eternal rest in God's love as a result of their steadfast faith and endurance. Those who choose to ignore the good news about Jesus, don't repent, don't change their lives, continue to do evil will suffer the consequences (Luke 11:23, John 12:48). The bible is clear on our need to follow Jesus and repent, but people who don't will get farther and farther from Jesus' light until they can no longer see it. Not only do we want to *stay* in the light of Jesus' ways, as His followers, but we also want to *encourage others* to do the same.

John 8:12, GW

12 Jesus spoke to the Pharisees again. He said, "I am the light of the world. Whoever follows me will have a life filled with light and will never live in the dark."

2 Corinthians 4:3-4, ICB

3 The Good News that we preach may be hidden. But it is hidden only to those who are lost. 4 The devil who rules this world has blinded the minds of those who do not believe. They cannot see the light of the Good News—the Good News about the glory of Christ, who is exactly like God.

November 1
Not All Are Believers

John 11:25-26, ESV

25 Jesus said to her, "I am the resurrection and the life. Whoever believes in me, though he die, yet shall he live, 26 and everyone who lives and believes in me shall never die. Do you believe this?"

John 6:63-65, ERV

63 "It is the Spirit that gives life. The body is of no value for that. But the things I have told you are from the Spirit, so they give life. 64 But some of you don't believe." (Jesus knew the people who did not believe. He knew this from the beginning. And he knew the one who would hand him over to His enemies.) 65 Jesus said, "That is why I said, 'Anyone the Father does not help to come to me **cannot come.'**"

"Who lives and believes in me," so often when reading this it can be easy to skip over the 'lives' part of this phrase made by Jesus to a Samaritan woman in the book of John. Living 'in' Jesus is living our lives like He did, righteously, or least as righteous as we can. All of our needs are provided for by God, the bible reassures us (2 Corinthians 9:8), but many people think they need things that are unimportant to the Lord. Scripture is important to read and understand, as all of our direction comes from the Holy Spirit, and the word of God. Scripture tells us that when we pursue God's righteousness through Jesus, things like food, shelter, clothing, and other necessities to our survival will be taken care of, as the Lord our God knows full well what we need (Matthew 6:31-33). Only human pride and ignorance leads us to believe that *we* need to take care of our needs here on our tiny portion of Earth.

If you don't believe you *need* to change your life for Jesus, you might believe *in* Him but you're not *'living in Him,'* as Jesus Himself refers to in the above scripture. People who aren't trying to emulate their life after Jesus have all sorts of reasons for not submitting their lives to Him, perhaps they're unaware they were supposed to, or maybe they don't want to admit they need to follow someone other than themselves. The bible tells us that if God knows we aren't going to believe in Him the way He is asking, we will be left to our own devices and ultimately die without eternal life in Heaven, we may even end up in hell for not repenting for our sins (John 8:24, Revelation 21:8). God is all we need to seek, we are told, and we are urged to rest in our faith that He'll provide all we require to thrive. This is the essence of faith, and to stop seeking our needs on our own, but to rest and live in Him.

Romans 1:28, CJB

28 In other words, since they have not considered God worth knowing, God has given them up to worthless ways of thinking; so that they do improper things.

John 5:44, ESV

44 How can you believe, when you receive glory from one another and do not seek the glory that comes from the only God?

November 2
Expectations & Understanding

Psalm 118:8, ESV

8 It is better to take refuge in the Lord than to trust in man.

Isaiah 2:22, ICB

22 You should stop trusting in people to save you. People are only human. They aren't able to help you.

It's hard not to have expectations, we expect to be satisfied after eating a meal, or after praying, we expect the sun to rise each morning and set each evening. Just like we can subconsciously develop expectations, we can sometimes develop our own interpretations of what justice needs to look like in order to satisfy our vengeance, or our need to right what we consider an injustice. As humans, we cannot see the whole picture, every side to every story, but only one part of it in our limited understanding. Yet, even though we don't have all the information, some people jump to conclusions and judgements regarding one another in ignorance. Sometimes, the most difficult thing for any of us to do is sit back, let life unfold before us, and accept that God does all the planning and judging.

Solving our own problems appears to have all the sound reason of a person with a great deal of integrity. Whether we seek help from another in a time of need or strife, or we figure out a solution to our problems independently, cleaning up after ourselves is an axiom many people would accept. Admirable? Not according to the bible. The Lord expects us to lean on His understanding, putting *all* of our anxieties at His feet and *not* leaning onto any human rationalizations (Proverbs 3:5-6). This also puts us all in a humble position, as we are asked to yield to the guidance of the Holy Spirit inside of us and not our own goals and desires. Helping one another when we're in need or down is just exactly what we're called to do, but *expecting* it from another is wrong. Anything that causes us to turn away from the Lord's guidance, support and direction is wrong, including our own solutions and expectations. All we can expect is one life, one death, and one judgement in front of a merciful God (Hebrews 9:27), and all we need to ever understand will come from the Spirit of the Lord within us.

Jeremiah 17:5, GW

5 "This is what the Lord says: "Cursed is the person who trusts humans, who makes flesh and blood His strength and whose heart turns away from the Lord."

November 3
Creation Versus the Creator

Genesis 1:1, 11-12, 14-16, KJV/ESV

1 In the beginning God created the heaven and the earth. 11 And God said, Let the earth bring forth grass, the herb yielding seed, and the fruit tree yielding fruit after His kind, whose seed is in itself, upon the earth: and it was so. 12 And the earth brought forth grass, and herb yielding seed after His kind, and the tree yielding fruit, whose seed was in itself, after His kind: and God saw that it was good. 14 And God said, "Let there be lights in the expanse of the heavens to separate the day from the night. And let them be for signs and for seasons, and for days and years, 15 and let them be lights in the expanse of the heavens to give light upon the earth." And it was so. 16 And God made the two great lights—the greater light to rule the day and the lesser light to rule the night—and the stars.

The universe is fascinating, the stars, the planets and galaxies, people dedicate their lives to studying them. Eliminating or dismissing God's declaration in Genesis is already disbelief, and places the majesty of the creation of the universe awkwardly on itself. For those who place their faith and trust in the tangible results of proven Historical facts, evidence, God's majesty will remain hidden (Romans 1:28). The need for proof is distrust, disbelief, skepticism, and dwells inside of those who are not God's children. Without God, there is no forgiveness of sins, and Hell awaits us (Hebrews 9:22). If that's not enough to put the fear of God into someone, Jesus assures that not one word of the scriptures will be changed until 'the heavens and earth disappear' (Matthew 5:18).

Our time on earth is limited, and the earth's time is limited too, apparently. So, as fascinating as the solar system is, the bible tells us that it didn't create itself, God did, so we should be humbling ourselves before Him. To declare ourselves king of the natural species, and therefore, above every other living thing on earth is pompous and arrogant. We may be at the top of the intellectual food chain, and dominant over every other species on earth, but that's because God made it that way (Genesis 1:26), after He made everything, including humans. God is the creator of all things (Colossians 1:15-17), and expects us to not only recognize that, but to respect that by worshiping Him above everything else. When we give credit to the *creation* instead of the creator we're guilty of serving a false God, we aren't putting God above all things. Everything physical is temporary, so faith is our **only** salvation.

Romans 1: 21-22, 25, ERV/GW

21 They knew God. But they did not give glory to God, and they did not thank him. Their thinking became useless. Their foolish minds were filled with darkness. 22 They said they were wise, but they became fools.25 These people have exchanged God's truth for a lie. So they have become ungodly and serve what is created rather than the Creator, who is blessed forever. Amen!

John 6:63-64, GW

63 "Life is spiritual. Your physical existence doesn't contribute to that life. The words that I have spoken to you are spiritual. They are life. 64 But some of you don't believe." Jesus knew from the beginning those who wouldn't believe and the one who would betray him.

November 4

Get to Know God

Deuteronomy 4:39, ESV

39 Know therefore today, and lay it to your heart, that the Lord is God in heaven above and on the earth beneath; there is no other.

Isaiah 66:2, ERV

2 "I am the one who made all things. They are all here because I made them," says the Lord. "These are the people I care for: the poor, humble people who obey my commands."

Those of us who believe in God don't have much trouble accepting that He created all living things. Many of us also readily welcome the holy scripture as containing the word of God, and that it's meant to be used as a guide in our lives. However, we know far less about God than some people are able to find comfort in, and there is controversy in this mystery that some people just can't accept. If we love God, and are earnest in showing Him that we are devoted to Him, we'll want to learn, and understand our relationship with Him, as well as His will for us. We do this through prayer, listening to the Holy Spirit, and reading the word of God. When we read the bible, we learn that God has had a tumultuous relationship with the humanity He created (Genesis 6:7), that He can show great wrath (Psalm 78:59), and is full of compassion (Psalm 103:13-14). All-knowing, and all-powerful, God wants us all to want to know Him better, but always keeps us from knowing too much. We are given free will to make our own choices, because forced love isn't really love. God wants us to choose Him first, and love Him more than we love ourselves.

The humanity God created found ways to sin, and sought to follow their own goals and desires instead of being faithful to God (Psalm 81:10-13, Jeremiah 8:6). Humans are stubborn though, and we are constantly straying from God, focusing on ourselves and the world around us. God wants all people to repent, to return to Him and be healed, and offers forgiveness to all who seek Him (2 Chronicles 7:14). Correcting us through tribulations, and purifying us through hardship, many people have difficulty abiding in a God who utilizes pain and calamity. Only arrogance prevents us from accepting our role as children of God, and fosters the feeling of indignance and outrage when things go wrong in our world. Many people use their free will as rationale for their autonomy against God's will, even though God gave us that free will to show Him how obedient we are. Just because we can make our own choices based on what we desire for ourselves, doesn't mean we should be. If we truly love God, we yield to His command, as He is in charge, not us. God humbled Himself for us by sending a piece of Himself down in the form of Jesus to die for His broken humanity (Romans 5:8, John 10:30). Only with humble, repentant hearts can we approach the Lord, begin to understand Him, or feel His salvation in our hearts.

Micah 6:8, ESV

8 He has told you, O man, what is good; and what does the Lord require of you but to do justice, and to love kindness, and to walk humbly with your God?

November 5
God in Human Form

Colossians 1:19, ERV

19 God was pleased for all of himself to live in the Son.

For many of us, the belief in a higher power is a no-brainer, an axiom, something we easily accept. For anyone who has read anything in the bible, Jesus came to Earth as the example of the perfect, most holy human and died for the sins of all humanity (1 John 3:5, 1 Peter 1:19). For many of us, the life and times of Jesus here on Earth provides the story of the forgiveness of our sins through the ultimate sacrifice, but what some may not know is that Jesus was actually God in human form. Jesus prayed to God and called him 'Father' though, how can that be if he was actually God Himself? As if to take a piece of Himself and implant it in the virgin Mary, God allowed Jesus to become a human being to talk with us, educate us, and to experience everything that we do. (Hebrews 2:14-18) God is more powerful than any mortal human can possibly understand, and trusting in His unseen supremacy is the essence of our faith.

Humans have been making one bad choice after another throughout history, choosing greed and money over love for one another, and re-writing God's version of right and wrong for ourselves (Malachi 3:18). When we do these things we are turning away from God's love and support, like an unfaithful partner (Psalm 78:56-57). In our lives here on Earth sin, greed, temptation, pride, wickedness and corruption are all around us, but God's love sustains us. God came down here as a human out of love for us in the form of Jesus (John 1:18). Walking among the people whom he created, scorned and ridiculed and eventually put to death by those very same people, all our creator wants is our love and devotion (Jeremiah 24:7). God loved humanity so much He took human form in Jesus Christ, and saved us all from eternal damnation by dying for the sins of all humanity. Now, *that's* love!

Colossians 2:9-10, CEB

9 For the entire fullness of God's nature dwells bodily in Christ, 10 and you have been filled by him, who is the head over every ruler and authority.

Ephesians 2:4-5, ERV

4 But God is rich in mercy, and he loved us very much. 5 We were spiritually dead because of all we had done against him. But he gave us new life together with Christ. (You have been saved by God's grace.)

November 6

The Miracles of Jesus

Mark 1:32-34, ESV

32 That evening at sundown they brought to him all who were sick or oppressed by demons. 33 And the whole city was gathered together at the door. 34 And he healed many who were sick with various diseases, and cast out many demons. And he would not permit the demons to speak, because they knew him.

John 3:1-2, NIV

1 Now there was a Pharisee, a man named Nicodemus who was a member of the Jewish ruling council. 2 He came to Jesus at night and said, "Rabbi, we know that you are a teacher who has come from God. For no one could perform the signs you are doing if God were not with him."

We can't help it that we were born two thousand years *after* Jesus was here on Earth performing miracles, but that doesn't make them any less valid or miraculous. All of Jesus' disciples, twelve very different men, each saw Jesus perform these miracles, and more, during His ministry. Jesus healed people with skin diseases (Mark 1:40-42), cast out demons from those who were possessed (Mark 7:26-30), healed a deaf man (Mark 7:31-35), fed a multitude of people with only five loaves and two fish (Matthew 14:14-21), healed a man who was paralyzed (John 5:3-9), and brought a deceased man back to life (John 11:17-45). These scriptures are firsthand accounts of God's power through Jesus. We know that Jesus was God in human form from the many accounts from the bible (Colossians 2:9, John 20:28, Titus 2:13, Matthew 1:23), as well as Jesus' own words (John 8:58, John 10:30), and these miracles prove it.

The same God that made the universe, that allows the sun to rise each morning, loves *us* each enough to want us to come back to Him in faith. We really are that important to God, even if He's no longer walking around the Earth with us making life better one person at a time. God's power is evident all around us if we know where to look; in the laughter of a child, the love between newlyweds, the sunset, in the miracle of the human soul, the mountain ranges that seem to touch the sky, and in the stars that light up the Heavens. For the unrighteous, these share no significance or connection, but for the righteous this moves and humbles us because we know of the power and majesty that God can work in our own lives.

John 15:9, ICB

9 "I loved you as the Father loved me. Now remain in my love."

November 7

Our Whole Heart, Not One Ounce Less!

1 Chronicles 28:9, NASB

9 As for you, my son Solomon, know the God of your father, and **serve Him wholeheartedly** and with a willing mind; **for the Lord searches all hearts**, and understands every intent of the thoughts. If you seek Him, He will let you find Him; but if you forsake Him, He will reject you forever.

Deuteronomy 6:5, ESV

5 You shall love the Lord your God **with all your heart** and with all your soul and with all your might.

For those who believe in the grace and majesty of our all-knowing, and all-powerful God, saying we love Him comes easily. Praying for daily guidance, reading the scriptures, even repenting our sins gives us feeling of satisfaction knowing we're being candid with Christ, our Lord. But, are we? Deep inside, there are places we don't readily talk about to our friends, or immediate family, where we may keep some things about ourselves hidden. Secret truths…Perhaps we're hiding because we're afraid of something, or trying to avoid facing something else, or simply unaware of a sin we've committed, but we all hide more than we realize. The bible tells us that all secrets will be revealed (Luke 8:17), that God see's every hidden secret (Daniel 2:22), so there can be no reason for any of us to hide from God. Denial, ignorance, and stubbornness keeps us from humbling ourselves before God. Humility seems to be difficult for humanity to achieve, and maintain.

If we're not fully trusting in God, if we're holding anything back, He knows. Trusting God's changes in the face of His unknown plan is too risky for some people to give up their autonomy to serving Him. Half-hearted efforts to connect with God still shows Him a certain degree of faithlessness, and indicates a lack of trust. What's in our heart is what our priority is (Matthew 6:21); are we serving ourselves, trying to reassure ourselves through the effort we put into our worldly goals? Or, are we fully committed to God, putting Him first? We make time for the things we consider important in our lives, so the amount of time we spend with God tells Him how much of a priority He is to us. When we pray, we should be more open with our creator about what's troubling us, what we're afraid of, and what we aren't sure of. If we aren't open to following instead of leading, abiding in Him instead of negotiating, complying with Him instead of deciding our paths for ourselves, we aren't serving God, or putting Him first. If we aren't ready to uncover all of the pain and darkness inside of us, to hand over to our Lord and Savior, we aren't giving Him our whole heart either (Revelation 3:15-16). No relationship we'll ever have will be as rewarding, or as challenging, as the one we have with our God. Be humble, be penitent, and search your hearts in the name of the Lord, brothers and sisters.

Hebrews 4:12-13, ESV

12 For the word of God is living and active, sharper than any two-edged sword, piercing to the division of soul and of spirit, of joints and of marrow, and **discerning the thoughts and intentions of the heart**. 13 And no creature is hidden from his sight, but all are naked and exposed to the eyes of him to whom we must give account.

November 8
Speak Softly

Colossians 4:6, ESV

6 Let your speech always be gracious, seasoned with salt, so that you may know how you ought to answer each person.

Titus 3:2, ERV

2 Tell them not to speak evil of anyone but to live in peace with others. They should be gentle and polite to everyone.

Who do you know that always speaks with graciousness, kindness, politeness, and with few words? Probably not many people. Words are powerful and permanent, and too often underestimated. Humans tend to use too many, and use them before thinking thoughts completely through. Evil tongues are everywhere, spreading rumor and inuendo, hatred and division. Crude humor is a vile waste of time and intellect, according to the bible, and the righteous shouldn't partake of it (Ephesians 5:4). This can be difficult when it's all around you, on the lips of your friends and colleagues, the music people listen to and the shows, videos and apps people watch. God calls us to have self-control, and when we *must* speak, to speak with gentleness (Proverbs 17:27). These can seem like strict, harsh even, rules that we might not see the importance of. God made the universe, God made all of humanity, so God makes the rules. Besides, who are we, as corrupt sinning humans, to judge what righteousness should and shouldn't *look* like?

Thinking should take more of our time than speaking, especially when one is trying to understand the bible *correctly,* a deliberate yet complicated work. Our words should be thoughtful and kind, and used to build one another up in spirit. Love and forgiveness should be the motivation behind our words, not greed, pride, lust, envy, gluttony or vanity. We need to *check* ourselves throughout the day, as we are constantly surrounded and bombarded by the temptation to let down our guard, and not allow the evil around us to corrupt us (Lamentations 3:40, Ephesians 6:13). Our words represent what's in our hearts, and we represent Christ with our words. Choose words wisely, brothers and sisters.

Luke 6:45, ESV

45 The good person out of the good treasure of His heart produces good, and the evil person out of His evil treasure produces evil, for out of the abundance of the heart His mouth speaks.

Matthew 12:36-37, ESV

36 "I tell you, on the day of judgment people will give account for every careless word they speak, 37 for by your words you will be justified, and by your words you will be condemned."

November 9
What Makes a Person 'Impure'

Job 4:17, ESV

17 'Can mortal man be in the right before God? Can a man be pure before his Maker?

Romans 8:7, ESV

7 For the mind **that is set on the flesh** is hostile to God, for it does not submit to God's law; indeed, it cannot.

Our world is made up of many different kinds of people. It can be difficult to understand, relate to, or even accept some groups of people due to differences in customs, cultures, priorities, and attitudes. We need to remember that when Jesus picked His twelve disciples, He chose a tax collector, which at the time was the most hated person in society. Jesus also healed lepers, exorcised demons from people, both men and women, and forgave a thief who was hanging on the cross next to Him during His crucifixion (Mat. 8:2-3, Luke 11:14, Luke 8:1-3, Luke 23:39-43). It's clear, that human beings have a harder time with other human's sins than Jesus apparently does. Jesus looks at our *hearts*, what is truly *inside* of us, to places most of us never want to look. To be quite frank, 'sexual impurity,' *according to the bible*, includes more examples of fornication (Hosea 9:1-2, Numbers 25:1), adultery (Luke 16:18, Hosea 3:1), rape (Genesis 34:2, Judges 19:25), incest (2 Samuel 13:1-39, Ezekiel 22:9-11), polygamy (Exodus 21:10, 2 Chronicles 13:21), and prostitution (1 Kings 22:46, 14:24, Judges 16:1), than it does homosexuality (Rom.1:23-27). What's more, at the time the bible was written, the word 'homosexuality' didn't exist, and the scriptures regarding same-sex activity had more to do with false God worship (Jeremiah 13:26-27, Hosea 4:12-14) than a monogamous, loving, relationship. Impurity stems from our human desires to give into our wicked physical pleasures, to have more than another, and to take what isn't ours. We can only combat our natural tendency to commit sins with the power of Jesus' grace, self-control, forgiveness, and love. **Impure thinking occurs when the thirst for exerting one's own thinking, power, and dominance over others eclipses this true, honest, love.**

As much as we'd like to know, and understand people by just looking at them, or listening to them a couple of times, it takes much more than careful, practiced, mortal profiling to know the heart of another human being. It takes a lifetime to know *ourselves*, we can't possibly know *other people* like we assume we do. The stories illustrated in the bible present us with a moral code of behavior in regard to what we should be doing with our lives, and our bodies: that we should treat ourselves, and one another with respect, and no one's sinful desires forced upon another. Faith, not only to one another, but to God's *covenant*, or adultery, is also covered at length in the bible. Instead of promoting, or condemning a certain group of people or individuals, the bible clearly illustrates that the lack of self-control, desire to dominate another, and lack of respect for love is what results in immorality, and all forms of impurity. Very few of us can admit to not giving into a sinful desire at some point in our lives. We all have an equal need for the Lord's forgiveness, cleansing, and grace, as well as equally share the potential for salvation through our Savior, Jesus Christ. Lord, prevent our arrogance from creating more hypocrisy. Praise be to God, great is your faithfulness. AMEN.

James 1:27, ESV

27 Religion that is pure and undefiled before God, the Father, is this: to visit orphans and widows in their affliction, **and to keep oneself unstained from the world**.

November 10
True Intensions

Romans 8:2-4, ICB

2 I am not judged guilty because in Christ Jesus the law of the Spirit that brings life made me free. It made me free from the law that brings sin and death. 3 The law was without power, because the law was made weak by our sinful selves. But God did what the law could not do. He sent His own Son to earth with the same human life that others use for sin. He sent His Son to be an offering to pay for sin. So God used a human life to destroy sin. 4 He did this so that we could be right as the law said we must be. Now we do not live following our sinful selves, but we live following the Spirit.

Just because our sins were forgiven by Christ on the cross, doesn't give us carte blanche to live any way we want, with reckless disregard to sin and wickedness. Though we believe in Christ, and through His death on the cross for our sins we have forgiveness, God is not deceived by our poor choices. Our hearts reveal our true natures, which cannot escape God's omnipresence. We are told in the bible that whatever we reap, so will we sow (Galatians 6:7), and to nourish our spirits instead of our flesh (Galatians 5:16). Many people plow through life with reckless disregard to this warning, fooled by the devil's trickery, their own pride and lack of fear in our one, Almighty God. Even though we're forgiven, we must not take our sins lightly, without regard to the sacrifice made for that forgiveness. We should be using our mistakes to learn, and make better choices with each new opportunity. What's more, we must constantly *renew* our commitment to keep our focus on Jesus, and not ourselves or others.

Jesus calls us to be better people, righteous and holy (Leviticus 11:44), modeling our spirits by His. If we're not really trying, or don't think we need to conform to a book written thirty-five hundred years ago, then we're in for a rude awakening on judgement day. We are all given one life, one death, and one judgement, no one is immune (Hebrews 9:27). The bible assures us of this, and urges us to pursue a more righteous lifestyle, driven by a heart that loves our neighbor as ourselves. Although we can all partake of eternal life through the salvation of Jesus Christ, we cannot take advantage of this gift because God knows our hearts (Psalm 44:21). God knows if we're truly seeking Him, or if we're just driven by self-preservation. If we only want the benefits that come from believing in God, but we don't think we need to invite Him into our daily lives, choices, and decisions then we're not truly devoted (John 14:15). We can fool others, hiding from them our true intensions and desires we mask by favorable behavior, but God knows what's really driving us. How pure will God see *your* intensions?

1 Chronicles 28:9, NASB

9 As for you, my son Solomon, know the God of your father, and **serve Him wholeheartedly and with a willing mind**; for the Lord searches all hearts, and understands every intent of the thoughts. If you seek Him, He will let you find Him; but if you forsake Him, He will reject you forever.

November 11
Christs Is Enough

2 Corinthians 12:9, ESV

9 But he said to me, "My grace is sufficient for you, for my power is made perfect in weakness." Therefore I will boast all the more gladly of my weaknesses, so that the power of Christ may rest upon me.

Romans 9:32, ERV

32 They failed because **they tried to make themselves right by the things they did. They did not trust in God to make them right.** They fell over the stone that makes people fall.

Being a kind, and forgiving person in a cold, cruel, world can seem like trying to catch the wind; foolish and impossible. As followers of Christ Jesus, we are called to love others as ourselves, forgive enemies, and turn the other cheek (Mat. 22:39, 5:44, 5:39). Trying to maintain our self-control when we're angry can seem impossible sometimes. Attempting to stay graceful when nothing seems to be going our way, we have too much to do, and not enough to get through it all, can test our nerves. In our everyday lives we can feel pressed, disrespected, ignored, left out, persecuted, mistreated, and misunderstood. Human beings are self-focused, in a hurry, like to make things easier, faster, better, and don't always treat one another with love and kindness (Luke 6:31). We are flawed, each and every one of us, trying to stay righteous in an unrighteous world can seem like too much, and being holy the way God asks us can seem like an impossible job.

No one is too broken for Jesus. No matter what has gone wrong in our lives, our relationship with our Savior is spiritual, and no one can take that from us. Mistakes will be made, good people suffer sometimes, we can all feel like we're not good enough, and we will experience pain (John 16:33). Humans can't be holy without God (Matthew 19:26), and the journey to true righteousness will be fraught with many hardships. Not only are we made to need Jesus, we can't do anything righteous without Him (John 14:6, 15:5-6). Better behavior, more contrite choices, and the kind of attitude that wins God's heart can all be learned by following the life of Christ Jesus more closely. The patience, grace, and self-control we need to stay righteous, even when we're under pressure, comes from Jesus. Repeat prayer, and humble attitudes, will go a long way when we are struggling to get through a situation. We can derive comfort, guidance, and unload the painful baggage taking up residence in our hearts and minds to the Lord in prayer. Our faith assures us we will be heard in our time of need (Psalm 34:15). No matter how rejected we may feel, no matter how badly the world treats us, no matter how deep the pain, our relationship with God can sustain us through anything, and can always be repaired. Nothing, no one, is impossible for God. No one will ever love us the way our creator can, and when we truly seek Him in our hearts, He feels it too. Talking to our Heavenly Father about our hurt, our trouble, our triumphs, and our struggles will yield the strong relationship we will be able to rely on. Lord in Heaven, reinforce us with your Mighty power and grace. Fill us, gracious Lord, with the patience, faith, endurance, and understanding we need to sustain us through our tribulations. All glory and honor to God, most High, our Lord and Savior. AMEN.

Isaiah 65:24, ERV

24 "I will answer them before they call for help. I will help them before they finish asking."

November 12
Assurance

2 Corinthians 3:4-5, ESV

4 Such is the confidence that we have through Christ toward God. 5 Not that we are sufficient in ourselves to claim anything as coming from us, but **our sufficiency is from God**.

Joshua 1:9, ESV

9 (The Lord said) "Have I not commanded you? Be strong and courageous. Do not be frightened, and do not be dismayed, for the Lord your God is with you wherever you go."

As a human race, our self-awareness, the trust we have in our own abilities, and judgement is a delicate, and dynamic state of mind. Human self-confidence is fragile, mercurial, and can often be situational. Arrogant people can think of many reasons why they fail, but seldom take responsibility for any of them. Confident people, however, can acknowledge their weaknesses without interpreting them as personal failings. There are such fine differences between arrogance, confidence, and insecurity. Insecure people are eager to represent themselves differently than what they believe they are, and can suck up a great deal of attention in doing so. On the other hand, Confident people often listen more than they speak, they are secure enough to listen and respond appropriately to a situation. Where we derive our confidence says a lot about what is truly in our hearts. Both arrogant, and insecure people often derive their confidence from themselves, and the world around them (Jeremiah 17:5). Confident followers of Christ derive their confidence from His grace (Hebrews 10:35-36).

A truly humble person, with complete self-control, who derives all their confidence from the Lord all the time is a fantastical person. The only one who was ever able to maintain this completely righteous, and holy state of mind was our Lord and Savior, Christ Jesus. In this holy confidence, we don't let negative thinking stop us, or dominate us. Within the divine grace of Jesus' love, we will always know our limits, have firm boundaries, and will be able to say 'no' appropriately. Wouldn't it be wonderful to always have the right amount of self-discipline, and self-control? We are all imperfect though, and designed to be repeatedly reminded of our need for God. We must continue to look inward, at our flaws and mistakes, this is where we need more of the Lord. What a precious gift of knowledge it is to know, specifically, what we need to pray for? When we can be confident in our relationship with Christ, we will become people who are self-assured, let our accomplishments in the Lord speak for themselves, and won't feel the need to brag or boast. True confidence comes from our faith.

Jeremiah 17:7, CSB

7 The person who trusts in the Lord, whose **confidence indeed is the Lord**, is blessed.

Proverbs 3:26, ESV

26 **For the Lord will be your confidence** and will keep your foot from being caught.

November 13
Sin & Purity

Matthew 5:48, ESV

48 You therefore must be perfect, as your heavenly Father is perfect.

James 3:2, NLT

2 Indeed, we all make many mistakes. For if we could control our tongues, we **would be** perfect and could also control ourselves in every other way.

For many people, focusing on, and eliminating their sins is how they make themselves righteous, and identify as a follower of Jesus Christ. Some religious groups are staunch in their beliefs about sin, as if to create a set of standards, ostracizing those who don't quite fit into their mold. Jesus befriended, and even chose people who were looked down on by their societies, like tax collectors and prostitutes (Luke 5:30), calling for all people to repent and come to Him (Isaiah 45:22, Acts 17:30). Although we understand that we cannot be perfect, Jesus calls us to be just that, so what is a human to do? To some, it may seem like God has set us up for failure, and we all handle failure differently. We are only able to be perfected through Jesus, this is how we're designed, to need Him. Make no mistake, to those who are letting Him in, Christ is re-forming us, molding, and shaping us, He is making us holy. We can see Christ at work in us through our prayers of repentance, through our kindness to others, through our changed actions, words, and behaviors. We can see this purification process at work, through our better decisions and choices, and with each righteous choice He makes us want to be *more and more* like Him. Devotion is a word of action, likewise, through daily prayers of repentance and petition, and through better listening, we can *show* our devotion to our Lord and Savior, whom we love so much. Just because we believe in Jesus, or even because we *follow* Him, doesn't make us free from sin. There is no freedom from sin without genuine, humble repentance through Christ.

It's not overcoming our sin that makes us clean, or right with God, because we will **always** sin. We don't automatically stop sinning because we believe in Jesus, and accept Him into our hearts. *It is by the grace of Jesus that we're forgiven for the sins we commit, not because we're so awesome to be believers, or because we no longer sin, but because Jesus is greater than anything we could ever do or say.* It is our devotion to the Lord, and the purity of our hearts in Christ Jesus that makes us pure, it's our heart that we're being judged on. Our human hearts, the central core of what motivates each of us, what makes our souls individual and unique, this is what God is trying to purify. How often we pray for strength when we're weak, how often we pray for someone who wrongs, or betrays us, how many times we stop to help someone else in need, how often we trust in the Lord when our world is crashing down around us, how many times we pray and say, 'thank you' for what we've been given, these are the things we'll be judged on. How many times we committed fornication, or how many times we've lied, or how many times we've coveted something that didn't belong to us, are less important than how many times we ask the Lord to forgive us, and to teach us how to make better choices by listening more closely to the Holy Spirit. After all, devotion to the Lord is something we **feel** with our hearts, our souls, and not something we do, or not do, with our bodies (John 6:63).

Hebrews 10:14, ERV

14 With one sacrifice Christ made His people perfect forever. They are the ones who are **being made holy.**

November 14
The Fear of God: Spiritual Death?

Romans 6:16b, ICB

16b You can follow sin, or obey God. **Sin brings spiritual death.** But obeying God makes you right with him.

Matthew 10:28, ESV

28 And do not fear those who kill the body but cannot kill the soul. Rather fear him **who can destroy both soul and body** in hell.

Revelation 20:14, ESV

14 Then Death and Hades were thrown into the lake of fire. This is the second death, the lake of fire.

The price for one life is one death, an unpleasant reality for us all. Actually, it's our sin that causes us to die, according to scripture (Romans 5:12). If we all die once, what is second death? We can all admit wanting to change an aspect of our physical bodies at one point in our lives, and these bodies eventually fail us in the end. What makes each person an individual is the unique assembly of characteristics and desires that inhabit a person's spirit. We cannot *see* our souls, but we know that we have them. Because Adam and Eve disobeyed God, all humanity was destined to sin as a result, and that changed everything for humanity. Not every human will end up serving God, so not every human will get into His everlasting Kingdom. When our bodies fail, they return to the earth from which they came, but our spirits sleep until Jesus comes again (1 Thessalonians 4:13-18). When Jesus comes a second time, He'll be collecting us for our final judgement.

Who we are, what we ultimately become is within our spirits, not our bodies, of course. What fuels our desires, motivates us, if we loved others, if we helped those in need, these are the things we'll be judged on. We all commit sins, but who actually felt bad about their sins, and who repented? God can not only destroy our bodies, but our spirits as well. Those who don't get into the Heavenly Kingdom can only hope for spiritual death, or suffer eternally in the lake of burning sulfur, not a pleasant thought. For those who are of God, this puts the fear of God in our hearts. To those who don't align with God, this may feel like a cruel ultimatum. We are God's creation, and He expects those who enter His Kingdom to present with the proper humility, and purity of heart. Our spiritual future is the one we're fighting for here, and we're made to struggle amongst a sinful, wicked world in order to prove our devotion to the one, true God. Allow yourself to be humbled, fear God, repent, and give your spirit eternal life through Jesus Christ.

Romans 8:10, ESV

10 But if Christ is in you, although the body is dead because of sin, the Spirit is life because of righteousness.

1 Corinthians 15:22, ESV

22 For as in Adam all die, so also in Christ shall all be made alive.

November 15
Rejected

Daniel 4:35, ERV

35 People on earth are not really important. God does what he wants with the powers of heaven and the people on earth. No one can stop his powerful hand or question what he does.

When life beats us up, and we feel nothing but rejection, pressure, fear, and oppression, the compound interest can leave us questioning, "Why is this happening to me?" We will be tested, broken, used, and corrected as God purifies and refines our souls. This Almighty 'decontamination' can be painful, confusing, and disheartening, leaving our spirits drained of hope and joy. It can be easy to fall prey to self-pity, thinking we've done nothing to warrant such painful circumstances, insurmountable tribulations, and intense heartbreak. Our lives are in the hands, and under the will of our Lord, God, and all that happens to us is meticulously choreographed by Him (Proverbs 19:21, Isaiah 14:24). When life hurts us beyond what we feel can be repaired, we can seriously question our relationship with God. When we don't understand why we are made to suffer, the pain can feel like relentless punishment, rejection and unjust cruelty.

No choice exists without God, as He fills the Heavens and all the earth (Jeremiah 23:24). God knows the end from the beginning (Isaiah 46:10), no need to change His mind, as He can make anything happen (Ephesians 1:11). Maybe God inflicts pain in our lives to test our faith in Him, to teach us something, to correct a wicked thought process or behavior, or a combination of reasons. No matter how dark our worlds become, we cannot forget that those of us who believe in the blood of Jesus are God's children (John 1:12-13-*below*), and God will never forsake His children (Psalm 37:28). This is our faith in God, that we trust Him even though we cannot feel His mercy and grace through our blinding hurt. So we must keep trying to do good, in order to please the Lord. We must continue to pray, and ask the Lord to show us our sins, so that we can bring them to Him in repentance. We will wait on the Lord to restore our souls (Isaiah 40:31). **WE** may feel like we need comforting, reassurance, and love, but will only get what the *Lord* wishes us to have. We must not begin to believe that we are not loved by God, because the bible tells us that the Lord loves us (Jeremiah 31:3). This is how we trust in the Lord over mankind.

No matter where we stand in our relationship with Christ, whether disciplined, tested, or blessed, how we handle these circumstances should be consistent, and always righteous. We can't decide to give in to wickedness, sin, and self-pity just because we feel we've been wronged (Ephesians 4:26-27). We can't know, we cannot see, the whole picture that God does, and we need to trust His judgement over our emotions. Wrong choices are still wrong, even, and especially when we're hurting. All we have, all we feel, all we go through without understanding, should be brought to the Lord. Even if we **feel** we've been rejected by God, *it doesn't mean we have been*. There should be no reason to stray from the Lord, no matter what we are feeling, or going through. Stay strong in the waiting, dear brothers and sisters, and know that you are never alone in how you are feeling. Lord, forgive our ignorance and sin, please allow us the wisdom to know our wrongs so we may come to you in repentance. Mighty Christ, give us endurance to withstand the trials we do not fully understand. Merciful Jesus, fortify our strength so that we may endure by your grace. Gracious Lord, restore our souls, that we may feel your divine love and grace once again. All praise, and glory, be to the Father through the son. AMEN.

John 1:12-13, GW

12 However, he gave the right to become God's children to everyone who believed in him. 13 These people didn't become God's children in a physical way—from a human impulse or from a husband's desire to have a child. **They were born from God.**

November 16
Under Pressure-Refining Us

Proverbs 17:3, ICB

3 A hot furnace tests silver and gold. In the same way, the Lord tests a person's heart.

Pressure is a part of many people's lives, pressures from work colliding with family, social, and personal taxations take a great deal of our attention. Fixated on what we can accomplish, what people are expecting of us, and trying to live up to our own, individual expectations can all tempt us to take our main focus away from our Lord and Savior. We all sin, and when we sin we learn something else that the Lord wants from us, or **doesn't** want from us. As we go through tests, trials, and tribulations we will either call on our Lord for comfort and direction, or lean onto our own understanding (Proverbs 3:5-6). Some people that go through painful experiences become embittered against God, unable, or unwilling, to accept His grace and judgement. God's will is going to be done, here on Earth as well as in Heaven, our resistance only hurts ourselves. Pushing God away because we don't think we can handle all He's given us is not fully trusting in Him, or accepting His will for us.

Each painful occurrence can be a learning experience that we can use to become more righteous in the eyes of God. Our bad habits, attitudes and choices invites trouble into our worlds, and when we allow ourselves to be humbled by God we can see where we've made those mistakes (Romans 7:7). With this information we can repent for those mistakes, and work toward recognizing them better the next time, in order to avoid making them altogether. Sometimes we even blame God for the poor choices that we made, angry and bitter that He isn't listening to us. The bible tells us that when we sin, we're turning away from God, so when we've sinned we've only ourselves to blame (Proverbs 5:23). Instead of feeling sorry for ourselves, we should be praying for guidance and support from God to get us through. Instead of retreating into ourselves in stony, self-righteous silence toward God, we need to accept the humility He's placing on us, and allow Him to continue to refine us. Sinful people cannot be in God's presence, so God is trying to refine all of us for readiness for eternal life. No one can bring out the holy in us like our own creator, we should pray for strength and help one another through those tough, painful times. Stick together, brothers and sisters, but above all, stick it out! AMEN

Isaiah 48:10-11, GW

10 "I have refined you, but not like silver. I have tested you in the furnace of suffering. 11 I am doing this for myself, only for myself. Why should my name be dishonored? I will not give my glory to anyone else."

1 Peter 1:6-7, GW

6 You are extremely happy about these things, even though you have to suffer different kinds of trouble for a little while now. 7 The purpose of these troubles is to test your faith as fire tests how genuine gold is. Your faith is more precious than gold, and by passing the test, it gives praise, glory, and honor to God. This will happen when Jesus Christ appears again.

November 17
Comfort & Mercy

Lamentations 3:31-32, ERV

31 He should remember that the Lord does not reject people forever. 32 When he punishes, he also has mercy. He has mercy because of His great love and kindness.

Psalm 119:50, ESV

50 This is my comfort in my affliction, that **your promise** gives me life.

With words like 'reject, punish, and affliction,' in the above scriptures, it's a wonder why some people expect life to be comfortable, or fair. Where was it written that life was going to be a complete and total pleasure experience where all of our dreams should naturally come true? As humans, we constantly set ourselves up for disappointment, distracted by our dreams, wishes, desires, and expectations. If we were *always* comfortable, *all* of the time, how would God know we would truly seek Him in our times of need? Life isn't supposed to be comfortable, we're being tested. Or rather, our faith is (Jeremiah 9:7).

Pain, suffering, disappointment, regret, and guilt are all experiences we are brought to by God, for the bible assures us over and over that **His** will be done. On Earth, in Heaven, three and a half thousand years ago, and right now, always and forever, God's will is done. Life is never going to be about our comfort, it's about our creator's intension to bring all of humanity back to Him through repentance. We are included in 'all humanity,' since we are humans. As such, we are subject to God's discipline and reproval in order train us in His version of righteousness. When we're hurting or disappointed, we tend to turn to our fellow man. Some of us talk with family or friends, others vent to co-workers or social media when we're distressed, distracted or annoyed. Knowing other people understand what we're going through is comforting to us, somehow. No one can restore the balance in our lives like our Savior in Christ Jesus, however.

When we say we have faith we're resting in the trust that no matter what happens to us, the Lord is watching, and is the Mighty hand that holds our ultimate fate. The bible tells us not to worry about what man can do to the body, because it's our spirit that God's really interested in (Matthew 10:28). All of our bodies have an expiration date, but our spirits have the opportunity to live forever with God. Essentially, we're all hoping we're going to be considered good enough to be worthy of the kingdom of Heaven. Having other people in our environments to share our burdens, help ease our load and suffering, are blessings. But God is our provider, the one that nourishes our souls with wisdom, forgiveness, and grace through our faith. In the end, our judgement will be between us and God, the bible doesn't say 'in the presence of thine family, or friends, or close supporter,' just us, and God. Prayer, repentance, correction, service, repeat. Amen!

Deuteronomy 31:8, ESV

8 "It is the Lord who goes before you. He will be with you; he will not leave you or forsake you. Do not fear or be dismayed."

November 18
In Control

Psalm 135:6, ESV

6 Whatever the Lord pleases, he does, in heaven and on earth, in the seas and all deeps.

Proverbs 16:33, ERV

33 People might throw lots to make a decision, but the answer always comes from the Lord.

Many people have pre-conceived notions about people who are devoted to God as strange, celibate monks or nuns, in a monastery or other daunting, isolated stone building in a far off land, living too sparce for common comfort. Here we go, forming judgements based on assumptions, ideas and stereotypes of what a certain group of people may be like. We are all different, and yet, all of us are capable of a deeper devotion to God. Not all of us are going to end up as monks or nuns, realistically, so what are we *really* afraid of in getting closer to God? Some people have trouble giving up any kind of control over their lives, including, and especially, God. In order to get closer to God we must humble ourselves, expose and repent all of our sins, and change our ways. Some people don't fully trust God's unknown, don't realize they're just as worthy as the next sinner, or fear change for the risk of potentially having to give up something we don't want to. Still others don't want to examine anything negative about themselves, especially sins they may be trying to hide.

Without knowing what's going to happen next, it's difficult to think we can control any aspect of our lives. God knows all, see's all, and if we think we can hide our sins we are only fooling ourselves. God's will is going to be done, the bible tells us. God made us, made the Earth, made everything, so everything, therefore, is in His control. When we think we're making our own choices as the masters of our own destinies, we're actually straying away from God and His grace. When God attempts to put us back on our path through strife, affliction, pain and gentle discipline we can sometimes misunderstand this. We are all ripe candidates for the devils trickery, trying to fool us, deceive and tempt us from our path with God. The power of Jesus' sacrifice on the cross can never be taken from us, cannot be thrown away *by* us, and offers us forgiveness and mercy when we return to acceptance of God's will.

1 Corinthians 2:9, ESV

9 But, as it is written, "What no eye has seen, nor ear heard, nor the heart of man imagined, what God has prepared for those who love him"

Isaiah 45:7, ESV

7 "I form light and create darkness; I make well-being and create calamity; I am the Lord, who does all these things."

November 19
'Sleeping'

Hebrews 9:27, ICB

27 Everyone must die once. After a person dies, he is judged.

John 11:25-26, ESV

25 Jesus said to her, "I am the resurrection and the life. Whoever believes in me, though he die, yet shall he live, 26 and everyone who lives and believes in me shall never die. Do you believe this?"

We have all lost people to the inevitability of death. There are so many misconceptions about death, causing fear deep down inside of many of us. Our bodies are made in God's image, but they are only temporary. We are only given one life, one death, and one final judgement. When Jesus says, 'whoever *lives* and believes in me will have everlasting life,' He is talking about our quest for righteousness. As a corrupt race, humans aren't Holy enough to be in the presence of God, we must **earn** our spot in Heaven (Hebrews 12:14, Jeremiah 9:7). We are also told in the bible that Heaven is a place of everlasting peace, where no suffering can be felt, only love. We have all imagined what it might be like at the end, perhaps a bright light at the end of a tunnel, a feeling of peace, or maybe the face of Jesus welcoming us. Over and over, the bible refers to death as 'sleep,' until Jesus comes back for us (Job 14:10-12, Daniel 12:2, Isaiah 26:19, John 11:11-14).

While we live we make choices, learn from mistakes, and are given an opportunity to live in paradise forever with our maker at the end of it all. We must follow the laws of God's covenant, though, keeping the commandments, as Jesus pleads with us to do in the bible (John 14:15). This is how we 'live for Jesus,' by modeling our lives after His. During our time here on Earth, we will be tempted repeatedly and relentlessly by evil trying to separate us from God's good news, and we will endure suffering and not always know why. Our faith is being tested (Deuteronomy 8:2). Although it is most sad for the living when someone we love has died, we cannot know what their judgement will yield, and don't always know how to comfort each other. This is the fear of God, and we all feel it (Matthew 10:28). As followers of the one true Messiah, **while** we remain 'awake' we can continue to prove to God that we will turn to Him for **all** of our needs; our training in righteousness, for continued repentance, to deepen our faith, for the comfort we need, and to show continued good works.

1 Thessalonians 4:13-18, ERV

14 We believe that Jesus died, but we also believe that he rose again. So we believe that God will raise to life through Jesus any who have died and bring them together with him when he comes. 15 What we tell you now is the Lord's own message. Those of us who are still living when the Lord comes again will join him, but not before those who have already died. 16 The Lord himself will come down from heaven with a loud command, with the voice of the archangel, and with the trumpet call of God. And the people who have died and were in Christ will rise first. 17 After that we who are still alive at that time will be gathered up with those who have died. We will be taken up in the clouds and meet the Lord in the air. And we will be with the Lord forever. 18 So encourage each other with these words.

November 20
Hearing the Word/Spirit

Job 33:14-18, ERV

14 But maybe God does explain what he does but speaks in ways that people don't understand. 15 He may speak in a dream, or in a vision at night, when people are in a deep sleep lying in their beds. 16 He may whisper something in their ear, and they are frightened when they hear his warnings. 17 God warns people to stop them from doing wrong and to keep them from becoming proud. 18 He does this to save them from death. He wants to keep them from being destroyed.

Romans 10:17, ESV

17 So faith comes from hearing, and hearing through the word of Christ.

We're told to pray, often, to place our burdens upon the Lord, for repentance of our sins, for comfort in times of affliction, and for guidance and direction. The bible tells us that the Holy Spirit communicates to Jesus for us, a gift of His crucifixion and resurrection. The above scripture tells us that God uses different mediums to communicate His will, in a dream, a vision, or a thought that's not our own telling us the more righteous way of doing things as we move along through our lives. When we're frazzled, confused, upset, or distracted we aren't focused on God, we're focused on our lives, and we may not hear the Holy Spirit communicating to us. If we're studying the word of God, and reading our bibles, we will begin to understand what attitudes we must have, and what behaviors the Lord despises. Once we know this, we can begin to apply it to our lives, and use this knowledge when we speak to others and make choices.

If we're only listening to others read the scriptures in church, and not reading them for ourselves, we can't possibly be getting the complete picture the way God intended for us. In the bible, we discover that not everyone will go to Heaven, that there **is** a hell, and that there is one sin that cannot be forgiven (Matthew 7:21, Revelation 21:8, Matthew 12:31-32). We also learn from the bible, that not one word contained therein will be added or taken away in meaning or significance, and that there is a planned end for humanity. If we aren't reading from Genesis to Revelation for ourselves, we're missing out on the ongoing and tenuous relationship between God and Israel, which could be seen as an allegory for God's ongoing relationship with humanity itself. When we listen to theologians and scholars, they can provide incredible insight, but they cannot provide the personal relationship that develops when we submerge ourselves in the scriptures at our own pace and understanding. God should be our priority, knowing Him and obeying Him, and if one reads the bible they should *want* to. Prayer is the best way for us to communicate to God, and always through Jesus (John 14:6), but the Holy Spirit is the one who'll be communicating to us.

1 Corinthians 2:13, ERV

13 These things also we speak, not in the words which are not based on man's wisdom. Instead, we use the Spirit's teachings. We explain spiritual things to those who have the Spirit. We explain spiritual things in spiritual words.

Isaiah 30:21, ERV

21 If you wander from the right path, either to the right or to the left, you will hear a voice behind you saying, "You should go this way. Here is the right way."

November 21
Judgement

Matthew 7:1-2, ERV

7 "Don't judge others, and God will not judge you. 2 If you judge others, you will be judged the same way you judge them. God will treat you the same way you treat others."

John 7:24, ESV

24 "Do not judge by appearances, but judge with right judgment."

In reading the scriptures, it can appear to be sending mixed signals with regard to judging. Do we judge, or do we not judge? Interacting with others, engaging in conversation for business or pleasure, listening to words along with body language, the human mind forms conclusions and opinions. Forming opinions is forming judgements, according to the dictionary, and the bible is ambiguous regarding judgement. When we form a judgement or opinion we must ask ourselves what are we forming this judgement **for**? Are we using this opinion to determine the amount of righteousness someone is truly seeking, or to build them up in knowledge or faith? Are we using our rationale to clarify a lesson from a situation, or to understand how to better help one another? Or are we using our judgement to classify ourselves among others for our own gain? Sometimes we form opinions, classify people unjustly without knowing all of the facts, and begin to view them in a poorer light as a result (James 5:9).

In the bible, everyone is called to repent and be forgiven, no matter the sin (Acts 17:30-31). Forming opinions and speculations on one another may be an inevitable human trait, but what we **do** with that judgement will reflect how Holy our hearts are. Are we helping to build one another up, supportive and loving to our fellow sinners, or are we condemning them quietly in our hearts while we smile to their faces? The bible does make it clear that there is only one final judge, and He is the giver and destroyer of life. This is definitely not anyone human, thank goodness. We humans need to retrain our hearts and minds to be kinder, more accepting, more forgiving and less assuming of one another. This is what Jesus calls us to do, and it is what is right and just. After all, Jesus is the final judge of us all! (John 5:22)

James 4:11-12, ESV

11 Do not speak evil against one another, brothers and sisters. The one who speaks against another or judges another, speaks evil against the law and judges the law. But if you judge the law, you are not a doer of the law but a judge. 12 There is only one lawgiver and judge, he who is able to save and to destroy. But who are you to judge your neighbor?

November 22
The Day of the Lord

Mark 13:7-10,32,33, ICB

7 (Jesus said) "You will hear about wars and stories of wars that are coming. But don't be afraid. These things must happen before the end comes. 8 Nations will fight against other nations. Kingdoms will fight against other kingdoms. There will be times when there is no food for people to eat. And there will be earthquakes in different places. These things are like the first pains when something new is about to be born. 10 But before these things happen, the Good News must be told to all people. 32 No one knows when that day or time will be. The Son and the angels in heaven don't know. Only the Father knows. 33 Be careful! Always be ready! You don't know when that time will be."

Sometimes reading the bible can feel more like trying to decipher an elaborate code. 'Only wise people will understand,' refers to people who are focused on the righteous mindset established by Christ, and dutifully studying the bible. God enlightens us all in His own timing, and we only know what He allows us to at any given time. Nothing lasts forever, the bible tells us, not even the world we currently live in (Matthew 24:35). If we know we're living on borrowed time, the smart decision would be to adhere as closely to our creators commands as possible. Many people appear to be living like they have all the time in the world to clean up their attitudes, choices, and unwholesome desires. Perhaps people think that their opinion of themselves is the only one that matters, but they don't control the final judgement.

"Well, I don't know if I truly believe in God, so that stuff doesn't really apply to me," is a common, yet invalid, excuse many people use. God's will is superior to humans, and God's will is what is done. The message is clear: Wake up and repent, trade in that selfish pride for humility, and learn how to follow Jesus more closely. We all fall short in the eyes of God (Romans 3:23), so we could all stand some improving. God wants us **all** to repent, to need and rely on Him for all of our needs, not just the moments of desperation and panic. Whether we want to admit it or not, we will all face God's judgement based on what's truly in our hearts when we're called (Matthew 24:29-31). We are told that we're either going to live forever in God's kingdom or to be disgraced and sent to the lake of fire (Rev. 20:15). If the wonder of the sunrise, or the cry of a newborn baby, or the mist floating mysteriously over a serene mountain lake isn't enough to inspire devotion to God, than this ominous warning should. What is it going to take to change the hearts of mankind?

Daniel 12: 1b-4,7b, ESV/ICB

1b "It will be a time of trouble unlike any that has existed from the time there have been nations until that time. But at that time your people, everyone written in the book, will be rescued. 2 Many sleeping in the ground will wake up. Some will wake up to live forever, but others will wake up to be ashamed and disgraced forever. 3 Those who are wise will shine like the brightness on the horizon. Those who lead many people to righteousness will shine like the stars forever and ever. 4 "But you, Daniel, close up the book and seal it. These things will happen at the time of the end. Many people will go here and there to find true knowledge. 7b When the power of the holy people has been completely shattered, then all these things will be finished."

November 23

When Time Runs Out?

Isaiah 24:3, NIV

3 The earth will be completely laid waste and totally plundered. The Lord has spoken this word.

Matthew 24:35, ESV

35 "Heaven and earth will pass away, but my words will not pass away."

God is all knowing, all powerful, the bible tells us this and creation backs this up, and He has a purpose for all mankind (Isaiah 46:8-10). From the majesty and wonder of the Earth, the stars, the mountains and the universe to the whistle of the wind, the smell of the rain, and the wail of a newborn cry, God is all around us. The invisible energy force that binds us, penetrates us and formed us, few of us truly understand. The bible also tells us, that only God knows when the 'end of time' will be, indicating everything we know to be steady and sure about the world we live in has an expiration date (Matthew 24:36). We also read in the Gospel of Luke that, 'many will not be able to enter the kingdom of Heaven.' (Luke 13:22-24) Plainly said, Jesus tells us that not everyone will get to Heaven. This may not seem fair to some, but the story of humanities infidelity to God has been going on for thousands of years, the bible chronicles this (Leviticus 20:1-5, Jeremiah 32:35, Judges 3:7, Acts 7:43), and some people never come to understand their role in it all. We are all God's children, His creation, and He calls us to be righteous so that we can live eternally in His presence in Heaven. Some people have a difficult time with faith which is unseen and intangible, or belief in a superior being of *any* kind, or trouble following the path of righteousness, or believing that they need to do anything other than believe and prosper.

God knows and sees all. He knew that some of them would stray away from Him, and sent Jesus to die for the one's that would return to Him so that we could have eternal life with Him in Heaven. God wants our *hearts*, not just our belief, but true devotion (Mark 12:30-31). God wants us to be different than the people who obliviously go about their lives not giving a passing nod to Jesus in their own. We are called to be different from our sinful pasts before we accepted Jesus into our hearts, and live more righteously like Jesus did, and to *seek* Him in this way (Proverbs 8:17). Jesus explains that the shepherd walks away from His 99 sheep to find the one lost sheep; God leaves no potential believer behind (Matthew 18:12-14). As our Heavenly Shepherd watches over us while the hourglass of Earth's time ticks by, God is hoping that more of His children will repent and come back to Him in good faith. The beauty about the bible is that the moral teachings are all in parables, or stories, and the moral message never gets stale, but remains timeless. Reading and understanding the scriptures that have been provided to us can teach us priceless knowledge about the moral code of living a more Holy life, as we are called to do (Matthew 4:4), and to ignore or bypass that is a gross miscalculation. Today, there is a format of bible that every level of understanding can accommodate, there is no excuse not to know what's in it. Eventually, time runs out for all of humanity, and usually faster than we think. We are never too old to learn something new, to be more humble, to be more loving, to be less judging of others. Will your spirit be ready when God's final will is imposed?

Matthew 28:19-20, NIV

19 "Therefore go and make disciples of all nations, baptizing them in the name of the Father and of the Son and of the Holy Spirit, 20 and teaching them to obey everything I have commanded you. And surely I am with you always, to the very end of the age."

November 24
Giving Thanks and Praise

Hebrews 12:28, ESV

28 Therefore **let us be grateful** for receiving a kingdom that cannot be shaken, and thus let us offer to God acceptable worship, with reverence and awe.

Hebrews 13:15-16, GW

15 Through Jesus we should always bring God a sacrifice of praise, that is, words that acknowledge him. 16 Don't forget to do good things for others and to share what you have with them. These are the kinds of sacrifices that please God.

We have so much to thank our Heavenly Father for! If the earth, love, and life itself isn't enough, everlasting life in Heaven with our creator is called Heaven for a reason. God gave us Jesus and the Holy Spirit, for the chance at eternal salvation. Righteousness is nearly impossible for a sinful humanity, but God loved us enough to send Jesus to die for all our iniquities. Upright, contrite, Holy and without sin, Jesus came to Earth to fulfill God's promise (Isaiah 54:10). Instead of just saving His chosen people, God arranged for all humans to have a chance to earn His approval (Matthew 28:19). Through trials, difficulties, and pain the Lord God purifies and refines us in righteousness (Isaiah 48:10). We have the written word of God, the bible, as a manual for life, and Jesus as a model to live by. Teaching us the relationship between God and humanity, and our place in the world He's created, the bible is invaluable to us.

May sharing, love for others, generosity and humility dwell inside of our hearts by the grace of the Lord. We must never forget to carry the words of the Lord on our lips, to help others who may be struggling in their faith, or to exalt the Lord in praise. As followers of Christ, we must represent Him with our words, our forgiveness, our generosity, and our love (James 1:22-25). We must never forget that we are all sinners, and God wants every soul to return to Him in good faith, so we shouldn't discriminate against anyone. Never underestimate the power of planting a small seed in a non-believer, and encourage the exploration of God on one's own. Reading the bible is our best defense against false prophesy and backsliding in our faith. The Lord is faithful to those who are faithful to Him. All praise and glory to God, our creator and most high. AMEN.

Psalm 107:21, CSB

21 **Let them give thanks to the Lord** for His faithful love and His wondrous works for all humanity.

Revelation 14:7, GW

7 The angel said in a loud voice, "Fear God and give him glory, because the time has come for him to judge. Worship the one who made heaven and earth, the sea and springs."

November 25

'Those Who Have Ears, Let Them Hear'

John 1:1, GW

1 In the beginning the Word already existed. The Word was with God, and the Word **was** God.

James 1:19-21, ICB

19 My dear brothers, always be willing to listen and slow to speak. Do not become angry easily. 20 Anger will not help you live a good life as God wants. 21 So put out of your life every evil thing and every kind of wrong you do. Don't be proud but accept God's teaching that is planted in your hearts. This teaching can save your souls.

Words communicate, describe, and can build up or tear down. Once spoken, our words cannot be taken back. A permanent representation of what's in our hearts, our words reveal a lot about us. People who value their intelligence like to use many words, and sometimes struggle to get people to understand them. God's words are the ones we should be living by. If we only listen to the words that come out of our world, filtered through the imperfections of one another, we aren't following the word of God but the word of man (Act 5:29). Likewise, if we're only listening to another person's representation of God's word, we are actually hearing the **filtered** version of God's word. Second hand information is never really reliable, and when the salvation of our soul is in the balance, words are life and death. Reading the bible is the answer to learning God's word, but praying for understanding is important in comprehending how we can apply it's wisdom to our lives. Parables, stories, analogies, and allegories make up the lessons the bible teaches, and can be interpreted differently by different people. Speaking less offers us a greater opportunity to listen, and listening garners knowledge and information. When we listen wholeheartedly to another person's words, we must ask ourselves is this supportive of God's word, or mans?

If we aren't praying for a deeper understanding of God's word, we are setting ourselves up for a gross misunderstanding (Matthew 13:15). If we aren't reading the bible, we won't know the difference between God's word, and someone else's understanding of God's word. If we're really listening, we will know by their words if a brother or sister is with God, or still lost. We should be listening *more* than we speak, after all, we were given two ears but only one mouth.

Romans 10:17, NIV

17 Consequently, faith comes from hearing the message, and the **message is heard through the word about Christ.**

Psalm 119:73, GW

73 Your hands created me and made me what I am. **Help me understand** so that I may learn your commandments.

November 26

Jesus: Immortal Savior in a Mortal Body

John 14:6, ERV

6 Jesus answered, "I am the way, the truth, and the life. The only way to the Father is through me."

Jesus was a divine immortal spirit of God in a mortal body, was born of a human woman named Mary, and is our everlasting Messiah (John 10:30, Matthew 1:18-23)(Revelation 1:8). He came to preach the good news of the eternal kingdom of God, and to offer His life as a ransom for many (Matthew 20:28). Surrounded by the power of the Roman empire, Jesus and His disciples had an uphill battle spreading Christ's ministry, and were killed for it. Many people did not believe that God could take human form and walk among them, or be resurrected from death, and some still do not believe in Jesus to this day. People have trouble with trust and change, both of which our faith in God requires. The bible teaches that with God, all things are possible (Matthew 19:26). Believing in God's mighty power is more easily accessible when we're celebrating the birth of a child, or when we're watching mother nature's incredible beauty. Believing in God when we're suffering, or when we're watching someone we love suffer can be more challenging. Some people even believe that just believing in God should automatically make everything better in their lives. **Faith isn't a magic wand, it's a journey in change of spirit.** We derive comfort from our faith, and we strengthen our faith through our tribulations, this is how we grow in Christ. We praise God for the blessings He's given us through Jesus each day, and this shows God our love, through our devotion.

God sent Jesus to die on the cross for the sins of all humanity, the perfect and final sacrifice for those who would come to believe. This is why we pray to Jesus, and the bible reflects this in the passage above. There is no other way to Heaven, people, none. No matter how tough the bible is to understand, or accept, sometimes, we cannot add, change, or take away from what has already occurred and been said (Matthew 5:18, Revelation 22:18-19). By praying to *anyone else* we would be *departing* from the faith of Jesus Christ and making it into something it was never intended to be. There is no reason to complicate the already complicated, one either believes in Jesus or they don't. If they don't, there is no help for them, really there isn't (John 3:36). As followers of Christ, Jesus isn't *just* the way to eternal salvation, but the *template* for the perfect human being. We learn how to treat one another, how to pray, how to live our lives through His word and the scriptures from His disciples. Jesus asked His disciples to preach the world to 'All Nations,' (Matthew 28:19) meaning anyone who believed and renewed their spirit through Christ **Jesus** could be **saved**.

John 11:25-26a, ERV

25 Jesus said to her, "I am the resurrection. I am life. Everyone who believes in me will have life, even if they die. 26a And everyone who lives and believes in me will never really die."

John 15:5, ERV

5 Jesus said, "I am the vine, and you are the branches. If you stay joined to me, and I to you, you will produce plenty of fruit. But separated from me you won't be able to do anything."

November 27
Only Through Jesus

Romans 8:5-7, GW

5 Those who live by the corrupt nature have the corrupt nature's attitude. But those who live by the spiritual nature have the spiritual nature's attitude. 6 The corrupt nature's attitude leads to death. But the spiritual nature's attitude leads to life and peace. 7 This is so because the corrupt nature has a hostile attitude toward God. It refuses to place itself under the authority of God's standards because it can't.

Matthew 6:24, ESV

24 No one can serve two masters. Either you will hate the one and love the other, or you will be loyal to the one and have contempt for the other. You cannot serve God and mammon.

Some people are always going to be chasing after wealth, possessions, prosperity, affluence and abundance. Many people brag about being 'self-made,' and believe they deserve all they've managed to work to obtain, and more. If we're telling ourselves we just want to have some financial security, that we won't allow whatever fortunes we're able to acquire to corrupt our hearts, we're lying to ourselves. Other people don't think there is anything wrong with wanting to be 'comfortable.' These people either don't read the bible at all, or don't understand what they've read. The bible tells us that even chasing after, or wanting more of anything tangible that this world offers is chasing after sin, and not of God (James 4:4, 1 John 2:15-17). God provides all we require, and to want more is to court greed.

If we think we can pursue worldly comforts like wealth and status, and still able to stay in God's good graces, we're fooling ourselves. What Jesus is trying to tell us is that *truly* righteous people do not engage in materialistic pursuits of acquisition and profit, they pursue humility and modesty by following the life of Christ. Jesus Christ preached humility, self-control, modesty, forgiveness, and love. If we're chasing after an extravagant lifestyle we are greedy, selfish, and in love with worldly things, these things are not of God, and we can't go two opposing directions at the same time. This is why the pursuit of righteousness is a sacrifice, and filled with turbulence and persecution, and why not everyone is going to stick with it. Jesus also makes it pretty clear that if someone isn't with Him, they're actually opposing Him. To truly love Jesus is to do our very best, each day, to relinquish our desires for more holy choices, and become the people He calls us to be. Jesus teaches us all the way of righteousness, He forgives the repentant, He alone is our atonement and propitiation, He comforts, He sustains, and He alone will judge us (John 5:22). May we never grow weary of doing what is right in Christ's name, AMEN.

Matthew 12:30, NLT

30 Jesus said, "Anyone who isn't with me opposes me, and anyone who isn't working with me is actually working against me."

November 28
In the Righteous Hands of Jesus

Daniel 4:34-37, ERV

34 Then at the end of that time, I, Nebuchadnezzar, looked up toward heaven, and I was in my right mind again. Then I gave praise to God Most High. I gave honor and glory to him who lives forever. God rules forever! His kingdom continues for all generations. 35 People on earth are not really important. God does what he wants with the powers of heaven and the people on earth. No one can stop his powerful hand or question what he does. 36 At that time God gave me my right mind again, and he gave back my great honor and power as king. My advisors and the royal people began to ask my advice again. I became the king again—even greater and more powerful than before. 37 Now I, Nebuchadnezzar, give praise, honor, and glory to the King of Heaven. Everything he does is right. He is always fair, and he is able to make proud people humble!

It may not be much, but what we have we are protective over, whether it be our families, possessions, acquisitions or positions. Many people are reluctant to engage in a deeper devotion to God because they don't want to relinquish the control they think they have over their lives. Some people are content to say they 'believe' in God, but aren't comfortable discussing anything farther. Arrogant people don't think they need God, and turn away from Him (Psalm 10:4). Deceived by the world into thinking that being humble is the sign of a weak person, some never see that it takes a great deal of love and strength to deny what we want, and to put others before ourselves. We cannot pursue our own goals and desires, and still say we are following Jesus, we may be able to fool ourselves, but the Lord can't be fooled (Hebrews 4:13).

How we are remembered by others is secondary to how our souls are going to be perceived by our Lord, who has watched every move we've made, and heard every word that has come out of our mouths. Jesus is calling us to deny ourselves the things we want in our lives, and live a life **He's** called us to. Perhaps we're already doing what we were meant to, or perhaps the Lord has been trying to incorporate more charity, generosity, goodwill, or community service into our hearts. We can't follow the Lord, or abide by what He commands for us if we aren't paying attention. We must remain humble *despite* the world, pray often, repent for our sins, and listen to the Holy Spirit inside of us, guiding our thoughts to more wholesome and righteous choices. Trusting in Jesus brings direction, comfort, forgiveness, wisdom and love, and leads us to true righteousness. When we let go of our pride and arrogance, a peace envelops the heart as we rest in the faith that our lives are in the very capable, righteous hands of the Lord.

Matthew 16:24-26, ERV

24 Then Jesus said to his followers, "If any of you want to be my follower, you must stop thinking about yourself and what you want. You must be willing to carry the cross that is given to you for following me. 25 Any of you who try to save the life you have will lose it. **But you who give up your life for me will find true life**. 26 It is worth nothing for you to have the whole world if you yourself are lost. You could never pay enough to buy back your life."

November 29
Devotion Over Sin

Psalm 14:2, ESV

2 The Lord has looked down from heaven upon the sons of men To see if there are any who understand, **Who seek after God.**

Lamentations 3:25, ESV

25 The Lord is good to those who wait for him, **to the soul who seeks him.**

As humans, we can assume a great deal of knowledge without really understanding how it all fits together. The bible is layered, complex, and uses symbolism within its text, much like a secret code. We will never fully grasp all that God intended, and some people have more difficulty with this than they can admit. Following God is confusing, challenging, and, at times, frustrating! We are meant to be challenged, our faith journey to understanding our God is intended to be hard. All knowledge and understanding is a gift from God (Proverbs 2:6), we know what He allows us to. If we could become righteous on our own, through our own wisdom and acquired knowledge, or just sheer determination, then Jesus died for no reason (Galatians 2:21). God sent Jesus to save us, because nothing we could do on our own could (1 Corinthians 15:57).

Just how does Jesus make us right with God? People might think that believing in Jesus, trying not to sin, and praising God on occasion in church is sufficient to maintain our faith. Wrong. Jesus makes us right by cleansing, and renewing our spirits, and by the pain and trials we go through. Jesus' death gave us the Holy Spirit, which lives inside of us, guiding and educating us (Titus 3:5). When we listen, and abide by the Holy Spirit, we can learn, grow, and mature in our faith. Not everyone wants to listen, and many people have difficulty with abiding in anyone else but themselves, they don't accept correction through trials (Proverbs 1:7). When we learn how, or why we are sinning we can pray for the Lord to help us in that area, this is seeking Him. When we accept our faults, and genuinely *want* to be better people through Christ, we purify our thinking in this way. When we perform works of faith to the underserved or needy because it gives our spirit joy to help someone else, we are actively showing our devotion to God out of a heart that truly loves their neighbor as themselves. When we pray to the Lord for guidance and direction before we make a choice or decision, we are also actively showing our love and devotion to God by acknowledging His place in our lives. We are made incomplete, to need our God, that is the way He has designed things. Our devotion to improving, through Christ Jesus our Lord, making changes, repeated repentance for our ongoing sins, and giving Him praise and thanks are all the ways in which we **maintain** our devotion.

Acts 17:26-27, NASB

26 And He made from one man every nation of mankind to live on all the face of the earth, having determined their appointed times and the boundaries of their habitation, 27 **that they would seek God**, if perhaps they might feel around for Him and find Him, though He is not far from each one of us.

November 30

Got Faith?

Hebrews 11:6-7, 27-31, 39a, ERV

6 Without faith no one can please God. Whoever comes to God must believe that he is real and that he rewards those who sincerely try to find him. 7 Noah was warned by God about things that he could not yet see. But he had faith and respect for God, so he built a large boat to save His family. With His faith, Noah showed that the world was wrong. And he became one of those who are made right with God through faith. 27 Moses left Egypt because he had faith. He was not afraid of the king's anger. He continued strong as if he could see the God no one can see. 28 Moses prepared the Passover and spread the blood on the doorways of the people of Israel, so that the angel of death would not kill their firstborn sons. Moses did this because he had faith. 29 And God's people all walked through the Red Sea as if it were dry land. They were able to do this because they had faith. But when the Egyptians tried to follow them, they were drowned. 30 And the walls of Jericho fell because of the faith of God's people. They marched around the walls for seven days, and then the walls fell. 31 And Rahab, the prostitute, welcomed the Israelite spies like friends. And because of her faith, she was not killed with the ones who refused to obey. 39a God was pleased with all of them because of their faith.

We believe in one God, all-powerful, as the creator and guardian of our universe. There are so many important aspects of our daily lives that we know exist, but cannot see. Many powerful things in life are unseen, like gravity, wind, and human emotions, for instance. An all-knowing, omnipresent, and yet, unseen power, God is all around us, and a part of every aspect of our lives. Our faith is the strength of our belief that God hears us, and will never reject us (Deuteronomy 31:8). From the bible we are given many examples of people who were right in the eyes of God because of their acts of great faith. Rahab was a prostitute, and yet God saw her faith and saved her. Matthew was a tax collector, and socially despised, but was chosen by Jesus to be one of His disciples (Matthew 9:9-13). Great Historical figures aren't great because they were more talented, more learned in their faith, or less sinful, but because of the depth of their faith, and the purity of their hearts. Only God knows *why* someone sins, and how important He truly is to them (1 Samuel 16:7, Psalm 14:2).

We aren't guaranteed anything in life, and we can take many of our Heavenly Father's gifts for granted. Our capacity to learn, for instance, as well as our capacity to love, the force of nature, and the soul within us that makes us all individuals, are all invisible, gifts, from God. When we turn to the Lord for all of our needs, guidance, comfort, strength, wisdom, patience, grace, self-control, we show Him our devotion. When we turn to the Lord when we're hurting, suffering, waiting, doubting, oppressed, persecuted, wronged, grief-stricken, or without hope, we show Him our faith. When we feel we're lacking in a certain aspect of our lives, instead of turning to the world for answers we should be turning to Jesus Christ. Nothing this world can accomplish will ever come close to the power and grace of our Lord and Savior. Is **your** faith strong enough to ensure *you're* right with God?

December 1

The Key to Understanding

Genesis 6:5, ESV

5 The Lord saw that the wickedness of man was great in the earth, and that every intention of the thoughts of His heart was only evil continually.

Jeremiah 9:7, GW/ERV

7 So the Lord All-Powerful says, "A worker heats metal in a fire to test it **and see if it is pure**. I will **now refine them with fire and test them**. What else can I do for my dear people?"

Present in spirit form since the beginning of time as we know it, God created the universe and everything in it (Genesis 1:1-2). All humankind came from the first two humans (Acts 17:26), so when they disobeyed God, they cursed all that would come after them into perpetual sin (Romans 5:12). Humans ate from the tree of knowledge, the one tree in the Garden of Eden from which God instructed them not to (Genesis 2:16-17). From our youth, we long to make our own choices in life, having seized autonomy away from God in the Garden of Eden, so we naturally desire to go through our lives without regard to God's plan for us (Jeremiah 8:6, Ecclesiastes 7:29). And, it may seem as though we suffer through tribulations throughout our entire lives no matter what we do, this is because God is trying to purify our sinful hearts (Isaiah 48:10). God is in control of every aspect of our lives (Isaiah 45:7), having planned our course before we were born (Psalm 139:16), and is greater than the belief, or disbelief in our hearts (1 John 3:20). Jesus was sent to teach us all the truth about God's Heavenly Kingdom, what it's going to take for us to make it there, and to die as the perfect, and final, sin offering to His fledgling humanity (Hebrews 1:3, Matthew 28:18, John 7:16, John 3:16). It is through our belief in Jesus Christ that brings us closer to God in the way that He desires.

Although we are all brothers and sisters under one God (Genesis 9:18-19), not all of us have hearts that desire to be close to God (John 6:64). Many people just want to be comfortable in life, and don't want to substitute their quest for worldly comforts for the sacrificial, modest, humility the Lord desires from us (1 John 2:15). Many people don't invest in reading, and understanding fully, the bible in its entirety, so they don't know the full story (Matthew 22:29). In the bible, burnt offerings were accepted as atonement, or compensation, for sins committed (Leviticus 1:4). To understand God is to understand that He wants us to change our hearts and minds, instead of focusing on the sins we commit, and our penance for them (Hosea 6:6). Jesus came to explain this (Matthew 9:13). Many people don't realize that throughout our lives we will **all** be tested, we will **all** be judged, and at the end we will all be *sorted* (Matthew 13:40-43). Only God knows when this will happen (Matthew 24:36), and He desires all of us to turn back to Him in repentance. Jesus even warns us that many will NOT get to Heaven (Luke 13:23-24), and encourages us to follow Him' through learning and abiding by His commands (Matthew 16:24-26). God isn't just stern, frightening and final, He's loving, forgiving, and generous as well

(Deuteronomy 5:29, Job 5:18, Isaiah 45:22). **Pick up a bible,** and begin the lifelong journey to learning, **and understand**ing, all that **God** has intended for us, brothers and sisters. The Lord be praised for all His love, patience, and graciousness toward us all, AMEN.

Matthew 13:15, ERV

15 "Yes, the minds of these people are now closed. They have ears, but they don't listen. They have eyes, but they refuse to see. If their minds were not closed, they might see with their eyes; they might hear with their ears; they might understand with their minds. Then they might turn back to me and be healed."

December 2
Almighty God

Daniel 2:21-22, ESV

21 He changes times and seasons; he removes kings and sets up kings; he gives wisdom to the wise and knowledge to those who have understanding; 22 he reveals deep and hidden things; he knows what is in the darkness, and the light dwells with him.

Psalm 111:10, ESV

10 The fear of the Lord is the beginning of wisdom; all those who practice it have a good understanding. His praise endures forever!

As adult humans, we should have no excuse for not knowing the scriptures better. The only way to know God, know what He expects of our commitment to Him, and to know the good news of Jesus Christ is to read it in the bible. Aside from churches, in general, the world isn't designed with God in mind. Competition, greed, money and power is what drives and motivates the world economies, countries, laws, and struggles. In God's Heavenly kingdom, love for our neighbor, humility, forgiveness, and peace govern over all, and no one is excluded. Short-sided and selfish, many people are so focused on their own lives, their own turmoil, their own goals and needs that they don't have time to take an honest look at their relationship with God.

Mist over the stillness of a morning lake as the amber sun rises over the horizon, the beauty and majesty of an eagle soring over a lush, green canopy of trees sparks wonder and awe in many people. The soft, sweet grasp of a babies tiny hand over a grandparents weathered finger brings a tear to the eyes of scores of God's children. Witnessing the terrifying splendor of nature's whirling vortexes of wind and rain, the thundering rumble of the earth splitting, and the deadly churning of powerful seas both hypnotizes, bewitches and ignites fear in all of us. It was the hand of the creator that made all that surrounds us, supports us, and allows humanity to continue on. It is the creator that generates joy, strife, tears, majesty, pain and love, in the lives of all humanity. It was by His great and holy power that we live and breathe today, and in the very image of our almighty God. If that doesn't move you to a more obedient love for your God and creator, the Heavenly kingdom isn't right for you anyway.

Colossians 1:15-17, ESV

15 Christ is the image of the invisible God, the firstborn of all creation. 16 For by him all things were created, in heaven and on earth, visible and invisible, whether thrones or dominions or rulers or authorities—all things were created through him and for him. 17 And he is before all things, and in him all things hold together.

1 Peter 5:6, ESV

6 Humble yourselves, therefore, under the mighty hand of God so that at the proper time he may exalt you.

December 3
Fact or Fiction

Genesis 1:1-3, GW

1 In the beginning God created heaven and earth. 2 The earth was formless and empty, and darkness covered the deep water. The Spirit of God was hovering over the water.3 Then God said, "Let there be light!" So there was light.

Doctors and nurses help people to heal, teachers and professors educate, shopkeepers and tradespeople make and sell usable goods, and archeologists dig for tangible pieces of History. As we try to offer something to the world in trade for the things we need, we hope to feel relevant and useful along the way. Science plays an important role in helping us to understand the planet we live on, and can fuel the insight we need to improve our health and environment. Scientists and archeologists search for tangible clues they can touch and study that may reveal new discoveries about our ancient ancestors. Among old bones, pottery shards and remnants of old structures we can learn a great deal about the cultures of the past. Likewise, new discoveries in medicine and health can help create a better quality of life for everyone in the present age. While some people hold more faith in science, needing to have proof and reluctant to trust what they don't understand fully, others view science as an interesting but irrelevant component of our world that has nothing to do with faith in God (Hebrews 11:1-3). When scientific discoveries are uncovered, many people love to debate how the findings validate, or invalidate, the events written about in the bible. Finding actual ruins and remnants that resemble biblical cities is exciting to some, and at the very least interesting, but the *need* for this proof highlights the absence of faith.

No matter what we discover, or how we change our world, God's will is always going to be the bottom line, in the lives of believers and non-believers alike (Proverbs 19:21). True followers of Christ don't need to see the actual ruins of Sodom and Gomorrah to believe the message that we derive from the story: that we shouldn't want to turn away from righteousness, and to always obey God. Noah's ark doesn't need to be found, cataloged and turned into a major tourist destination for Christ-followers to remain steadfast to their covenant with God. When we pray and feel listened to, that's the Holy Spirit inside of us, and the Holy Spirit is from God through Jesus (Romans 8:9). Learning about our environment and our past is necessary to understand our History and, hopefully, avoid repeating mistakes made by those who've come before us. Nothing is going to stop the plan God has for us, no matter what we humans discover or uncover. The truths we set our convictions by, however, should always come from the word of God. After all, will we believe what man has built and said, or what God tells us?

Hebrews 11:1, ESV

1 Now faith is the assurance of things hoped for, the conviction of things not seen.

Hebrews 11:6 GW

6 No one can please God without faith. Whoever goes to God must believe that God exists and that he rewards those who seek him.

John 20:29, GW

29 Jesus said to Thomas, "You believe because you've seen me. Blessed are those who haven't seen me but believe."

December 4
A 'True' Follower

Matthew 7:4, GW

4 How can you say to another believer, 'Let me take the piece of sawdust out of your eye,' when you have a beam in your own eye?

Let me propose a question to you, would you know a fellow Christ follower if you saw one? People notice many things about one another, like their walk, the way they talk, the way they drive, or the way they order their coffee. Humans are social creatures, we want to bond with like-minded people, and want to feel secure in our surroundings. Someone's grace, patience, poise, or kindness is often overlooked amongst the hurried frenzy and self-serving, stubborn pursuit of one's own choices and desires. Most people will never know the amount of self-control, patience, or restraint it takes a follower to say or behave righteously in a situation. We are all tempted, under pressure, and probably more focused on ourselves than we really should be. Our focus should be on our walk with the Lord, our decisions, priorities, actions, behaviors and words aligned with His teaching. We really shouldn't be focused on another person's sins or choices, and how they relate to, or affect, our own. Even if we're wronged by someone else's sin we're asked to forgive, to turn the other cheek (Matthew 5:38-48). What's more, when we're focused on ourselves, or others, we're not focused on the Lord. More than that, when we put ourselves in the position of the judge we're putting ourselves in the position that rightfully belongs to the Lord.

Teasing someone behind their back, gossiping, making fun of someone else's differences or quirks, a silent desire for another, discord or arguing, pride in our appearance, the demand, or expectation of respect, and looking down on another, are all examples of how sin plays a role in our everyday lives. We may know that someone practices a sinful lifestyle by what we see and hear, but we cannot know how many times that person prays for repentance, and growth, in Christ daily. Maybe someone has committed a crime in their past, or they gamble, or they're battling addiction, are these people now unqualified for the exclusive club of people who are graced by Christ's love and salvation? Hey, no one is left out of Jesus' love, He calls all people to repent. Some people may think that just because they accept Jesus into their hearts, and they're trying hard to be a good person, that they're more pure than others. Wrong (Proverbs 30:12). Jesus calls all people to repent because, like it or not, all people are sinners (Genesis 6:12, Romans 3:10, Ecclesiastes 7:20). When we pass judgement on others, no matter the reason, we are hypocrites, because we sin too (Romans 2:1). So, the answer to the question, 'Would you know a fellow Christ follower?' Is that it shouldn't matter, because *everyone* deserves to be treated like a fellow Christ follower, with love, tolerance, and forgiveness.

James 4:11-12, ERV

11 Brothers and sisters, don't say anything against each other. If you criticize your brother or sister in Christ or judge them, you are criticizing and judging the law they follow. And when you are judging the law, you are not a follower of the law. You have become a judge. 12 God is the one who gave us the law, and he is the Judge. He is the only one who can save and destroy. So it is not right for you to judge anyone.

December 5

Wisdom: Changing Our Hearts and Minds

James 3:13-18, GW/ERV

13 Do any of you have wisdom and insight? Show this by living the right way with the humility that comes from wisdom. 14 But if you are bitterly jealous and filled with self-centered ambition, don't brag. Don't say that you are wise when it isn't true. 15 That kind of wisdom doesn't come from above. It belongs to this world. It is self-centered and demonic. 16 Wherever there is jealousy and rivalry, there is disorder and every kind of evil. 17 However, the wisdom that comes from above is first of all pure. Then it is peaceful, gentle, obedient, filled with mercy and good deeds, impartial, and sincere. 18 People who work for peace in a peaceful way get the blessings that come from right living.

Our intellects are crucial in helping us function effectively as we navigate our ever-changing environments. This brainpower helps us to understand, and recognize danger, how to interact successfully with others, and how and where to obtain the things we need. But, what is the difference between wisdom and intelligence, and, does it matter? Intelligence is knowledge, wisdom is the ability to put that knowledge into practical use. In the above verse from the book of James, chapter three, we are encouraged to show our wisdom by living humbly. All around us we see people thriving, successful, as we wonder when we'll have **our** turn to thrive. Envy, jealousy, pride, and the drive to compete with the status of another is unrighteous, and wicked according to the bible. Many of us read that and think to ourselves, "I'm glad I'm not envious," but many of us are just as guilty as the next person when it comes to wishing we had something that someone else has. Being appreciative for what we have is difficult when we're more focused on what we'd *like* to have.

Our world is the result of thousands of years of self-exploration, and the need to have things bigger, faster, more efficient, cheaper, and with less work. The result of our years of collective wisdom has created a humanity with the natural propensity toward dissention, hostility, defiance, and the need for independent autonomy apart from the Lord. People can be fascinating, but no one offers the perfection Jesus Christ offers. No matter how much someone loves us, only Jesus died for our spiritual salvation and eternal life. Completely opposite of the world we've created for ourselves, Jesus offers grace, patience, tolerance, acceptance, forgiveness, peace, and love. Humankind will always be imperfect, Jesus remains pure eternally. Wisdom is recognizing this, and reshaping our priorities accordingly.

True wisdom comes from the Lord, He gives us the ability to transform our lives from our intelligence (Proverbs 2:6). Learning from the mistakes the Israelites made, which is documented at length in the bible, and reading what Jesus and His disciples describe as righteous behavior is a good foundation for spiritual wisdom. However, just reading the bible, even *understanding* the bible, doesn't make us wise in the eyes of the Lord. Recognizing that the Lord has supreme control over every aspect of our lives, and fearing that He can change, eliminate, or alter anything He wants at any time is intelligence (Proverbs 1:7). What we do with this knowledge tells the Lord how wise we are in Him. Actually repenting, praying, remaining devoted to the Lord through ALL we experience, and learning what God wants from us *by those scriptures* is wisdom. Gracious Lord, grant us the knowledge to remain obedient to you, the hearts to desire so, and the wisdom to put that to use in our lives. AMEN.

December 6

Love, Honor, and Obey

Deuteronomy 13:4, ERV

4 You must follow the Lord your God. Respect him. Obey His commands and do what he tells you. Serve the Lord your God, and never leave him.

Proverbs 19:3, ERV

3 People ruin their lives with the foolish things they do, and then they blame the Lord for it.

Jeremiah 42:6, ERV

6 It doesn't matter if we like the message or if we don't like the message. We will obey the Lord our God. We are sending you to the Lord for a message from him. We will obey what he says. Then good things will happen to us. Yes, we will obey the Lord our God.

To not misunderstand, or misinterpret the scripture, while carrying a constant heir of humility and service in a world full of wickedness, following God's laws and commandments can seem extremely difficult at times. If God's expectations seem too difficult to be realistic, that's because they are. Through suffering, God tests us to see who places all their faith and devotion to Him, and who obeys His commands (Isaiah 48:10). When we are hurting, or frustrated, or lost, we are to rely on God, sending all our concerns through Jesus in prayer. Patiently we wait, then, and we don't rely on our own understanding or schemes (Proverbs 3: 5-6).

Our world is built on money, greed, and acquisitions, not on giving, service, and love as God's Heavenly kingdom is (Mat 20:25-28). Conceit, wealth, pride, arrogance, disrespect, lust, and opulent lifestyles are the status quo, and many people blindly follow this without regard to their salvation. We cannot call ourselves righteous if we *have no regard* for the *culpability* of our wicked behaviors, attitudes and lifestyles. We make our own choices, but who we're listening to, and what's motivating that choice determines how we're ultimately judged. Are we doing what **we** want to do, or are we doing what the **Lord** has *guided* us to? Not just our choices and decision making should we be trusting completely in the Lord, but in our everyday actions and words. We show the Lord our love by living the way He's asked us to (John 14:15), and His word has no expiration date. If the Lord says He's the beginning and the end, then this indicates there will be an end (Revelation 21:6-7). Will He judge us as faithful, or deviant to His Word?

Proverbs 19:16, GW

16 Whoever obeys the law preserves His life, but whoever despises the Lord's ways will be put to death.

Luke 6:49, ICB

49 "But the one who hears my words and does not obey is like a man who builds His house on the ground without a foundation. When the floods come, the house quickly falls down. And that house is completely destroyed."

December 7
Deceived

2 Corinthians 4:3-4, ERV

3 The Good News that we tell people may be hidden, but it is hidden only to those who are lost. 4 The ruler of this world has blinded the minds of those who don't believe. They cannot see the light of the Good News — the message about the divine greatness of Christ. Christ is the one who is exactly like God.

Proverbs 24:16, ERV

16 Good people might fall again and again, but they always get up. It is the wicked who are defeated by their troubles.

We all have troubles, sometimes financial, sometimes ethical, and still other times we find ourselves in a 'no-win' situation, caught between a rock and a very hard place. When we are under pressure it can be easy to become discouraged in our faith. Discouragement, disappointment, unmet expectations, and our own poor decisions can cause us to question whether God is really listening, or actually hears us each time we pray. If, sometimes, it feels like our prayers aren't being answered, it may be because they aren't. God sometimes won't listen to our prayers (James 4:3, Isaiah 59:2, John 9:31, Proverbs 28:9, Zechariah 7:11-13). If we want to be saved, and stay in the Heavenly family, we must exist humbly, and give praise and obedience to our Almighty God. Doing what we're told by our Heavenly Father, and creator, is only a difficult and painstaking task to those who are reluctant to relinquish their wickedness. God isn't going to reward bad behavior, and He knows who approaches Him with humility, and who is arrogant in their hearts. When we're corrected by God, we suffer. If we are stubborn to God's discipline, or reluctant to change or repent we will remain deceived, and because of our wickedness our prayers may not be heard.

Thinking we have more control over our lives, our successes, than we actually do, many people don't understand that they have always been under God's Sovereign power. Resistance is futile to our omniscient creator, we will either come to know and respect His power in our lives or die fighting it. Hell is described by Jesus as a place like a blazing furnace, where there will be weeping and gritting of teeth (Matthew 13:50), why would anyone want to risk going there? Pride and arrogance, wealth, respect from other people, and worldly conquests only lead to hell, and the salvation of our spirits should be worth more to us. If we repent for our sins, for our arrogance, our pride, our planning, and our poor decisions, we may be allowed to understand better how to change in the way God calls us to. God rewards good behavior, hearing the prayers of the righteous, by granting us grace, by enlightenment & wisdom, peace, and opportunities to those who are faithful to Him. When we remain humble *through* our trials, we can learn from them, and this brings a deeper awareness of our spiritual Father in Heaven. Trouble and pain are likely going to be uncomfortable, unpleasant, and trying, but we cannot let them turn us away from God.

2 Timothy 2:25b-26, ESV

25b God may perhaps grant them repentance leading to a knowledge of the truth, 26 and they may come to their senses and escape from the snare of the devil, after being captured by him to do His will.

Daniel 12:10, ERV

10 Many people will be made pure—they will make themselves clean. But evil people will continue to be evil. And those wicked people will not understand these things, but the wise people will understand them.

December 8

Repentance-Atonement-Penance

Proverbs 28:13, ESV

13 Whoever conceals His transgressions will not prosper, but he who confesses and forsakes them will obtain mercy.

2 Corinthians 7:10, GW

10 In fact, to be distressed in a godly way causes people to change the way they think and act and leads them to be saved. No one can regret that. But the distress that the world causes brings only death.

Stealing something that didn't ring up at the grocery store, lying, lusting for another in our hearts, vengeance toward another, bitterness toward God for pain suffered, and chasing after worldly comforts are common sins that can sneak into our lives. God calls us to repent, meaning to apologize and promise not to commit those sins again, and to be sincere about this in our hearts. this can be difficult, as we often commit the same mistakes over and over, repeating patterns of poor choices. Our human hearts require reconditioning to actually want to be righteous the way God calls us to be. We need to want to change for God's better version of ourselves to take shape. When we do what pleases us, it often doesn't please God, and something's got to give. We all make choices, and many of us don't even think about God when we make them. We all make mistakes (James 3:2).

Since the penalty of sin is death, according to God, the forgiveness of sins is an incredible gift (Romans 6:23). If we repent, and are forgiven, many people believe this gives them carte blanche to commit any sin they want. After all, we'll be forgiven anyway. We must actually try to avoid committing the sin we're asking repentance for, or we're not really sorry. God knows our hearts, He knows if we're really remorseful and seeking Him, or just seeking to clear a guilty conscience. We can fool others, we can even fool ourselves, but we cannot fool God. Unless we're humble, remorseful, and truly seeking God, we're still chasing sin and wickedness. Sin and wickedness leads to death, and eventually hell. God's eternal promise, God's word, and His love are far more powerful than the human stubbornness that prevents a deeper faith.

Acts 3:19, ESV

19 Repent therefore, and turn back, that your sins may be blotted out.

Isaiah 65:2, ERV

2 "All day long I stood ready to accept those who turned against me. But they kept doing whatever they wanted to do, and all they did was wrong."

December 9

One Spiritual Family

Proverbs 11:29, ESV

29 Whoever troubles His own household will inherit the wind, and the fool will be servant to the wise of heart.

1 Timothy 5:8, ESV

8 But if anyone does not provide for His relatives, and especially for members of His household, he has denied the faith and is worse than an unbeliever.

From the many conflicts of divorce, disputes over family events, stepparent issues, money, in-law quarrels, and the care of an elderly parent, family can be a source of great stress for many of us. Family members aren't chosen, we're born into a group of related people, and though we have the same DNA, we can all be very different people. Shaped by our environments, opportunities, and disappointments, we are all driven by different passions, boundaries, and dreams. God's word calls us to love, forgive, and do right by our family members. Some of the ways we can do this is making sure our family is provided for, loving and forgiving them, and helping them to stay faithful to Christ Jesus.

When we accept Jesus into our hearts, we become members of His chosen family, and we're called to be righteous (Galatians 3:29). By submitting to the Lord's cleansing, we learn of the iniquities we are called to leave behind. All of Christ's chosen people will be cleansed of their unrighteousness, and in this process we are all humbled. Because of our faith, we are one family under God, no shared DNA required. Our family is the body of people who are faithful and devoted to Christ Jesus. Not every member of our own families may want to devote their lives to Christ, and we're told wickedness and righteousness cannot coexist (2 Corinthians 6:14). We can urge family members to submit to the will of the Lord, we should certainly pray for them, but changing their heart must come from within themselves. We are all God's creation, and anyone who needs help should be helped, any way we **can** help them. We don't need to know all about their life to know that we should all be more loving, more forgiving, and more willing to help one another. No matter who joins our spiritual family, or who turns away from it, we are all Christ's, and we all have the same Father in Heaven.

Galatians 3:26-28, ERV

26-27 You were all baptized into Christ, and so you were all clothed with Christ. This shows that you are all children of God through faith in Christ Jesus. 28 Now, in Christ, it doesn't matter if you are a Jew or a Greek, a slave or free, male or female. You are all the same in Christ Jesus.

Ephesians 2:17-19, GW

17 He came with the Good News of peace for you who were far away and for those who were near. 18 So Jewish and non-Jewish people can go to the Father in one Spirit. 19 That is why you are no longer foreigners and outsiders but citizens together with God's people and members of God's family.

December 10
In His Own Words

Ezekiel 22:6-12, ESV

6 "Behold, the princes of Israel in you, every one according to His power, have been bent on shedding blood. 7 Father and mother are treated with contempt in you; the sojourner suffers extortion in your midst; the fatherless and the widow are wronged in you. 8 You have despised my holy things and profaned my Sabbaths. 9 There are men in you who slander to shed blood, and people in you who eat on the mountains; they commit lewdness in your midst. 10 In you men uncover their fathers' nakedness; in you they violate women who are unclean in their menstrual impurity. 11 One commits abomination with His neighbor's wife; another lewdly defiles His daughter-in-law; another in you violates His sister, His father's daughter. 12 In you they take bribes to shed blood; you take interest and profit, that is, profit that comes from charging interest to the poor and make gain of your neighbors by extortion; but me you have forgotten," declares the Lord God.

The bible makes it pretty clear, in the old testament (Genesis 6:5, Ecclesiastes 7:20), as well as the new (Romans 3:10, James 3:2), that humans are sinful, prone to making wicked choices by turning away from God. Over and over, the Lord asks people to repent (Isaiah 30:15, Acts 3:19), and return to Him (Ezekiel 18:32, Isaiah 44:22). Many people take the scripture laws of the old testament (Gen., Ex., Lev., Num., Deut.) and use them to categorize, condemn, label and exclude other people from their worship circles and communities. Anytime we categorize, condemn, label or exclude other people we are judging, and taking away from the fact that we are all children of the one, Almighty God, **all of us saved by Jesus.** Jesus didn't love one group more than another (Deuteronomy 10:17, Acts 10:34), He didn't exclude anyone (Mark 2:16-17, John 4:7-10), He didn't forgive one repentant sinner and ignore another (1 John 2:2), we shouldn't either.

The decency, and humility, of the human heart, or lack thereof, is the whole point of repentance in the eyes of God. Again and again, the Lord implores humankind to change their hearts, and in this way, their actions, words and behaviors. Quite frankly, *any* sin we commit takes our eyes away from God, as we're focused on ourselves, whether it's due to fornication, lust, greed, pride, envy, hate, or revenge. What we should all be focused on is the fear of God in our hearts, and His ability to determine our fates. We should also be aware of our sins, enough to feel badly that we've committed them, and enough to want to change ourselves for the better. We should always be aware of the power of God in our lives, and be thankful to Him for all that we have. We shouldn't use our sins against ourselves, or others, which only impedes progress, doesn't allow for forgiveness, and spreads hate. We all want to be loved, forgiven, included, and to feel relevant, so that's how we should treat others (Matthew 7:12). *When we read the bible in its entirety, we find that humility, love and repentance are the repeated themes, and that individual sins are merely the variable that reminds us all just how much we need our Lord and Savior.*

December 11

Looking for Love in All the Wrong Places

Exodus 20:5a, ERV

5a "You shall not worship them or serve them; for I, the Lord your God, am a jealous God."

Colossians 3:17, ERV

17 **Everything you say and everything you do** should be done for Jesus your Lord. And in all you do, give thanks to God the Father through Jesus.

We often tweet, chat, or text our circle of friends with our keen observances of common work, social, and environmental ques, eager to share our opinions on what we've seen, or heard, with our network of friends. We share common interests and goals with friends, attitudes, outlooks and concerns. When we're looking for love and affection, we often seek it from our spouses, family, or loved ones. It is our immediate family who see us behind closed doors, and often know about the private battles we all face. Many of us obtain our spiritual guidance from our local pastor, minister, reverend, priest, rabbi, or preacher, often in scheduled, weekly fellowship. Our jobs, our social circles, and our family provide a plethora of reassurances we often don't pay much attention to. In a million different ways, the people who are the closest to us reassure us daily that we are trusted, relevant, necessary, appreciated, heard, and loved.

Churches offer a place for fellowship, bible study, philanthropic works, and even spiritual counsel and guidance for those who are troubled and don't want to confide in close friends or family. However, if we say we are devoted to God, but we only seek Him through the opinions of others, in a setting not controlled by ourselves, and only a couple of times a month, how devoted are we, really? Often friends and close family are the ones who see us go through the trials of our lives, and we usually find their encouragement, advice, and trust a blessing. If we say Jesus is our rock and redeemer, but we only seek the counsel of our family and close friends when we're struggling or in pain, is He really?

Jesus tells us that anyone who chooses to follow Him must give up their own goals and desires (Luke 9:23), but He doesn't stop there. If we love God, believe in Jesus, and want to serve our Lord, we will accept His place as first in our lives. Putting God first means going to Him first for all of our spiritual guidance, conflict resolution, and personal reassurances. This means pursuing a relationship with the Lord outside of church, through reading the bible, prayer, and reflection. When we feel we don't have enough of something, whether it be patience, grace, opportunity, forgiveness, understanding, or humility, we first pray. Confiding in those we love, and trust is a beautiful expression of a shared love, but it shouldn't be our first instinct. God tells us that He is a zealous and jealous God, and seeks our devotion to Him (Deuteronomy 4:24, Luke 10:27). When we are truly placing God first in our lives, we are seeking His counsel first, over our jobs, our kids, our best friend, even our spouses. Lord, help us to seek you first, and to place you first in our hearts. Praise God through Jesus Christ, AMEN.

Luke 14:26, ERV

26 "If you come to me but will not leave your family, you cannot be my follower. You must love me more than your father, mother, wife, children, brothers, and sisters—even more than your own life!"

December 12
Healthy Boundaries

1 Timothy 5:13, ERV

13 Also, these younger widows begin to waste their time going from house to house. They also begin to gossip and try to run other people's lives. They say things they should not say.

Proverbs 20:19, ESV

19 Whoever goes about slandering reveals secrets; therefore do not associate with a simple babbler.

The bible teaches us to help one another, love one another and lift one another up in Christ, but not everyone wants, or thinks they need help. Not everyone will be saved, unfortunately, and we need to know when to move on. It is painful, but true, that not everyone will be willing to give up certain sins, or forgive others, or give up control of their lives to the Lord (John 12:48). Boundaries are important to our mental, physical, and emotional well-being, or, what we will and won't tolerate from others. In the bible we are told over and over again to love one another, to bear one another's burdens, and to forgive one another. As followers of Christ Jesus, we need to understand that not everyone will want help, to assist those who accept help, and pray for all.

Learning and growing in Christ can come from stories and advice of others, from the scriptures, and certainly from prayer. We are all imperfect, but we are all learning, and we all have something to offer to another. We should be treating one another the way we would *like* to be treated, as we are instructed in the bible (Matthew 7:12). Our actions are an extension of the convictions in our hearts; loving and forgiving others is understanding and respecting their boundaries, while contempt for others is arrogance. Some people may never be comfortable discussing Jesus Christ, we cannot force the Lord onto people who aren't accepting, but we can pray for them. We cannot impose advice onto people who don't want it, this causes dissention and distrust, but we can pray for them. A more open-minded heart, greater acceptance for others, and readiness to forgive is the new, righteous mindset we need to be operating from. Our boundaries will change as what we will, and won't tolerate from others changes, but we should *always* be praying for the salvation of those around us as well as ourselves and our loved ones.

1 Peter 3:8-12, ESV

8 Finally, all of you, have unity of mind, sympathy, brotherly love, a tender heart, and a humble mind. 9 Do not repay evil for evil or reviling for reviling, but on the contrary, bless, for to this you were called, that you may obtain a blessing. 10 For Whoever desires to love life and see good days, let him keep His tongue from evil and His lips from speaking deceit; 11 let him turn away from evil and do good; let him seek peace and pursue it. 12 For the eyes of the Lord are on the righteous, and His ears are open to their prayer. But the face of the Lord is against those who do evil.

December 13
Importance of the Bible

Ezekiel 33:5, ERV

5 They heard the trumpet, but they ignored the warning. So they are responsible for their own deaths. If they had paid attention to the warning, they could have saved their own lives.

Ezekiel 33:7-9, ERV

7 "Now, son of man, I am choosing you to be a watchman for the family of Israel. If you hear a message from my mouth, you must warn the people for me. 8 I might say to you, 'These evil people will die.' Then you must go warn them for me. If you don't warn them and tell them to change their lives, those evil people will die because they sinned. But I will make you responsible for their deaths. 9 But if you do warn the evil people to change their lives and stop sinning, and if they refuse to stop, they will die because they sinned. But you have saved your life."

Full of promises that don't ever end, warnings of life and death, and unspecified limits on time, the bible is mysterious, relevant, and still vital no matter what century we're reading it in. *The weight of the importance of the bible should be on one's spiritual guidance, and direction, and not a complete, literal, or even historical, anthology to set maps and charts by.* God tells us how He wants us to live, what He expects of His people, and His great love for us all through His relationship with the nation of Israel. What began as a local relationship between the only country who worshiped one supreme God, spread throughout the entire world by the gospel of Jesus' disciples (Matthew 24:14). When Jesus died on the cross, what was just Israel's ongoing spiritual relationship with God became a global opportunity for all who would come to know and follow Jesus. Following Jesus comes with tests of faith, trials of suffering, and blessings of unknown natures. In Ezekiel 33:7-9 we see that God requires specific things from us sometimes, and that failing to hear, or understand His warnings won't save us.

Truth is, only the mercy of Jesus can save us, any of us, all of us. Whoever believes in Jesus, follows Him, and lives righteously with love for others as themselves will have eternal life (John 5:24). Following Jesus' example sounds easier than it really is, because the world we live in is completely opposite of what Jesus values (James 4:4). Unless we understand what Jesus wants, what His life and ministry says, we live in a world of confusion masked by the devil's deceit. The bible is the word of God, and transcribed per His command, and given to humanity as a *code of ethics* to model our lives by (2 Peter 1:21). Although the bible was not meant to be a Historical timeline, rather, a collection of stories, lessons, and sermons, prayers and songs of praise that God wanted all of us to know and understand. In reading the bible, one can truly grasp the truth as God tells it, and not how man has interpreted it. Read on, pray, repent, and gain enlightenment in the name of the Lord. AMEN! Read on brothers and sisters.

Psalm 119:9, ESV

9 How can a young man keep His way pure? By guarding it according to your word.

Mark 13:31, ESV

31 "Heaven and earth will pass away, but my words will not pass away."

December 14
RECAP

God is in control of our lives, not us. We can only show Him how devoted we are to Him as we endure, learn, and grow in Him. Trust is fragile, but is the essential foundation to a solid faith that can withstand the pressures the Lord places upon us.

> Isaiah 45:5-7, NIV/KJ21
>
> 5 "I am the Lord, and there is no other; apart from me there is no God. I will strengthen you, though you have not acknowledged me, 6 so that from the rising of the sun to the place of its setting people may know there is none besides me. I am the Lord, and there is no other. I form the light, and create darkness; I make peace, and create evil; I, the Lord, do all these things."

Humility is opposite of pride, and required to be considered righteous in the eyes of the Lord. Most of us are more arrogant than we'd like to admit, assuming we have more control over our lives than we actually do. When we accept our station as subservient to the one, true, Almighty God, we place ourselves favorably before the Lord.

> Luke 14:11, ESV
>
> 11 (Jesus said) "For everyone who exalts himself will be humbled, and he who humbles himself will be exalted."

Jesus is the only way to be saved, and the only way to God, and eternal salvation. God came down to Earth in human form, to die for the sins of the humanity He created. As a result, the Holy Spirit was born, allowing us access to the one, true, Almighty God individually. An incredible gift for all who would come to believe.

> Philippians 2:5-7, CEV
>
> 5 And think the same way that Christ Jesus thought: 6 Christ was truly God, but he did not try to remain equal with God. 7 Instead he gave up everything and became a slave, when he became like one of us.

Following Jesus is the only way to true righteousness. As humans, we are fallible, imperfect, and prone to sin. Therefore, only Jesus can advocate to the Father for us, and is the only one we should be following. Other people can inspire us, and even help us on our life journeys, but no one can offer the forgiveness, salvation, and perfect example of righteousness that our Lord and Savior can.

> John 14:6, ESV
>
> 6 Jesus said to him, "I am the way, and the truth, and the life. No one comes to the Father except through me."

December 15
The Verdict

Luke 6:37, DLNT

37 "Do not judge, and you will not be judged; and do not condemn, and you will not be condemned; pardon, and you will be pardoned."

Hebrews 9:27, NASB

27 And just as it is destined for people to die once, and after this comes judgment.

Constantly assessing our physical environment for potential threats, as well as opportunities, we can form judgements and opinions on one another almost automatically. We can form judgements of other people simply based on their appearance, punctuality, speech, and one-time encounters. We are so comfortable in our judgements, we can be indignant when those expectations are unmet. In the bible we learn the God will have revenge for the wicked, not us (Hebrews 10:30). We also learn in the bible, that all judgement has been given to Jesus, who will sort us all out at the end of time (Matthew 25:31-46). Some people just aren't prepared to accept, let alone plunge into the depth, and many layers, of the Holy Bible. When we learn what is truly right according to God, we're able to see more clearly the mistakes we've made in our own lives.

Don't give in to the wicked. Many of us would accept this advice as an axiom, a no-brainer. What we, as a society, classifies as wicked may not be the same as God's description of wickedness, however. We have been living in a morally backward society for so long, it may surprise many to learn that the things the world values as important like knowledge, wealth, power, status, and control are completely opposite of the things God values (1 John 2:15-16). Instead of placing value on loud personalities, sharp opinions, conquest, and showy displays of wealth, the Heavenly Kingdom places value on self-control, modesty, peace, forgiveness, and humility. Many people would even be floored to learn that the world was in control of the devil (1 John 5:19), and has many people confused about a great many things (Luke 8:12). If all people read their bibles, all of society would know that wickedness according to God includes physical pleasures, pride, greed, stubbornness, loud opinions and crude humor, competition, deception, and wealth by example. We can all have difficulty seeing our own choices in that long list of biblical sins, but that doesn't mean we don't commit any (Jeremiah 17:9). Human judgement is naturally flawed, fueled by stereotypes, our personal desires, an unrighteous sense of justice, and individual prejudices.

The verdict: humanity has been sinful since we were created (Gen. 3:9-19), and because of that incident in the Garden of Eden all humans would be sinful continually (Genesis 6:5). As a result, God gives all good and bad in our lives (Isaiah 45:7), to see who will turn to Him (Psalm 53:2), and show Him true devotion.

James 4:12, ICB

12 God is the only One who makes laws, and he is the only Judge. He is the only One who can save and destroy. So it is not right for you to judge your neighbor.

2 Corinthians 5:10, ESV

10 For we must all appear before the judgment seat of Christ, so that each one may receive what is due for what he has done in the body, whether good or evil.

December 16
No Editing Required

Deuteronomy 6:13-14, GW

13 You must fear the Lord your God, serve him, and take your oaths **only in His name.** 14 Never worship any of the gods worshiped by the people around you.

Exodus 20:9-10a, ESV

9 "Six days shalt thou labor, and do all thy work: 10a But the seventh day is the sabbath of the Lord thy God: in it thou shalt not do any work."

All places of organized worship serve the purpose of housing a mass of people for celebrating and worshiping God, something many of us could all use more of in our lives. We have all seen beautiful, ornate statues of important religious people (Deuteronomy 4:16), and opulent furnishings, fancy religious dress robes, or gold furnishings in these places of worship. Silent meditation, songs of praise, scripture readings and sermons, reverence of various persons or objects, and prayer are all different ways people worship. People have accumulated many different customs, celebrated by different religious groups, causing many kinds of arguments. It's important to note, that anyone who doesn't dismiss God, or Jesus, entirely is another brother or sister in faith, and it's not our place to judge, label, or scorn them. We need to keep our focus on the Lord, not on the differing opinions, sins, or iniquities that we all have. In the bible, God makes it pretty clear that **He** is the only one we should be worshiping, and the way to do that is through Jesus (John 14:6). As a significant form of worshiping the one true, Almighty God, we should be praying to only Jesus. Many important people came before us with bravery and tremendous acts of faith, it can be difficult to avoid looking up to them. We all need to keep in mind, however, the difference between respect and gratitude, and revering, exalting, or *worshiping* other humans. The only person who lived completely sin-free was Jesus (1 Peter 2:22), and He is who we pray to, and model our lives by.

God asks a lot from humans, and many people give up, finding it impossible to follow all of His divine rules and commandments (John 6:64-66). Many of us can admit to working on the Sabbath, and not thought about it as being wrong in the eyes of God. Some people might think that the greatness in religious leaders provides a suitable replacement for Christ's example because they are more tangible and accessible (Jeremiah 17:5). Jesus instructs us to pray to our Father in private (Matthew 6:6, 7:13), emphasizing the personal nature of our relationship with God. We can't change God's rules, He is the only one we are to worship or revere, and His laws cannot be changed, tweaked, modified or ignored. Revering, idolizing, admiring are all synonymous with worship, and this is considered idolatry. Christ's life is all we should be admiring, revering, worshiping, and setting our lives by. Just because we are grateful for someone's works, or humbled by their sacrifice doesn't place them as better, or more worthy than Christ Jesus, our Lord and Savior. We read and understand Christ's life by reading about Him in the scriptures, and praying to Him through the Holy Spirit. We can't ignore verses because they're difficult to follow, and we can't ostracize groups of people who might also be devoted to God, but sin differently. Worship is a beautiful experience for faithful followers **to share**, and people like to celebrate differently. What should remain unchanged is our contrite devotion to our one Almighty God: we're either going to obey, or walk away. Choose wisely.

Revelation 22:18-19, GW

18 I warn everyone who hears the words of the prophecy in this book: If anyone adds anything to this, God will strike him with the plagues that are written in this book. 19 If anyone takes away any words from this book of prophecy, God will take away His portion of the tree of life and the holy city that are described in this book.

December 17
When Time's Up

Isaiah 24:19-20, ESV

19 The earth is utterly broken, the earth is split apart, the earth is violently shaken. 20 The earth staggers like a drunken man; it sways like a hut; its transgression lies heavy upon it, and it falls, and will not rise again.

If something we read in the bible sounds too farfetched to believe, it's alright to interpret it any way we like, right? Um, no. If the bible reads a little frightening, it's supposed to be. We only get one life, then we go through one death to face our one judgement. God shows no partiality, desires us all to repent, and see's all we do, this should frighten us, if only a little. Sometimes, the bible's allegorical and heavily symbolic prose leaves many people scratching their heads, arguing the meaning or moral code, or even walking away in disbelief or frustration. All life comes to an end, the bible assures us. Even taking symbolism into account, 'the earth will fall and never rise again,' is an ominous prophecy, at best. What are we to take away from this? God desires us to change our hearts and lives, and walk humbly in the shadow of Jesus (Micah 6:8, Matthew 11:29). We must ask ourselves, are we really taking seriously, and living up to, the standards set by God?

What does it take to really appreciate what we have in our lives? We've been given a chance at eternal life with our creator, where there is no more suffering or pain, despite our perpetual nature to sin. God gave us personal instruction on how to live and treat one another in the form of Jesus, and died for *all* of those who believe, serve, and love Him wholeheartedly. We are also given the Holy Spirit once we come to follow Christ Jesus, accepting Him into our hearts, which is our own personal piece of God inside our souls, guiding us to the right choices (Acts 2:38). If we're to achieve eternal life, we must repent, take heed to the warnings that have come before us. The bible's words are a guide, meant to both inspire hope and fear equally, and warns us all to live a life of service and love to God. Time is running out for us to turn our lives completely around, no halfhearted efforts or false platitudes, and show God we can be faithful to Him. 'Like a thief in the night,' is meant to inspire us to make the best use of our time here on earth. Every choice we make reflects the purity of our hearts, and we'll be held accountable for all we do and say (Matthew 12:36-37). *Only time will tell* if we're truly devoted to God, or just full of half-hearted deception.

2 Peter 3:9-10, KJV

9 The Lord is not slow in doing what he promised—the way some people understand slowness. But God is being patient with you. He does not want anyone to be lost. He wants everyone to change His heart and life. 10 But the day of **the Lord will come as a thief in the night**; in the which the heavens shall pass away with a great noise, and the elements shall melt with fervent heat, the earth also and the works that are therein shall be burned up.

December 18
The Fear of God

Psalm 33:6-11, ERV

6 The Lord spoke the command, and the world was made. The breath from His mouth created everything in the heavens. 7 He gathered together the water of the sea. He put the ocean in its place. 8 Everyone on earth should fear and respect the Lord. All the people in the world should fear him. 9 because when he speaks, things happen. And if he says, "Stop!" — then it stops. 10 The Lord can ruin every decision the nations make. He can spoil all their plans. 11 But the Lord's decisions are good forever. His plans are good for generation after generation.

The fact that God is the Almighty, all-knowing King of the universe isn't much of an argument, most people would accept that there is a higher power in the lives of all humans. From here, though, people's beliefs stem in all directions from the completely devout, to the non-believer. Some people believe the meaning they derive from scriptures whole-heartedly, while others incredulously focus on trying to prove that the events described actually took place. Even though the bible was written by men, admitted sinners, these men were spoken to by God, visited by God or angels on His behalf, and others spent spiritual time, or actual time training with Jesus personally (2 Peter 1:16-21). The authors of the bible were called by God to fulfill His purpose so that we could all partake in the knowledge, the good news, of God's word for every generation. (Matthew 24:35).

God loves all of His creation, which includes all humans, and His intention is to cleanse us all of our sins (Jeremiah 9:7). When we do something the Lord doesn't agree with, we are punished, and our lives get more tumultuous and difficult to manage. Stress, trouble, pain, disappointment and failure greet us when we stray from the Lord's will. The bible has been warning humans of their despicable behavior since we first sinned on 'page one' of the bible, in Genesis (Gen. 3). It shouldn't be a surprise to learn that we do many things wrong in the eyes of God, and that we need His forgiveness, grace, and blessings to complete a fulfilling life **in Him**. When we refuse to accept God's will, become angry, or bitter from the punishment we receive from Him we are only bringing on more darkness and strife. This is because when we stubbornly refuse to humble ourselves before the Lord we're foolishly *turning away* from God's grace and forgiveness. Living in fear of the Lord means we understand and respect God's Sovereign power, and we willingly submit to His grace, as well as His correction.

Hebrews 12:25-26, ERV

25 Be careful and don't refuse to listen when God speaks. Those people refused to listen to him when he warned them on earth. And they did not escape. Now God is speaking from heaven. So now it will be worse for those who refuse to listen to him. 26 When he spoke before, His voice shook the earth. But now he has promised, "Once again I will shake the earth, but I will also shake heaven."

Proverbs 1:7, ESV

7 The fear of the Lord is the beginning of knowledge; fools despise wisdom and instruction.

December 19
Good Fish, Bad Fish

Matthew 12:36-37, ESV

36 (Jesus said) "I tell you, on the day of judgment people will give account for every careless word they speak, 37 for by your words you will be justified, and by your words you will be condemned."

Matthew 13:41-43, 47-49, ERV

41 (Jesus said) "The Son of Man will send His angels, and they will find the people who cause sin and all those who do evil. The angels will take those people out of His kingdom. 42 They will throw them into the place of fire. There the people will be crying and grinding their teeth with pain. 43 Then the godly people will shine like the sun. They will be in the kingdom of their Father. You people who hear me, listen. 47 Also, God's kingdom is like a net that was put into the lake. The net caught many different kinds of fish. 48 It was full, so the fishermen pulled it to the shore. They sat down and put all the good fish in baskets. Then they threw away the bad fish. 49 It will be the same at the end of time. The angels will come and separate the evil people from the godly people."

In this last passage we can derive several facts according to the words spoken by Jesus to His disciples in the book of Matthew. Referring to 'the end of time' is a phrase thrown around by lovers and other poets, but few people understand the concept of life on earth ceasing to exist. Repeatedly, we are clued in by Jesus about the mortality of the planet we all call home (Matthew 5:18, Mark 13:31, 2 Peter 3:10). Instead of focusing on the doomsday scenario, Jesus warns us to prepare our **souls** (Hebrews 12:1-2). We are all sinners, and If we aren't repenting, we aren't going to be forgiven (Luke 13:3, Acts 17:30). When our hearts are full of remorse and shame for the wrong we've done, God see's that in our hearts.

From the above passage we are also informed that we will all be collated, sorted, and classified into one of two groups of people at our final judgement based on how we lived our lives. We are told we will either be seen as wicked and sinful, or we are going to be seen as godly. The bible repeatedly calls us to change the way we live, (2 Peter 3:9, 2 Chronicles 7:14, Isaiah 55:7) and offers plenty of scripture telling us how to live right (Isaiah 1:17, Matthew 22:37-40, Matthew 5:3-12). We should, therefore, do what our creator has told us to do, or we are guilty of submitting to wickedness. Jesus tells us that if we're not for Him, we're against Him, so even if we believe in Jesus as our Messiah we still need to repent. It isn't our belief alone that saves us, but knowing we must live a holier, more righteous life as Jesus calls us to (Mark 8:34). We are only given a finite, and unknown, amount of time to devote our hearts to Jesus, and there are many distractions and temptations along the way. At the end of our lives, will we be classified as godly, or tossed out with the rest of the 'bad fish?' Pray on, be humble, repent, and repeat, AMEN!

Matthew 12:30, ERV

30 (Jesus said) "Whoever is not with me is against me. And anyone who does not work with me is working against me."

December 20
Heartbreak and Fairness

Matthew 5:3-4, ESV

3 Jesus said, "Blessed are the poor in spirit, for theirs is the kingdom of heaven. 4 Blessed are those who mourn, for they shall be comforted."

Matthew 5: 21, ESV

21 Jesus said, "You have heard that it was said to those of old, 'You shall not murder; and whoever murders will be liable to judgment.'"

Faith is difficult. We all suffer setbacks and anguish in our lives, but sometimes we suffer unimaginable pain that leaves us devastated beyond any reasonable repair, and can sometimes make us question or even walk away from our faith. We all know someone who has been touched by death, maybe we, ourselves have suffered the loss of someone we care about. Losing someone always hurts, their absence replaced by memories that don't quite fill the holes left behind in our hearts. All death is sad for those left behind, but some deaths are more unexpected, tragic or, difficult to process when a crime or act of violence has been committed. Murder, rape, suicide, cancer, Alzheimer's, drunk drivers and other ghastly harbingers of death hover over our world like an ominous cloud of injustice. Human beings have an innate sense of justice that isn't always congruent with our God and creators idea of justice, but we have more trouble with this fact than God does.

When someone we love is taken from us we feel a range of mixed emotions from gut-punched, lost, devastated, and sad, to angry, confused, vengeful and outraged. Life doesn't seem fair, and is sometimes just down right cruel, so where does God stand in the midst of all this tragedy? Humans can't define or understand God's justice as a simple cause and effect, clearly defined, specific and outlined punishment fits the crime, every situation, every time, practice of divine order. God sees things we cannot. Our world makes it pretty clear that not every cancer patient, or rape, or suicide victim will die, and not every murderer will receive the same punishment. Good people suffer while sometimes sinful people seem to thrive, and it can be easy to feel left behind, forgotten, and forsaken. The bible explains that humans will be constantly tested, and do not fully understand God; His will is going to be done despite the level of someone's individual faith in Him. What the bible does assure us of is that *every* human falls short in the eyes of God, that He accepts repentance, grants mercy *and* forgiveness to all that seek it. God is loving, will judge us all on an individual basis, and asks all to come to Him as our main source of comfort. All lives will have both blessings and strife, according to the bible, and this is going to look different in each person's life. God calls us all to seek Him, for comfort, guidance, repentance, and mercy no matter *what* He plans for our lives.

Jeremiah 17:10, ERV

10 "But I am the Lord, and I can look into a person's heart. I can test a person's mind and decide what each one should have. I can give each person the right payment for what they do."

December 21
A Perpetual State of Learning

Romans 3:19-20, 28, 31, ICB

19 The law commands many things. We know that those commands are for those who are under the law. This stops all excuses and brings the whole world under God's judgment, 20 because no one can be made right with God by following the law. The law only shows us our sin. 28 A person is made right with God through faith, not through what he does to follow the law. 31 So do we destroy the law by following the way of faith? No! **Faith causes us to be what the law truly wants.**

1 John 2:6, ICB

6 Whoever says that God lives in him must live as Jesus lived.

When we are explaining something to someone else it can be easy to feel smarter, especially if they're not readily understanding us. Similarly, if we're polite and gracious but still feeling superior in our minds, we're displaying arrogance in the eyes of the Lord. No one is better than anyone else, we just have different skills and talents (Romans 2:11). Even if we just think unwholesome thoughts but never act on them, we are still guilty in the eyes of God (Matthew 5:27-28). God's rules govern our moral code of living, how we should love and treat one another. If we believe in God, if we *love* God, we should want to purify ourselves like He's asked us to (1 Peter 1:15-16, 1 John 3:3). We can't ignore the laws and commandments just because they were written long ago, morality laws that are meant to guide humanity don't expire.

Many of us can admit we don't discuss the commandments often, or at all, and not all of us have passed them on to our children, or family (Deuteronomy 6:6-7). Some people behave as if God's commandments are more important than their devotion to Him. God's commands can show us how to behave, and in doing so highlights what we're each doing wrong. In learning what we've done wrong, we see that we're in need of a Savior, and this is what should fuel our devotion to the Lord. Those that *are* aware of what God is asking of us, many have come to realize that no one can follow **all** of God's rules **all** of the time. If we care about our relationship with God we should feel badly enough about our sins to try and do better by Him. We are meant to feel bad about our sins, and return to the Lord with sincere hearts. If we don't know and fully understand God's commandments, then we won't know when we're breaking them. In this way, our repeated sins, or our lack of trying to improve shows we're not really sorry. If we're only repenting because we know we have to, or because it'll clear our guilty conscience, this is self-preservation, and a sin. Since the bible was written thousands of years before we were all born, and it applies to all humans, and doesn't expire, not one of us has a legitimate reason for **not** knowing the word of God. When we suffer, we learn. Whether we committed a sin and are being disciplined, or our faith is being tested, we are all in a perpetual state of learning under **God's** control, direction and will.

1 Corinthians 10:23, GW

23 Someone may say, "I'm allowed to do anything," but not everything is helpful. I'm allowed to do anything, but not everything encourages growth.

December 22
Sit Back, and Leave the Driving to God

Proverbs 16:1, ICB

1 People make plans in their hearts. But only the Lord can make those plans come true.

Jeremiah 23:23-24, ICB

23 "I am a God who is near," says the Lord. "I am also a God who is far away." 24 "No one can hide where I cannot see him," says the Lord. "I fill all of heaven and earth," says the Lord.

Who and what are we living our lives for? We are teachers, politicians, healers, peacekeepers, stock brokers, firemen and women, and chefs. We are also parents, children, bosses, aunts and uncles, humans bring meaning and service into their lives in many ways. Are we doing what we are because that's what we want to do, or because something larger from within us 'compelled' us to do the work we do? What we strive for in our lives tells us what motivates us—do we search for the comfort and security the world provides, or are we searching for spiritual growth in Christ? Despite what we may think, we cannot have both (James 4:4). We would all like a nicely padded nest to live in, but everything on earth is temporary, we cannot take anything with us when we die. Some people are content to seek worldly comforts thinking they might as well be comfortable while they're here, not thinking this has anything to do with God. We are called to trust in the Lord for everything, to be content with what we're given, and not to go looking for more anywhere else.

Something larger than ourselves is trying to drive our lives, and if we let it, God will bring us to a potential we could never reach on our own. Submitting to the Lord is required if we want our souls to live forever, and eventually go to Heaven. When we trust in man, we suffer under a curse from God, and we don't really have to know what that is to know it's probably unpleasant. God is going to have His way in our lives (Jeremiah 10:23), and the more we struggle with this the more unpleasantness we bring on ourselves. Just because He doesn't appear before us, or speak to us from the shadows of our bedrooms, doesn't mean He isn't aware of absolutely everything. Human stubbornness and pride continue to separate people from God. No matter what God gives us or presents us with, we still need to do the work. What we have may have come from our hard work, but the opportunity as well as the grace to fulfill it was from God. Until we all come to learn and understand this, we will continue to be corrected and redirected by God.

Jeremiah 17:5-6, ICB

5 this is what the Lord says: "A curse will be placed on those who trust other people. It will happen to those who depend on people for strength. Those are the ones who have stopped trusting the Lord. 6 They are like a bush in a desert. It grows in a land where no one lives. It is in a hot and dry land with bad soil. They don't know about the good things that God can give."

December 23
Steadfast Faith

Matthew 4:1-10, ESV

1 Then Jesus was led up by the Spirit into the wilderness to be tempted by the devil. 2 And after fasting forty days and forty nights, he was hungry. 3 And the tempter came and said to him, "If you are the Son of God, command these stones to become loaves of bread." 4 But he answered, "It is written, "'Man shall not live by bread alone, but by every word that comes from the mouth of God.'" 5 Then the devil took him to the holy city and set him on the pinnacle of the temple 6 and said to him, "If you are the Son of God, throw yourself down, for it is written, "'He will command His angels concerning you,' and "'On their hands they will bear you up, lest you strike your foot against a stone.'" 7 Jesus said to him, "Again it is written, 'You shall not put the Lord your God to the test.'" 8 Again, the devil took him to a very high mountain and showed him all the kingdoms of the world and their glory. 9 And he said to him, "All these I will give you, if you will fall down and worship me." 10 Then Jesus said to him, "Be gone, Satan! For it is written, 'You shall worship the Lord your God and him only shall you serve.'"

Sometimes, just when all is going well with Christ, we're praying regularly, trying to speak less wickedness, another challenge, a pressure placed upon us when we least expect it sucks every last ounce of grace right out of us. Life is a series of challenges, and God is relentless in His pursuit of cleansing our unrighteousness in preparation for our final judgements. Whew! Just when we can't handle one more crisis, we learn something else that stops us dead in our tracks. Where is God at this moment, some of us ponder? A good thought is Jesus, He is always the answer. When we're mad, we need to take a deep breath and realize we're being challenged. Now we must ask ourselves, how do we want to handle this situation? We should want to handle it by handing it over to our Lord, with the understanding that things happen according to His purpose, and not our own. When we're worried, overwhelmed, or panicked, we need to remember that the Lord is faithful to hear all of His sheep who are lost, hurt, or in distress (Luke 15:4 -7).

How we handle ourselves through, and in the midst of a crisis reveals who we truly have our faith in. If we're faithful to God, and truly believe in Him, we will naturally want to pray. When we pray with an abundance of emotion we need to remember these feelings too will pass, but our words cannot be taken back. It is always a good idea to begin and end a prayer with thanks and praise to the Lord for all He's done, and keep our concerns short and sincere (Matthew 6:7). When Jesus walked the earth He too was tempted, and put through physical, emotional, and spiritual stresses. No stranger to suffering, Jesus was beaten, mocked, and paraded through town with a crown made of thorns (John 19:1-7). Through it all, Jesus preached the word of God, performed miracles, and remained sin-free and completely devoted to God. We aren't ever going to be like Jesus, but we're expected to genuinely want to, and we're expected to try, no matter what.

December 24
Our Shepherd

Ezekiel 34:11-12, 15-16, GW

11 This is what the Almighty Lord says: "I will search for my sheep myself, and I will look after them. 12 As a shepherd looks after His flock when he is with His scattered sheep, so I will look after my sheep. I will rescue them on a cloudy and gloomy day from every place where they have been scattered. 15 I will take care of my sheep and lead them to rest, declares the Almighty Lord. 16 I will look for those that are lost, bring back those that have strayed away, bandage those that are injured, and strengthen those that are sick. I will destroy those that are fat and strong. I will take care of my sheep fairly."

Of all the animals mentioned in the bible, the lion sounds more attractive, the jackass sounds more appropriate, but the sheep is used to represent humanity. Full of pride and arrogance, the human race leans toward carving their own rules of justice, often forgoing morality for wealth and conquest. It's no wonder, then, that God pleads with us to repent and be reformed, or be destroyed. We are His creation, so He makes the rules, many humans still haven't gotten past this very, simple fact. Hey, we aren't as superior as we think we are, God *only allowed* us dominion over all the creatures of the earth (Genesis 1:29-30). He also set rules for us to follow, which we disobeyed almost immediately, forever fracturing the trust between God, and His humanity. We brought our discipline on by disobeying, because we didn't like, or didn't fully trust God's rules. Being able to take care of oneself, and not being a burden for another, but to be in a better position to help another in need, is the righteous version of independence. Retooling, reshaping, or rewording the divine message God is sending just to suit our own personal needs and ideas is arrogance, and a sin.

Our shepherd, Christ Jesus, looks after our spirits through the use of the Holy Spirit (John 14:26). Guiding our moral thoughts, and effecting the outcome of our actions, decisions, attitudes and words, the Holy Spirit creates and removes barriers in order to guide us on the path of true righteousness. When we're lost, we are put in positions where we are reminded of our need for Christ, whether we need His guidance, His comfort, His rules, His mercy, His grace, His strength, His power, or His forgiveness. We need to be humble, and remind ourselves of this often, because we cannot be in a position to pray for anything without humility (1 Peter 5:6). Once we realize our futility, our need for a divine presence to watch over us, we can pray. Repenting for our sin, our arrogance, our lack of faith through prayer is always the first, best step toward a stronger relationship in Christ. On the other side of the Lord's correction, reforming and discipline is His justice, mercy, healing and abundant love that awaits all who are patient through their affliction.

John 10:11, GW

11 "I am the good shepherd. The good shepherd gives His life for the sheep."

John 10:27-28, KJV

27 "My sheep hear my voice, and I know them, and they follow me: 28 And I give unto them eternal life; and they shall never perish, neither shall any man pluck them out of my hand."

December 25
The Love of God

1 Corinthians 13:4-7, GW

4 Love is patient. Love is kind. Love isn't jealous. It doesn't sing its own praises. It isn't arrogant. 5 It isn't rude. It doesn't think about itself. It isn't irritable. **It doesn't keep track of wrongs**. 6 It isn't happy when injustice is done, but it is happy with the truth. 7 Love never stops being **patient**, never stops believing, never stops hoping, never gives up.

1 John 4:9-10, CSB

9 God's love was revealed among us in this way: God sent His one and only Son into the world so that we might live through him. 10 Love consists in this: not that we loved God, but that he loved us and sent His Son to be the atoning sacrifice for our sins.

Humans are capable of many kinds of love; we love our families, our friends, our pets, our spouses, and of course, our Lord and Savior. The way we express each kind of love is different based on customs, differences in cultures, differences in relationship norms, and degrees of faithfulness. God is the ultimate example of love, sending Jesus to be the appropriation for the sins of all humanity. The bible explains what love is, and what it isn't, and the depth of human emotion can certainly complicate our perceptions of love. The bible explains that our first love should be for God (Matthew 22:37-39).

Dynamic and ever-changing, our emotions can often influence our choices, and these stem from the desires of our heart. We all want to feel accepted, appreciated, and relevant to others, we all want to be **loved**. God offers us tough love, purifying our naturally sinful hearts with one's that are more contrite, one's that seek Him (Ezekiel 36:25-27). If we love someone, no matter what kind of love it is, we should be **faithful** to that love. Many people get into trouble when they give into seduction, lust, and physical impulses, which come all too naturally to all of us. Scientifically speaking, love, attraction, and even lust, are all caused by the release of hormones in our brains: and we can't control what our hormones do. What we *can* control, is how we treat one another.

No matter what kind of love we're talking about, trust, faithfulness, kindness, patience, and forgiveness are the nutrients that fortify, and sustain, our love. Even if we disagree with our loved ones, we display tolerance, understanding, and forgiveness, without thinking our thoughts or beliefs are superior. We do this *because* we love them. This is the example that Jesus gave us, that we forgive, and accept one another **despite our imperfections**, because His divine **love** paid the price for **all** of our sins.

1 John 4:7, GNV

7 Beloved, let us love one another: **for love cometh of God**, and everyone that loveth is born of God, and knoweth God.

Isaiah 54:10, GNV

10 For the mountains shall remove, and the hills shall fall down; but my mercy shall not depart from thee, neither shall the covenant of my peace fall away, saith the Lord, that hath compassion on thee.

December 26
All Love

1 John 4:7-8, ESV

7 Beloved, let us love one another, for love is from God, and whoever loves has been born of God and knows God. 8 Anyone who does not love does not know God, because God is love.

Deuteronomy 7:9, ESV

9 Know therefore that the Lord your God is God, the faithful God who keeps covenant and steadfast **love with those who love him and keep His commandments**, to a thousand generations.

Love is an ambiguous, complicated word, representing many different kinds of emotions, levels of commitment, and not always guaranteed to be reciprocal. Family love, parent and child love, spousal love, and friendship are all very different forms of love. We all show our love in different ways, through kindness, commitment to one another, forgiveness, understanding, and sometimes physical contact in the form of hugs, handshakes, or kisses. There are certainly forms of physical contact that aren't really loving, but sinful, and people interpret this differently. Certainly, adultery, fornication, or any other type of *uninvited* physical contact isn't really love, but lust. However, according to the bible, anything that doesn't include a commitment, anything done *outside* of the sanctity of a marriage, or desiring something that belongs to another, is considered lust. (Hebrews 13:4, Colossians 3:5) In a faithful, loving, monogamous relationship, where two devoted people commit themselves to Christ, there is no such thing as 'sinful love,' for All love is from God. All relationships take effort, and not everyone puts in the same amount of effort, not everyone has a pure heart. Only God knows what someone's true level of commitment is, because only the Lord knows what's really in our hearts (Jeremiah 17:9-10).

Love and commitment are synonymous, no one wants a *temporary* loving relationship. People in committed relationships are loyal to one another through both good, and not so good times. People in committed relationships are loving, forgiving, and supportive to their friends, family, and loved ones. People who don't truly love aren't loyal, or supportive, or forgiving (1 Corinthians 13:4-8). All of us are capable of love in some form, as well as forgiveness, and judgement only comes from ignorance and arrogance. If two people love each other, even if they're from different cultures, races, or backgrounds, then it's the commitment they share and bring before God that truly matters. It's this principal, along with the commitment to loyalty, that can only come from real love that truly matters, not their race, or sex, or cultural background, or personal history. We aren't capable of judging another's relationship, we can't know another's level of devotion to the Lord, and we shouldn't try to think of one another as rivals. Not all sinners will welcome Christ, but all sinners who *do* welcome Christ shouldn't be excluded because of their sins (Matthew 12:31-32). After all, we should be focused on loving and forgiving one another, and forwarding Christ's message, not focused on sin and dissention.

1 John 4:16, ESV

16 So we have come to know and to believe the love that God has for us. God is love, and whoever abides in love abides in God, and God abides in him.

December 27
Christat Will Judge Everyone

John 5:22 , ESV

22 The Father judges no one, but has given all judgment to the Son

Hebrews 9:27, ESV

27 And just as it is appointed for man to die once, and after that comes judgment.

Proverbs 15:3, ERV

3 The Lord sees what happens everywhere. He watches everyone, good and evil.

Our world has a category for everything, labels and brands for clarification, a group or genre for every type of person, and prefers to have things in nice, neat, predictable packages. We like to think we control our own destinies, and can't help but find ourselves looking around to others, comparing what *we* have to what we think *they* have. Some of us compare ourselves to others, wondering if we're doing things right, while other people like to see how much they've accomplished compared to another. Anytime we're focused on *ourselves*, or *other people*, we're taking our hearts away from Christ. If we truly love the Lord, then we know that all we have is because of **His will**, and we can live with knowing we'll never be forsaken by Him. It's only when we're *not sure* if God will deliver to us all that we desire that we go seeking it in the world around us, and *this* is sin. Focusing on others causes us to feel other forms of wickedness like envy, pride, deceit, competition, judgment and gossip. Building one another up, praising God in fellowship or worship, forgiving another, or helping another strengthen their faith are all ways we can help our brothers and sisters instead of putting a stone in their path to stumble over.

Just because we can't see the Lord watching over us doesn't mean He isn't. We're expected to work diligently at being more righteous on our honor. Not only does the Lord see all we *do*, but He sees all that's in our hearts, He knows if we're faking it (Proverbs 21:2). Since Christ has the final judgement on all of us, we should be focused on pleasing Him and not everyone in our world. If we're *following* Christ, we'll be exhibiting the loving, patient, graceful, service-oriented kindness that will make people feel loved. Competition is a creation of our world, and pits brother against brother to highlight one's superiority. No one human is more superior to another in the eyes of God, only the devil spreads dissention among Christ's followers. We *cannot* judge another, because we don't have the authority to, because God will use our own judgements against us, and because we sin also. Just because someone sins differently doesn't mean they're better, or worse, than another. We are all on a journey with Christ, some closer than others, but we're **all** lost, sinful sheep in His flock.

Romans 2:1-3, GW

2 No matter who you are, if you judge anyone, you have no excuse. When you judge another person, you condemn yourself, since you, the judge, do the same things. 2 We know that God's judgment is right when he condemns people for doing these things. 3 When you judge people for doing these things but then do them yourself, do you think you will escape God's judgment?

December 28
You Are Not Alone

Ezra 10:4, ESV

4 "Arise, for it is your task, and we are with you; be strong and do it."

Psalm 23:4, ESV

4 Even though I walk through the valley of the shadow of death, I will fear no evil, **for you are with me**; your rod and your staff, they comfort me.

Galatians 2:20, ESV

20 I have been crucified with Christ. It is no longer I who live, **but Christ who lives in me**. And the life I now live in the flesh I live by faith in the Son of God, who loved me and gave himself for me.

It can be difficult to feel like Christ is with us sometimes, our lives can be fraught with disappointment, difficulty, and painful experiences. Our prayers don't always feel answered, hope can be a struggle some days, and we often have more questions than answers when it comes to God and our faith. We are never alone when struggling to understand our relationship with God better, or in thinking you're in the shrinking minority of people who are actually trying to put God first in their lives. Faith is trust, and that takes time to develop. God is spirit, and our relationship with Him is something that is not easily understood. It can be difficult to know what the truth is, with many different avenues of thought available in the world to provide answers that only the Lord can provide. We're not alone when tripping over our sins, committing the same ones over and over. We're not alone when doubting that God still loves us at times, especially when we're hurting and don't know the lesson God is trying to teach us (Proverbs 3:11-12). Every relationship takes work, and our relationship with our Lord and creator is certainly no different!

When we accept Jesus into our hearts we become His followers, and are expected to deny what we may want for ourselves so that we may do what He is going to ask of us (Matthew 16:24). But when we do follow Jesus, trying to live a more righteous lifestyle in the way that He asks, we are blessed with the Holy Spirit as a guide (John 14:23). Knowing that the Spirit of God dwells inside of us should provoke some improved behavior, choices, words and attitudes from all of us (1 Corinthians 3:16). No matter how dark the world around us has become, no matter how lost our hope may seem, the Lord is always with us. We must never forget that in the midst of our tribulation and heartache, the Lord waits for us to seek Him. When we pray to the Lord for comfort in our time of pain, for guidance, for wisdom, and purer hearts, and then thank Him for His love and generosity, we are returning love through our devotion.

Matthew 28:19-20, ESV

19 (Jesus said) "Go therefore and make disciples of all nations, baptizing them in the name of the Father and of the Son and of the Holy Spirit, 20 teaching them to observe all that I have commanded you. And behold, **I am with you always**, to the end of the age."

December 29

Time

Ecclesiastes 3:11, GNT

11 He has set the right time for everything. He has given us a desire to know the future, but never gives us the satisfaction of fully understanding what he does.

2 Peter 3:8-9, NIV

8 But do not forget this one thing, dear friends: With the Lord a day is like a thousand years, and a thousand years are like a day. 9 The Lord is not slow in keeping His promise, as some understand slowness. Instead he is patient with you, not wanting anyone to perish, but everyone to come to repentance.

We never seem to have enough time; to get all of our errands done, goals accomplished, bonds formed, to travel to the places we long to see, or to enjoy a beautiful moment just once more. Humans like to think they have everything figured out, an answer for everything under the sun and beyond. Scholars study ancient documents, scientists perform tests, and archeologists dig for clues to explain the whole universe. Only dominant among God's *other* creations on the earth, humans have been deceived by the devil in thinking they have more dominion than we actually have (John 8:44, 2 Corinthians 11:14). It's human arrogance, and grossly misplaced pride, that makes us think we can handle our lives successfully without God. Humans weren't given free will to compete with one another for world domination and conquest, but to test the hearts to see if they would remain loyal to God through all their conflicts (2 Chronicles 16:9a).

Our time is controlled by God, not only the time of our lives, but the time of the earth, and all its inhabitants (Matthew 24:35-36). When we think of time, we can't help but recognize our mortality, and realize, to our chagrin, just how much of our lives is out of our control. It's difficult to remain positive in our faith when we see arrogant, greedy, wicked people succeed while we wait for the Lord in pain and anguish. God calls on us to do just that. We aren't told a lot about the Kingdom of Heaven, and life on earth doesn't offer much comfort along the way. While we have all been distracted by the superficiality of our own lives, God has been concerned with the condition of our souls. Sins are helpful to remind us how, and where we are deficient, but should inspire us to realize just how much we need our Heavenly Father's grace and justice. Rather than focus on the minutia of our individual sins, or life circumstances, we should be focused on our devotion to the Lord, and the spiritual morality guiding our hearts. God shifts our life circumstances to bring us to places He needs us to be in our faith walk with Him (1 Peter 1:7). We may not understand how it all works now, but in the end we'll be glad we never gave up on the quest for righteousness through Jesus.

Righteousness will be worth the wait

Malachi 3:17-18, GNT

17 "They will be my people," says the Lord Almighty. "On the day when I act, they will be my very own. I will be merciful to them as parents are merciful to the children who serve them. 18 Once again my people will see the difference between what happens to the righteous and to the wicked, to the person who serves me and the one who does not."

December 30
Spiritual Rebirth

Mark 16:6, ESV

6 And he said to them, "Do not be alarmed. You seek Jesus of Nazareth, who was crucified. **He has risen**; he is not here. See the place where they laid him."

Matthew 18:3, ESV

3 And said, "Truly, I say to you, unless you turn and become like children, you will never enter the kingdom of heaven."

Romans 12:2, ESV

2 Do not be conformed to this world, but be transformed by the renewal of your mind, that by testing you may discern what is the will of God, what is good and acceptable and perfect.

Toddlers mischievously peek around the corner to their parents room, afraid to be caught in their natural, precocious, curiosity and scolded. We seek, and find, direction in many places along our interesting lives. As kids, we are resilient, flexible, and full of wonder. As we get older, we find change more difficult, as we form solid opinions, boundaries, and convictions. Some of us delude ourselves into thinking, 'Well, if I think I'm a good person, then God must also.' If we're afraid to approach God, we should be, we call Him 'God' for a reason (Matthew 10:28). Forgiving, persistent, graceful, all-knowing, and merciful, God only wants us to return to Him (Joel 2:13). As parents, many of us would tell our wandering children, "I don't care what you **think** you've done, just come home."

The bible assures us that we are spiritually reborn through our belief in Jesus (2 Corinthians 5:17). Some of us are too stuck in our ways to think we can change anything for the Lord, others might be too skeptical to confide their innermost dreams and fears in a God they don't fully trust. Even though many people believe in God, some people misunderstand, or misinterpret, and hesitate to devote their lives to God. We are all in different places in our faith journey, and trust is like the wind. God can create the earth, and all its inhabitants, and resurrected Jesus from death after three days, He is capable of anything. No one is too broken for the Lord to heal, no one is capable of judging life fairly, and no one is perfect. We are all equal in the eyes of the Lord, just not ourselves. Anger can turn to patience, self-loathing into self-love, humility can replace the arrogance, vengeance can be replaced by forgiveness, and grace can replace the pride-through Christ Jesus. Stay faithful, brothers and sisters. AMEN.

Ephesians 4:21-24, ESV

21 assuming that you have heard about him and were taught in him, as the truth is in Jesus, 22 to put off your old self, which belongs to your former manner of life and is corrupt through deceitful desires, 23 and to be renewed in the spirit of your minds, 24 and to put on the new self, created after the likeness of God in true righteousness and holiness.

December 31
Final Advice

2 John 8, ESV

8 Watch yourselves, so that you may not lose what we have worked for, but may win a full reward.

Hosea 14:9, ERV

9 A wise person understands these things, and a smart person should learn them. The Lord's ways are right. Good people will live by them. Sinners will die by them.

In our ignorance we didn't understand that we serve the Lord, He doesn't serve us (Matthew 4:10, John 12:26). In our infancy we didn't realize that merely believing in Jesus wasn't enough to save our souls (James 2:18-20a). In reading the bible, we finally understand that all humanity is evil and prone to sin (Genesis 6:5), constantly tempted to blaze new trails without adhering to the Lord's laws and commands (Hosea 7:13). As we grew in our faith, we came to realize that the whole world is in the power of the devil (1 John 5:19), and we must remain strong in our faith, with our eyes constantly on Jesus to be, and remain, righteous in the eyes of the Lord. Studying further, we realize that all we know and understand about the world we live in is scheduled for termination at an unknown time (2 Peter 3:10). Learning that not everyone will get to heaven was sobering (Matthew 7:21), and that nonbelievers will be thrown down to hell with the rest of the wicked (Revelation 21:8). After we die, we don't immediately float up to Heaven under the escort of the Heavenly hosts, but we are 'sleeping' until the Lord calls us *all* for judgement (Daniel 12:2, 1 Thessalonians 4:13-14). So many revelations come from **a closer study** of God's world, revelations that certainly **helps us to understand** our unique, and individual relationships with **God.**

None of us know how much time we have, so every second of our lives count. **Now is the time to decide**, once and for all, just how devoted we are, and if we're ready **to give Jesus our life.** We don't get to make up the rules, or change them, and humility and submission will always be an uncomfortable challenge for a sinful humanity. We must ask ourselves, 'Just how much is our soul worth to us?' because that's what life is all about, the salvation of our souls. God wants our soul, the devil wants to keep it from Him, and we don't always want to be the one that has to decide the outcome. Each person's journey with God looks different, we can only accurately compare our journeys to Christ's, since He is the one we're trying to be more like. Our focus should always be on the Lord, and what He desires from our lives, for we all have something to offer Him in service. Continue on in good faith, brothers and sisters, striving for the contrite, righteous hearts, forged by the will of the Lord. In His name we praise, our Lord and Savior, King of the universe who provides all things. AMEN.

Matthew 13:15, ERV

15 "Yes, the minds of these people are now closed. They have ears, but they don't listen. They have eyes, but they refuse to see. If their minds were not closed, they might see with their eyes; they might hear with their ears; *they might understand with their minds. Then they might turn back to me and be healed.*"